Britain at Work

As depicted by the 1998 Workplace
Employee Relations Survey

Mark Cully, Stephen Woodland,
Andrew O'Reilly and Gill Dix

London and New York

First published 1999
by Routledge
11 New Fetter Lane, London EC4P 4EE

Simultaneously published in the USA and Canada
by Routledge
29 West 35th Street, New York, NY 10001

Reprinted 2000, 2002

Routledge is an imprint of the Taylor & Francis Group

© Crown Copyright / Economic and Social Research Council / The Policy
Studies Institute / The Advisory, Conciliation and Arbitration Service,
1999.

Typeset in Garamond by
HWA Text and Data Management, Tunbridge Wells
Printed and bound in Great Britain by
St Edmundsbury Press Ltd, Bury St Edmunds, Suffolk

British Library Cataloguing in Publication Data
A catalogue record for this book is available
from the British Library

Library of Congress Cataloging in Publication Data
Britain at work : as depicted by 1998 workplace relations
   survey / Mark Cully ... [et al].
      p.   cm.
   Includes bibliographical references and index.
   1. Employee attitude surveys – Great Britain. 2. Industrial
surveys – Great Britain. 3. Industrial relations – Great Britain
Statistics. 4. Personnel management – Great Britain – Statistics.
5. Labor – Great Britain Statistics.   I. Cully, Mark.
HF5549.5.A83875   1999   99-34133
331'.0941–dc21   CIP

ISBN 0-415-20636-7 (hbk)
ISBN 0-415-20637-5 (pbk)

Contents

Technical appendix   303

Figures

Tables

Foreword

This book presents the first comprehensive account of findings from the 1998 Workplace Employee Relations Survey (WERS 98), the fourth in a series of surveys that began in 1980.

Over this period, the economic, political and institutional context to employment relations has changed greatly. The survey was first conceived in the late 1970s when British industrial relations was dominated by collective workplace institutions and characterised by voluntarism. The 1990 survey suggested a significant decline in traditional forms of collective representation. Most of the available evidence has pointed to further change since 1990.

As the world changes, so must the instruments we use to measure it. WERS 98 is the outcome of a rigorous re-appraisal. This has led to some substantial changes to its design. Perhaps most fundamental is a re-casting of the management questionnaire, with less emphasis on the institutional aspects of employment relations and a greater emphasis on management policies and practices. Further innovations included reducing the size threshold for the survey to workplaces with 10 or more employees and, for the first time, including a survey of employees. In designing and implementing these changes, we learned from the experience of the research team involved in the second Australian Workplace Industrial Relations Survey.

Change inevitably leads to some loss of continuity. In part, though, continuity has been preserved through a separate panel study which involved a survey of workplaces interviewed in the 1990 survey. The focus of the questionnaire was on change between 1990 and 1998. A brief taster of the results is given in Chapter 10 of this book. A more extensive discussion of change will be presented in *All Change at Work?*, the companion to this volume.

Another development, as significant in its own way, was the move to computer-aided personal interviewing. This has considerably improved the quality of the data obtained, as well as enabling greater sophistication in questionnaire design within the setting of a 'live' face-to-face interview. It has also – without discounting the efforts of the authors – helped to reduce greatly the turn-round time on delivery of results. We published first findings from the survey four months after the final interview and, compared with the last survey, we have trimmed a year off the time taken to produce the source book.

While the survey itself continues to evolve and improve, it remains a collaborative enterprise between the four sponsors: the Department of Trade and Industry (which now has responsibility within government for employment relations); the Economic and Social Research Council (ESRC); the Advisory, Conciliation and Arbitration Service (ACAS) and the Policy Studies Institute (PSI) supported in part with funds from the Leverhulme Trust. Not only does co-sponsorship spread the costs, it also ensures that the survey reflects a variety of interests – including those of policy makers, practitioners, and academics. And it safeguards the independence and credibility of the survey findings.

This survey has been overseen from inception to completion by a Steering Committee of the four sponsors. Zmira Hornstein chaired the committee until her retirement in spring 1998, and, on behalf of the entire Steering Committee, I wish to record my thanks for her unique and valuable contribution. Other members of the Steering Committee have been: Bernard Carter, representing DTI policy interests; W.R. Hawes and, lately, Peter Syson, representing ACAS; Pam Meadows, Margaret Blunden and Jim Skea who successively represented PSI; and Christine McCullough, Jeremy Neathey and Paul Marginson representing ESRC. Their constructive approach has contributed greatly to the success of this project.

Nevertheless, a Committee cannot steer without people willing and able to row the boat. The Steering Committee has been fortunate indeed in its choice of oarsmen and women. Mark Cully from DTI led the research team, which also comprised Stephen Woodland and Andrew O'Reilly from DTI, Gill Dix from ACAS, and Alex Bryson, Neil Millward and John Forth from PSI (the latter two now based at the National Institute for Economic and Social Research). Professor John Godard of the University of Manitoba joined the research team for a three-month period during the intensive process of questionnaire design and added greatly to the work of the team.

Fieldwork for the survey was contracted, after competitive tendering, to Social and Community Planning Research (SCPR). Particular recognition must go to Colin Airey and Rosemary Hamilton of SCPR, who have worked on all four surveys to date, together with Anthony McKernan, Jon Hales, Pauline Burge and Susan Purdon. They were backed up by a first-rate team of interviewers and data processors.

Over 30,000 managers, worker representatives and employees gave freely of their time in contributing to this survey. The Steering Committee has always taken great pride in achieving a high response rate for the survey, and in this respect the outcome of the fourth survey is again a source of satisfaction. Credit must go to both the research team and SCPR; but the response rate also says much about the importance of the subject to those at the sharp end of employment relations.

This book and its companion volume are by no means the final words on the survey. By necessity, it is a broad overview. The authors write in a personal capacity and some readers will arrive at different interpretations of the survey results – if they did not, it would be a dull read indeed. The Steering Committee hopes that, over the coming months and years, the survey data will be subjected to further analysis and reflection. The survey data has been deposited at the ESRC Data Archive for precisely this purpose.

In the spirit of continuous improvement, the authors have provided their own recommendations for the design and conduct of a fifth survey (see Chapter 13). The impact the survey results have on policy and academic debate, together with the feedback we receive from readers and users of the data, will be important factors in determining the future course of workplace surveys in Britain.

Mark Beatson
Chair, WERS Steering Committee
April 1999

List of abbreviations

ACAS	Advisory, Conciliation and Arbitration Service
BWDS	Basic Workforce Data Sheet
CAPI	Computer Aided Personal Interview
DTI	Department of Trade and Industry
EETPU	Electrical, Electronic, Telecommunications and Plumbing Trade Union
EPQ	Employee Profile Questionnaire
ESRC	Economic and Social Research Council
HRM	Human Resources Management
IDBR	Inter-Departmental Business Register
IiP	Investors in People
ONS	Office for National Statistics
PAYE	Pay As You Earn
PSI	Policy Studies Institute
RIDDOR	Register of Injuries, Diseases and Dangerous Occurrences Regulations
SCPR	Social and Community Planning Research
SIC	Standard Industrial Classification
TUC	Trades Union Congress
USDAW	Union of Shop, Distributive and Allied Workers
VAT	Value Added Tax
WERS 98	The 1998 Workplace Employee Relations Survey
WIRS	Workplace Industrial Relations Survey

1 Introduction

This book presents an up-to-date portrait of the diverse nature of employment relations in the workplace in contemporary Britain. It does so through the 1998 Workplace Employee Relations Survey (WERS 98), a large and complex edifice constructed to collect, collate and classify what might otherwise remain disparate and diffuse. In this introductory chapter we give a short account of how the survey was carried out, setting it in the context of the times in which it took place.

The worth of this project might best be illustrated by the fact that it is the fourth time the consortium of government, executive agencies and research bodies has joined together to fund it. The first was conducted in 1980, with further surveys in 1984 and 1990. Costly they may be, but there is a demonstrable need to periodically update our stock of knowledge about employment relations at the workplace. We need to be able to say, with reasonable accuracy, what proportion of workplaces (and employees) might be affected by government initiatives, whether innovations have taken root, whether change has occurred, how widespread good practice is, and whether the findings of sector or organisation-based studies can be generalised from the particular to the whole.

Besides this need to replenish our knowledge base, it must also be renewed. Since 1990 many of the issues confronting practitioners and policy makers have altered. In place of concerns over 'macho' management and searching for human resource management, most commentators are now interested in the constellation of management practices and whether they cohere into identifiable sets. It is also now well-established that the British labour market and many firms are highly flexible – debate now centres on how this meshes with employment standards and how individuals preserve their 'employability'. Unions have responded to declining membership by reviewing their approaches to serving members at the workplace.

The 1998 survey is well-placed to measure the new: the subject matter is more wide-ranging and the scope of the survey has been broadened to include very small workplaces and, also, a fresh employee perspective. One change that should be highlighted from the start is the title of the survey. Previous surveys are referred to as the Workplace Industrial Relations Survey (or WIRS for short), but now 'employee' has been substituted for 'industrial'. This change was made for two reasons. First, in approaching workplace managers to take part in the survey, they were told it was a survey of 'employee relations practices' (as, indeed, were managers in all past surveys). We decided that to be consistent we should persist with this title. Second, we considered 'employee relations' to be a better reflection of the content of the 1998 survey.[1] In general, we make only passing reference to the survey title, and mostly use the more general term 'employment relations'. Irrespective of the title, it should be apparent from the structure of the survey and the content of this book that pluralism has been a guiding motif.

The series to date has attracted some criticism, most notably (and ironically, as he pioneered workplace surveys in Britain) by McCarthy (1994: 321). According to McCarthy, the surveys are 'unlikely to provide us with much more than limited monitoring of changes that we already know about'. The subject, he says, 'cries out for a case study approach' as only this is capable of yielding 'imaginative insights'. Such criticisms have often been applied to surveys: forty years ago Wright Mills (1959) warned of the problems of what he called 'abstracted empiricism', which to his mind constituted a 'withdrawal from the tasks of the social sciences', and produced results that 'no matter how numerous, do not convince us of anything worth having convictions about'. We see the position of McCarthy as a retreat into methodological nihilism. Surveys are an essential part of social enquiry, capable of generating new insights and validating old ones, as well as providing a focus for future case studies.

This volume constitutes our primary analysis of the 1998 survey.[2] We hope that it satisfies the objective set by the consortium's Steering Committee for a book which would inform government policy development, as well as stimulate and inform debate among employers, workers and the wider community. The survey will continue to enrich and enhance our understanding of employment relations through secondary analysis of the data, which is publicly available for all to use. And we trust that in-depth case studies will help to establish the conditions under which the statistical associations we have found arise.

The social, economic and political landscape in 1998

Chapter 10, which uses the 1998 survey and its predecessors to quantify the extent of change in employment relations over the past two decades, provides an overview of the main changes to the social, economic and political landscape over the period. In this section, our purpose is to give a short account of the topography at the time of the conduct of the 1998 survey.

In 1998, Britain was at the tail end of an economic upturn that had begun in 1992 following the substantial devaluation of sterling that occurred after exiting the European exchange rate mechanism. There were more Britons in paid work in 1998 than ever before and unemployment (as measured by the claimant count) was at its lowest level since 1979. Inflation was low, the underlying rate running between 2.5 and 3.2 per cent, more or less in line with the target set for the Bank of England's Monetary Policy Committee. Growth in average earnings, while above inflation, was also relatively modest, running between 4.3 and 5.7 per cent. Industrial action in 1998 was rare indeed with only 12 days per thousand employees being lost in the year, less than 1 per cent of the average level in the late 1970s.

Given such circumstances, one might conclude that it was a time when employment relations and working life were relatively trouble-free. There were, however, undercurrents of disquiet. Unemployment still remained high – around 1.8 million were actively seeking work – much of it concentrated in some cities and regions. There were several high profile large-scale redundancies in 1998. Many commentators pointed to evidence of heightened job insecurity. Almost one in twelve workers were in jobs of a temporary kind. Many people were working very long hours – 13 per cent worked in excess of 48 paid hours a week, a higher proportion of employees than any other country in the European Union. Allied with concerns about long working hours on people's health, the consequences of work on life outside the workplace also came to the fore.

As if to symbolise this disquiet, there had been several recent enquiries conducted by august bodies into work and working life. The Council of Churches for Britain and Ireland conducted a major study into unemployment and the future of work, the Royal Society of Arts set about redefining work, and the Fabian Society sponsored a royal commission style investigation into the changing character of work. Research foundations also made more funds available to study the future of work. It may have been a bout of pre-millennial fever, but the nature of work was on the political agenda in a way that had not been so for many years.

Part of the prominence of debates over the nature of work might be traced to a change in the political climate. Indeed, it is tempting to see 1998 as a distinctive year, coming as it did only months after the advent of a new Labour government some 18 years after that party was last in office. This is especially so in the field of employment relations because of the flurry of legislative and other activity which the new government brought to this area. Working time regulations were introduced and steps were taken to establish a national minimum wage. A range of proposals were announced in the 1998 *Fairness at Work* White Paper (Department of Trade and Industry, 1998a) to extend the coverage and range of individual employment rights, allow for a statutory union recognition procedure, and encourage new ways of working through a Partnership Fund. With one minor exception though,[3] none of this new legislation was enacted until after the survey had been conducted.

That is not to say that, in some areas, there had not been adjustments made in anticipation of new legislation, or wider changes to practice in keeping with the new government's espousal of partnership at work. For example, a study conducted for the Low Pay Commission in early 1998 showed some organisations to be revising pay structures to give above average pay increases to those at the bottom of the scales (Incomes Data Services, 1998). Similarly, a survey of trade unions suggested that prospective changes to legislation had led to a perceived increase in the number of recognition deals throughout 1998 (Trades Union Congress, 1999). Several new partnership agreements were also well publicised, like that between Tesco and the Union of Shop, Distributive and Allied Workers (USDAW).

However, one should not overstate these adjustments. The scale of changes made in advance of new legislation was probably modest.

Thus, 1998 may or may not have marked a distinctive break from the past in the arena of employment relations. That is for future historians to judge. What can be said with certainty at this stage is that WERS 98 represents a benchmark against which the legislative changes introduced can be assessed. It is also clear, looking backwards, that the landscape in 1998 differed markedly from 1980. In preparing for the 1998 survey we recognised that so much had altered in British employment relations since the series began that it was time to re-consider the issues which informed the structure of the survey and the design of the questionnaires.

Our approach was to ensure that there was sufficient continuity to map the core features of workplace employment relations and changes in them over time, but beyond that to use the survey to address several themes. These were to:

- examine the state of the contemporary employment contract;
- explore how employee relations and practices at the workplace impact upon its performance and competitiveness; and
- assess whether there has been a transformation in workplace employment relations in Britain.

The first two themes are covered in this book, notably in Chapters 7 and 8 (the employment contract) and Chapters 6 and 12 (workplace performance and employment relations climate). Change is the subject of Chapter 10, and constitutes only an initial analysis of this topic, which is given a more detailed treatment in Millward *et al.* (2000). Reporting on the 'core' of the survey constitutes the bulk of this book. Discussion of the topics under investigation, together with a more specific exposition of the main issues confronting practitioners, policy makers and researchers in the area, is left to the individual chapters. Before proceeding to the analysis it is necessary to give a short account of how the survey was designed and conducted. A fuller, and more technical, account is given in the Technical Appendix.

Design of the survey

Trivial though it may seem, we need to begin by explaining what is meant by a *workplace* survey. There are two elements to this. First, the basic analytical unit is a workplace, which we defined as 'the activities of a single employer at a single set of premises'. A branch of a bank or high street store are workplaces in their own right, as are the head offices of those organisations. Workplaces are subsets of organisations, except where the workplace is the sole one in an organisation and it is only here that the terms 'workplace' and 'organisation' are interchangeable.

To enumerate employment relations in the British workplace, we needed to generate a statistically representative sample of workplaces. One approach, the basis for a recent American study (Kalleberg *et al.*, 1996), is to generate a random sample of employers by asking a random sample of employees for details of whom they work for. This approach has elegant statistical properties (Parcel *et al.*, 1991), but is fraught with practical problems, notably in getting sufficiently detailed and accurate information from workers about their employers.[4] In Britain we are fortunate in having a ready-made sampling frame of workplaces: the Inter-Departmental Business Register (IDBR), held by the Office for National Statistics. This register contains details on all going concerns (both privately-owned and publicly-owned) operating in the UK by accumulating details from PAYE and VAT registrations. It is hierarchically organised with its basic 'local unit' conforming to our own definition of a workplace in all but a very small proportion of cases.[5]

Second, a workplace does not speak with a single voice, but with a Babelesque din. The problems confronting the survey researcher in wishing to analyse the workplace are akin to that of studying households: are all members surveyed or just one, and if just one then who should it be? Many household surveys overcome this problem by only interviewing the 'head', who speaks on behalf of the household. Our solution was analogous. We identified certain people within the workplace who, by dint of their position, could speak for the workplace. The two respondents were the manager at the workplace with day-to-day responsibility for personnel and employment relations matters, and a senior worker represent-ative. However, although it was mostly personnel managers and union representatives who were interviewed, it was not a survey of them but of their workplaces. That is, the respondents acted as informants of what went on in their workplace, and they were chosen because of the role they occupied within the workplace.[6] In addition, however, and for the first time in the series, we directly surveyed a number of employees within each workplace irrespective of their position within the workplace – this innovation is discussed in more detail below.

The basic structure, then, was the same as the others in the series: a sample survey of managers and worker representatives in their roles as informants answering questions about the state of employment relations at their workplace. Figure 1.1 summarises the main elements of the survey structure. As can be seen from this, while we have used the term 'survey' in the singular throughout, the project consisted of two distinct elements totalling four distinct surveys, three of which (i.e. the 1998 cross-section) are linked.

The 1998 cross-section

We refer to the main element as the 1998 cross-section, which is representative of all British workplaces with 10 or more employees (with some minor exceptions).[7] Previous surveys had an employment threshold of 25 employees. This had been seen as the limit below which it would not be possible to easily administer a structured survey, in situations where the employment relationship is often characterised by a high degree of informality (Scase, 1995). Uncovering and

Figure 1.1 Structure of the survey

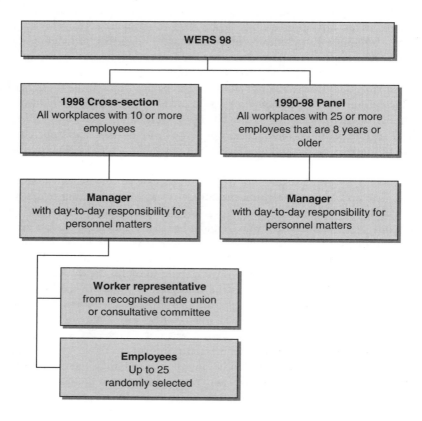

measuring informal rules is a major challenge for survey research. Early piloting work showed that it *was* possible to administer the survey in workplaces with as few as 10 employees.

Dropping the size threshold to 10 employees has the paradoxical effect of increasing the heterogeneity of the survey population while reducing the variability within it. This is because there are as many workplaces with between 10 and 24 employees as there are with 25 employees or more. If we opted to present results for all workplaces with 10 employees or more, we would have had to qualify a large proportion of the findings by noting that they were mostly a feature of very small workplaces. We did not wish to do this. Given this, and for reasons of consistency with past surveys in the series, most of this book is limited to analysis of workplaces with 25 employees or more. In Chapter 11 there is a separate treatment of small *business* employment relations where the sample of workplaces with 10 to 24 employees is drawn upon.

As already noted, the IDBR was used to select the sample. The IDBR was first stratified by workplace employment size and by industrial activity. Workplaces were randomly selected within a particular category of size band and industry (e.g. education workplaces with 100–199 employees). Across the sample as a whole, however, larger workplaces were given a greater chance of being selected than smaller workplaces to enable comparisons to be made between them. Similarly, workplaces within some industries (i.e. those with relatively few workplaces, such as electricity, gas and water) were given a slightly greater chance of being selected than those in other industries to allow comparisons across all major industry groups. The variation in the probability of selection of workplaces has been corrected for by weighting the data so that its size and industry profile after weighting matches that of the IDBR. A fuller account of the sampling design and weighting is given in the Technical Appendix.

For the cross-section the intention was to survey around 2,250 workplaces, to be split between 2,000 workplaces with 25 or more employees – roughly the number included in each of the previous surveys – and 250 workplaces with between 10 and 24 employees. In each workplace selected, an interview was to be conducted with the manager who had day-to-day responsibility for personnel matters. There were then two further aspects of the cross-section – the worker representative interview and the survey of employees. They are displayed beneath the management box in Figure 1.1 because we were dependent on management: first, to identify eligibility in the case of worker representatives; second, for permission to interview worker representatives and to survey employees; and, third, to provide the information necessary to contact them.

A workplace was defined as having participated in the survey so long as a management interview was conducted. The next section provides details on the number of people who took part at each stage.

Interviewing worker representatives has been an integral element of the survey series throughout. There are two reasons why a worker representative perspective continues to remain important. First, although the bulk of questions are 'factual', differences in frames of reference mean that answers between management and worker representatives are not always consistent. For example, a manager may state that the workplace operates a staff suggestion scheme, but a worker representative may think it dormant or non-existent if no-one has made a suggestion for several years. The difference in perspective may lead to differences in response and it is desirable, where this occurs, to give both management and worker representative accounts. Second, much of our interest is in what worker representatives do, and in this they are obviously the best placed informant. Chapter 9 discusses in more detail the objectives of the worker representative interview and the rules for eligibility and selection.

The third, and novel, element of the cross-section was the survey of employees. Although managers and worker representatives are employees of the workplace, they were not interviewed to provide an employee perspective. Moreover, in 1990, about half (49 per cent) of all workplaces had no worker representative interview to counter the account provided by management. All pointers were that this percentage would have increased by 1998. Surveying employees within all sampled workplaces was a solution that resolved both issues. Having studied closely the outcome of a recent Australian national workplace survey, which successfully incorporated a survey of employees within it (Morehead *et al.*, 1997), we too decided to extend the project in this way.

Our approach differed somewhat from that used in the Australian study. In each workplace the management respondent was asked to provide a list of all employees at the workplace. From this list, however ordered or arranged, the interviewer was to randomly select 25 names – or all if there were fewer than 25 employees – and these employees were then sent a pack containing a short questionnaire, a leaflet describing the purpose of the survey and a reply-paid envelope. This approach was easy for interviewers to implement and had the merit of giving employees in all workplaces a broadly equal chance of selection.[8]

It should be apparent from this account of the cross-section that each of the three parts are linked by the workplace. This gives us a design of uncommon power, as we have three distinct perspectives on employment relations, and through matching responses (i.e. within the same workplace) we also have the facility to explore interactions between workplace and individual-level effects.

The 1990–98 panel

The second strand to the project, as shown in Figure 1.1, was the panel. A panel is where the same 'unit' takes part in two or more separate waves of a survey conducted over time. In tandem with the cross-section it can be used to learn more about the dynamics of change. Without a panel, it would not be possible to say whether changes observed between two snapshot surveys are due to changes in the population of workplaces or to changes in the behaviour of ongoing workplaces.

The sample for the panel was the 2,061 workplaces which took part in the 1990 survey. We selected a random 1,301 of these, aiming to achieve interviews with a management respondent – defined in the same way as for the cross-section – with about 1,000. In addition, all of the 2,061 workplaces were to be traced to see what fate had befallen them over the previous eight years. The knowledge that some workplaces had not 'survived' is very powerful retrospective information, as the responses from 1990 (when the workplace *was* a going concern) can be examined for any predictive patterns.

Questionnaire design

Unlike the approach adopted in the 1990 survey, where the management interviews for the cross-section and panel used identical questionnaires, the two strands this time went down separate design paths. The panel questionnaire was largely based on the 1990 management questionnaire. It was necessary for questions to remain more or less identical so as to establish whether change had occurred. However, the 1998 cross-section questionnaires were cast in a new mould.

New to the survey were topics such as equal opportunities, training, team-working and performance monitoring. There was more extensive questioning in areas such as flexible working and performance appraisal. Given the constraints of interview length, some topics were allocated less time than in the earlier surveys. These included areas to do with union organisation, pay determination and industrial action. Part of the time 'savings' also arose through dispensing with parallel questions for manual and non-manual workers, a distinction seen as having less salience in 1998 than it did in 1980. Where a sharper focus was required, questions were asked instead about the largest occupational group.

The worker representative questionnaire was also recast, with less space given to duplicating management questions (in areas where we thought that managers were likely to be the better informant) and more given to exploring the role and activities of worker representatives. The employee questionnaire was designed from scratch and benefited from a round of cognitive testing.

Each of the three interview-based questionnaires were conducted using computer-aided interviewing. The research team's paper questionnaires were converted into computer programmes prior to two pilot surveys undertaken in the summer of 1997. They were then refined, along with the questionnaire for the employee survey, before fieldwork began in the autumn.

Conduct of the survey

The survey was conducted between October 1997 and June 1998 – we use WERS 98 as the shorthand label as only 20 per cent of the interviews were conducted at the tail end of 1997. As with each of the three previous surveys in the series, the contract to undertake the survey fieldwork was won by Social and Community Planning Research.

A summary of fieldwork outcomes is provided in Table 1.1. For the cross-section 2,191 workplaces took part, representing a response rate of 80 per cent, slightly lower than the 83 per cent achieved in the 1990 survey. The management interview in these workplaces averaged more than an hour and a half. The 2,191 participating workplaces was a slight shortfall from our target of 2,250 workplaces. This shortfall only occurred among workplaces with 25 employees or more, of which 1,929 took part, 71 fewer than the target of 2,000. The response from very small workplaces slightly exceeded the target of 250, with 262 taking part.

Table 1.1 Fieldwork outcomes

	Total responses	*Response rate*	*Average duration*
	Number	*%*	*Minutes*
1998 cross-section			
Management questionnaire	2,191	80	108
Worker representative questionnaire	947	82	47
Survey of employees	28,237	64	–
1990–98 panel			
Management questionnaire	882	85	66

From the 2,191 participating workplaces, interviews were conducted with 947 worker representatives. This amounted to a response rate of 82 per cent of eligible cases. In 1,880 of the workplaces (85 per cent), the management respondent agreed to the conduct of the employee survey.[9] In total, 44,283 questionnaire packs were distributed to employees and 28,237 were returned in a usable state. This represents a response rate of 64 per cent when expressed as a percentage of those distributed, though a rate below half once we take into account those workplaces which did not take part in the survey at all and those which refused to allow the survey of employees to proceed. By any measure, though, this novel element must be deemed a success. Its purpose, to capture a genuine employee voice, chimed with many employees, one noting 'this questionnaire is a good idea because it asks us how we feel – something that does not happen much at my workplace'.

Finally, interviews were conducted with managers in 882 of the 1,301 sampled workplaces for the panel. Most workplaces where no interview was conducted were ones that had not survived over the intervening eight years (40 per cent), and only 15 per cent of those that could take part did not yield a productive interview (9 per cent being refusals). In productive workplaces the interview took, on average, slightly longer than one hour.

Plan and approach of the book

The book is divided into three broad parts. The next five chapters give a detailed account of contemporary workplace employment relations, relying entirely on data collected in the course of the management interview. Chapter 2, by way of background, draws a profile of workplaces – how many are large, how many are small, and so on – so that readers can gain an idea of the main features and structural characteristics of the population of workplaces with 25 employees or more. In Chapter 3 the analysis proper commences by looking at how labour is deployed across workplaces. In particular, we look at the means by which management attempt to attain flexibility in their use of labour, whether through the use of 'non-standard' labour or by innovations in the form of work organisation. Chapter 4 then examines more closely the direct management of employees, from when they are recruited through to their exit from the workplace. In Chapter 5 attention shifts to the institutional arrangements for regulating the employment relationship at the workplace, notably the role played by trade unions and joint consultative committees. Then, in Chapter 6, we look at how workplace performance is monitored and measured and explore indicators of workplace well-being.

The second broad part, covering Chapters 7–9, introduces the other two elements of the 1998 cross-section. Two chapters are devoted to the survey of employees. In Chapter 7 we examine the substantive content of employees' jobs, covering such matters as job influence, access to training and participation in workplace decision-making, as well as the 'bread and butter' issues of hours and pay. Chapter 8 moves into the realm of the 'psychological contract' and explores the underlying motives which guide employee behaviour. Finally, in Chapter 9, we change sources once more, this time turning to the account of employment relations provided by worker representatives. Particular attention is paid to their role and function within the workplace.

After this there are three discrete chapters which address some contemporary themes in employment relations. Chapter 10, as already noted, provides an initial account of the main changes which have transpired in workplaces over the past two decades. It serves as an appetiser for the full volume on change (Millward *et al.*, 2000). In Chapter 11 we incorporate data from the very small workplaces – those with between 10 and 24 employees – to examine whether employment relations in small businesses are distinctive, and, if so, whether this is by virtue of their size or their ownership structure. Chapter 12 draws on data from all three groups of respondents to explore the associations between how a workplace is organised and managed, how well it performs and the climate of employment relations. The final chapter offers some conclusions.

Conventions used throughout the book

Before proceeding further it is necessary to explain some of the conventions used in reporting numbers and identifying differences between two or more of them.

In common with all sample surveys, assigning figures to the proportion of respondents with a given feature implies a degree of precision which may not be warranted. There are two types of 'error'. The first is sampling error, which arises because of the chance that the workplaces surveyed may not, by the inclusion of atypical cases, exactly match the population from which they were drawn. This can be quantified through the calculation of standard errors and confidence intervals. We can then state, for example, that we are 95 per cent confident that a given number falls within a range, with the width of the range determined by the size of the standard error. What this means is that, had a different sample been drawn, in nineteen out of twenty cases the estimate given would fall within the range. To give an example, in Chapter 5 we report that 45 per cent of workplaces recognised trade unions for bargaining over pay and conditions. If we were to be wholly precise, we should say that we are 95 per cent confident that between 41.6 and 48.2 per cent of workplaces recognised unions. However, to adopt this approach for every result presented would be cumbersome and tedious. Readers who are interested in this further should see the Technical Appendix where a ready reckoner table is provided to calculate average standard errors.

The second source of error is measurement error arising from answers being given 'wrongly' by respondents or entered wrongly by interviewers. For the most part this reflects flaws in questionnaire design: using poorly-worded questions or not allowing for all contingencies in available responses. An example from the management questionnaire was asking managers whether the workplace was privately- or publicly-owned, a question which respondents in some non-government organisations found awkward to answer. We have endeavoured to minimise measurement error through the use of computer-aided questionnaires

Table 1.2 Table and figure conventions

	Interpretation
Symbol/text	
0	Less than 0.5 per cent, including none
–	Not applicable
( )	Number should be treated with caution, as unweighted base is between 20 and 50 observations
*	The unweighted base is fewer than 20 observations and is too low to produce any reliable estimate

which incorporate logic and consistency checks and reduce the possibility of interviewer mistakes, and remedy it through data editing. Yet a residue of measurement error will remain and we alert the reader where we consider it important.

A special case of measurement error is where questions were not answered, either because the respondent refused to provide an answer, or did not know the answer. Generally, the scale of this throughout the survey was small. Where it was substantial, or some other reason warrants it, we mention the scale of these missing responses; otherwise, we ignore them. Changes in the number of observations upon which tables are based vary from table to table – where the base is not the same, this is due to differences in the number of missing responses. By not including them within the table we have made the implicit assumption that, had the respondents answered the question, their responses would have conformed to the same pattern as those that did answer.

Our convention, then, is mostly to report exact percentages for convenience but also, for stylistic variation and to (implicitly) acknowledge that survey figures are estimates, to make extensive use of qualifiers: 'around', 'about', 'almost', 'approximately' and so on. However, this is not to call into question the validity of the findings. In particular, where we highlight a difference or mention an association this has been tested to establish if it is statistically significant (i.e. the difference or association is almost certain to be true in the wider population).[10] Generally we have satisfied ourselves that where a statistical association has been uncovered it is robust.

Table 1.2 explains the interpretation of symbols and notes which feature in the tables. To economise on space and to highlight the main associations, the tables often exclude categories. Numbers are rounded and will therefore not always sum to 100 per cent.

A final introductory word

We hope that this book will be the starting point for a body of work which will enhance our understanding of the world of work. If, in places, our treatment seems unduly superficial, this has only been because of our desire to highlight the breadth of issues covered in the survey and the possibilities for further analysis. It is a fundamental precept of this series that the data is publicly available for all interested researchers to use, and we urge all who are inspired or goaded by these results to do so – see the Technical Appendix for further details.

Notes

1 Our use of this phrase is consistent with that used by Flanders (1964: 17) in his analysis of the Fawley Productivity Agreements. Industrial relations, he said, had 'come to be associated with the formal institutions regulating relations between employers and employees', whereas employee relations 'covers a company's relations with all its employees'.

2 Preliminary results from WERS 98 were published in the *First Findings* (Cully *et al.*, 1998) booklet in October 1998. Note that the results published in this volume may differ slightly from similar figures in that booklet. This is for two reasons: first, a handful of observations have since been dropped from the data set; second, in some cases, extreme values have been trimmed. The first of these changes should not in general affect point estimates; trimming, however, will mean that estimates of rates in this volume (e.g. of dismissal rates, or applications to Industrial Tribunals) are lower than those published in the *First Findings* booklet.

3 This was the Deregulation (Deduction from Pay of Union Subscriptions) Order 1998, which altered the procedure for employer collection of union dues. These changes were introduced in June 1998 at the very end of fieldwork.

4 For example, Kalleberg *et al.* (1996: 29–30) were unable to survey 21 per cent of the employers from the information provided by 1,427 employees due to refusals, missing information or erroneous information. Moreover, there is a further problem with this strategy of cumulative attrition as the initial survey of employees is, itself, subject to non-response.

5 The SCPR Technical Report (Airey *et al.*, 1999) describes the procedures followed in the event that a local unit on the IDBR did not correspond to an entire workplace or was made up of two or more workplaces.

6 Some background information was collected on the individual respondents. This provides useful contextual data allowing researchers to locate the respondents' 'frame of reference' in answering questions as respondents are actors as well as informants, and this will shape their interpretation of events.

7 The survey population excluded the following Standard Industrial Classification divisions: A (Agriculture, hunting and forestry), B (Fishing), C (Mining and quarrying), P (Private households with employed persons) and Q (Extra-territorial organisations). In total, these industries accounted for just 1.5 per cent of employment in December 1997. Note also that the strict definition of a contract of employment was used to identify employees, and this means that in division L (Public administration and defence) military personnel were not included.

8 The probability of selection of individual employees across all workplaces is relatively uniform as the high probability that a large workplace was selected offsets the low probability that an employee in that workplace would be selected. The converse applied in small workplaces. A workplace sample that was selected with probability proportionate to employment, which WERS 98 approximated, would yield a sample of employees with exactly equal probabilities of selection given this fixed sample number per workplace approach.

9 This is the number recorded as agreeing to the employee survey by interviewers, but of these 97 (4 per cent) yielded no returns at all from employees.

10 Unless otherwise stated, the threshold we have used for testing statistical significance is at the 5 per cent level. Many of the associations are significant to a greater level than this.

2 A profile of workplaces in Britain

This chapter sets the scene for the detailed analysis of workplace employment relations that follows. It provides an overview of the main structural characteristics of workplaces in Britain with 25 or more employees. These include the number of employees at a workplace, the industry to which it belongs and whether the workplace is privately- or publicly-owned. Such features provide the basis for much of the discussion, scrutiny and analysis in later chapters, and an examination of them will help to ground that discussion. They help to illuminate, as well as explain, some of the variation in employment relations practices.

Throughout the survey we relied upon self-classification, accepting managers as best placed to answer questions about the way in which work is organised, their relationship with employees and other broader workplace and organisational structures. However, for a small number of questions, *all* responses were subsequently checked to verify the information. This included most of the characteristics examined in this chapter. For example, while most managers correctly classified their workplace as being positioned either within the private or the public sector, a minority were unsure. This was especially so in the case of charities, where the perception was that of providing a public, rather than a private, service. In such cases we scrutinised and recoded the data as appropriate.[1]

Workplace and organisation size

As the three previous studies in this series have amply illustrated, the size of both the workplace and the wider organisation is crucial to understanding a wide range of employment relations phenomena. Sisson and Marginson (1995: 100) argue that size matters, all other things being equal, because larger units increase the complexity of the management task, and:

> [t]he more complex the management task, the greater the need for rules and procedures to achieve consistency of behaviour on the part of individual managers. The greater the need for rules and procedures, the greater the need for workers and workers' representatives to accept their legitimacy.

Figure 2.1 Distribution of workplaces and employment, by workplace size

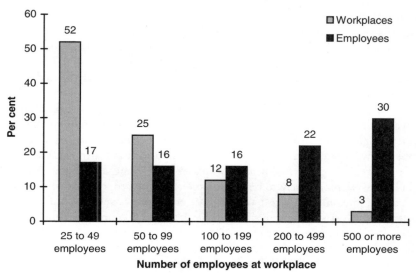

Base: All workplaces with 25 or more employees.
Figures are weighted and based on responses from 1,929 managers.

Workplace size

Size is defined here by the total number of employees at the workplace. The definition of employee used was strictly those people with a contract of employment with the employer.[2] Representatives, sales people and similar employees were included if their principal reporting point was the sampled workplace. However, freelance workers, home or out-workers, and casual workers who did not have a contract of employment were excluded. Additionally, workers who performed tasks at the workplace, but were employed by *another* organisation, for example agency workers and contractors, were also excluded.[3]

The distribution of workplaces with 25 employees or more is highly skewed, as can be seen in Figure 2.1. The smallest workplaces, those employing 25–49 workers, accounted for over half of all workplaces while the largest, those with 500 employees or more, formed just 3 per cent of the total. However, the distribution is far more even when employee coverage is examined, with the largest size band of workplaces accounting for almost a third of all workers, and the remaining two-thirds more or less evenly spread across the remaining size bands.

The difference between these two distributions means that care needs to be taken when interpreting some of the survey results. For example, something that affects a high proportion of workplaces might apply to a much lower proportion of employees if it is found mainly among smaller workplaces. Thus, where appropriate, we present results for both the proportion of workplaces and the proportion of employees affected.

Organisation size

The number of employees at a workplace is only one indicator of size. The workplace must also be located within its wider organisational context – covering matters such as ownership, and the number of employees and separate sites in the organisation as a whole – to gain a fuller understanding of how it functions. Marginson (1984), for instance, has shown that organisational size has a distinct effect, one that is independent of workplace size.

We first sought to establish if a workplace was an independent organisation in its own right ('stand-alone sites'), or one of a number of different workplaces within a single organisation. If the latter, we then obtained information on the number of workplaces and employees across the organisation in the UK.[4] Just over a quarter (27 per cent) of all workplaces were stand-alone sites. Smaller workplaces were more likely to be stand-alone, but even so, over two-thirds (70 per cent) of the smallest size band (25–49 employees) were part of a larger organisation. Most stand-alone sites had fewer than 100 employees and only 2 per cent had 500 employees or more.

Turning now to those workplaces that were part of a wider organisation, around half (47 per cent) of those with 25–49 employees were part of organisations with over 100 different sites. This compares with under a third (29 per cent) of those with 500 or more employees. This picture is reversed when it comes to the number of employees in the organisation. Here, as shown in Table 2.1, larger workplaces were more likely to belong to very large organisations. Most workplaces though, irrespective of their size, belong to large or very large organisations.

Differences between workplaces that are part of a wider organisation can be attributed to more than just employment size. Much may depend on 'distance' from the head office where ultimate control functions lie. Of course, this also depends on whether or not the workplace itself *is* the head office, which was the case for 11 per cent of workplaces that were part of a wider organisation.

To summarise, most workplaces were small but more employees worked in larger than smaller workplaces. Most workplaces were also part of a wider organisation, but were less likely to be so where small. However, small workplaces that were not stand-alone sites were, in common with larger workplaces, usually part of very large organisations (with at least 100 sites and 10,000 employees across the UK).

Industry

Industry is one of the common ways of categorising workplaces. The output of a workplace, and the type of environment in which it operates, are likely to be significant determinants of how work is organised and the character of employment relations. Allen and du Gay (1994: 269), in contrasting manufacturing with services, note 'the relative intangibility of most service output and the fact that the consumption of a service is less easily divorced from its production'. This has implications for the division of labour and the organisation of work.

Table 2.1 Workplaces that are part of a wider organisation, by organisation size and workplace size

	Number of employees in organisation			
	Less than 100	*100 to less than 1,000*	*1,000 to less than 10,000*	*10,000 or more*
	% of workplaces	*% of workplaces*	*% of workplaces*	*% of workplaces*
Workplace size				
25–49 employees	11	15	36	38
50–99 employees	9	23	35	34
100–199 employees	–	27	36	36
200–499 employees	–	17	36	48
500 or more employees	–	6	42	52
All workplaces that are part of a wider organisation	7	18	36	38

Base: All workplaces that are part of a wider organisation with 25 or more employees.
Figures are weighted and based on responses from 1,450 managers.

Managers were asked to provide details of the *main* activity undertaken at the workplace,[5] and their responses were coded using the 1992 Standard Industrial Classification. The design of the sample, as outlined in Chapter 1, allows for analysis of the survey data at the level of industry divisions and Table 2.2 shows the distribution of workplaces and employment across the twelve divisions. This provides an opportunity for more detailed analysis than possible in past surveys, and allows practitioners to benchmark practices within their own broad industry group.

Manufacturing and wholesale and retail were the industries with the most workplaces, followed by education and health. The lowest number was found in electricity, gas and water (0.4 per cent). Looked at in terms of the distribution of employment, the results differ somewhat. In particular, manufacturing accounted for a quarter of all employment, almost as much as both wholesale and retail and health combined. This means that there are differing patterns in the size and distribution of workplaces across industries. For example, manufacturing (32 per cent), electricity, gas and water (55 per cent) and public administration (42 per cent) all had a high proportion of workplaces with 100 or more employees, while the fewest were found in hotels and restaurants and health (both 13 per cent). These differences are reflected in the average number of employees per workplace, which was three times higher in electricity, gas and water than in hotels and restaurants.

Turning to the distribution of single or multiple site workplaces within industries, Table 2.2 shows two distinct clusters. Stand-alone workplaces were relatively common in construction, other business services, other community services and

Table 2.2 Workplace characteristics, by industry

	All workplaces			Workplaces that are part of a wider organisation
	Workplaces Column %	Employees Column %	Average number of employees	Workplaces Row %
Industry				
Manufacturing	18	25	150	60
Electricity, gas and water	0	1	191	98
Construction	4	3	84	40
Wholesale and retail	18	14	84	86
Hotels and restaurants	6	3	62	75
Transport and communications	5	6	120	89
Financial services	3	4	123	86
Other business services	9	9	112	57
Public administration	6	9	162	97
Education	14	10	77	85
Health	13	14	116	65
Other community services	4	3	78	57
All workplaces	100	100	108	73

Base: All workplaces with 25 or more employees.
Figures are weighted and based on responses from 1,929 managers.

manufacturing. By way of contrast, nearly all workplaces in electricity, gas and water and public administration were part of a wider organisation. A similar pattern was evident when examining organisation size by industry. Confining attention just to workplaces that were part of a wider organisation, very large organisations predominated in education (where 59 per cent of workplaces are part of organisations with 10,000 employees or more),[6] financial services (also 59 per cent) and hotels and restaurants (51 per cent). This latter industry had a most unusual distribution in having both a high proportion of stand-alone workplaces and a high proportion of workplaces that were part of very large organisations.

Patterns of ownership and control

The ownership and control of workplaces have important implications for management structure and work organisation. Organisational policies and practices and the extent to which they impinge on an individual workplace's ability to make decisions may depend on the structure of reporting and account-ability within the organisation. For example, workplaces that are more remote from the head office, such as foreign-owned workplaces, may exhibit greater autonomy in their practices by adhering to local rather than overseas norms.

Private/public sector status

Important differences are likely to arise depending on whether a workplace is operating in the private sector attempting to maximise returns for shareholders or in the public sector operating within the confines of pre-determined operating budgets. Even within these sectors, there are important differences in the character of ownership and control. Within the private sector there are partnerships, non-government organisations, co-operatives, private companies and publicly listed companies. However, it is within the public sector that changes in the character of ownership and control have been most profound over recent years. In particular, there has been considerable devolution of authority to local managers in education and health through systems of grant-maintained schools and the creation of National Health Service trusts. This nuance and complexity we leave in the background, instead concentrating on the simple dichotomy of private and public sector workplaces.

The public sector accounted for 28 per cent of all workplaces, nearly all of which (95 per cent) were part of a wider organisation. Among the 72 per cent of workplaces in the private sector, around a third (36 per cent) were stand-alone sites. Overall, public sector workplaces were somewhat larger than those in the private sector, as they employed 32 per cent of all employees. This is reflected in the average employment size, 103 employees in the private sector and 121 in the public sector. There was no great difference in the distribution of workplaces by employment size within the two sectors except at the top end, where there were a considerable number of very large workplaces in the public sector. Indeed, 39 per cent of public sector employees worked in workplaces with 500 or more employees compared with a quarter (25 per cent) of private sector employees.

Sector is very strongly associated with industry with the bulk of workplaces within an industry falling into either the public or the private sector. All or almost all of the workplaces surveyed in manufacturing, wholesale and retail, hotels and restaurants and financial services were in the private sector. Similarly, all public administration workplaces were in the public sector. Industries with relatively large numbers of workplaces found in both sectors include health (with 57 per cent in the private sector), other community services (71 per cent) and transport and communications (78 per cent).

Foreign ownership

Variations in employment relations policies and practices within foreign-owned workplaces may reflect the cultures and management styles imported into, or adapted to fit in with, British employment relations. Moreover, Cooke (1997) shows that US multinational companies' decisions on where to invest are very much guided by the character of the host country's industrial relations system.

In the private sector, 81 per cent of workplaces were found to be wholly UK-owned, 6 per cent were partly foreign-owned and 13 per cent predominantly (i.e. 51 per cent or more) or wholly foreign-owned. As shown in Table 2.3, the larger the workplace, the more likely it was to be foreign-owned.

Table 2.3 UK and foreign ownership in private sector workplaces, by workplace size

	Wholly UK-owned	Partly foreign-owned	Predominantly or wholly foreign-owned
	% of workplaces	% of workplaces	% of workplaces
Workplace size			
25–49 employees	82	7	11
50–99 employees	85	4	10
100–199 employees	72	6	22
200–499 employees	74	7	19
500 or more employees	59	12	28
All private sector workplaces	81	6	13

Base: All private sector workplaces with 25 or more employees.
Figures are weighted and based on responses from 1,308 managers.

Another indicator of the pattern of control, and whether or not it originates from outside the UK, is the location of the controlling head office. Among all private sector workplaces that are part of a wider organisation, 87 per cent had their controlling head office in the UK (which includes those workplaces that *were* the head office of the organisation). Among the fifth of private sector workplaces which were not wholly UK-owned, half still had a UK head office with the remainder having head offices in the United States (23 per cent), European Union member states (15 per cent), other European countries (11 per cent) and Japan (1 per cent).[7]

Working owners

A different aspect of ownership (that we use primarily in Chapter 11) is the presence of a working owner. The working owner is a provider of both capital and labour. This raises dilemmas about how proprietorial authority mixes with face-to-face relations, especially in the context of small businesses (Scase, 1995). Alternatively, where owners are absent it becomes necessary to develop more explicit supervisory control through formal structures and procedures.

An individual or family had a controlling interest in 28 per cent of private sector workplaces, defined as those being at least half owned by the individual/family. Among these, over two-thirds (70 per cent) had a full-time owner-manager on site, so that a fifth (20 per cent) of all private sector workplaces had a working owner present. Working owners were more common in stand-alone sites (45 per cent) and were relatively over-represented in construction (35 per cent), health (32 per cent) and manufacturing (27 per cent). Similarly, working owners were mostly found in small workplaces, though even in the largest private sector workplaces they formed a significant minority (7 per cent).

Figure 2.2 Workplace age

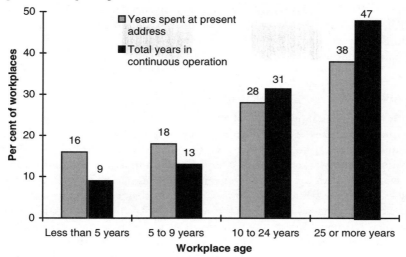

Base: All workplaces with 25 or more employees.
Figures are weighted and based on responses from 1,902 (present address) and 1,872 (continuous operation) managers.

Workplace age

The final area that we examine is the number of years a workplace has been operating. We can measure workplace age in two ways: first, the number of years in existence at its present address; and second, the total number of years it has been in existence, adding in any years spent at a previous location. The pattern is broadly similar, as shown in Figure 2.2. Most workplaces have been in operation for many years – one workplace in the sample reported that it had been in continuous operation since 1333.[8]

Public sector workplaces were, on average, older than private sector workplaces. Just 6 per cent of public sector workplaces were new (i.e. less than five years old) using the second of the definitions above, while around two-thirds (67 per cent) had been in existence for twenty-five years or more. The comparative figures for the private sector were, respectively, 11 per cent and 40 per cent. Newer workplaces were disproportionately found in construction (22 per cent), public administration (15 per cent) and hotels and restaurants (13 per cent), while education had the highest proportion of relatively old workplaces (83 per cent).

There has also been much recent interest in 'greenfield' sites (Guest and Rosenthal, 1993), in part because past surveys in this series have shown them to have quite distinct patterns of employment relations, notably in being without a union presence (Millward, 1994). A particular form of this is where a workplace re-locates from one location to another with newly built premises. This might allow management the opportunity to implement changes to working practices 'freed from the constraints of tradition and custom and practice' (Guest and Rosenthal, 1993: 13), especially if the move involved a change in the workforce. Overall, 19 per cent of all workplaces had moved to a new address at some stage during the past ten years, and of these around two-fifths (40 per cent) had switched to premises built on a greenfield site.

Conclusion

As this chapter has shown, the WERS 98 survey population is diverse. Using structural characteristics as a means of unravelling the patterns in employment relations is one way to make sense of this diversity. In particular, it allows practitioners and workers alike to compare and contrast the situation in their own workplace with the generality of other like workplaces. Nevertheless, such analyses should be treated with some caution, as they can obscure significant differences between workplaces with the same, or similar characteristics. Moreover, while they can reveal interesting patterns, it would be wrong to assume that a particular form of employment relations arises *because* of a workplace's structural characteristics. Part of the purpose of the remaining chapters is to identify other features of the workplace that affect the pattern of employment relations, independent of these structural characteristics.

Notes

1 The data editing instructions are described fully in the SCPR technical report (Airey *et al.*, 1999).
2 This is the legal definition of employee. Clarifying employment status can be difficult, especially among those working in non-standard employment (Burchell *et al.*, 1999).
3 This is not to say agency and contract workers were not represented in the survey since the sampling frame included contracting and employment agency workplaces in their own right.
4 A high proportion (15 per cent, unweighted) of managers in workplaces that were part of a wider organisation were unable to answer this question. We therefore use the number of employees in the organisation, where there were 7 per cent unable to answer, as our preferred indicator of organisation size.
5 There may have been more than one activity undertaken at the workplace but it is the main activity that is used. Similarly, where a workplace is part of a wider organisation, there may be considerable differentiation in activity across workplaces in that organisation, but that is something we chose not to investigate.
6 It is likely that some of the respondents in the education sector took the 'wider organisation' to mean the local authority, rather than the local education authority, in which they were located.
7 Since controlling head offices may not be located in the country in which the parent organisation is head-quartered, reliance on this question may be less useful for understanding the diffusion of overseas employment relations practices than the question on foreign ownership.
8 Due to an error in question routing, we have had to impute the total years in continuous operation for work places at their current address for 10–24 years, but which have moved at some stage. The results may also be slightly biased towards older workplaces. The precise interval between the drawing of the sample and the close of fieldwork is uncertain, but is likely to be over one year (Airey *et al.*, 1999: 46). Smaller workplaces were more likely to have closed in that time and our analysis shows these are, on the whole, relatively young workplaces (if in the private sector).

3 Workforce composition and employers' labour use

How employers structure their workforces, how they attempt to attain flexibility and how they organise work are all issues of considerable academic and policy interest. These three issues are explored in this chapter. The distinct contribution this survey can make, unlike household surveys such as the Labour Force Survey, is to look at how the labour process is structured *within* workplaces. Of course, this is a partial analysis, as we capture only the employer dimension. For example, if the proportion of hospitals employing predominantly female nurses is high (as it is), we cannot say whether this arises from employer preferences or because of other social factors which lead more women than men to opt for nursing as a vocation. Nonetheless, employers face and exercise choices in how they compose and deploy their workforces, and these choices have ramifications for workers and the conduct of employment relations within, and across, workplaces.

Workforce composition

Most of the information in this opening section is drawn from the Employee Profile Questionnaire (EPQ), a four-page form sent to managers prior to interview, which sought details of actual numbers of people employed at the workplace broken down into a range of different categories, such as occupation, hours of work, and gender. Information was also collected on earnings, labour turnover, absenteeism and union membership. Data from the EPQ was obtained at the start of the management interview, and any inconsistencies were clarified and corrected at that time.[1] As a result the information obtained was of high quality. We use it to look at the extent to which employees cluster in non-random ways across workplaces, looking first at individual characteristics and then at job characteristics.

Gender

It is well-established that, across the economy, women earn less than men and are less likely to occupy positions of high status (Hakim, 1996; Crompton, 1997). Both of these indicators of women's relative standing have been causally related to the extent of occupational segregation; that is, some jobs are so predominantly male or female that there are, in effect, separate labour markets for them which produce differing outcomes on things like pay. The social origins of occupational segregation have been heavily debated, but that is not what concerns us here; our focus is on uncovering evidence of segregation within workplaces, and determining whether this is in any way related to employer policies.

Overall, men accounted for 52 per cent, and women 48 per cent, of employment in workplaces with 25 or more employees. This aggregate figure varied across workplaces, as shown in Table 3.1. Most marked are the sectoral differences: women accounted for around three-fifths of employment in the public sector and a little over two-fifths in the private sector. An alternative way of presenting this information is to look at the share of female employment *within* workplaces, which is the second column in Table 3.1. In roughly half of all workplaces women constituted a majority of the workforce. The pattern is consistent with the first column, but is even more marked. There were relatively few workplaces in manufacturing, electricity, gas and water, construction and transport and communication where at least half the workforce were women. By contrast, almost all workplaces in education and health had majority female workforces.

The final column in Table 3.1 shows the percentage of workplaces where the female share of workplace employment was less than half the industry average. For example, 26 per cent of employees in manufacturing workplaces were women. Table 3.1 shows that, in around a third (34 per cent) of manufacturing workplaces, women made up less than half of this percentage, i.e. in these workplaces their employment share was below 13 per cent. This indicates the extent to which workplaces in a given industry are out of step with the industry average. Overall, a fifth of workplaces fell into this category, but the proportion in the private sector was almost double that in the public sector. However, it is at the industry level that the findings become more significant. The predominance of women in education and health is largely uniform across workplaces with almost no workplaces in these industries having a relatively low female presence. In contrast, somewhere between a third and over half of workplaces in manufacturing, electricity, gas and water, construction, and transport and communication had a relatively low female presence, even taking account of the (relatively low) industry average.

These findings suggest that some of the differences in the patterns of female employment are due to factors over and above certain industries being 'gendered'. Cockburn (1983) has shown, for instance, that a male culture operates at the workplace in certain sub-sectors (like printing in her case studies) so as to exclude suitably-qualified women. We examine two possibly related factors: first, if the workplace was covered by an equal opportunities policy; and, second, whether as a matter of practice the workplace keeps records on the number of jobs held by men and women.

Some two-thirds (64 per cent) of workplaces were covered by formal written equal opportunities policies that dealt with equality of treatment or discrimination. Half that number (32 per cent) kept records. Workplaces covered by an equal opportunities policy were more than three times as likely to keep records as those

Table 3.1 Employment of women, by main classifications

	Female share of employment	Mostly women (over half) at workplace	Low female presence (under half of industry average)
	% of women in employment	*% of workplaces*	*% of workplaces*
Workplace size			
25–49 employees	55	55	19
50–99 employees	47	51	23
100–199 employees	46	50	18
200–499 employees	45	46	21
500 or more employees	48	47	16
Organisation size			
Less than 100 employees	46	44	20
100–999 employees	40	31	30
1,000–9,999 employees	47	52	24
10,000 employees or more	52	73	12
Sector			
Private	42	43	23
Public	61	77	12
Organisational status			
Stand-alone workplace	50	48	19
Part of a wider organisation	47	54	20
Industry			
Manufacturing	26	11	34
Electricity, gas and water	27	8	55
Construction	15	3	38
Wholesale and retail	54	46	31
Hotels and restaurants	57	65	3
Transport and communications	21	13	36
Financial services	58	73	15
Other business services	50	46	26
Public administration	45	51	20
Education	68	96	0
Health	82	97	1
Other community services	45	50	14
All workplaces	48	53	20

Base: All workplaces with 25 or more employees.
Figures are weighted and based on responses from 1,914 managers.

without, 43 per cent compared to 13 per cent. Even so, the correspondence between policy and practice was not high, confirming the findings of earlier case study work in this area (Jewson *et al.*,1995).

Figure 3.1 illustrates the differences we found across workplaces. Both the operation of an equal opportunities policy and the monitoring of employment were associated with lower proportions of workplaces with a relatively low female presence (i.e. horizontal segregation).

These policies and practices might also be associated with vertical segregation. Our measure of vertical segregation looks at whether female managers are over- or under-represented in the workplace. A ratio was calculated of the proportion of female managers (among female employees) relative to the proportion of male managers (among male employees). If this figure equals one, then managerial jobs were equally distributed between men and women – that is, in proportion to their employment in the workplace. If it is less than one, men disproportionately held managerial jobs, while the opposite is true if the figure is greater than one. For example, if women made up a third of the workforce in a workplace, but only accounted for a quarter of the managerial positions, the ratio is less than one.

There were disproportionate numbers of male managers in 70 per cent of workplaces. There was no difference between the private and public sectors, save that the public sector had a higher proportion of workplaces with only female managers and the private sector had a higher proportion with only male managers. Having an equal opportunities policy in place appears to have two distinct effects: it was associated with, first, a lower proportion of workplaces with only male managers and, second, a higher proportion with only female managers. It was *not* found to be associated with any difference in the broader gender composition of management as male managers were relatively over-represented in around 70 per cent of these workplaces. Finally, the fact that a workplace had a relatively low female presence had no bearing on the representation of female managers. Women are under represented at managerial rank in all types of workplaces.

Other individual characteristics: ethnic origin and age

There are a variety of other ways in which the composition of a workforce may differ from one workplace to the next. Two that are known to be important for the conduct of employment relations are ethnicity and age. Race, for example, has been found to be a factor associated with low pay and higher levels of redundancies (Jenkins, 1989), and is also covered by legislation outlawing discrimination. Likewise, age is related to both union membership and earnings; young workers tend to have more frequent job turnover; and there is emerging concern about older workers experiencing discrimination in redundancy selection and recruitment (Taylor and Walker, 1994).

Overall, the shares of employment for these three groups were 6 per cent for those from an ethnic minority background, 6 per cent for young workers (aged under twenty one years), and 16 per cent for older workers (aged over fifty years). Table 3.2 shows the proportion of workplaces in different categories where the

Figure 3.1 Low female presence at the workplace, by equal opportunities policy and record keeping

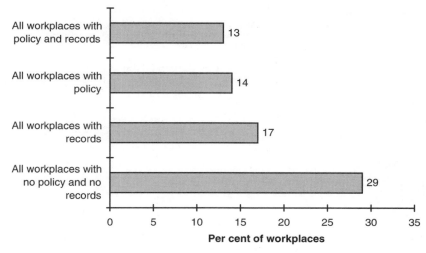

Bases: All workplaces with 25 or more employees.
Figures are weighted and based on responses from 1,910 managers.

workplace share for each of these groups is at least a tenth. In 12 per cent of cases workers from ethnic minorities made up a tenth or more of the workforce, compared with 22 per cent where younger workers made up at least a tenth, and 61 per cent of workplaces with at least the same proportion of older workers.

There was a remarkable disparity in the employment of young workers between the public and private sectors, with it being very rare for any workplaces in the public sector to employ a significant proportion of young people. In fact, almost two-thirds (65 per cent) of public sector workplaces employed *no one* under the age of twenty-one. These differences were even more marked in a few industries, such as hotels and restaurants, where younger workers made up at least a tenth of the workforce in 81 per cent of workplaces, compared with below 5 per cent in electricity, gas and water, public administration and education.

There were not such pronounced patterns in the clustering by size and sector of workers from ethnic minorities. It was notable, however, that, as workplace size increased, so too did the proportion of workplaces where ethnic minority workers made up at least a tenth of the workforce. There was a similar association with organisation size.

The distribution of the employment of older workers is partly a mirror image of the distribution of employment of younger workers. Here, the public sector exceeded the private sector in its employment of older workers. There were some industries with high proportions of workplaces where both younger and older workers made up a tenth or more of the workforce – wholesale and retail and other community services – and some with low proportions on both counts – notably, financial services.

Table 3.2 Employment of ethnic minorities, young workers and old workers, by workplace size and sector

	Workplaces where a tenth or more of the workforce are:		
	From an ethnic minority	Aged under 21	Aged over 50
	% of workplaces	% of workplaces	% of workplaces
Workplace size			
25–49 employees	11	24	58
50–99 employees	12	23	58
100–199 employees	12	17	70
200–499 employees	18	21	67
500 or more employees	21	8	71
Sector			
Private	12	31	56
Public	13	2	71
All workplaces	12	22	61

Base: All workplaces with 25 or more employees.
Figures are weighted and based on responses from 1,864 (column 1), 1,896 (column 2) and 1,893 (column 3) managers.

Workplaces with an equal opportunities policy employed proportionately more workers from ethnic minorities, but fewer younger workers and fewer older workers than workplaces without a policy. Thus, in the two areas where there is anti-discrimination legislation (i.e. sex and race), equal opportunities policies were associated with greater employment of the affected groups; in the non-statutory field of age there was no such association.

Occupation

As with information on sex, race and age, the breakdown of employment by occupation was obtained via the EPQ. Managers were asked to divide their workforce into nine occupational groups (based on the 1990 Standard Occupational Classification).[2] The average workplace employed people in five of the nine occupational groups. This number increased with workplace size, from four occupational groups in the smallest workplaces to six in the largest. Figure 3.2 shows the proportion of workplaces in which each of the nine groups were found.

Almost no workplace could make do without managers – indeed, it may even be seen as something of a novelty that 7 per cent of workplaces did not employ any managers.[3] Similarly, most workplaces employed people in clerical and/or secretarial positions. The least common occupations found across the breadth of workplaces were those in protective and personal services and operative and assembly work.

Figure 3.2 Occupations employed at the workplace

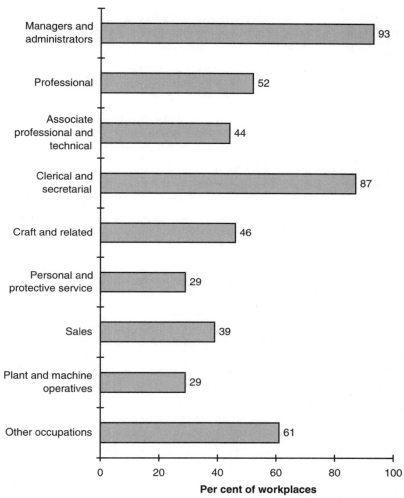

Base: All workplaces with 25 or more employees.
Figures are weighted and based on responses from 1,904 managers.

There were substantial differences in the occupational make-up of workplaces across industries. For example, professionals were represented in nearly all education workplaces (99 per cent), but were found in only about a fifth of workplaces in wholesale and retail and hotels and restaurants (both 22 per cent). Similar extremes can be found for many of the other occupational groups, and the patterns are mostly unsurprising, bar some minor anomalies (which we may put down to the whimsy of respondents, many of whom would have confronted the occupational classification for the first time). It might be thought, for example,

Table 3.3 Largest occupational group at the workplace, by industry

	Occupation with the most employees	% of workplaces
Industry		
Manufacturing	Plant and machine operatives	48
Electricity, gas and water	Craft and related	45
Construction	Craft and related	41
Wholesale and retail	Sales	51
Hotels and restaurants	Personal and protective service	29
Transport and communications	Plant and machine operatives	45
Financial services	Clerical and secretarial	64
Other business services	Clerical and secretarial	30
Public administration	Clerical and secretarial	49
Education	Professional	69
Health	Personal and protective service	60
Other community services	Other occupations	34

Base: All workplaces with 25 or more employees.
Figures are weighted and based on responses from 1,929 managers.

that almost every workplace engaged in public administration employs clerks of some description, yet 6 per cent did not according to our results.

From the EPQ, it was possible to identify the occupation which accounted for the greatest proportion of non-managerial employees, the 'largest occupational group'. Throughout the remainder of the questionnaire, there were many questions asked solely with reference to this group. In some areas we would expect there to be differences within a workplace – in, for example, the organisation of work – with occupation being the main source of difference. Asking questions with reference to the largest occupational group was adopted as a heuristic device to prevent the interview becoming unduly long and unwieldy by having to repeat questions for each occupational group present at the workplace. Conversely, it necessarily constrained our view of diversity across groups within a workplace.

On average, employees in the largest occupational group made up 61 per cent of all employees and 67 per cent of non-managerial employees at the workplace. In 73 per cent of workplaces, the largest occupational group made up more than half of the non-managerial workforce, and in a further 24 per cent between a third and a half. By definition, they are numerically the most important, but we also take it as a proxy for the 'core' workforce – that is, those most likely to be engaged in the main business activities of the workplace – in common with the approach adopted by Osterman (1994). This is readily apparent from Table 3.3 which shows, for each industry, the occupation most likely to have constituted the core. In manufacturing, for example, operative and assembly workers were the largest occupational group in about half of workplaces.

Using the information on occupation we are also able to explore the skill mix of the workforce in each workplace. Glynn and Gospel (1993: 121) attribute what they call the 'low skill equilibrium' of the British labour market to a 'failure by British firms to demand, employ, and develop well educated and trained workers'. We explore the demand and employ dimension of this statement below – development and training are covered in the next chapter.

For each workplace we summed the number of employees falling into the three occupational groups that require the most extensive levels of vocational training or post-schooling qualifications: professionals, associate professional and technical occupations, and craft and related occupations (Office of Population Censuses and Surveys, 1990). This figure was used to calculate the proportion of non-managerial employees who were 'skilled' workers in each workplace. Table 3.4 shows how these were distributed across industry. Nearly a third of all workplaces have a majority skilled workforce, while a further third employ 10 per cent or fewer skilled workers.

Among the industries with a very high proportion of workplaces with no skilled workers were wholesale and retail, and financial services, both industries with a high female share of employment (see Table 3.1). By contrast, education also employed many women but has a high proportion of workplaces with skilled workers. This suggests a possible sectoral divide. In the private sector there was a strong inverse association between the proportion of female employees and the proportion of skilled workers. In the public sector there was no such relationship.[4] For example, in private sector workplaces where women were in the majority,

Table 3.4 Proportion of skilled employees at the workplace, by industry

	Skilled* employees as a proportion of non-managerial employment:				
	No skilled employees	*10% or less*	*More than 10% to 25%*	*More than 25% to 50%*	*More than 50%*
	% of workplaces	*% of workplaces*	*% of workplaces*	*% of workplaces*	*% of workplaces*
Industry					
Manufacturing	4	17	23	20	37
Electricity, gas and water	2	2	6	21	68
Construction	19	2	10	14	54
Wholesale and retail	40	26	12	10	12
Hotels and restaurants	21	23	38	9	8
Transport and communications	33	32	10	9	15
Financial services	57	9	14	13	7
Other business services	12	11	7	23	47
Public administration	27	15	16	13	29
Education	0	0	2	42	55
Health	22	7	26	23	22
Other community services	17	23	13	16	31
All workplaces	19	15	16	20	30

Base: All workplaces with 25 or more employees.
Figures are weighted and based on responses from 1,862 managers.
* Skilled employees represent the sum of 'professional', 'associate professional and technical' and 'craft and related' occupations as a proportion of all employees at the workplace.

skilled workers were also in the majority in 14 per cent of workplaces, compared with 34 per cent where men were in the majority. In the public sector the respective figures were 41 per cent and 48 per cent.

We use this measure of skill throughout the remainder of this chapter (and elsewhere in the book) to look at other aspects of employers' labour use.

The deployment of labour

We have looked at the types of people employed, and the jobs they do, across British workplaces and how they cluster in particular ways. It is also the case that jobs, even the same type of jobs, will be organised differently from one workplace to the next, and even within workplaces.

Recent years have seen an extensive debate on the changing nature of work. Official statistical sources show increases over the 1980s and 1990s in the number of people working part-time, in self-employment, working for an agency, or engaged in some other form of temporary work. Discussions on this topic often omit nationally representative data on how employers adopt and use these various forms of labour (though see Hakim (1990) and Beatson (1995) for exceptions). A substantial block of questions was devoted to this area in the survey. We begin by looking at employers' use of part-time labour, then turn to a discussion about the use of different forms of so-called non-standard employment and the extent of work that is outsourced.

Hours of work: full and part-time work

We divided the workforce into full- and part-time based on the official statistical convention of 30 hours or more per week used in Britain. Across all workplaces, full-timers accounted for 75 per cent of employment, and part-timers 25 per cent. Women held 81 per cent of the part-time jobs (which accounted for 42 per cent of all women's jobs). In Table 3.5, we report two workplace-based measures of working hours: workplaces where all employees were full-time; and workplaces where part-time employees accounted for over half of all employees.

Overall, 16 per cent of workplaces employed only full-timers, followed by a further quarter (26 per cent) of workplaces employing relatively few (less than 10 per cent) part-timers. Another quarter (26 per cent) of all workplaces had a workforce where part-time workers were in the majority. This distribution, however, varies a lot between different types of workplace.

There were very high proportions of workplaces in wholesale and retail, hotels and restaurants, and education and health, where part-time workers constituted a majority.

Table 3.5 also shows a pronounced association with organisation size: around half of all workplaces belonging to very large organisations have workforces that are mostly part-time. There is also a relationship between part-time work and low skills among workplaces in the private sector. Part-time employees were in the majority in 43 per cent of private sector workplaces with no skilled employees,

Table 3.5 Part-time employment, by main classifications

	Proportion of part-time employees at workplace		Part-time share of employment
	None	*Over half*	*All workplaces*
	% of workplaces	*% of workplaces*	*% of employees*
Workplace size			
25–49 employees	18	32	32
50–99 employees	17	22	25
100–199 employees	9	15	22
200–499 employees	11	23	24
500 or more employees	6	17	23
Organisation size			
Less than 100 employees	24	18	21
100–999 employees	22	11	17
1,000–9,999 employees	14	24	21
10,000 employees or more	5	48	32
Sector			
Private	20	25	22
Public	5	30	30
Organisational status			
Stand-alone workplace	20	20	28
Part of a wider organisation	14	29	24
Industry			
Manufacturing	36	1	4
Electricity, gas and water	51	0	5
Construction	39	0	5
Wholesale and retail	14	43	45
Hotels and restaurants	3	55	47
Transport and communications	23	4	9
Financial services	20	5	15
Other business services	23	7	26
Public administration	9	1	12
Education	0	40	40
Health	1	50	44
Other community services	8	51	36
All workplaces	16	26	25

Base: All workplaces with 25 or more employees.
Figures are weighted and based on responses from 1,914 managers.

compared with just 6 per cent of workplaces where the majority of workers were also in skilled occupations. There was no such association in the public sector.

Sub-contracting and non-standard forms of labour

In contemporary labour markets there are a variety of different contractual forms under which labour can be performed. The conventional or 'standard' form is for employers to hire people under a contract of employment, be it full- or part-time. It is also standard for that contract to be open-ended, with notice periods built in on both sides of the contract if either party wishes to terminate it. Two 'non-standard' variants which have grown rapidly over the past decade (although they still make up only a small fraction of the employed labour force) are fixed-term contracts and 'zero-hours' contracts. Under the first of these, the contract runs for a specified period instead of being open-ended. The parties to the contract can choose to renew the contract when it expires. Zero-hours contracts are of a more casual kind, where there may be an ongoing employment relationship but no guaranteed regularity in hours worked.

There are also non-standard forms of labour where the employer contracts for services to be provided, some of which may be for labour-only services. It has become increasingly common for services to be outsourced (e.g. cleaning, security), particularly in the wake of compulsory competitive tendering regulations applied to local authorities. Labour-only services may also be provided by freelancers or homeworkers or through a third contracting party, an employment agency.

Thus far in examining employment levels we have used as our definition all those with a contract of employment with the employing workplace. This might have the effect of excluding several forms of non-standard labour from our employment figures – they would either be self-employed or employment status could be indeterminate, a 'mixed question of law and fact' (Court of Appeal in O'Kelly *v* Trusthouse Forte plc, cited in Deakin and Morris, 1995: 145). This is often the case with homeworkers. Others, such as agency workers, will be employed from another workplace.

We asked questions about each of these ways in which labour might be deployed. Table 3.6 summarises the use of non-standard forms of employment across all workplaces, comparing differences between the public and private sectors. Far and away the most common category identified was sub-contracting, undertaken by 90 per cent of workplaces. We look in more detail at this below. The next most widely used category was fixed-term contracts, found in almost half of all workplaces, followed by temporary agency workers ('temps') in just over a quarter of workplaces. There was more modest use of freelancers, home-workers and employees on zero-hours contracts.

In most categories, the incidence of non-standard work was slightly greater in the private than the public sector, with the notable exception of fixed-term contracts. Almost three-quarters of public sector workplaces had some employees on fixed-term contracts compared with a third of private sector workplaces.

Table 3.6 Sub-contracting and use of non-standard labour, by sector

	Sector		All workplaces
	Private	*Public*	
	% of workplaces	*% of workplaces*	*% of workplaces*
Sub-contract one or more services	91	88	90
Temporary agency workers	29	26	28
Fixed-term contract employees	34	72	44
Freelance workers	16	7	13
Homeworkers	8	3	6
Zero-hour contract employees	6	2	5
None of these used	5	6	5

Base: All workplaces with 25 or more employees.
Figures are weighted and based on responses from 1,914 managers.

Summarising the overall use of non-standard labour, about three-fifths of workplaces used both contractors and one other form of non-standard labour, and a little under a third used contractors only. Much smaller proportions did not use contractors but did use some other form of non-standard labour, and just 5 per cent of workplaces used no non-standard labour of any kind.

There was a positive association between each of the forms of non-standard labour and the skill level of the workforce, with the sole exception of workers on zero-hours contracts. Even after taking account of workplace size, we found that the use of temps, workers on fixed-term contracts and freelancers was greater the higher the proportion of skilled workers at the workplace. For example, 38 per cent of workplaces where skilled workers were in the majority used temps, compared with 15 per cent of workplaces with no skilled workers. Each of these different forms of non-standard labour can be thought of as a means by which employers attain numerical flexibility – that is, employers' ability to adjust the size of the workforce in line with short-term variations in the demand for labour.

Another way in which it is possible to make short-term adjustments is by shifting employees between tasks, sometimes referred to as functional flexibility. Managers were asked what proportion of employees in the largest occupational group were formally trained to be able to do jobs other than their own. In well over half of workplaces, the answer was none (29 per cent) or just a few (29 per cent), and in only just under a quarter (23 per cent) of workplaces was there a clear majority who were trained to be functionally flexible.

Ackroyd and Procter (1998) highlight the rise in British manufacturing of what they call the 'new flexible firm'. This is contrasted with the original notion of the flexible firm put forward by Atkinson (1984). His model suggested that flexible firms pursued a joint strategy of functional flexibility for the 'core' workforce and numerical flexibility for the 'periphery'. Ackroyd and Procter argue that both means of securing flexibility have now intruded into the core. We take up some of these issues below, looking in more detail at sub-contracting and the use of temps and workers on fixed-term contracts.

Managers were asked to identify which services were sub-contracted at their workplace from a list of eleven possible activities. On average, workplaces had sub-contracted four of these eleven services. Foremost among these were building maintenance (61 per cent), cleaning (59 per cent), transporting of documents or goods (39 per cent), training (37 per cent) and security (35 per cent). It may be that such services have never been undertaken at the workplace – small workplaces, for example, are unlikely to provide or require catering – so the actual incidence of sub-contracting, in this sense, may be slightly understated.

Of all workplaces that were five or more years old, 28 per cent had contracted-out some services which five years earlier had been done by direct employees of the workplace (or parent organisation).[5] This proportion was higher in the public sector – 36 per cent compared with 25 per cent in the private sector – and was particularly pronounced in electricity, gas and water (77 per cent), public administration (47 per cent) and financial services (45 per cent).

Of these workplaces, about a third – giving an overall proportion of 10 per cent of workplaces were five or more years old – were using contractors that included former direct employees of the workplace (or parent organisation). These cases constitute a direct transfer of employment from one employer to another within the confines of the activities of a single workplace. Again, this proportion was higher in the public sector (19 per cent of workplaces more than five years old) than in the private sector (6 per cent).

In workplaces where managers had contracted out services, they were asked the reasons for doing so. Although structured surveys are not an ideal tool for exploring motivation, some robust findings emerged. Around half (48 per cent) of all workplaces that had contracted out services previously undertaken by direct employees had done so to make cost savings. This was, by far, the most common reason given. Others included the ability to focus on core business activities (27 per cent) and to offer an improved service (21 per cent).

In the public sector, among workplaces that had moved towards subcontracting, 38 per cent said they did so because of government-led initiatives or regulations. Although this might imply that contracting out was foisted upon the public sector, there was no difference between the proportions of workplaces in the private and public sector saying they were motivated by potential cost savings.

Cost savings appear to have been realised. Overall, 42 per cent of workplaces said they made cost savings through contracting out, but 31 per cent were now paying *more* for the same services with the remainder paying about the same. Where the motivation for contracting out was to make cost savings, these were more likely to have been realised – two-thirds (66 per cent) had saved money, while only a tenth (11 per cent) were paying more. Similarly, government initiatives to stimulate contracting out appear to have led to net savings – 42 per cent of these workplaces were paying less and 18 per cent were paying more. The most common stated motivation for contracting out among those workplaces where the service now costs more was to obtain an improved service (35 per cent).

Savings in labour costs did not feature prominently in reasons for engaging temporary agency workers or employees on fixed-term contracts. For workplaces using temps, the most commonly cited reasons for doing so were short-term cover (59 per cent) and adjusting the size of the labour force in line with demand (40 per cent). The latter reason was also the most common explanation for the use of fixed-term contracts (39 per cent of workplaces). Other reasons for using fixed-term contracts were to obtain specialist skills (21 per cent), a freeze on permanent staff numbers (18 per cent) and as a trial for a permanent job (17 per cent). Cover for maternity leave was also an important category for the employment of both temps (22 per cent) and those on fixed-term contracts (11 per cent).

Where temps and fixed-term contracts were used, they were most likely to be engaged alongside workers in the largest occupational group. Table 3.7 shows, for each occupation, that the proportion of workplaces employing people on fixed-term contracts was always greater where they were in the largest occupational group. For example, a third of workplaces where clerical workers were the largest occupational group also had clerks on fixed-term contracts. In comparison, across workplaces generally, just 13 per cent employed some clerks on a fixed-term basis.

Table 3.7 Use of employees on fixed-term contracts and temporary agency workers, by occupation

	Any in largest occupational group	Any in workplace
	% of workplaces	*% of workplaces*
Employees on fixed-term contracts		
Managers and administrators	–	6
Professional	61	15
Associate professional and technical	24	5
Clerical and secretarial	33	13
Craft and related	13	3
Personal and protective service	24	5
Sales	28	4
Plant and machine operatives	14	3
Other occupations	21	6
Temporary agency workers		
Managers and administrators	–	1
Professional	19	5
Associate professional and technical	30	5
Clerical and secretarial	40	16
Craft and related	8	2
Personal and protective service	10	2
Sales	3	0
Plant and machine operatives	23	4
Other occupations	8	5

Base: All workplaces with 25 or more employees.
Figures are weighted and based on responses from 1,868 (fixed-term) and 1,891 (agency workers) managers.

This pattern persisted across workplaces for all occupational groups, with the most widespread use of people on fixed-term contracts being found in core workforces.

The degree of correspondence was, overall, slightly lower between the occupations in which temps were used and the largest occupational group at the workplace, but was still very high. It was highest among workplaces where clerical workers were the largest occupational group and lowest for craft and skilled manual workers. In workplaces where technical workers, craft and skilled manual workers and sales workers were the largest occupational group, it was most common for temps to be engaged in clerical activities; nonetheless, in these cases the second most common use of temps was found in the largest occupational group. It appears that the use of non-standard forms of labour is more closely related to employment *within* the core than outside it.

Moreover, with the exception of sub-contracting, there was a statistically confirmed negative association at the workplace level between the different forms of non-standard labour (numerical flexibility) and functional flexibility.[6] The positive association between sub-contracting and functional flexibility is consistent with the argument that employers dispense with non-core activities leaving them free to concentrate on developing the skills of the core workforce. Otherwise, these results are at odds with Atkinson and with Ackroyd and Procter, both of which would suggest a positive association between numerical and functional flexibility. Ackroyd and Procter are half right though: where numerical flexibility is pursued it is more likely to be within the core workforce. Taking managers' motivations at face value, it also appears that the use of non-standard labour in the core workforce is more to do with buttressing that workforce and making short-term adjustments to the size of it, than in making permanent changes to its status.

Work organisation

Debates about the organisation of work have been at the forefront of industrial sociology for more than a decade. One strand, referred to as labour process theory, has its roots in Braverman's *Labour and Monopoly Capital* (1974), which argued that increasing division of labour would lead to a continual de-skilling of the workforce. Another strand, popularised by Piore and Sabel (1984), suggested that a new form of work organisation, one based on 'flexible specialisation', was emerging. Much of the debate is situated within manufacturing and the research is characterised by ethnographic and detailed case studies, usually conducted within factories. For instance, the so-called 'lean production' model, which has considerably influenced contemporary debate, was based on the organisation of work within Toyota.

We focus on three issues in this section, namely the extent of multi-tasking, job influence and teamworking. Other aspects of new forms of work organisation – specifically the 'fit' with the management of employees – are investigated in the next chapter. Our data is more general than can be obtained from case studies but lacks the depth of this method of analysis. In looking at the organisation of work for the core workforce, the occupational group clearly needs to be taken into account. Rather than providing a separate account for each of the eight (non-managerial) groups, we will give an overall perspective and highlight the main occupational differences.

Multi-tasking and job responsibilities

The occupational groupings we have used are relatively broad, and it may be that there are distinct sub-groupings or classifications within a workplace. The scale of this is of interest as one of the features of new forms of work organisation is a reduction in job demarcations, with workers supposedly becoming multi-skilled and able to undertake a variety of tasks within a workplace. While we are unable to explore the process of change, we can look at the number of distinctly different job classifications within the largest occupational group and see how it is associated with different types of workplace. The number of job classifications ranged from 1 to 70 within our sample, with 91 per cent of workplaces having fewer than ten, and an overall median of four and a mean of five. The factor most closely associated with the number of job classifications within a workplace was employment size. As employment size increased, so too did the number of job classifications, and this was consistent for each of the eight occupational groups. After taking account of employment size, workplaces where associate professional and technical workers and craft and related workers formed the core workforce had the highest number of job classifications. Where craft and related occupations formed the core workforce, manufacturing workplaces had the same average number of job classifications as workplaces in other industries. It was higher, however, in manufacturing workplaces where operative and assembly workers were the core (compared with workplaces in other industries). Again, we are unable to capture any trend towards multi-tasking and reduced job demarcation with our data, but its spread would appear on the basis of this measure to be no more widespread than elsewhere in the manufacturing industry, supposedly at the forefront of changing work organisation.

How employees are informed of their job responsibilities should say something about the character of work organisation. Supervision was the dominant mode, with 84 per cent of workplaces using this to convey job responsibilities to workers in the largest occupational group. Formal documentation which prescribes how a job is to be conducted was also very much a norm – 59 per cent of workplaces had standard operating procedures, 58 per cent a staff manual and 39 per cent both. Specifying individual objectives and targets was one of the least common ways of making individuals aware of their job responsibilities, used in 41 per cent of workplaces.

There were important variations in the means used to convey job responsibilities, depending on the occupation concerned. Supervision was most commonly used where personal service workers made up the core workforce (94 per cent) and least common, but still a very high proportion, for clerical workers (77 per cent). The greatest variation was to do with setting individual targets, which was most common where the largest occupational group were professionals (63 per cent) or sales workers (60 per cent), and least common where it was routine unskilled manual workers (16 per cent) or operative and assembly workers (19 per cent).

We have already discussed aggregate figures on the proportion of the core workforce trained to be able to move from one job to another ('functional flexibility') and now we explore this in more detail. There is, foremost, a great deal of difference depending upon which occupation makes up the largest group. The lowest levels of functional flexibility are found among workplaces where technical and scientific workers make up the core workforce – in over 80 per cent of these cases either no or very few workers had been trained to be functionally flexible, and in only 7 per cent of cases were most so trained. By way of contrast, in workplaces where sales workers constituted the core workforce, 45 per cent had trained most of these workers to be functionally flexible while 36 per cent had none or few so trained.

Job influence

The degree of job influence is one of the key factors identified by those advocating new forms of work organisation. Lean production is said to be 'a superior way of making things ... it provides more challenging and fulfilling work for employees at every level' (Womack *et al.* cited in Hampson, Ewer and Smith, 1994: 237). Figure 3.3 shows three different measures of job influence – task variety, autonomy, and control over the pace of work. The level shown is the proportion of managers stating that workers within the largest occupational group have 'a lot' of influence in these domains. Parallel measures were collected in the employee survey and are discussed in Chapter 8.

We would expect some occupations, notably those where the entry-level qualifications are high, to have more job influence than others. This is broadly what Figure 3.3 shows. In workplaces where professional workers formed the core workforce, they had considerably greater levels of job influence than where routine unskilled workers ('other occupations') were the largest occupational group. Consistent with this pattern, the relative *lack* of job influence was greatest in those workplaces where operative and assembly workers and routine unskilled workers formed the core workforce. For example, in over two-fifths of workplaces where routine unskilled workers were the largest group, they had little or no influence on job variety, discretion over how work was done, or the pace of work.

We next examined whether there were any factors associated with particular occupations having higher or lower levels of job influence (as reported by managers) in comparable workplaces (i.e. those where they form the same core workforce). When we related the methods of transmitting job responsibilities to the different elements of job influence, some consistent patterns emerged. Where individual objectives and targets were used, job influence was higher; where supervision and standard operating procedures were used, it was generally lower. Target setting

Figure 3.3 Level of job influence in core workforce, by occupation

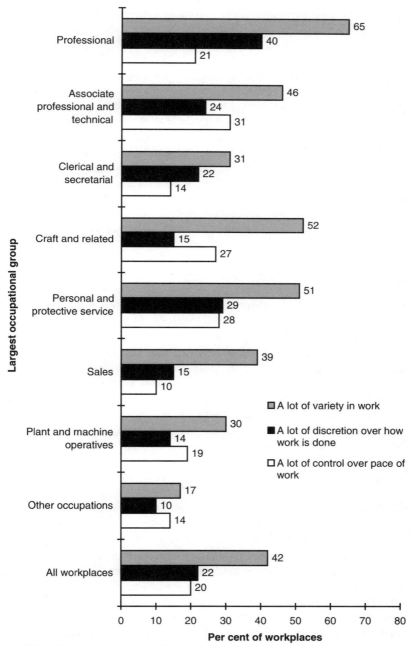

Bases: All workplaces with 25 or more employees.
Figures are weighted and based on responses from 1,922 managers.

was associated with greater job variety within each of the eight occupational groups, and with greater job autonomy and control over the pace of work for four of the occupational groups. Supervision was associated with lower job variety for four of the occupational groups, lower autonomy for six of the occupational groups, and lower control over the pace of work for four of the occupational groups. A similar pattern is also evident where standard operating procedures were used.

The occupational picture reveals some of the complexities. In workplaces where technical and scientific workers formed the core workforce, the relationships set out above hold: if they were supervised or had to follow standard operating procedures, job influence was lower, whereas if they were in workplaces where individual targets were set, they had higher job influence. Workplaces where sales workers were the core provide an interesting counterpoint. Here, supervision was associated with greater task variety and autonomy (but lower control over the pace of work), while individual target setting was also associated with greater job influence. In workplaces where clerical workers formed the core the pattern was even more complex. For this group, each of the three alternative methods of conveying job responsibilities was associated with higher levels of task variety but lower levels of control over the pace of work.

Teamworking

Teamworking is a central element of the new forms of work organisation. It has been most closely associated with the automotive industry where it first emerged from Volvo plants in Sweden in the 1970s, and in combination with other elements such as just-in-time inventory control became the basis of the lean production model used in Toyota. Hampson, Ewer and Smith (1994) argue that the Scandinavian version of teamworking is distinct from the Japanese version in the degree of autonomy afforded to workers and Murikami (1997) demonstrates this empirically in a comparative study of teams in nineteen automotive plants.

A series of questions were asked about teamworking in the survey. Overall, 83 per cent of managers stated that at least some employees in the largest occupational group worked in formally designated teams, and in 65 per cent of workplaces most employees in the group worked in teams. We were concerned to see to what extent teamworking corresponded to the archetype.

Figure 3.4 shows how the two-thirds of workplaces where most employees in the core workforce worked in teams is whittled progressively down to just 3 per cent of workplaces where these teams correspond in full to the model of autonomous teamworking. First, in a small proportion of cases, team members did not work with one another! Second, in a larger number of cases, the team did not have responsibility for a specific product or service. Third, and central to the theoretical underpinnings of teamworking, just over half of workplaces with teamworking allowed team members to jointly decide how work was to be done. Cumulatively, therefore, around a third (35 per cent) of all workplaces operated teams that corresponded approximately to a model of semi-autonomous teamworking. However, it is the final stage which truly signifies a real break in forms

Figure 3.4 From teamworking to fully autonomous teamworking

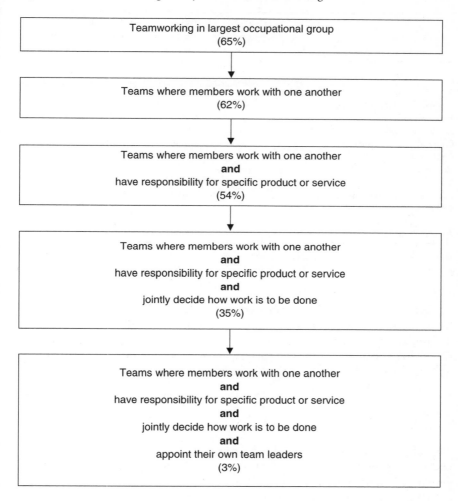

Teamworking in largest occupational group
(65%)

Teams where members work with one another
(62%)

Teams where members work with one another
and
have responsibility for specific product or service
(54%)

Teams where members work with one another
and
have responsibility for specific product or service
and
jointly decide how work is to be done
(35%)

Teams where members work with one another
and
have responsibility for specific product or service
and
jointly decide how work is to be done
and
appoint their own team leaders
(3%)

of work organisation. Just 5 per cent of workplaces with teams allowed the team members to appoint their own team leaders. The 3 per cent of workplaces which met all four criteria we label as fully autonomous teamworking.

Table 3.8 shows there to be considerable variation in teamworking, and the form it took, depending upon which occupation formed the core workforce. It was least common where craft and related workers, and operative and assembly workers formed the core. This statement continues to hold true when we discount the workplaces with teams that do not correspond to fully-autonomous or semi-autonomous models – for example, where professionals were the core group around three-fifths had (at least) semi-autonomous teams, compared with under a fifth of workplaces where operative and assembly workers constituted the core.

Table 3.8 Type of teamworking in core workforce, by occupation

	Fully autonomous teams	Semi-autonomous teams	Other types of teams	No team working
	% of workplaces	% of workplaces	% of workplaces	% of workplaces
Largest occupational group				
Professional	4	53	37	7
Associate professional and technical	1	46	50	4
Clerical and secretarial	2	36	53	8
Craft and related	2	21	45	32
Personal and protective service	4	33	39	23
Sales	6	31	51	12
Plant and machine operatives	5	13	56	26
Other occupations	2	17	59	22
All workplaces	3	31	48	17

Base: All workplaces with 25 or more employees.
Figures are weighted and based on responses from 1,907 managers.

Consistent with the model of teamworking, the level of job influence among the largest occupational group was greater where teams were fully autonomous.

Somewhat surprisingly, the incidence of (at least) semi-autonomous teams was lowest in manufacturing workplaces, in common with hotels and restaurants and transport and communication. In these industries, it amounted to no more than a fifth of workplaces.

Conclusion

This chapter has looked at workforce composition, the deployment of labour and the organisation of work, all of which contribute to our understanding of employers' labour use. This concluding section summarises the main findings, drawing them together by examining how employers seek to attain flexibility in labour use and to what extent this is associated with low-cost labour. The measure of low pay that we use is the proportion of non-managerial employees at the workplace who were earning below £3.50 per hour. Overall, two-thirds (65 per cent) of workplaces had no low-paid employees and in a tenth (9 per cent) a quarter or more of the workforce was low-paid.

Throughout the chapter we have shown consistent sectoral differences in employers' labour use. In the public sector around three-quarters of workplaces had a majority female workforce. Two-fifths of workplaces had a majority skilled workforce. Part-time employment was also substantial, with just under a third of workplaces having a majority part-time workforce. There were no significant relationships between the number of women employed and the number of skilled workers, or between the number of part-time workers and skilled workers.

The situation was quite different in the private sector. Here, about two-fifths had a majority female workforce, a quarter had a majority skilled workforce and a quarter also had a majority part-time workforce. The more women working at a workplace, the lower the number of skilled workers. Similarly, the more part-timers working at a workplace, the lower the number of skilled workers.

Sectoral differences also carried over in part to the deployment of labour. Only a small fraction of all workplaces did not sub-contract any services or use one of the various forms of other non-standard labour. The public sector made much more use of employees on fixed-term contracts, while use of the other non-standard forms was generally higher in the private sector. A more important finding in this section, though, was that use of non-standard labour was greater *within* than *outside* the largest occupational group, and this was positively associated with the skill level of the workforce.

The final section examined the organisation of work. Multi-tasking, job influence and teamworking were all strongly dependent on which occupation formed the largest group at the workplace. After taking occupation into account, it was notable that job influence was associated with the method by which job responsibilities were transmitted.

The pattern of labour use is strongly related to the incidence of low pay, particularly within the private sector, as shown in Figure 3.5. Across the private sector as a whole, 13 per cent of workplaces had a quarter or more of the workforce earning below £3.50 per hour. This was higher where more women were employed and where part-time workers were in the majority. It was lower where the workplace was relatively high skilled. It was also lower where each form of non-standard labour was used, and especially low where fixed-term contract employees or temporary agency workers were used in the core workforce. It was higher where most employees in the core workforce had been trained to be functionally flexible, but was unrelated to teamworking.

What are we to make of this? There appear to be two routes to flexibility for private sector workplaces. One is based on minimisation of labour costs through extensive use of part-time, female, relatively low-skilled employees. This is most likely to be found among workplaces in wholesale and retail, hotels and restaurants and financial services. Typically, these workplaces were part of very large organisations. The other route appears to be based on numerical flexibility through the use of sub-contracting and other forms of non-standard labour. In these workplaces, employees on fixed-term contracts and temps are found in the core workforce, and a more skilled workforce at that. These workplaces are less likely to have trained the core workforce to be functionally flexible. Low pay is much scarcer among this second group of workplaces. This route to flexibility was most commonly found among workplaces in electricity, gas and water and other business services.

The picture within the public sector is less straightforward as so few workplaces within the public sector – just 7 per cent – had *any* low paid employees. We have shown that direct transfers of employment were three times greater in the public than the private sector. The main motivation in contracting out services was to

Figure 3.5 Labour use and low pay in private sector workplaces

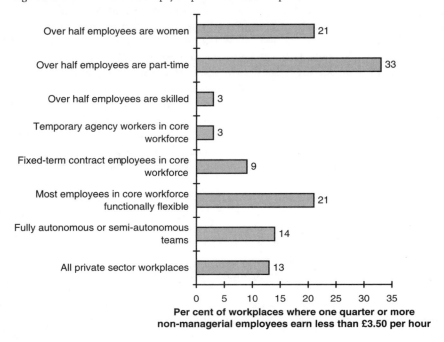

Over half employees are women — 21
Over half employees are part-time — 33
Over half employees are skilled — 3
Temporary agency workers in core workforce — 3
Fixed-term contract employees in core workforce — 9
Most employees in core workforce functionally flexible — 21
Fully autonomous or semi-autonomous teams — 14
All private sector workplaces — 13

0   5   10   15   20   25   30   35

Per cent of workplaces where one quarter or more non-managerial employees earn less than £3.50 per hour

Base: All private sector workplaces with 25 or more employees.
Figures are weighted and based on responses from 1,275 managers.

achieve cost reductions. One conclusion that might be drawn from this is that the public sector has managed to effectively transfer low paid jobs into the private sector.

Notes

1 As noted in Chapter 1, the face-to-face interviews were conducted using laptop computers. This allowed us to incorporate a number of logic and consistency checks, so that any problems could be solved at source.
2 In past surveys an alternative occupational classification was used, which divided the workforce into manual and non-manual groups. The continuing usefulness of this distinction was questioned (Cully and Marginson, 1995), and it was decided for consistency with other major surveys to adopt the current official statistical standard.
3 The industries with the greatest proportion of workplaces without managers are education (17 per cent) and construction (14 per cent). Here, it is possible that respondents completing the EPQ were more likely to categorise themselves in their vocational specialism rather than as managers (e.g. head teachers labelling themselves as professionals).
4 For the private sector $r = -0.27$ ($p = 0.000$), and for the public sector $r = -0.05$ ($p = 0.204$).
5 We did not ask about any movement in the opposite direction. However, in a separate question, 26 per cent of managers reported that the overall use of sub-contracting had increased in their workplace

over the past five years and 3 per cent said that it had gone down. Given these figures, the scale of any 'contracting-in' is likely to have been modest.

6   The association was measured using gamma, a summary measure of the linear association between two ordinal variables. It was lowest for fixed-term contracts (gamma = −0.063), and greatest for homeworkers (gamma = −0.459), and for contracting out it was positive (gamma = 0.215).

4 The management of employees

Possibly no issue in the British workplace has received as much attention in the past decade as the implementation or otherwise of 'human resource management' (HRM). The term, which in academic discourse at least has largely supplanted 'personnel management', originated in the United States and began to make headway in the UK in the latter part of the 1980s (Legge, 1995). At the time this survey was last conducted in 1990, HRM symbolically announced its arrival with the advent of the *Human Resource Management Journal*. It was notable that none of the articles appearing in the first number made reference to the WIRS series. At first glance this might be considered rather puzzling, as past surveys had always examined management and the bulk of the data was, in fact, gathered from managers. However, the range of issues outlined by the editor perhaps makes it clear why the survey did not feature as a source. They covered: the flexible organisation; the integration of the management of employees into the overall management of the business; the role of line management in personnel; how to gain employee commitment; and the shift in focus away from management–trade union relations to management–employee relations. The latter of these was identified as the most important as 'historically, most managements have put the emphasis on "collectivism"' (Sisson, 1990: 6). As with management, so too the survey; but if management had rediscovered the individual, then the focus of the survey also had to shift.

The pursuit of flexibility was covered in the last chapter, and this chapter – together with the next, which deals with the collective aspects of the employment relationship – covers the remaining issues identified by Sisson. In the first part, we examine how the personnel function is organised within workplaces. We then look at how different events in an employee's working life are managed, starting from the time they are recruited through to the possible termination of their contract. The chapter then concludes by bringing together much of the information detailed in this and the last chapter, to see how far British management might be said to be 'strategic' in its approach to managing employees, or whether it remains largely opportunistic and pragmatic as is often argued (Sisson and Marginson, 1995).

Who manages employees: the location and operation of the personnel function

In this section we look at how the personnel function is organised, examining in particular the degree of autonomy of workplace managers and, within the workplace, of line managers.

The presence of specialist personnel managers at the workplace

Almost nine out of ten workplace managers interviewed said they were the person 'primarily responsible' for employee relations matters at the workplace.[1] Of the 11 per cent who were not, most described themselves as either general managers (33 per cent) or company secretaries (26 per cent). While most workplaces had someone for whom employee relations formed part of their job, considerably fewer had a manager based at the workplace who was specifically dedicated to this task.

To see how many respondents could be described as a personnel specialist, answers were combined from two questions: one that asked for the formal job title of the respondent and another that asked about the proportion of time spent dealing with employee relations issues.

Just over a fifth (22 per cent) had titles that inferred direct responsibility for employee relations matters. Within this group we have our first indicator of the diffusion of the HRM style of managing employees – 7 per cent of managers were called 'human resource managers',[2] compared with 15 per cent with the more traditional 'personnel manager' label, while just 1 per cent were entitled 'employee relations manager' and a further 1 per cent were called 'industrial relations managers'. Human resource managers were more likely to be found in larger workplaces (29 per cent) and most often in workplaces in electricity, gas and water (44 per cent). They were also more common among workplaces that were partly or wholly foreign-owned (25 per cent). Public administration remains the last bastion for personnel managers, where they were found in 31 per cent of workplaces. Among the four-fifths of managers without specialist titles, about half (52 per cent) classified themselves as general managers and 14 per cent were also the owner, proprietor or managing director of the workplace.

The average manager we interviewed spent 35 per cent of their time on employee relations matters, with a median of 25 per cent. Just a fifth (21 per cent) spent more than half their time on it. A considerable proportion of managers allocated very little of their time to employee relations matters, 30 per cent spending less than a tenth. Even after discounting those who said they were not primarily responsible for employee relations at the workplace, this figure barely altered (29 per cent).

A personnel specialist was defined as a manager who had any of the following job titles – Employee Relations Manager, Industrial Relations Manager, Human Resources Manager, Personnel Manager – *or* who spent more than half of their time on employee relations issues. In just under a third (30 per cent) of all workplaces there was someone based at the workplace who was a specialist using this definition. Of those without a specialist title, just 9 per cent spent over half of their time on employee relations matters.[3] The spread of specialists across workplaces was closely related to workplace size, as is shown in Table 4.1. Small workplaces, stand-alone sites in particular, were most likely to rely on a non-specialist to handle personnel issues.

The presence of a personnel function varied considerably across industries. Around a tenth of private sector workplaces in education (7 per cent) and construction (14 per cent) had a specialist on site. Of the other industries, electricity, gas and water (74 per cent), public administration (54 per cent) and financial services (43 per cent) were most likely to have specialists at the workplace. Differences between public and private sectors in aggregate were small, the proportions with specialists being 27 and 31 per cent respectively.

Workplaces that were partly foreign owned were more likely to have a personnel specialist than wholly UK owned workplaces, and where the share of foreign ownership exceeded half they were twice as likely. Even after taking into account workplace size, substantial differences remain.

Personnel management across the wider organisation

We next examined how the personnel function was structured across organisations, looking only at workplaces that were part of a larger organisation, and excluding

Table 4.1 Presence of personnel specialist at the workplace, by organisational status, workplace size and foreign ownership

	Stand-alone workplaces	Part of a wider organisation	All workplaces
	% of workplaces	% of workplaces	% of workplaces
Workplace size			
25–49 employees	11	19	17
50–99 employees	25	29	28
100–199 employees	31	51	46
200–499 employees	66	77	75
500 or more employees	82	89	88
Ownership of private sector workplaces			
Wholly UK owned	18	33	27
Partly foreign owned	*	55	41
Predominantly or wholly foreign owned	*	51	51
All workplaces	20	34	30

Base: All workplaces with 25 or more employees.
Figures are weighted and based on responses from 1,721 (size and all workplaces) and 1,190 (ownership) managers.
Note: Excludes interviews not held at the workplace.

those which were head offices in their own right.[4] The overall picture for these 'branch sites' was that 31 per cent had a personnel specialist at the workplace, 78 per cent had access to a specialist at a level above the workplace, 54 per cent had both and 14 per cent had neither. Table 4.2 shows how these figures were related to a range of workplace characteristics, including workplace and organisation size.

As already shown, the larger the workplace the more likely there was to have been a personnel specialist on site. In contrast, an opposite relationship was found between workplace size and no specialist presence at the workplace, but at a higher level. Two-thirds of the smallest branch sites had access to a specialist not at the workplace, but at a higher level, compared with around one in ten of the largest workplaces.

Both of these relationships altered when examined against organisation size. Workplaces that were part of small organisations were most likely to have no specialist either at the workplace or at a higher level. Branch sites of very large organisations were most likely to have access to a specialist at a higher level in the organisation. However, the effects of workplace and organisation size were not wholly independent of one another. The larger the workplace was relative to the size of the wider organisation, the more likely it was that a specialist would be at the workplace, and there only. The reverse relationship was found for small workplaces in large organisations. Finally, specialists at both levels were more common the greater the number of employees in both the workplace and the organisation.

We are now in a position where we can summarise, for *all* workplaces (be they stand-alone sites, or branch sites, or head offices) whether there was a personnel specialist either at the workplace or at a higher level in the organisation. This is shown in the final column of Table 4.2. Overall, a third of workplaces did not, and this was most common in workplaces that were part of very small organisations, typically stand-alone sites. Other than manufacturing and construction, over half of all workplaces in each industry had access to a specialist.

Tasks of managers responsible for employee relations

All managers responsible for employment relations matters[5] – irrespective of whether they were a personnel specialist or not – were asked to elaborate on the tasks and responsibilities performed in the course of their work (or the job of someone who they were responsible for). To do this, they were presented with a list of nine tasks covering various aspects of the management of employees. Their responses are shown in Figure 4.1. Handling grievances, recruitment of employees, dealing with equal opportunities issues, and staffing or manpower planning were the most common duties. Tasks associated with pay were the only matters where less than four-fifths said they, or their subordinates, covered these tasks.

The number and type of duties a manager was responsible for varied according to the type of manager. Over a third (39 per cent) of personnel specialists said they were responsible for all nine issues. Where the number was somewhat less the tasks most likely not to be undertaken were responsibility for payment systems,

Table 4.2 The structure of the personnel function, by main classifications

	Branch sites				All workplaces
	Personnel specialist at workplace only	Personnel specialist at workplace and higher level	Personnel specialist at higher level only	No personnel specialist	Personnel specialist at workplace or higher level
	% of workplaces	% of workplaces	% of workplaces	% of workplaces	% of workplaces
Workplace size					
25–49 employees	3	16	66	15	57
50–99 employees	6	21	54	19	63
100–199 employees	13	33	41	13	74
200–499 employees	19	57	18	6	89
500 or more employees	24	60	12	4	95
Organisation size					
Less than 100 employees	*	*	*	*	17
100–999 employees	16	21	21	42	53
1,000–9,999 employees	6	27	51	15	87
10,000 employees or more	3	26	66	4	95
Sector					
Private	10	28	43	19	53
Public	3	19	71	7	91
Organisational status					
Stand-alone workplace	–	–	–	–	20
Part of a wider organisation	7	24	54	14	80
Industry					
Manufacturing	20	24	15	41	37
Electricity, gas and water	7	62	26	5	97
Construction	(22)	(35)	(25)	(18)	32
Wholesale and retail	7	29	57	7	71
Hotels and restaurants	6	34	35	24	58
Transport and communications	7	31	45	18	59
Financial services	3	36	62	0	90
Other business services	7	27	53	13	60
Public administration	5	43	49	3	95
Education	2	5	83	10	79
Health	3	24	63	9	70
Other community services	(4)	(22)	(67)	(8)	58
All workplaces	7	24	54	14	64

Base: All branch sites belonging to a wider organisation that are not head offices (columns 1–4) and all workplaces (column 5) with 25 or more employees.
Figures are weighted and based on responses from 1,116 (columns 1–4) and 1,910 (column 5) managers.
Note: Excludes interviews not held at the workplace (columns 1–4).

Figure 4.1 Employee relations responsibilities of managers

Base: All workplaces with 25 or more employees.
Figures are weighted and based on responses from 1,494 managers.
Note: Excludes managers without primary employee relations responsibility and interviews not held at the workplace.

and health and safety. A similar proportion of general managers (35 per cent) had responsibility for all tasks, and they were least likely to be responsible for the two pay issues. In contrast, well over half (59 per cent) of owners or proprietors assumed responsibility for all nine issues, though it is not possible to comment on the extent to which these may have been delegated to other managers to handle on a day-to-day basis.

Apart from simply knowing whether there was a personnel function at the workplace, we also collected information about the size of the personnel department, specifically, the number of staff assisting the respondent in their duties. On average, between two and three employees worked with the manager, with the number higher in the public sector (3.3 staff) than the private sector (2.5 staff). A fifth (18 per cent) of managers in the private sector did not have any assistance, whereas in the public sector it was only a tenth (8 per cent). Personnel specialists had more staff working for them on average than non-specialists, 3.2 staff compared with 2.5 staff.

Autonomy of workplace managers in branch sites

The structure of the personnel function within organisations does not, of itself, tell us anything about the autonomy of local managers. It is not necessarily the case that authority to make decisions at the local level diminishes as structures become more elaborate. The activities of large organisations may be too diverse to lend themselves to a highly-centralised structure. An alternative form is the divisional structure which is 'loose' in the sense that local management have greater freedom to make decisions but 'tight' in the extent of monitoring of the local unit from the centre (Marginson *et al.* 1988). We examine two aspects of autonomy. First, whether the degree of local autonomy differs according to the issue being dealt with – are local managers more likely to have discretion when recruiting compared with, say, health and safety? Second, we examine how autonomy is related to the structure of the personnel management function.

Taking the same range of employee relations issues used above, managers were asked whether they had to follow a policy set by managers elsewhere in their organisation; whether they had to consult managers elsewhere before making a decision; and whether they had an obligation to regularly report to managers elsewhere on these matters. It should be noted that workplace managers may tend to overstate their own authority. For example, Edwards and Marginson (1988) found that managers tended to overstate their authority in relation to specific issues such as the handling of redundancy and the introduction of new technology.

For each of the nine issues, a majority of managers in branch sites had to follow policies set at a higher level in the organisation. Differences across issues were small although managers were less likely to have to follow a policy on operational matters – training (52 per cent) and recruitment (65 per cent) – than they were on issues with organisation-wide implications – pay or conditions of employment (81 per cent) and payment systems (75 per cent). Local managers in the public sector were somewhat more likely to have to follow polices than their counterparts in the private sector.

Fewer managers also had to consult elsewhere in their organisation before acting on an issue. However, there was more variation by issue. They were least likely to have to consult on operational matters, with around a quarter having to consult before making decisions on recruitment (27 per cent), performance appraisals (27 per cent) or training (17 per cent). In contrast, workplaces with an external policy guiding their actions were more likely to have consulted someone else in their organisation. For example, three quarters (73 per cent) of managers did so when making a decision about systems of payments.

Finally, requirements for local managers to regularly report on employee relations issues to higher levels in the organisation were slightly less widespred than requirements for them to consult. Only on one issue, health and safety (48 per cent), did around half of managers in branch sites have to regularly report. A quarter (27 per cent) said they did not have to report on any of these issues. There was little difference across the range of issues.

Having looked broadly at the type of discretion afforded to local managers, we now turn to a summary measure of autonomy in order to explore how it varied according to the structure of the personnel function. It would have been too complicated to approach this issue by issue; instead, we group workplaces according to whether managers were required to follow a policy, consult before deciding and regularly report over *any* of the nine issues. Those that do not can be said to have autonomy in decision-making. The results of this analysis are shown in Table 4.3.

In branch sites where there was no specialist at a higher level, local managers had a good deal of autonomy. Around half of private sector branch sites and a quarter of public sector branch sites in this situation did not have to follow a set policy on any of the nine issues. Where there was a specialist at a higher level, however, managers in almost all branch sites, in both sectors, had to follow a policy on one or more of the issues. Where managers were free from the strictures of policy, the chances that they had to consult before making a final decision were higher, and *vice versa*. For example, nearly half of all private sector managers in branch sites without a specialist on site did not consult at a higher level on any of the nine issues. There was also a substantial proportion of branch sites in both sectors where managers at the local level did not have to report to managers at a higher level.

The most striking implication of Table 4.3 is the relative lack of autonomy of local managers in branch sites where there was a specialist at a higher level. This result was consistent on each of the dimensions of autonomy examined, and across both the private and public sectors. The conclusion is quite stark: the

Table 4.3 The locus of decision-making on employee relations matters, by structure of personnel function and sector

	Personnel specialist at workplace only	Personnel specialist at workplace or higher level	No personnel specialist
	% of workplaces	*% of workplaces*	*% of workplaces*
*Private sector branch sites**			
Do not follow policy set elsewhere in organisation	59	5	48
Make decisions without consulting elsewhere in organisation	35	18	45
Do not regularly report to elsewhere in organisation	61	19	49
*Public sector branch sites**			
Do not follow policy set elsewhere in organisation	29	2	25
Make decisions without consulting elsewhere in organisation	51	11	23
Do not regularly report to elsewhere in organisation	42	22	50

Base: All branch sites with 25 or more employees.
Figures are weighted and based on responses from 1,116 managers.
Note: Excludes interviews not held at the workplace.
*Branch sites are workplaces belonging to a wider organisation that are not head offices.

presence of a personnel specialist at a higher level plays a large role in circumscribing the activities of local managers, even where these are personnel specialists themselves.

One group of branch sites where managers appeared to have greater discretion were those which were wholly foreign owned. A third (38 per cent) did not have to follow a policy set elsewhere in their organisation, a quarter (27 per cent) did not have to consult before making a decision, and a third (37 per cent) did not have to report. The respective figures for wholly UK owned workplaces were 16 per cent, 24 per cent and 28 per cent. Taking the three of these together, 14 per cent of foreign owned workplaces said there was no higher level influence (on any of the nine issues) over their authority to manage employees. This compares with just 1 per cent in wholly UK owned workplaces.

Supervisors' responsibilities for employee relations

Delegation of employee relations management away from personnel departments has been a consistent theme among those writing about HRM. In this scenario 'every manager becomes a personnel manager' (Ezzamel *et al.*, 1996: 73). Yet supervisors have always been responsible for the performance of their subordinates; at issue is the degree of authority they hold, which in Britain has generally been slight (Lowe, 1992).

Nine out of ten (90 per cent) workplaces had at least some supervisory employees with 'people management' duties. This figure varied little across different types of workplaces. Supervisors were mostly responsible for training (86 per cent), health and safety (76 per cent), the conduct of performance appraisals (66 per cent) and the handling of grievances (62 per cent).[6] The only issues where supervisors played a limited role were those related to pay – only around a tenth of workplaces gave supervisors responsibility for either the pay and conditions of employment (13 per cent), or the system used to remunerate employees (8 per cent).

Allocating employee relations duties to supervisors does not equate to giving them decision-making authority. Managers were asked whether supervisors had the authority to make final decisions over three issues: recruiting people to work for them; deciding pay increases; and dismissing workers for unsatisfactory performance. The results are reported in Figure 4.2. In general, the answer was 'no' to all of these questions. Indeed, over two-thirds (70 per cent) of managers said that supervisors could not make a final decision on *any* of these issues. Around a quarter (27 per cent) of workplaces with supervisors gave them authority to make decisions on recruitment, but very few workplaces did so for pay increases and dismissals – just 3 per cent and 8 per cent respectively. Supervisors in the public sector had less decision-making authority than their counterparts in the private sector.

We also explored how well supervisors were equipped for their people management responsibilities. A low level of training was very evident in our results: almost a third of workplaces (30 per cent) had never given supervisors training in

Figure 4.2 Extent to which supervisors are given final say in decisions, by sector

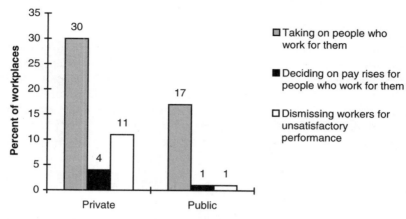

Base: All workplaces with supervisors and 25 or more employees.
Figures are weighted and based on responses from 1,756 managers.

people management skills, and a further quarter (25 per cent) had only trained a few employees. Where training had taken place, supervisors were more likely to make final decisions on recruitment but were no more likely to decide pay increases or dismissals.

Employee relations in the wider business context

The proponents of the so-called 'hard' version of HRM argue that it becomes effective 'only when human resource strategy is integrated with wider business strategy' (Guest and Peccei, 1994: 220). Integration might be captured in different ways: whether human resource issues are incorporated into strategic plans; whether it is covered at the board (i.e. senior management) level; and, more recently, whether the workplace – either directly or through the parent organisation – has applied for and been accredited as an 'Investor in People' (IiP). We look at each of these issues.

Two-thirds of all managers (68 per cent) said the workplace had a formal strategic plan that covered, among other things, the issue of 'employee development'.[7] Larger workplaces were more likely to have a plan of this kind, as were workplaces that were part of a larger organisation, though here the association was more pronounced. Public sector workplaces (83 per cent) were also more likely to have such a plan.

A further indicator of how human resource matters are incorporated into wider business plans is the involvement of employee relations managers. This was widespread. In workplaces where the plan covered employee development issues, over four-fifths of managers (83 per cent) said they, or someone else responsible for employee relations issues, was involved in the preparation of the plan. Overall, then, 56 per cent of workplaces have an 'integrated employee development plan'. Again, this was positively associated with workplace size such that over two-thirds (70 per cent) of the largest workplaces had an integrated plan with an employee development dimension.

Matching strategy with practice, it is argued, requires the strategy to be 'owned' up and down an organisation's hierarchy. We did not attempt to measure this directly in the survey – Legge (1995: 116) points to the 'conceptual problematics and fuzziness that permeate the major strategy models'. What we can show, for private sector workplaces only, is whether anyone on the board of directors had specific responsibility for employee relations issues. Around two-thirds (64 per cent) of private sector workplaces that were part of a wider organisation had someone at this level with this remit. This was strongly related to the size of the organisation: workplaces in the largest organisations were nearly three times more likely than those in the smallest organisations to have an employee relations director on the board.

The final indicator of integration is the attainment of the Investors in People (IiP) award. The IiP award is given to workplaces or organisations – by independent assessors from Training and Enterprise Councils in England and Wales, and Local Enterprise Companies in Scotland – which have in place a planned approach to setting and communicating business objectives and developing people to meet those objectives. Assessors have a list of twenty-three indicators by which they judge the commitment, planning, action taken, and systems of evaluation in place to meet objectives.

We divided workplaces into those that held an IiP award (either in their own right or through the parent organisation); those that had applied at some stage in the previous five years, but were not successful in gaining the award; and those which had never applied. Overall, just under a third (32 per cent) of all workplaces were IiP accredited. A further 16 per cent of workplaces had applied for the award but were not successful.[8] Slightly over half (53 per cent) of all workplaces had never applied for the award. Accreditation was very closely associated with organisational size – 8 per cent of workplaces that were part of organisations with less than 100 employees had been accredited, compared with 62 per cent of those in the largest organisations. It was not at all related to workplace size. This suggests that initiatives to gain the IiP award are driven from the centre of (large) organisations, not directly from workplaces.

The scheme has made far greater inroads into the public sector than the private sector. Three-fifths (61 per cent) of private sector workplaces had never applied for the award, compared with a third (30 per cent) of public sector workplaces. The proportion of public sector workplaces holding the award is greater, 47 per cent compared with 26 per cent, but so too was the 'failure' rate. Excluding those which had never applied for the award, 32 per cent of workplaces in the public sector had failed to gain the award, compared with 28 per cent in the private sector.

In Figure 4.3 we show the extent of integration of employee relations into wider business strategy among workplaces that are part of a wider organisation in

Figure 4.3 Indicators of integration of employee relations into wider business strategy in private sector workplaces that are part of a wider organisation

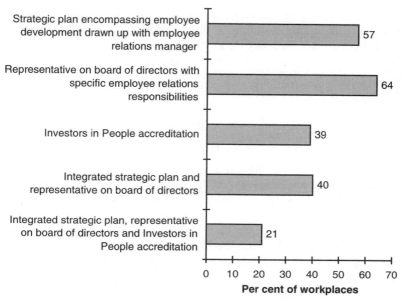

Base: All private sector workplaces that are part of a wider organisation with 25 or more employees. Figures are weighted and based on responses from 822 managers.

the private sector.[9] A fifth of these workplaces had all three elements. This proportion did not vary much by workplace size but did so by industry, where it ranged from 9 per cent in manufacturing to 47 per cent in financial services.

To summarise, the body of evidence examined thus far suggests that employee relations are generally an important aspect of management. Over half of all workplaces had an integrated employee development plan – one which encompassed employee development and was drawn up with the aid of an employee relations manager. Three-fifths of all workplaces had a personnel specialist, either at the workplace or at a higher level. Small, stand-alone sites were the least likely to have a specialist, but among branch sites nearly nine in ten had access to a specialist.

Where there was a wider organisational structure to the personnel function, there was a much lower degree of autonomy for local managers. Most were required to observe policies set elsewhere in their organisation and to consult before making decisions. There was even less evidence of authority having been delegated to supervisors. Many may have had a broad range of employee relations responsibilities, but they were mostly ill-prepared for the task and were not entrusted with decision-making powers. The broad picture is thus one of relatively well-developed structures for the management of employees, with control largely retained by personnel departments in the centre of organisations.

How are employees managed?

In the next part of this chapter we turn from structures and strategy to the actual practice of managing employees. We follow a broadly chronological approach by looking at management from recruitment through to the possible termination of the employment contract. In doing so, we take heed of how important structure and a strategic approach appear to be in explaining differences in management practice.

Recruitment

Methods of recruiting employees can be a good indicator of management style and, at the very least, can tell us something about the formality of the employment relationship. For instance, seeking out a new employee via a recommendation from another employee implies a rather different style to that where all vacancies must be advertised. We approach the topic of recruitment by looking at the factors management take into account when recruiting and the use of psychometric and aptitude testing to screen recruits. The latter indicates the extent to which employers are prepared to invest in identifying committed employees or, as one management guru prosaically put it, what they do 'to put off many of the less committed' (Peter Wickens, cited in Legge, 1995: 232).

Managers were first asked whether there had been any vacancies at the workplace in the preceding 12 months only 3 per cent said there had not. They were then shown a list of eight factors that might be taken into account when choosing between potential recruits. Most managers said they used several of these indicators of employability, as shown in Table 4.4, which is broken down according to whether the workplace was covered by a formal equal opportunities policy. The top three factors, for workplaces with and without a policy, were skills, experience and motivation.

More pointedly though, in the absence of laws prohibiting discrimination on the basis of age, 16 per cent of managers said they took this into account at the recruitment stage. Workplaces not covered by an equal opportunities policy were almost twice as likely to have this as a factor, though as we showed in the last chapter these workplaces also employed above-average numbers of both younger and older workers. Workplaces without a policy were also less likely to take references and qualifications into account, but paid greater heed to recommendations from other employees.

Age was most often cited as a recruitment factor by managers in hotels and restaurants (27 per cent). This industry is also notable for the importance managers placed on availability – almost three-quarters (74 per cent) regarded this as important, compared with an overall figure of around half. In this relatively low skill industry (see Table 3.4), high turnover rather than skill shortages is likely to be the explanation (see Chapter 6). Finally, managers in this industry were also the most likely to rely on personal recommendations (55 per cent).

As we have seen managers rated ability (as captured by skills and experience) and motivation to be of equal importance in selecting recruits. To what extent

Table 4.4 Criteria used in the selection of new employees, by presence of a formal equal opportunities policy

	Formal equal opportunities policy	No policy	All workplaces
	% of workplaces	% of workplaces	% of workplaces
Skills	91	86	89
Experience	90	88	89
Motivation	90	79	86
References	79	65	74
Qualifications	73	61	68
Availability	51	56	53
Recommendations	28	43	34
Age	13	23	16

Base: All workplaces with 25 or more employees.
Figures are weighted and based on responses from 1,904 managers.

did this feed into more formal methods of screening? Tests were separated into two types: those which purport to analyse a candidate's personality or attitude; and those which attempt to measure potential performance or competency. Just over a fifth of all workplaces (22 per cent) said they used the former and just over half the latter (53 per cent). Most workplaces using personality tests also used performance tests, with 16 per cent using both. This was most likely in larger workplaces. Private sector workplaces had a higher incidence of attitude tests than public sector workplaces, but the reverse was true for performance tests. Workplaces in financial services had a very high incidence of both screening methods (48 per cent and 64 per cent, respectively).

Personality tests were mostly used when hiring managerial staff, accounting for 70 per cent of all workplaces conducting these tests, and 17 per cent *only* used them on prospective managers. Just under a fifth of workplaces using these tests said they were routinely used for all occupations, giving an overall figure of 4 per cent of all workplaces.

The likelihood of having to undertake a personality test was closely related to whether the prospective recruit was to be in the largest occupational group at the workplace. Indeed, for each occupation (bar professionals), personality tests were always more common where it was the largest group. For example, where craft and related workers were the largest group, just over half (52 per cent) of workplaces would routinely use personality tests for vacancies in that occupation. However, where they were employed, but did not form the largest group, just over a third (34 per cent) of workplaces used them.

Performance-based tests were much more commonly applied to all grades of workers. Just 3 per cent of those conducting them reserved their use for prospective managers. These tests were routinely used in filling all vacancies in 14 per cent of workplaces using them (or 7 per cent of all workplaces). They were most commonly used for clerical workers, craft and related workers, and sales workers. As with personality tests, they were always more likely to be used for employees in the largest occupational group, irrespective of the occupation.

Training

Training is regarded as an important public policy issue because it is often cited as one (if not *the*) explanation for Britain's relatively low levels of labour productivity – see Rainbird (1994) for an overview of the arguments. Gospel (1992: 156) claims that an under-provision of workplace training in Britain has long been the case. He attributes this to management who 'were not particularly well-trained themselves and in part because of this they did not value the training of those below them'. We report on just two dimensions of the training issue: who was trained, and what the training covered.[10]

Managers were asked how many 'experienced' employees in the largest occupational group had received any formal 'off-the-job' training in the preceding twelve months.[11] On this definition training had taken place in 83 per cent of workplaces. In approaching half of these, giving 36 per cent overall, most employees in the largest occupational group had received some training. This proportion varied considerably across several workplace characteristics. It was higher in the public sector (57 per cent of workplaces) and in workplaces that were part of very large organisations (47 per cent). Similarly, it was also positively associated with having a personnel specialist at the workplace or at a higher level in the organisation (43 per cent), having an integrated employee development plan (45 per cent) and holding an Investors in People award (42 per cent). Finally, it was also higher in workplaces with recognised trade unions (48 per cent), consistent with other studies (Green *et al.*, 1999) that show a discrete union effect.

This broad picture, however, masks considerable variation by occupation (which was the reference point for the questions). Table 4.5, therefore, looks at training by occupation, but also validates the association highlighted above between training and the presence of an integrated employee development plan. As can be seen from the 'all workplaces' column, workplaces where relatively low-skilled occupations were the largest group – plant and machine operatives and other occupations – were the least likely to have provided training for most employees in these groups. In contrast, where professionals were the core workforce, around three-quarters of workplaces had provided most of them with training in the past year.

After taking occupation into account, the workplace characteristics identified above were still important in explaining differences. An integrated employee development plan was associated with a higher proportion of workplaces providing training for seven of the eight occupations. Recognition as an Investor in People was also associated with a higher proportion of workplaces providing training in seven of the eight occupations, as was the presence of a recognised union at the workplace.

It has been argued that a focus purely on formal, off-the-job training could be misplaced; the acquisition of workplace-specific knowledge through learning by

Table 4.5 Off-the-job training for most employees in core workforce, by occupation and presence of an integrated employee development plan

	Integrated employee development plan	No integrated employee development plan	All workplaces
	% of workplaces	% of workplaces	% of workplaces
Largest occupational group			
Professional	77	58	73
Associate professional and technical	45	15	32
Clerical and secretarial	37	30	34
Craft and related	35	23	28
Personal and protective service	50	29	41
Sales	45	18	34
Plant and machine operatives	19	20	20
Other occupations	27	17	22
All workplaces	45	25	36

Base: All workplaces with 25 or more employees.
Figures are weighted and based on responses from 1,849 (columns 1 & 2) and 1,863 (column 3) managers.

doing could be more valuable for employer and employee alike (Williamson *et al.*, 1975). We measured the scale of these 'idiosyncratic' skills by asking managers how long a new recruit to the core workforce would take to become as competent in their job as existing employees. In general, the greater the level of workplace-specific skills (i.e. the more time it took to become fully competent), the more off-the-job training also took place. This relationship held for five of the eight occupational groups.

Training, thus far, has been treated as some kind of generic good, but the content of training is clearly important. For instance, initiatives such as Total Quality Management require people to be trained in so-called 'soft' skills like customer service, rather than technical skills (Collinson *et al.*, 1998). In the four-fifths of workplaces where some training took place, managers were shown a list of ten items that training might have covered. The results are shown in Figure 4.4. All apart from 5 per cent of managers said training covered at least one of the ten areas, with two-thirds (65 per cent) providing training in three or more.

The content of training was closely related to the activity of the workplace. For example, 89 per cent of workplaces in hotels and restaurants had trained employees in customer service activities. This was much less widespread in manufacturing (9 per cent), where training in the operation of new equipment was most common (65 per cent). Perhaps of more interest was the way in which some topics combined. Combinations of training in teamworking, improved communication, and problem-solving methods were apparent, with a third (34 per cent) of workplaces providing training in at least two of these areas. Similarly, training in problem-solving, reliability and meeting deadlines and quality control clustered together with approximately a fifth (21 per cent) of workplaces covering

Figure 4.4 Areas covered by training

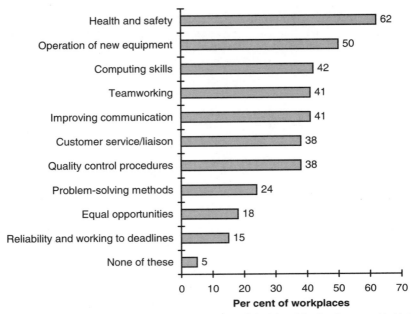

Base: All workplaces with 25 or more employees where off-the-job training has been provided in last 12 months.
Figures are weighted and based on responses from 1,642 managers.

at least two of these matters. A third grouping was training in communications and customer service which went together in 25 per cent of workplaces. These groupings imply different management approaches. The first is consistent with a participative approach to work organisation, whereas the second is more closely associated with a 'hard' quality management approach.

Often, though, training was provided in just one area. Where it was, it was most likely to be in health and safety (40 per cent), the operation of new equipment (27 per cent) or computing skills (14 per cent). These three are closest to what might be considered the technical requirements of a job. In comparison, the 'softer' or people-oriented skills such as improving communications or problem solving nearly always appeared as part of a wider package of training.

Talking to employees

This sub-section, together with the next two, covers the range of practices which go under the broad banner of 'employee involvement'. As defined by Marchington *et al.* (1992: 7) these are practices 'initiated principally by management, and are designed to increase employee information about, and commitment to, the organisation'. The term is contrasted with industrial democracy and collective bargaining, both of which imply some sharing of power with employees. In this first sub-section, we look at the range of downward communication practices. The following two sub-sections (following the division adopted by Marchington *et al.*) look, respectively, at upward problem-solving forms of communication and financial participation. Broadly, these three areas constitute what is termed direct employee participation, though the various forms need not be genuinely participative (Regalia, 1996) – the extent to which they are is a theme we explore. Indirect employee participation, through some form of employee representative structure is examined in the next chapter.

Managers communicate with their employees in a variety of ways and, doubtless, for a variety of purposes. We asked a series of questions about possible forms of downward communication and the results are presented in Figure 4.5. On each of the four specific methods asked about – team briefings, workplace-wide meetings, the 'cascading' of information via the management chain, and staff newsletters – there was widespread use, with almost all workplaces using at least one of these methods. In addition, one in ten managers identified other forms of downward communication including e-mail and notice boards. The five per cent of workplaces that ostensibly had no forms of downward communication were more likely to be: stand-alone sites (10 per cent); in manufacturing (14 per cent) or construction (18 per cent); those without a union presence (9 per cent); and those where there was no personnel specialist either at the workplace or at a higher level (12 per cent).

The use of the management chain and newsletters was greater in large workplaces. The use of team briefings and meetings with the whole workforce either did not vary by workplace size or did so in no apparent pattern. However, the smallest workplaces were, in each case, the least likely to use the method of communication.

Figure 4.5 Methods used by managers to communicate directly with employees

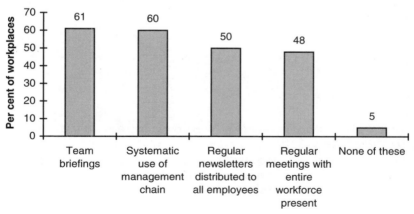

Base: All workplaces with 25 or more employees.
Figures are weighted and based on responses from 1,905 managers.

Most workplaces used a number of these communication methods. A tenth (11 per cent) were operating all four and a further 31 per cent had three of the four in place. Larger workplaces, those that were part of a larger organisation and those in the public sector, were all more likely to be using all these methods.

As well as asking about the different forms of communication we also enquired about the process, focusing our attention on team briefings. Over half (57 per cent) of all workplaces conducted briefings at the level of work group, section or team compared with a fifth (20 per cent) that held departmental meetings, and a further fifth (18 per cent) with a mixture of these two. A very small proportion of workplaces (2 per cent) conducted briefings for supervisors or managers only. Briefings mainly took place on a monthly (35 per cent) or weekly basis (31 per cent), though a large proportion of managers said they took place daily (18 per cent).

Briefings need not be participative events, given their principal function is to transmit information from managers to employees. Managers were asked how much time, if any, was typically allowed during briefing sessions for questions or other contributions from employees. In almost all cases (98 per cent) at least some time was set aside for this element, though it varied substantially. In half of cases, at least a quarter of the time was set aside for employee contributions, while 20 per cent limited employee participation to the bare minimum. This was unrelated to the level at which briefings were held or their frequency.

Getting employees involved

The second group of practices are those where information flows upwards in the workplace. These range from the rudimentary suggestion box through to problem-solving groups, which is where we commence our analysis.

Managers were asked whether the workplace had groups of employees set up to 'solve specific problems or discuss aspects of performance or quality'. Just under two-fifths (38 per cent) had such groups.[12] These groups went under a plethora of titles, including:

- Communicate for Quality
- Rapid Action Team
- Forward through Service group
- Let's Do It Better

This suggests that a variety of groups have been incorporated under this definition, from the allegedly passé quality circles (Legge, 1995) to groups set up as part of a fully-fledged 'kaizen' (continuous improvement) initiative.[13] Table 4.6 shows the types of workplaces in which these groups were to be found. Their incidence was almost twice as great in large workplaces than in small ones. In every industry bar construction and other community services, at least a quarter of workplaces were using these groups, and it was over half in electricity, gas and water, financial services and education.

Problem-solving groups were no more likely to be found in foreign-owned workplaces (where the parent organisation might have been a potential source for their diffusion, as has been the case for Japanese-owned automotive plants set up in Britain). They were, however, more likely to be found in workplaces with a personnel specialist in the organisation (41 per cent); those with an integrated employee development plan (48 per cent); and in workplaces with recognised unions (45 per cent).

We also examined how problem-solving groups functioned. Half of all workplaces with problem-solving groups operated them on a permanent basis. About a third (32 per cent) confined them to a finite life. The remainder had a mixture of both.[14] Not all employees within the workplace had the opportunity to participate in the groups. Two-fifths of workplaces with these groups involved at least most non-managerial employees, but in a fifth only a few participated.

There were also differences in how, if at all, employees were rewarded for 'outstanding suggestions' made by the group. About two-fifths (38 per cent) of workplaces with groups gave no direct reward. Of those that did, it was equally common to award a financial bonus, or an acknowledgment (e.g. via a staff newsletter) or a written note of thanks. Some gave employees gifts in kind, such as a bottle of champagne, while in a small proportion of cases managers said a note would be put on an individual's staff record. Financial rewards were much less likely in the public sector, where acknowledgments were more likely to be given.

Suggestion schemes may be a less formal way for managers to obtain ideas from employees. A little over two-fifths of workplaces used this method. Whereas problem-solving groups were strongly related to workplace size, there was less evidence of this with suggestion schemes (as can be seen from Table 4.6). Such schemes can be easier to administer and this may account for the relative uniformity of their spread, but it is also the case, unlike problem-solving groups, that they entail little active employee participation. There was a slight positive association with the presence of problem-solving groups, with 16 per cent of workplaces having both.

The final area examined in this section is the use of staff attitude surveys, a further means of seeking out the ideas and views of employees. Just under half of workplaces had conducted a survey of employees at least once in the past five years.[15] As Table 4.6 shows, they were more common in larger workplaces, possibly indicating a need to have formal mechanisms for collecting opinions when numbers are large. They were also more likely in workplaces that were part of a wider organisation, and it is this latter association which predominates. This may be because such surveys are administered from the centre of organisations, which would allow for a comparison of employee views across different sites within an organisation.

Surveys were more likely to have taken place where there was a personnel specialist either at the workplace or a higher level (56 per cent); where there was an integrated employee development plan (56 per cent); in workplaces accredited with IiP (60 per cent); and in workplaces with recognised unions (55 per cent).

Table 4.6 Direct employee participation, by main classifications

	Any non-managerial employees participate in problem-solving groups	Workplace operates a suggestion scheme	Formal survey of employees during the last five years
	% of workplaces	% of workplaces	% of workplaces
Workplace size			
25–49 employees	32	28	39
50–99 employees	37	36	43
100–199 employees	47	33	53
200–499 employees	56	53	64
500 or more employees	68	46	73
Organisation size			
Less than 100 employees	26	22	25
100–999 employees	44	27	44
1,000–9,999 employees	39	37	50
10,000 employees or more	47	45	62
Sector			
Private	35	31	40
Public	45	38	56
Organisational status			
Stand-alone workplace	28	20	28
Part of a wider organisation	41	38	51
Industry			
Manufacturing	43	30	36
Electricity, gas and water	54	46	86
Construction	21	11	14
Wholesale and retail	35	33	53
Hotels and restaurants	28	38	53
Transport and communications	29	40	47
Financial services	53	49	62
Other business services	39	24	38
Public administration	38	68	75
Education	54	23	50
Health	29	37	34
Other community services	17	27	29
All workplaces	38	33	45

Base: All workplaces (columns 1 & 2) five or more years old (column 3) with 25 or more employees.
Figures are weighted and based on responses from 1,906 (column 1), 1,928 (column 2) and 1,713 (column 3) managers.

Surveys might simply be an information-gathering exercise, but one indicator of them being part of a broader, participative approach is when the results are shared with employees. Of workplaces which had conducted surveys at some stage in the preceding five years, two-thirds (66 per cent) had made the full results available, in written form, to all employees. The proportion doing so was similar across most types of workplaces, except for those where there was no personnel specialist at the workplace or a higher level. In these workplaces, 27 per cent had conducted a survey and under half (42 per cent) had provided employees with the results.

Taking the three of these forms of upward communication together, just 12 per cent of workplaces had all in operation, a quarter had two of the three in place, but it was most common for schemes to be operated in isolation (35 per cent) or not at all (30 per cent). This last situation was most evident in smaller workplaces and in workplaces that were part of small organisations. Across industries, it was especially high in construction where over two-thirds (69 per cent) had no form of upwards communication.

Financial participation

The third, and final, area we deal with under the broad banner of employee involvement are the various schemes that give employees a financial stake in the business, namely profit-sharing and employee share ownership schemes.[16] There has been widespread interest in financial participation, mainly because it is thought to better align workers' interests with those of their employer, from which virtuous effects might follow. In Britain, government has at various times explicitly encouraged the growth of financial participation through the provision of tax incentives.[17] The evidence for superior performance arising from these schemes – some from studies based on earlier surveys in this series (Blanchflower and Oswald, 1988; Fernie and Metcalf, 1995) – is mixed. That need not concern us here; rather, we examine which types of (private sector) workplaces operate these schemes and the extent to which they are genuinely participative.

Three schemes were distinguished and the incidence of these by industry is shown in Table 4.7. Profit-related pay was the most widely-used scheme, found in just under a half of private sector workplaces. Of these, four-fifths were schemes that had been registered with the Inland Revenue (and were, thereby, eligible for tax relief). A quarter of private sector workplaces operated some form of employee share ownership scheme, and a much smaller proportion operated a deferred profit-sharing scheme (where profits are put in a trust fund to acquire shares in the company for employees).

All types of schemes were more prevalent in larger workplaces, in workplaces with a personnel specialist (at the workplace or a higher level), and in workplaces with an integrated employee development plan. As can be seen from the table, both electricity, gas and water, and financial services were notable for their high incidence of these schemes. Just 1 per cent of the former had no financial participation – this probably reflects the extensive amount of privatisation in this

Table 4.7 Incidence of financial participation schemes in private sector workplaces, by industry

	Profit-related pay of bonuses	Deferred profit-sharing scheme	Employee share ownership scheme	None of these
	% of workplaces	% of workplaces	% of workplaces	% of workplaces
Industry				
Manufacturing	50	2	22	46
Electricity, gas and water	81	13	80	1
Construction	29	9	9	68
Wholesale and retail	62	10	32	31
Hotels and restaurants	42	8	31	53
Transport and communications	61	3	30	27
Financial services	80	25	56	12
Other business services	45	5	23	50
Public administration	-	-	-	-
Education	8	0	0	92
Health	6	0	0	94
Other community services	28	4	28	63
All workplaces	47	6	25	48

Base: All private-sector workplaces with 25 or more employees.
Figures are weighted and based on responses from 1,313 managers.

industry in the 1980s and 1990s, where employee share ownership schemes tended to be part of the privatisation package. Employee share ownership schemes were also more common in younger workplaces.

Overall, the different forms of financial participation appear to go hand-in-hand rather than as substitutes for one another. A fifth (20 per cent) of private sector workplaces had both a profit-sharing scheme and an employee share ownership scheme in operation (and 50 per cent had neither).

An important indicator of the extent to which these schemes promote participation is the eligibility rules for employee share ownership schemes and the take-up rates among non-managerial employees. Figure 4.6 shows that in a sixth of workplaces these schemes were reserved for managers only. At the other end of the scale, four out of five workplaces with these schemes allowed most, or all non-managerial employees to purchase shares. Eligibility, however, did not always translate into participation, as the take-up rate was substantially lower. There was a substantial gap between eligibility and participation in schemes with wide eligibility. On a more positive note, in almost all workplaces where non-managerial employees were eligible to purchase shares, at least some had done so.

Ben-Ner and Jones (1995) have argued that these schemes may only be effective where they are operated in conjunction with other forms of employee involvement. Pendleton (1997), using data from the 1990 survey, examines this and shows financial participation schemes to be associated with other forms of employee involvement. We also found evidence of this. There were positive associations between profit-related pay and each of the downward and upward forms of communication examined. For example, a fifth of workplaces had both a profit-related pay scheme and problem-solving groups. Similar associations, though more muted, were found between the incidence of employee share ownership schemes and the various forms of communication.

Performance appraisal

In many work situations the monitoring of individual employee performance is difficult, especially where 'output' is not easily measured or able to be directly assigned to individuals. Performance appraisals are one means of overcoming these difficulties.

Formal performance appraisals were conducted in 79 per cent of workplaces. Appraisal systems were slightly more common in the public than the private sector, being found in 83 per cent and 77 per cent of workplaces respectively. In both sectors, they were also more likely to be found where the workplace was recognised as an Investor in People.

In workplaces where appraisals were conducted, they often not did not apply universally. Two-thirds (65 per cent) of workplaces conducting appraisals did so for all non-managerial employees, but around a quarter (23 per cent) only did so for some. Similarly, there was unevenness in their use across occupations. Table 4.8 shows the breakdown by sector of the proportion of workplaces conducting

Figure 4.6 Participation of non-managerial employees in employee share ownership schemes

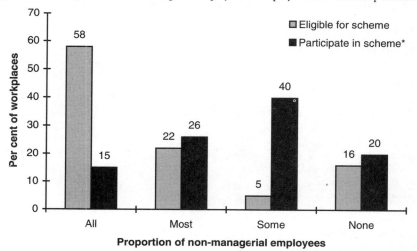

Base: All private sector workplaces with 25 or more employees operating employee share ownership schemes.
Figures are weighted and based on responses from 473 managers.
* 11 per cent of respondents were unable to answer the question.

appraisals for each occupational group (of those workplaces employing people in that occupation). It was most common for managers, professionals and sales workers to be formally appraised. For these occupations workplaces in the public sector were equally or more likely to conduct appraisals. Among the other six occupations, however, performance appraisals were more likely to be conducted in the private sector.

There were also differences in how frequently appraisals were conducted. Regular annual appraisals were reported in 65 per cent of workplaces and were more widespread in the private sector (68 per cent) than public sector (57 per cent). In the private sector, 12 per cent of workplaces conducted appraisals four or more times a year, and a further 14 per cent did so two or three times a year. In the public sector 9 per cent of workplaces fell into each group. There were also 5 per cent of workplaces where appraisals were conducted, but to no regular pattern.

Typically, performance appraisals were conducted by an employee's immediate supervisor. This happened in four out of every five cases (82 per cent), and was similar across most types of workplaces. The public sector had a relatively high proportion of workplaces, 13 per cent, where employees on the same level or grade took part in the conduct of the appraisal. Most of these workplaces were in education. In the private sector this 'peer review' element was negligible (2 per cent).

Much of the debate over appraisals centres on their purpose: are they to make the monitoring of performance more transparent and effective, or are they a means of individualising the workforce by imbuing employees with a more managerial ethos (Newton and Findlay, 1996)? More narrowly, are they tied in at all to payment systems? Managers were presented with a list of possible reasons why they appraise workers. The findings need to be interpreted with care as, over

Table 4.8 Regular performance appraisals, by occupation and sector

	Sector		All workplaces
	Private	Public	
	% of workplaces	% of workplaces	% of workplaces
Occupation			
Managers and administrators	68	74	70
Professional	63	78	69
Associate professional and technical	55	49	53
Clerical and secretarial	57	45	54
Craft and related	54	34	51
Personal and protective service	52	40	46
Sales	64	65	64
Plant and machine operatives	43	34	43
Other occupations	42	25	37
No appraisals conducted	23	17	21

Base: All workplaces with 25 or more employees.
Figures are weighted and based on responses from 1,921 managers.

time, managers and employees alike adjust their behaviour to accommodate the rules of the scheme. Managerial perceptions of stated purpose may not match the perceptions of employees, as Healy (1997) found for school teachers. According to managers, appraisals were most widely used to give feedback (93 per cent), to set objectives and review past performance (88 per cent), to identify training needs (88 per cent) and to talk about future prospects (82 per cent).

There was some evidence that performance appraisal was part of a wider approach to employee development. Where identifying training needs was one of the purposes of the system, just under half (44 per cent) of these workplaces had provided training to most non-managerial employees in the largest occupational group. In cases where the identification of training needs was not an explicit purpose the proportion was a third (30 per cent), and where no appraisals were conducted it was a quarter (24 per cent). Managers in workplaces with Investors in People accreditation were somewhat more likely to say that identifying training needs formed one of the purposes of the appraisal (71 per cent).

Finally, just over a third of managers said appraisals were used to determine the size of pay increases. This was more widespread in the private sector (37 per cent) than the public sector (20 per cent).[18] In both sectors, the presence of a recognised union at the workplace had no effect on the likelihood of appraisals being used in this way.

The same carrot for all?

'Single status' is a term applied where there is uniformity in non-pay terms and conditions across the workplace. On a symbolic level this might amount to all staff using the same canteen facilities. Harmonisation is thought to be a means of promoting employee commitment across all grades of workers. Brown *et al.* (1998), in a series of detailed case studies, show that firms consciously pursuing a strategy of individualising employment contracts tended to standardise non-pay terms and conditions.

Traditionally, discussions of the status divide have centred around differences between manual and non-manual work, or hourly-paid versus those on salary. Such distinctions have, over time, become less useful where much non-manual work shares many of the features of manual work – routinised tasks, relatively low-skilled entry points (Price and Price, 1995). Our focus, therefore, is on the divide between management and non-managerial employees. Managers were asked a series of questions about non-pay terms and conditions. They were asked to compare differing entitlements to various benefits between themselves and employees in the largest occupational group.[19] The results are summarised in Table 4.9. While most employers treat non-managerial staff the same as managers over entitlement to pensions, annual leave and sick pay, access to company cars and private health insurance is less equal. Private sector workplaces were much more likely to differentiate between managers and non-managerial employees than their public sector counterparts. This is not just because public sector workers of any grade rarely had access to some of the benefits. While this was the case for

Table 4.9 Entitlements to non-pay terms and conditions, by sector

	Sector		All workplaces
	Private	*Public*	
	% of workplaces	*% of workplaces*	*% of workplaces*
Managers entitled to:			
Employer pension scheme	78	93	82
Company car or car allowance	63	33	55
Private health insurance	61	7	46
Four weeks' or more paid annual leave	91	96	92
Sick pay in excess of statutory requirements	83	77	81
Employees in largest occupational group entitled to:			
Employer pension scheme	62	93	71
Company car or car allowance	12	17	14
Private health insurance	22	2	16
Four weeks' or more paid annual leave	81	95	85
Sick pay in excess of statutory requirements	64	76	67

Base: All workplaces with 25 or more employees.
Figures are weighted and based on responses from 1,925 (managers) and 1,927 (employees) managers.

company cars and private health insurance, the remaining three items were found in broadly the same proportions across both sectors. Where they were on offer in public sector workplaces, they were much more likely to have been available for both non-managerial employees and managers.

Taking the five items together, we produced a summary measure of single status. This is where, in a given workplace, there was no differential access to these entitlements, even where that meant there were no managers or non-managerial employees who were entitled to, say, four weeks or more annual leave.[20] Overall, two-fifths (41 per cent) of workplaces on this definition were single status. Such workplaces were more common where there was a recognised trade union at the workplace (54 per cent); if there was a personnel specialist within the organisation (48 per cent); and, where the workplace was covered by an integrated employee development plan (46 per cent). However, among private sector workplaces the presence of a recognised union made no marked difference.

Adapting to the needs of employees

In the previous chapter we showed that, across all workplaces, the composition of the workforce was very diverse. That diversity has increased over time, particularly as a result of the rising participation rate of women. Employers therefore have to adapt to the potentially diverse needs of workers if they are to attract and retain the workforce they need. Managers were asked about a range of practices at their workplace that fall under the broad heading of 'family friendly' initiatives. In Chapter 7 we also examine this from an employee perspective.

One way in which employers can accommodate the needs of employees is by giving them some flexibility over the times and places that they work. Managers were asked whether any non-managerial employees were entitled to: work at or from home in normal working hours; work only during school term times; switch from full to part-time employment; and share their job with another employee. Three-fifths (60 per cent) of all workplaces had one or more of these practices in place, though only 4 per cent had all four. The most commonly available was the ability to switch from full to part-time employment (52 per cent of workplaces), while the least common was working from home (14 per cent). In each area, there were more public sector workplaces offering these entitlements than those in the private sector. Half of all workplaces in the private sector did not offer any of these entitlements.

Where there was a relatively low female presence at the workplace (see Chapter 3) just a third (36 per cent) had one or more entitlements. Notably, just 1 per cent of these workplaces had term-time only contracts, compared with 19 per cent of workplaces overall.

Managers also provided details on the number of employees who took advantage of these entitlements, but we leave discussion of this for Chapter 7, where employees themselves can provide an account. It is worth noting, however, that around a quarter (23 per cent) of managers said that no employees had taken up any of these entitlements in the past year.

Cost is sometimes assumed to be a reason why employers do not offer family friendly policies. This was not, however, the perspective of managers in workplaces which had any of these entitlements in place. Approximately three-quarters (74 per cent) said there were no costs or they were minimal and this did not vary according to the number that were on offer.[21] Moreover, over four-fifths (84 per cent) said the entitlements were cost-effective, and this was largely unrelated to the scale of the costs.

It may be that costs are genuinely low; alternatively, it may be that managers had already factored in offsetting benefits when asked to think about costs. Most managers thought these policies brought benefits (just 7 per cent said there were no benefits). The most commonly mentioned was happier staff (50 per cent), but considerable proportions mentioned more tangible effects: 36 per cent said there had been an increase in the retention of employees and 24 per cent mentioned other improvements such as a reduction in absence levels. Typical comments were:

It allows us to encourage women back to work – takes note of fact people have lives outside work.
(Manufacturing, private sector, 200–500 employees)

You can retain your more efficient workers because you work around them and they are more reliable and settled in their job.
(Public administration, public sector, 25–50 employees)

Keeping staff with you so you keep turnover down, good for morale and motivation. People work better if they aren't worrying about their home life.
(Health, private sector, 100–200 employees)

Another area where we are able to explore how employers accommodate the needs of workers is how they generally respond to the situation where someone needs to take time off at short notice, such as when a child is sick. Table 4.10 shows how the responses varied by sector. One general point can be made – it was extremely rare to refuse permission to take time off [22] – but, besides that, the differences across the private and public sector are substantial. The greatest difference is that half of public sector workplaces provide special paid leave precisely for this type of circumstance, about four times the proportion of workplaces in the private sector. In the private sector the onus is largely on the employee to bear the cost of the absence, either by using up annual leave entitlements, making up the time later or taking time off without pay.

Handling disputes with employees

Whether viewed from a contractual or power perspective, the employment relationship can be subject to conflict and, ultimately, severed. This might be because the employee holds a grievance about some aspect of their working conditions; or it might be because management judges an employee's behaviour or action to be at fault, or their performance sub-standard. How these disputes are handled needs to be set against the legal framework. Since 1971 employees have had some protection against arbitrary dismissal through unfair dismissal

Table 4.10 Time off from work at short notice for family reasons, by sector

	Sector		All workplaces
	Private	*Public*	
	% of workplaces	*% of workplaces*	*% of workplaces*
Time off but has to be made up later	20	6	16
As leave without pay	22	8	18
As sick leave	3	5	4
As special paid leave	14	51	24
As annual leave	31	22	28
Depends on the circumstances	3	3	3
Individual decides	2	1	2
Other combinations of methods	3	4	4
Not allowed / never been asked	0	0	0

Base: All workplaces with 25 or more employees.
Figures are weighted and based on responses from 1,924 managers.

legislation, giving those with the necessary length of service the right to lodge an application against an employer with an Industrial Tribunal seeking re-instatement or compensation.[23] One of the consequences of this has been the formalisation of grievance and disciplinary procedures, which spread widely and quickly in the 1970s (Anderman, 1986).

Nine out of ten workplaces (91 per cent) had a formal procedure in place for dealing with individual grievances raised by non-managerial employees. Only stand-alone sites (74 per cent) had an incidence substantially below the average. Almost all public sector workplaces had a procedure in place (99 per cent). In the one in twelve workplaces without a procedure, managers were asked how problems were resolved. Overwhelmingly, responses were along the lines of 'they come to me and we sort it out'.

Procedures invariably covered all non-managerial employees at the workplace – less than complete coverage was found in no more than 2 per cent of cases. It was usual for employees to be made aware of the existence and content of these procedures through some form of written documentation, whether it be in the letter of appointment (47 per cent), a staff handbook (55 per cent) or via a notice board (10 per cent). Where they were not written down, which was the case in 13 per cent of workplaces, most managers said employees were made aware either at the time of their entry into the workplace or at some other time by their line manager or supervisor.

The general impression, then, is that most employees had access to a formal procedure to take forward any grievances they might have. This impression must be qualified, however, in two respects. First, employees may be reluctant to raise a grievance without some form of support – this is covered in the next chapter on employee representation where we look at whether employees could be accompanied when raising a grievance. Second, and possibly related to this last point, there was relatively little use made of grievance procedures in the year preceding the survey. Of workplaces with procedures, only a third (30 per cent) said that the procedure had been activated. This was very strongly associated with workplace size, ranging from 20 per cent in the smallest workplaces through to 79 per cent in the largest. One reason for this might be that employees had nothing to complain about. Another might be that the procedure is not a particularly effective mechanism for resolving problems, consistent with case study evidence from Earnshaw *et al.* (1998). Both were commonly advanced by managers when asked why they thought the procedure had not been used. Among the comments made were:

> Because we are quite happy to listen to them at any time and deal with problems before they develop.
>> (Other business services, private sector, 500+ employees)

> It's not part of the culture of this company.
>> (Construction, private sector, 500+ employees)

They haven't felt the need. If there is anything, they can usually sort it out without resorting to the procedure.

(Financial services, private sector, 50–100 employees)

Probably because they imagine nothing will change – lack of confidence in the procedure.

(Health, private sector, 100–200 employees)

Disciplinary procedures were as evident as grievance procedures, being found in 92 per cent of workplaces. They were distributed in an almost identical pattern. Indeed, of workplaces with a grievance procedure, 97 per cent also had a disciplinary procedure. They were also near identical in their workforce coverage, and the means by which employees were made aware of the procedure.

One of the arguments often made in favour of disciplinary procedures is that the outcome might be seen as fairer by both sides, when compared with the situation of management unilaterally deciding to sanction or dismiss someone. An important element of this 'natural justice' argument is that employees are able to appeal against decisions. Even workplaces without a procedure may allow an employee to appeal. Across all workplaces, 96 per cent allowed employees to appeal against decisions concerning discipline or dismissal. This was strongly related to the existence of a procedure. Almost all workplaces with procedures allowed appeals (99 per cent) compared with 71 per cent of workplaces with no procedures.

In Chapter 6 we go on to look at the extent of disciplinary sanctions and dismissals and any Industrial Tribunal claims that may have been lodged against the employer. This can be related to the incidence and use of procedures, and rights of appeal.

Job security and workforce reductions

The final area we examine is how employers juggle the sometimes conflicting objectives of providing job security for employees and retaining the flexibility to make reductions in the size of the workforce if needed. Job security has been a widely-discussed issue, especially in the wake of the recession in the economy in the early 1990s which affected employment across all grades (Gallie *et al.* 1998). Related to this has been substantial restructuring of employment within organisations, sometimes referred to as 'downsizing'. Much of this has been driven by technological change and the opening up of what were previously state-owned monopolies to wider competition. The experience of British Telecom is illustrative. In 1984 it was a state-owned monopoly and among the largest employers in the country with 245,000 employees. By 1998, post-privatisation and following a period of rapid advance in telecommunications technology, employment had halved to 125,000.[24]

Job security is often seen as vital to promoting employee commitment – in Chapter 8 this is explored from the perspective of employees. Employees may be more willing to accept change, for instance to working practices, if they believe their jobs are secure. But employers may be unable to offer such guarantees. We asked managers whether there was a policy at their workplace of guaranteed job security or no compulsory redundancies for any grade of non-managerial employees. Overall, only 14 per cent of workplaces had such a policy.[25] Workplaces in the public sector were about five times as likely as those in the private sector to have a job security policy, 32 per cent compared with 6 per cent. Within private sector workplaces, job security policies were more likely to be found in workplaces that were part of a very large organisation (17 per cent) and where a recognised union was present (13 per cent). Manufacturing workplaces (2 per cent) were the least likely to offer guaranteed job security, compared with half (49 per cent) of workplaces in electricity, gas and water.

The incidence of job security policies also differed by occupation. In 71 per cent of workplaces with job security policies, they applied to all non-managerial employees at the workplace, but in the remaining third only a sub-set was covered. Table 4.11 shows that, for each occupation, bar operative and assembly workers, employees were more likely to be covered by a job security policy if they were within the largest occupational group at the workplace. For example, in 17 per cent of workplaces where personal service workers formed the largest occupational group, they were covered by a job security policy, compared with an overall figure of 12 per cent in all workplaces where they were employed.

A third of all workplaces had made some reduction in the size of the workforce in the year preceding the survey.[26] Larger workplaces were nearly twice as likely as the smallest workplaces to have done so, 51 per cent compared with 28 per cent. There was no difference at all between the public sector and the private sector.

Table 4.11 Guaranteed job security, by occupation

	Largest occupational group	All workplaces
	% of workplaces	% of workplaces
Occupation		
Managers and administrators	-	12
Professional	20	14
Associate professional and technical	20	8
Clerical and secretarial	13	11
Craft and related	8	6
Personal and protective service	17	12
Sales	7	5
Plant and machine operatives	4	4
Other occupations	18	11
No guaranteed job security	86	86

Base: All workplaces with 25 or more employees.
Figures are weighted and based on responses from 1,881 (column 1) and 1,893 (column 2) managers.

Indeed, half of all workplaces in public administration had made workforce reductions.

The factors which prompted these reductions need not concern us here; our focus is on how these reductions were achieved and what type of protection a policy of guaranteed job security or no compulsory redundancies appeared to offer. The first point to make is that workforce reductions were equally common among workplaces with and without a job security policy. But were there differences in how these reductions were achieved?

Many workplaces making reductions had used several methods in doing so. Most common was 'natural wastage' (i.e. not replacing employees who resign) which happened in 57 per cent of cases, followed by early retirement or voluntary redundancies (37 per cent), redeployment within the organisation (32 per cent) and compulsory redundancies (27 per cent). With the exception of the latter, all were more common in the public sector than the private sector, notably early retirements or voluntary redundancies: public sector workplaces were twice as likely to use this method (63 per cent compared with 26 per cent). This pattern was reversed for compulsory redundancies. Private sector workplaces making workforce reductions opted for these in 32 per cent of cases, compared with 15 per cent in the public sector.

Broadly parallel differences were found between workplaces with a job security policy and those without. Most marked was the very low use of compulsory redundancies, used in just 5 per cent of workplaces with a job security policy, compared with 31 per cent of those without a policy. Of all workplaces with a guaranteed job security or no compulsory redundancy policy, just 2 per cent had made compulsory redundancies in the past year (compared with a tenth of workplaces without a policy).[27]

Conclusion

In this and the previous chapter, we have covered a lot of ground in terms of how work is organised and employees are managed. Where possible we have attempted to offer a sideways glance at how the various practices fit together. This concluding section draws together many of the facets discussed throughout the two chapters to paint an overall picture of the presence and prevalence of management practices. In doing so, we show how strongly related (or not) they are to the broad approach of the personnel management function discussed in the first two sections of this chapter.

Table 4.12 summarises the use of the range of relevant management practices discussed in this and the previous chapter. We will return to these practices at several points in this volume; therefore, we use the label 'high commitment management practices'. The reason for this label will become apparent. Where possible, we restrict our focus to the core workforce (that is the largest occupational group) as this is the best test of how deeply practices were embedded in the workplace. Some practices were widespread – procedures for dispute resolution, briefing meetings, performance appraisals, single status, family friendly working

Table 4.12 Management practices, by presence of personnel specialist and integrated employee development plan

	Personnel specialist and integrated employee development plan	Personnel specialist only	No personnel specialist or integrated employee development plan	All workplaces
	% of workplaces	% of workplaces	% of workplaces	% of workplaces
Largest occupational group has/have:				
Temporary agency workers	19	18	14	18
Employees on fixed-term contracts	38	32	12	28
Personality tests	17	10	5	11
Performance tests	42	34	17	35
Formal off-the-job training for most employees	51	30	18	36
Profit-related pay*	24	14	5	15
Employee share ownership scheme*	12	10	1	6
Regular appraisals	69	61	31	58
Fully autonomous or semi-autonomous teams	44	33	14	34
Single status for managers and other employees	51	42	22	40
Guaranteed job security	20	14	1	13
Workplace has:				
Formal disciplinary and grievance procedure	97	95	64	88
Group-based team briefings with feedback	65	52	48	59
Most non-managerial employees participate in problem-solving groups	20	11	6	15
Two or more family friendly practices or special leave schemes	59	45	15	41

Base: All workplaces with 25 or more employees.

Figures are weighted and based on responses from between 1,835 and 1,889 managers.

* Profit-related pay and employee share ownership schemes are based on responses from 1,287 and 1,291 private sector managers respectively.

arrangements – while others were much less so – employee share ownership schemes, personality tests at recruitment, profit-related pay, guaranteed job security.

Throughout the discussion it has been apparent that various structural features of the workplace – employment size (of the workplace and organisation), sector, and also the structure of the personnel management function – have been important in explaining differences in the use of management practices. Generally, all these high commitment management practices were more prevalent in larger workplaces, in workplaces (of all sizes) that were part of large organisations, in the public sector, and where there was a personnel specialist either at the workplace or at a higher level in the organisation. Similarly, the indicators we have of a strategic approach to employee relations – a strategic plan encompassing employee development which was drawn up with the aid of an employee relations manager, and Investors in People accreditation – were also associated with the use of these management practices.

Table 4.12 marries two of these indicators together – the presence of a personnel specialist and an integrated employee development plan – to see, across the board, how important they appeared to be in explaining differences in high commitment management practice. The differences are, for the most part, substantial and all are consistent. In each of the areas examined the practice was most likely to be found in workplaces covered by an integrated employee development plan and with access to a personnel specialist. They were least likely to be found in workplaces with neither.

Of course, such an exercise tells us little about how each of the practices fit together. It does not say whether workplaces are using packages or 'bundles' of practices that have an internal consistency or logic about how they combine, as opposed to being adopted and used in an ad hoc manner (Wood and de Menezes, 1998). However, what is logical and what is ad hoc is in the eye of the beholder. The use of any combination of management practice reflects the particular historical and social context in which they were first introduced, and the subsequent way in which they become modified and made to work. It is sufficient, we think, to demonstrate that these practices are not independent of either structure or strategy, and that there is evidence that a number of the practices consistent with a human resource management approach are well entrenched in many British workplaces.

Notes

1   In 10 per cent of cases, the interview was conducted with a manager who was not based at the sampled address, typically at a head office. These cases have been excluded from this analysis.

2   This is not an especially good indicator. Gennard and Kelly (1995), for instance, point to some reluctance on the part of management to adopt the HRM title even among those who would characterise their organisation as having adopted a HRM approach.

3   Of those who were owners, proprietors or managing directors this figure was also 9 per cent, accounting for 4 per cent of all specialists. These people were probably unlikely to be specialists in the intended sense, but we cannot preclude the possibility that they might have been.

4   Head offices were excluded as this would have overestimated the number of workplaces with a specialist at the workplace and underestimated the higher level presence of this function.

5   This section excludes the 11 per cent of managers who said they were not primarily responsible for employee relations matters at the workplace in addition to the 10 per cent of cases where the interview was not conducted at the sampled address.

6   This is likely to underestimate the role of supervisors in performance appraisal as not all workplaces had this system in place.

7   In total, 80 per cent of all workplaces said they had a formal strategic plan of which 12 per cent made no reference to employee development issues.

8   Our figures slightly underestimate those that have failed, as this category was based on a question only asked of managers at workplaces that were at least five years old.

9   This is because the information on whether there was a director on the board with a specific remit for employee relations was only asked in these workplaces.

10 In addition, managers provided information on their own training, the training of supervisors, induction programmes for new employees, the number of days' training and the acquisition of workplace-specific skills. Employees were also asked about training, and this is discussed at some length in Chapters 7 and 8.

11 Off-the-job training was defined as training away from the normal place of work, but either on or off the premises.

12 An additional 4 per cent of workplaces had problem-solving groups in which there was no input from non-managerial employees. We have disregarded this category.

13 Further evidence for this type of initiative is that just over a third (36 per cent) of workplaces with problem-solving groups also organised work along just-in-time principles.

14 In addition, 5 per cent of workplaces had abandoned the use of problem-solving groups in the preceding five years.

15 Of workplaces five years or older, to which the question was restricted.

16 We also asked about performance-related pay (either individual or group based) and *ad hoc* cash bonuses. Both of these can be distinguished from profit-sharing and employee share ownership schemes where the employee reward is explicitly and formally tied to the financial fate of the enterprise.

17 Most recently, the 1999 Budget contained proposals which would allow employees to purchase shares in employee share ownership schemes out of pre-tax salary, which can be matched with shares given by the company. The tax incentives introduced under the 1987 Finance Act, which saw 14,275 profit-sharing schemes (covering 4.6 million employees) registered with the Inland Revenue by 1998, are presently being phased out.

18 For all those who did not mention pay, respondents were then directly asked whether the performance appraisal system was used to determine pay increases, of which 10 per cent said that it was. The figure cited in Table 4.8 incorporates this data.

19 We cannot be absolutely sure that the exact entitlement was the same. Managers, for example, might have more generous pension provision in cases where both themselves and non-managerial employees had access to an employer pension scheme.

20 In fact, only 3 per cent of workplaces did not allow managers any of these five non-pay terms and conditions.

21 If we disregard the 10 per cent of managers who said it was not possible to measure the costs, then 79 per cent said costs were minimal or zero.

22 Data from the employee survey broadly confirms this point (see Figure 7.2).

23 In August 1998 Industrial Tribunals became known as Employment Tribunals.

24 Data from British Telecom Annual Reports.

25 A further 1 per cent of workplaces had such a policy, but it applied only to managers.

26 We did not ask, in this sequence of questions, by how much the workforce had been reduced. Elsewhere in the questionnaire, though, information was obtained on the number of employees at the workplace one year ago and five years ago, and the number of employees who resigned, were dismissed, were made redundant or otherwise left the workplace in the preceding year.

27 As we do not know in which occupational groups there were job losses, we cannot say definitively that these 2 per cent of workplaces had been unable to observe the guaranteed job security policy.

5   Employee representation

In this chapter we look more closely at the interaction between management and employees and how this relationship is mediated or shaped by worker representation and indirect forms of employee participation. Much of the focus is on the organisation and activities of trade unions at the workplace, but we also explore the extent of other forms of worker representation in the absence of unions.

Trade unions have long occupied a central place in British society and, unlike many other industrialised countries, it is at the level of the workplace where their influence and power has been exercised most. There are three factors which underpin the centrality of the workplace. First, unionism in Britain developed on the shop-floor with workplace-based activists being the lynchpins of organisation (Fox, 1985). Second, the framework of British labour law gives the state a comparatively limited role in setting the terms and conditions of employment. Third, the extent of national co-ordination in pay-setting arrangements has always been limited, and collective bargaining at the industry level has been on a long-term decline evident since the 1950s (Brown *et al.*, 1995). In short, the relative absence of statutory regulation and joint regulation at a national level leaves much scope for variation in union activity across workplaces. This survey is an ideal tool for exploring that variation.

If there is variation, what shape might we expect it to take? There are different views on this, all of them set against the backdrop of a substantial decline in union strength since 1979. One view is that, for much of the private sector, unions are now largely an irrelevance: to be tolerated where they are present but, otherwise, to play a marginal role in workplace activities. This is consistent with evidence showing increasing individualisation of the employment relationship in both union and non-union workplaces (Guest and Hoque, 1996), together with a modest amount of derecognition. Another view, closely associated with the position of the Trades Union Congress (TUC), is that 'new unionism' provides a feasible strategy for union renewal. Evidence on the introduction of high involvement management practices can be drawn on to suggest that unions can play a facilitative or partnership role in change (Bacon and Storey, 1993). Both views are plausible interpretations of the evidence, but are nonetheless inconsistent with one another. The crucial question, nicely posed by Claydon (1996: 170–1) is: 'Who is calling the tune here and what does a more co-operative stance imply for unions' ability to continue to represent their members' interests and retain their loyalty?'.

Another important area has been the recent challenge to the long-established practice that unions provide the single channel for promoting workers' interests. This has primarily come from measures adopted by the European Union. At the supra-national level the European Union has introduced consultation and information-sharing requirements via the European Works Council Directive. This applies to large multi-national undertakings, be they union or non-union. Proposals are afoot to require similar information and consultation mechanisms at the national level. Secondly, rulings in the European Court of Justice found that Britain had not adequately applied Directives dealing with the consultation of workers over health and safety matters and collective redundancies (and transfers of undertakings). The existing legislation had not made provision for worker representatives in situations where there were no recognised unions in a workplace, and the amending legislation made good this deficiency. Partly as a need to develop a response to these initiatives, the labour movement began to review its position on single channel representation. The TUC accepted the need for universal consultation rights over matters such as collective redundancies and health and safety, but fell short of embracing a more wide-ranging works councils agenda. Instead, they opted to pursue statutory rights to union recognition (Hall, 1996).

Our approach in this chapter is to set out the current state of employee representation and representative structures for employee information and consultation, termed 'indirect participation', at the workplace, and show how this is associated with the overall management stance towards unions and joint consultation. Is this one of exclusion or inclusion of a collective 'voice', and how is this related to union strength? The overall scope of joint regulation of the employment relationship is then examined, with further detail provided on pay setting arrangements. In the final section, we draw together the material presented in this chapter with that from the preceding two chapters to look at the interaction between high commitment management practices and the character of workplace trade unionism.

There are two points to be made about the data we draw on in this chapter. First, it comes only from the management interview. In Chapter 9, some of these issues are explored further, this time from the perspective of worker representatives. Second, as with the previous two chapters, the analysis is entirely based on the 1998 survey and makes no reference back to earlier surveys. Employee representation in Britain has changed substantially over the course of this series, and this is an important focus of discussion in Chapter 10.

Union membership

Union membership is related to the ability of unions to organise, recruit and present a united collective front to employers. It is also the case that management's attitude towards trade unionism, its permissiveness or hostility, may well shape union membership. Law guarantees freedom of association, but it cannot control the cultural environment in which union membership is encouraged to flourish, or is frowned upon.

Among workplaces with 25 or more employees, we found an aggregate union density of 36 per cent, which is a little below the comparable figure from the autumn 1997 Labour Force Survey of 38 per cent. It was also lower than levels reported by employees (see Chapter 7). This suggests that some workplace managers were not well informed about union membership in their workplace and therefore made best guesses.[1]

There was a wide degree of variation across workplaces in union density, ranging from 47 per cent of workplaces where there were no union members to 2 per cent where all employees (including managers) were union members. In between these two ends of the spectrum, there was a very even distribution of workplaces as shown in Figure 5.1.

There are two ways of looking at patterns in union density across different types of workplaces: one is to look at average levels of density in different categories of workplaces, the other is to calculate total membership as a percentage of total employment within a category ('aggregate density'). The two figures differ from one another because union density was generally higher in larger workplaces, meaning that aggregate density exceeds average workplace density. Table 5.1 shows both sets of figures across a range of workplace characteristics.

As mentioned above, union density is generally higher in larger workplaces, and we found a consistent increase from one size band to the next, ranging from one in four employees in the smallest workplaces to one in two in the largest. These differences were marked but not as pronounced as others, most notably whether the workplace was privately-owned or in the public sector. The average level of density across workplaces in the private sector was a lot lower than the aggregate density. This suggests that private sector union members were mostly found in larger workplaces, and this is indeed the case: 75 per cent of the smallest private sector workplaces had no union members, compared with 22 per cent of the largest workplaces. Within small private sector workplaces there was no real difference between stand-alone sites and those that were part of a larger organisation.

In some areas of the private sector, union membership was rare, at less than one in ten employees in hotels and restaurants and other business services. Indeed, union membership in the private sector was concentrated in workplaces that were previously nationalised, such as those in electricity, gas and water and transport and communications, as well as in large manufacturing workplaces and workplaces (of all sizes) in finance and banking services. There was much greater uniformity across the public sector.

One way of interpreting the strong association between density and both workplace and organisation size is that unions find it easier to make inroads where there is a greater concentration of workers. Another might be that management in large workplaces and large organisations find it beneficial to engage with unions. We are able to explore this through three attitudinal questions asked of managers.[2] First, they were asked to state whether they were in favour, or not in favour, of

Figure 5.1 Union density across workplaces

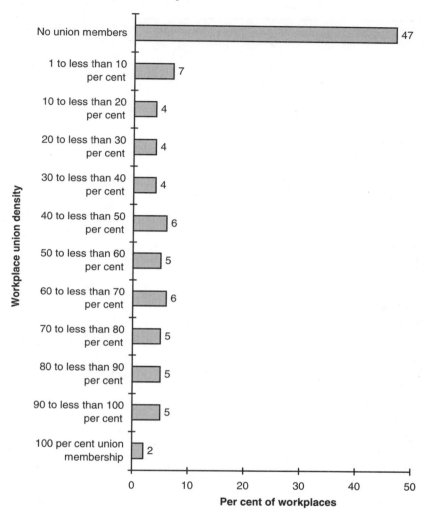

Base: All workplaces with 25 or more employees.
Figures are weighted and based on responses from 1,853 managers.

trade union membership at their workplace. In 29 per cent of workplaces managers said they were in favour of union membership, 17 per cent were not in favour and 54 per cent reported that they were neutral about it or that it was 'not an issue' at their workplace. Second, managers were asked whether they agreed or disagreed with the statement 'unions help find ways to improve workplace performance'. In 28 per cent of workplaces, managers either agreed or strongly agreed that unions could improve workplace performance, whereas 38 per cent disagreed or strongly disagreed with this statement. The third statement managers

Table 5.1 Trade union density, by main classifications

	Workplace average	Aggregate density
	Mean %	% of employees who are union members
Workplace size		
25–49 employees	23	23
50–99 employees	27	27
100–199 employees	32	32
200–499 employees	38	38
500 or more employees	42	48
Organisation size		
Less than 100 employees	6	8
100–999 employees	16	22
1,000–9,999 employees	38	39
10,000 employees or more	42	48
Sector		
Private	13	26
Public	61	57
Organisational status		
Stand-alone workplace	9	19
Part of a wider organisation	33	40
Industry		
Manufacturing	19	41
Electricity, gas and water	74	68
Construction	17	30
Wholesale and retail	8	14
Hotels and restaurants	2	4
Transport and communications	40	54
Financial services	42	32
Other business services	9	8
Public administration	66	63
Education	56	51
Health	34	43
Other community services	17	24
All workplaces	27	36

Base: All workplaces with 25 or more employees.
Figures are weighted and based on responses from 1,853 managers.

were asked to respond to was 'we would rather consult directly with employees than with unions'. The results here were stark: in 72 per cent of workplaces managers reported that they would prefer to consult directly with employees than with unions, and only 13 per cent disagreed with the statement. The results from the latter two statements raise the possibility that many of the managers who declared themselves neutral about union membership may hold negative views, but are reticent about saying so when asked directly.

Prior to the 1980s unions were able to sustain high levels of union membership by entering into agreements with management supporting, in effect, compulsory membership. These 'closed shops' were progressively outlawed, such that with the passing of the 1990 Employment Act it was unlawful to discriminate on the grounds of union membership or non-membership, and unions were unable to claim statutory immunity for any industrial action taken in support of these arrangements. It is no surprise, then, to find eight years later just 2 per cent of workplaces where managers said that employees had to be union members in order to get or keep their jobs.[3]

It remains entirely permissible for management to be supportive of, and encourage, union membership. Such support might reflect a view, widely held by employers in the 1970s, that unions assisted in the 'negotiation of order'. It might also be the case, though, that management tacitly supports what is a consensus among employees (Dunn and Wright, 1993). We found that, in 22 per cent of workplaces with union members, management 'strongly recommends' membership for at least some employees. These workplaces were much more likely to be found in the public sector (36 per cent) than the private sector (8 per cent).

A further way in which management facilitates union membership arrangements is by deducting membership subscriptions from pay, commonly known as check-off. In 1993 the continued operation of this practice became subject to individual authorisation by union members every three years.[4] Research conducted at the time suggested that check-off arrangements were mostly long-standing and changes were likely to be modest (Atkinson and Hillage, 1994). The legislation was opposed by unions (and others, including many employers) and was eventually repealed in 1998. At that time we found that two-thirds (66 per cent) of unionised workplaces had a check-off system in place.

Now that we know something of the management stance towards trade unions, we can examine how closely, if at all, it was related to levels of union density. Average union density was higher where workplace management was more favourable or encouraging towards trade unions. In the 17 per cent of cases where management were not in favour of union membership, average density was very low at 5 per cent. This compares with an average density of 62 per cent in workplaces where they were in favour. Among workplaces where managers were neutral or said that union membership was 'not an issue', the average density was again modest (15 per cent).

In workplaces without any union members, the vast majority of managers were either opposed or, at best, neutral to union membership. Table 5.2 therefore narrows the focus to those workplaces with union members. It shows that, even where there was a union presence, the average level of density was still influenced by the degree of management encouragement and the operation of a check-off system.[5] The overall difference in average density in this latter category might be explained by differences in the types of workplaces with a check-off system. In the public sector there was no clear association between workplace size, average density and check-off, but in the private sector there were differences. With the

Table 5.2 Average trade union density in workplaces with a union presence, by management stance towards unions

	Union members at the workplace	
	% of workplaces	Average density (mean % of employees who are union members)
Managers favour union membership:		
In favour	54	63
Neutral	41	37
Not in favour	5	29
Unions help find ways to improve performance:		
Agree	43	62
Neither agree nor disagree	26	43
Disagree	30	41
Managers would rather consult with employees than unions:		
Agree	58	41
Neither agree nor disagree	20	60
Disagree	23	65
Some employees have to be union members to get or keep their jobs:		
Yes	2	(59)
No	98	50
Management strongly recommend employees join a union:		
Yes	23	64
No	77	46
Union subscriptions deducted from employees' pay:		
Yes	67	55
No	33	40

Base: All workplaces with union members and with 25 or more employees.
Figures are weighted and based on responses from at least 1,235 managers.

exception of the largest workplaces, where there was no difference, average union density was higher in each size band (by between 13 and 25 percentage points) where check-off was in place. This might be because check-off arrangements, since the 1993 legislation, were more likely to endure in workplaces with a relatively high density. Alternatively, unions may have found it more difficult to retain members among workplaces where check-off was abolished.

Union recognition

We have already shown that in almost half of all workplaces there were no union members present. Among the remaining half of workplaces, we can now examine the incidence of multiple unionism and recognition, and also explore matters such as single-table bargaining. Figure 5.2 shows the distribution of the number of unions present per workplace across all workplaces, and across those with union members.

As can be seen from the figure, multiple unionism is a feature for a majority of unionised workplaces, although large numbers of unions are comparatively rare, perhaps following the period of union mergers and amalgamations in recent years. Around a quarter of unionised workplaces have four or more unions present, with fifteen being the largest number we recorded in a single workplace. Put in the context of all workplaces, about half have no unions present, a quarter have members from only one union, a tenth have members from two unions, and the remaining fifth have members from more than two unions.

Union recognition cannot be pre-supposed from union presence. This is because union recognition was, first, at the time of the survey, voluntarily agreed between the parties and, second, variable as to its scope and depth (Brown *et al.*, 1998).[6] There is a gradation in recognition arrangements, ranging from full regulation of the employment relationship through rights to collective bargaining, to a situation where there is no collective bargaining but representation rights over, for example, grievances and disciplinary cases. However, recognition covering the right to collective bargaining over pay and conditions remains the ultimate arbiter and is what unions aspire to in any agreement with employers. Our question on recognition is based on this definition and asked if management negotiated with unions

Figure 5.2 Number of trade unions at the workplace

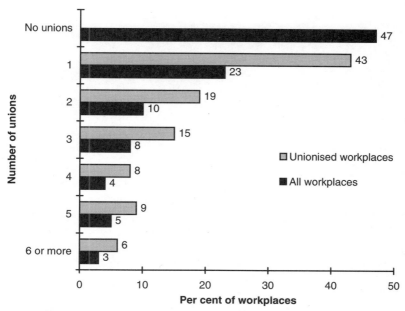

Base: All workplaces with 25 or more employees.
Figures are weighted and based on responses from 1,889 managers.

over pay and conditions for any sections of the workforce at the workplace.[7] Table 5.3 shows the make-up of workplaces by union status.

Among workplaces where there was some union presence, over four-fifths had a union recognition arrangement, representing 45 per cent of all workplaces. Union recognition was more common among larger workplaces, such that overall nearly two-thirds (62 per cent) of employees worked in workplaces with union

Table 5.3 Trade union presence, by main classifications

	No union present	Union present but no recognition	Recognised union
	% of workplaces	% of workplaces	% of workplaces
Workplace size			
25–49 employees	54	7	39
50–99 employees	48	11	41
100–199 employees	34	9	57
200–499 employees	23	10	67
500 or more employees	14	8	78
Organisation size			
Less than 100 employees	75	11	13
100–999 employees	60	11	29
1,000–9,999 employees	36	6	58
10,000 employees or more	21	7	73
Sector			
Private	64	11	25
Public	3	3	95
Organisational status			
Stand-alone workplace	70	11	19
Part of a wider organisation	38	7	54
Industry			
Manufacturing	60	10	30
Electricity, gas and water	2	0	98
Construction	55	8	37
Wholesale and retail	70	8	22
Hotels and restaurants	88	5	7
Transport and communications	41	7	52
Financial services	33	1	65
Other business services	74	7	19
Public administration	1	0	99
Education	5	9	86
Health	29	14	57
Other community services	51	8	42
All workplaces	47	8	45

Base: All workplaces with 25 or more employees.
Figures are weighted and based on responses from 1,889 managers.

recognition. Thus, a majority of employees have experience of a union role in workplace affairs, whether or not they themselves are union members or covered by collective agreements.

It is fair to state that union recognition is predominantly a public sector phenomenon: two-thirds of private sector workplaces were without a union presence, and only one in four recognised unions, compared with more than nine in ten public sector workplaces.[8] Within the private sector, recognition was closely associated with the size of the workplace and with the size of the organisation, but which was more important? Both had independent effects, of which workplace size had the larger. Thus, even in workplaces which were part of the largest organisations, there was a strong, positive association with workplace size. In such cases, recognition ranged from a third (33 per cent) in the smallest workplaces to three-quarters (76 per cent) in the largest.

There were 8 per cent of workplaces where unions had a presence, but were not recognised. An alternative way of expressing this is to say that, among unionised workplaces, there was a non-recognition rate of 16 per cent. There was a considerable amount of variation in this rate across different types of workplace. In the private sector it was 30 per cent, whereas in the public sector it was very small (3 per cent). Confining our attention just to the private sector for a moment, the non-recognition rate was especially high in stand-alone sites (41 per cent), other business services (49 per cent) and health (48 per cent).

One reason why unions may not have been recognised in these workplaces is that there was a relatively modest union presence. In fact, union density averaged 23 per cent (compared with 56 per cent in workplaces where unions were recognised), although less than half (44 per cent) had a density below 10 per cent. Overall, just 1 per cent of all workplaces had a majority of employees who were union members but where management had chosen not to recognise any union. Beyond that, there were a further 4 per cent of workplaces where union density was 10 per cent or more, but not in the majority. Some of these workplaces may be ones where unions seek to secure recognition over the coming years. Nearly all (85 per cent) of these workplaces are in the private sector.

Returning to the issue of multiple unionism, where there was more than one union present at the workplace, or where employers and unions took steps to avoid multiple unionism, we were able to explore how union recognition arrangements operated. Employers might wish to do so to avoid fragmentation in bargaining, and unions to secure members and prevent demarcation disputes over coverage. A great deal of importance has therefore been attached by some unions, employers and commentators to single union deals since they were pioneered by the Electrical, Electronic, Telecommunications and Plumbing Union (EETPU) in the early 1980s (Bassett, 1986). In workplaces which recognised only one union, 72 per cent of managers (or 24 per cent of all unionised workplaces) reported that they had done so through a formal single union agreement, rather than it simply having worked out that way.

More than half of unionised workplaces had two or more unions present. This feature, long common in British workplaces, has been identified as a possible source of friction. Machin *et al.* (1993) show, however, that it is not multiple unionism as such that may have deleterious consequences, but fragmented bargaining structures. Single union deals, evidently, overcome this, but so too does 'single table' bargaining where unions negotiate jointly with management. Multiple union presence was very strongly associated with multiple union recognition. Of workplaces with two or more unions present, 88 per cent also recognised more than one union.[9] We then asked whether management negotiated jointly with all of the recognised unions, or conducted separate negotiations with two or more bargaining units. Among workplaces which recognised two or more unions, around three-fifths (or 26 per cent of all unionised workplaces) conducted joint negotiations with all of the unions. A little below a fifth (17 per cent) of all unionised workplaces had a multiple union presence and negotiated separately with each union. The remainder had consolidated bargaining arrangements, but short of a 'single table'.

Thus, among unionised workplaces, single union deals and single table bargaining were equally common but found in different types of workplaces. Single union deals were twice as likely in the private sector (32 per cent compared with 16 per cent) while single table bargaining was over three times more likely in the public sector (40 per cent compared with 12 per cent). Over half the unionised workplaces in wholesale and retail, financial services and other community services had a single union agreement. The distribution of single table bargaining was more even, except for electricity, gas and water (83 per cent) where it was especially high.

To summarise these last two sections, for all bar a small proportion of workplaces, there are broadly only two types of arrangement. First, about half of all workplaces were entirely devoid of union members, or membership was very low and unions were not recognised. Second, in over two-fifths of workplaces union membership made up a significant proportion of the workforce and union recognition arrangements, mostly involving only one union or single table bargaining, were in place. There was a small residual group of workplaces with moderate to majority levels of union membership but without union recognition arrangements. The interactions between managerial attitudes and the ability of unions to organise, recruit and win recognition are clearly complex, and are independently associated with structural characteristics such as size and sector. However, our results show unambiguously that where management are predisposed towards unions, membership and recognition were far stronger than where management were opposed.

Worker representatives

One of the arguments commonly advanced in favour of unions is that they embody the collective 'voice' of workers (Freeman and Medoff, 1984). Similar arguments are also often made about the merits of joint consultative arrangements (Rogers and Streeck, 1995). To give rise to a voice, however, requires a spokesperson (or persons) from the union or workforce. This section looks at the presence of worker representatives, be they 'lay' union representatives or not. Its purpose is to give an overall perspective on the state of worker representation at the workplace based on information obtained in the management interview. Chapter 9, in contrast, focuses on the activities of worker representatives based on their own account.

To begin with, managers were asked about the presence and number of worker representatives at the workplace. A basic distinction was made between union representatives (of a recognised union) and other worker representatives, whom we label 'non-union' representatives – this distinction is important because, while some may be union members, they have no official status as representatives of the union.[10] Issue-specific representatives, like those dealing with health and safety matters, were excluded and these are covered later in the section. Table 5.4 shows the proportion of workplaces with worker representatives, broken down by the type of union presence.

Where there were worker representatives, they were most commonly union representatives, who were found in about three-quarters of workplaces with recognised unions (and, overall, in about a third of all workplaces). Non-union representatives were found in 12 per cent of all workplaces, and were equally common in workplaces with no union members and in those which recognised unions. They were slightly more likely to be found in workplaces where unions were present, but not recognised, though it is doubtful whether this presages any significant transition towards recognition – after all, four out of five of these workplaces had no representatives.

This highlights a more general point: almost three in five workplaces had no worker representatives of any kind, and this was the case for nine out of every ten workplaces where there were no union members. Workplaces without any worker representatives, therefore, follow much the same pattern as workplaces without union members (see Table 5.3), but there is an enhanced size effect as small workplaces with recognised unions were the least likely to have worker representatives. Thus, in the smallest workplaces, 65 per cent were without worker representatives while in the largest workplaces the proportion was 19 per cent.

Turning attention now to workplaces with recognised unions, a quarter do not have any lay representatives at the workplace. In about a third of these cases (or 8 per cent overall), union members have recourse to a worker representative based at another workplace in their organisation. This was most common among smaller workplaces that were part of a larger organisation. Table 5.4 also shows that one in ten workplaces with recognised unions had both union and non-union representatives at the workplace. These parallel channels of representation were somewhat more common in larger workplaces.

In 5 per cent of workplaces with recognised unions, there was someone who could be called a full-time representative – as distinct from a full-time union official who is an employee of the union, not of the workplace – by virtue of the fact that they spent all, or nearly all, of their working time on union activities. More than anything else, they were a feature of large workplaces, with one in three of the largest unionised workplaces having a full-time representative.

Among all workplaces with worker representatives, it was most common for

Table 5.4 Types of worker representatives, by trade union presence

	No union present	*Union present but no recognition*	*Recognised union*	*All workplaces*
	% of workplaces	*% of workplaces*	*% of workplaces*	*% of workplaces*
Both union and non-union representatives	–	–	10	4
Union representative only	–	–	64	28
Non-union representative only	11	19	1	7
No worker representatives	89	81	25	60

Base: All workplaces with 25 or more employees.
Figures are weighted and based on responses from 1,889 managers.

there to be several representatives, with the median being 3 and the mean 4.3 representatives. Naturally, the larger the workplace, the greater the number of worker representatives. In workplaces where they were present, the mean number of non-union worker representatives was greater than that for union represent-atives, 4.7 compared with 3.7.

Issue-specific worker representation: health and safety and collective redundancies

Under the Health and Safety (Consultation with Employees) Regulations 1996, employers are obliged to consult with their employees in good time about health and safety matters. The regulations filled a gap in earlier legislation which had not provided for consultation in workplaces without recognised unions.[11] The mechanisms for consulting are either with elected 'representatives of employee safety' or directly with employees. Employers were advised to 'choose whatever means suit you and your employees best' (Health and Safety Executive, 1996: 7), and suggested forms of consultation were said to include briefings, quality circles, notice boards, newsletters and e-mail. We are able to look at the precise arrange-ments adopted by all workplaces, unionised and non-unionised.

Over a third (39 per cent) of workplaces operated joint health and safety committees.[12] A slightly smaller proportion (29 per cent) consulted with safety representatives. A similar proportion (30 per cent) consulted directly, using a variety of means to do so. This leaves just 2 per cent of workplaces where, according to managers, no steps were taken to consult employees about health and safety matters. Having a committee in place was more common in workplaces with union recognition (47 per cent). More notable, however, was that among work-places without any union members, almost a third (31 per cent) had a joint committee and over a quarter (27 per cent) had elected safety representatives. These proportions were only slightly below those found across all workplaces. It appears, in this domain at least, that representative structures have been established in non-union workplaces.

The same cannot be said for consultations over collective redundancies. Case study research has shown that workplaces do not tend to operate standing structures for consulting workers over collective redundancies (Smith *et al.*, 1999). They either make use of permanent union or consultative structures or new ones are created as the need arises. Moreover, the need for these structures is transitory and they tend to be disbanded after the redundancies occur.

Overall, 17 per cent of workplaces had made some redundancies in the twelve months preceding the survey. It was most common for managers in these workplaces to consult directly with employees likely to be affected – this happened in 82 per cent of cases. Other methods used were to consult with union representatives (49 per cent); with a joint consultative committee (21 per cent); and with other employee representatives (4 per cent). Many employers used more than one avenue for consultation. In 12 per cent of workplaces where employees had been made redundant there was, ostensibly, no consultation – in nearly all of these cases fewer than twenty employees were made redundant in the year, which meant that managers were under no legal obligation to consult.

Under revised regulations introduced in 1995, managers in workplaces with recognised unions were given the option of bypassing unions and consulting employees by other means. Looking at this situation directly, we find that just over a third (36 per cent) bypassed recognised unions, either by consulting employees directly (23 per cent) or not consulting at all (13 per cent). Again, in very few cases were more than twenty employees made redundant, so consultation was not mandatory. However, the extent to which unions were bypassed suggests that some employers have taken the cue given in the 1995 regulations.

Accompaniment in grievance and disciplinary hearings

The final area we examine in this section concerns the role of worker represent-atives, if any, in assisting employees who wish to pursue a grievance, or are the subject of a disciplinary case. Procedurally, it is conventional to allow employees engaged in a dispute with their employer to be accompanied by a third party in any hearings, in line with common precepts of natural justice. This is recommended by, amongst others, ACAS in their guidance and codes of practice. We examined both grievance and disciplinary situations and found a near identical pattern between the two, so we confine our discussion to disciplinary cases which are, ordinarily, graver.

Just 4 per cent of workplaces do not allow employees to be accompanied by a third party in actions taken to discipline or dismiss them, and a further 2 per cent only allow the option of bringing a supervisor or line manager along – of little comfort if the dispute is centred around relationships with immediate managers, as they often are. Where they do allow the employee to be independently accompanied, 41 per cent of workplaces allow them to choose whoever they wish to accompany them. The remaining half of workplaces specify a variety of options, including trade union representatives (45 per cent), full-time union officials (27 per cent), and nearly all permit colleagues to join the employee (87 per cent).

There is a strong association between the type of union presence at the workplace and who can accompany employees. Workplaces with recognised unions were much more likely than others to specify that union representatives and full-time officials could fulfil this role. In workplaces where union members were present, but there was no recognition, nearly half (46 per cent) of managers said that workers could be accompanied by anyone of their choosing. Of those who specified the options open to employees, full-time officials were mentioned by a fifth (20 per cent) of managers, well below the comparable figure in recognised workplaces (51 per cent). Finally, almost all of the cases where there was no right to be accompanied, or where the option was confined to the immediate boss, were workplaces without any union presence at all.

Joint consultative committees

In the last chapter, we looked at the incidence of different forms of employee involvement, including direct participation and financial participation. Here, our interest is in joint consultative committees as a form of indirect employee participation. As Ramsey (1977) has demonstrated, interest in employee participation has waxed and waned according to the state of the labour market, what he refers to as 'cycles of control'. In tight labour markets, employers are more willing to cede some control over managerial prerogative through measures designed to promote employee participation. Marchington *et al.* (1992: 56–7), in the most recent set of detailed case studies, found that the current wave was for direct forms of participation with a 'lesser emphasis on representative participation'; though they also found that there 'was some synergy and complementarity' between joint consultation and union recognition.

A considerable amount of questioning in the survey covered consultative arrangements. This section provides an overview of it. In particular, we focus on the interaction with union presence, and the implications for single versus parallel channels of representation.

Incidence of joint consultative committees

Table 5.5 presents the overall picture on the incidence of differing forms of joint consultative arrangements. We asked about both workplace-level joint consultative committees,[13] and those that operate at a level higher than the workplace. We also asked about European Works Councils, and these are discussed below.

Just over half of workplaces had a committee which either operated at the workplace, or elsewhere in the organisation.[14] Less than a third of workplaces had a local committee and slightly more than a third had a committee at a higher level in the organisation. A tenth had both. The incidence of these committees conformed to some well-observed patterns: the greater the number of employees at both workplace and organisation level, the more likely was any form of

Table 5.5 Incidence of joint consultative committees, by main classifications

	No committee	Workplace committee only	Workplace and higher level committee	Higher level committee only
	% of workplaces	% of workplaces	% of workplaces	% of workplaces
Workplace size				
25–49 employees	52	11	8	29
50–99 employees	47	20	10	23
100–199 employees	37	27	14	21
200–499 employees	28	28	28	16
500 or more employees	23	43	23	11
Organisation size				
Less than 100 employees	80	16	0	4
100–999 employees	57	31	4	8
1,000–9,999 employees	31	17	14	38
10,000 employees or more	20	11	23	45
Sector				
Private	57	16	8	18
Public	18	20	19	42
Organisational status				
Stand-alone workplace	78	22	–	–
Part of a wider organisation	35	16	15	34
Industry				
Manufacturing	64	25	4	7
Electricity, gas and water	3	15	46	36
Construction	73	11	6	10
Wholesale and retail	48	8	15	28
Hotels and restaurants	54	11	12	22
Transport and communications	34	17	17	33
Financial services	37	6	8	49
Other business services	61	18	4	16
Public administration	11	18	39	31
Education	25	29	11	34
Health	45	11	8	36
Other community services	49	26	5	20
All workplaces	47	17	11	25

Base: All workplaces with 25 or more employees.
Figures are weighted and based on responses from 1,890 managers.

committee. Workplace level committees were most closely associated with workplace employment size, and higher level committees with organisation employment size.

Management disposition towards consultation and information-sharing appears to matter as well. Managers were asked whether they agreed or disagreed with the statement that 'those at the top are best placed to make decisions about this workplace'. Those agreeing with this sentiment were much less likely to have joint consultative committees within their organisation. Some 14 per cent of managers strongly agreed with the statement, and among these workplaces under a third (31 per cent) operated committees at either the workplace or a higher level. Only 3 per cent of managers strongly disagreed with the statement, and in these workplaces more than three-quarters (78 per cent) had committees.

The incidence of joint committees was also related to the type of union presence at the workplace. Workplaces with recognised unions had a much higher incidence of joint consultative committees than those without: three-quarters (74 per cent) of workplaces with recognised unions had a committee at either the workplace or at a higher level or both, compared with just a third (34 per cent) of workplaces with no union members. This is not just an artefact of employment size. If we confine our attention to the private sector, in each employment size band workplaces with recognised unions were more likely to operate joint consultative committees. In other words, workplaces without a union presence were substantially less, rather than more, likely to have put in place alternative mechanisms for consulting with employees on a collective basis. Union representation and indirect employee participation go hand-in-hand rather than being substitutes for one another.

Since 1994, large transnational companies operating in Europe have been required under a European Union Directive to establish consultation and information-sharing arrangements at a supra-national level.[15] These are commonly referred to as European Works Councils. Employees based in the United Kingdom were excluded from the Directive at the time of the survey as the previous government had declined to be party to the social chapter provisions of the Maastricht treaty.[16] Nonetheless, by dint of the size of their operations elsewhere in the European Union, substantial numbers of large transnational companies with a presence in the United Kingdom were covered by the Directive. While these companies were not obliged to include the UK workforce within the consultation arrangements put in place, there is evidence to suggest that, of around 250 such companies which had set up European Works Councils by late 1996, almost all had included UK workers (Marginson *et al.*, 1998: 21–2).

Our survey data gives an indication of the scale of these supra-national consultative arrangements in Britain, bearing in mind that we were unable to specifically identify those workplaces which might have been covered by the Directive. Among workplaces that were part of private sector transnational companies, 19 per cent of managers said that a European Works Council operated within their organisation. It should also be noted, however, that a high proportion (15 per cent) of workplace managers were unable to answer the question. This is, perhaps, unsurprising given the remoteness of European Works Councils from the workplace.

The operation of workplace level consultative committees

As well as identifying whether, and at what level, consultative committees operated, we also asked a series of questions that examined how workplace-based committees functioned. In combination they reveal something of the role these committees play at the workplace. One, perhaps symbolic, indicator of the function these committees serve is their title. We have not undertaken any detailed analysis of this data, but we were struck by the number of examples embracing contemporary trends, such as:

- Committee for Communication;
- Delivering Customer Promise;
- Partnership Committee.

A fairly general question identified the range of issues that were the subject of joint consultation at the workplace.[17] Foremost among these were working practices (88 per cent), health and safety (86 per cent), welfare services and facilities (83 per cent) and future workplace plans (also 83 per cent). Pay issues were among the least frequently mentioned (50 per cent), most likely as these are often considered to be a topic for negotiation rather than consultation.

There are a variety of ways in which employees might be appointed to sit on a joint consultative committee, possibly even multiple ways for the same committee. Figure 5.3 shows the results. There were some important differences between workplaces which recognised unions and those that did not. A similar proportion of both, just under half, had elected employee representatives. In almost a third (29 per cent) of recognised workplaces representatives were put forward by unions. A higher proportion of workplaces with no recognition had representatives appointed by management (28 per cent compared with 16 per cent), or called for volunteers (27 per cent compared with 18 per cent). In total, 52 per cent of workplaces without recognition had employee representatives whose only route to the committee was appointment by management or as volunteers. The respective figure for workplaces with recognition was lower at 30 per cent. For these workplaces, there may be some doubts about the independence of the employee representatives on consultative committees.

More direct evidence of the overlap between independent union structures and consultative arrangements comes from a further question which shows that in four-fifths (80 per cent) of workplaces with recognition, some or all of the employee representatives who sit on the consultative committee were also lay union representatives at the workplace. In workplaces with a union presence but no recognition, the existence of a joint consultative committee did not appear to be a springboard to full union involvement. In just 5 per cent of these cases did unions themselves choose any of the representatives for the committee.

Figure 5.3 How employee representatives are appointed to Joint Consultative Committees

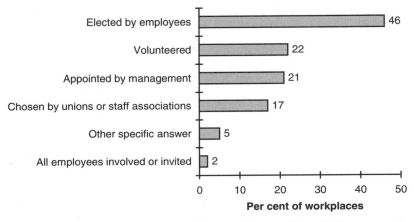

Base: All workplaces operating workplace-based joint consultative committees with 25 or more employees.
Figures are weighted and based on responses from 800 managers.

The frequency of meetings of consultative committees fell into three fairly even sized groups: just over a third (34 per cent) met once a quarter or less often; slightly under a third (29 per cent) met more often than once a quarter, but less often than once a month; and the remainder (37 per cent) met at least once a month. The committees met less frequently where they were located in a workplace with union recognition: the median number of meetings here was six in the past year, compared with ten where there was no recognition. This appeared to reflect the type of employee representatives who sat on the committee. Where unions themselves appointed the representatives, meetings occurred much less often – in 47 per cent of cases it was quarterly or less, compared with just 17 per cent of cases where management appointed the employee representatives.

Finally, we asked managers to make a subjective assessment of the influence of the committee in workplace decision-making. This was also related to how employees were appointed. Managers were much more likely to regard the committee as being 'very influential' where the employee representatives were appointed by management (56 per cent) than if they were put forward by trade unions (16 per cent) or were volunteers (22 per cent). Committees were also more likely to be regarded as very influential the more frequently meetings were held. Where committees met monthly or more often, 46 per cent of managers thought them very influential compared with 16 per cent where meetings were quarterly or less frequent.

These results appear to suggest that joint consultative committees function more effectively from *management's* viewpoint where they have more control over the appointment of worker representatives to sit on them. Where unions have been able to put forward the worker representatives, meetings are held less frequently and managers regard the committee as being less effective.

Negotiation, consultation and information-sharing in practice

In the opening part of this chapter we looked at the institutional structures of representation at the workplace. This only gives a partial picture of the degree of joint regulation of the employment relationship. As already noted, recognition of trade unions cannot be equated to full joint regulation. Similarly, the establishment of formal worker representative structures in non-union workplaces does not imply or guarantee a joint consultative approach to all workplace issues. In this section we examine the scope and depth of bargaining and joint consultation at the workplace. However, as we showed in Chapter 4, managers in relatively few workplaces that are part of a wider organisation have complete discretion over decision-making, and we use this data to qualify our findings.

Figure 5.4 presents information on the extent to which there is joint regulation of the employment relationship with worker representatives. The left-hand side of the figure refers to workplaces with recognised unions and with a lay union representative on site. The right-hand side refers to workplaces which did not recognise unions, but which had non-union worker representatives sitting on workplace-based joint consultative committees.[18]

Managers were asked to indicate for each of nine issues whether they negotiated, consulted, informed or did not involve worker representatives in dealing with the issue. The line between these categories is blurred and it would be misleading to attach too high a degree of importance to any given percentage figure. However, the questions are robust and distinct enough to identify several patterns arising from the data.

First, the scope of joint negotiation at the workplace is quite modest. Among workplaces with union representatives the only issue over which negotiations occurred in a substantial proportion of workplaces was pay and conditions. Well below that was the handling of grievances and health and safety. Among workplaces with non-union representatives negotiations took place most frequently over health and safety.

Just over a fifth (22 per cent) of workplaces with union representatives negotiated with them over pay and one or more non-pay issues. A further fifth (17 per cent) negotiated only over pay, while 13 per cent negotiated only over non-pay issues. This leaves half of such workplaces where, according to managers, no negotiations occurred with union representatives over any of the nine issues. In most of these workplaces, consultation occurred over four or more of the issues listed (19 per cent) or fewer than that number (19 per cent). In 4 per cent of cases there was some information-sharing. This left a residual 7 per cent of cases where union representatives were not involved in any of the issues at all – that is, no negotiation, consultation or information-sharing. Among workplaces with non-union representatives, negotiation over pay matters was relatively rare (13 per cent), but a higher proportion engaged in non-pay negotiations (38 per cent), and there was also a substantial proportion (31 per cent) where consultation occurred over four or more issues.

Figure 5.4 The scope of negotiation, consultation and information-sharing, by type of worker representative

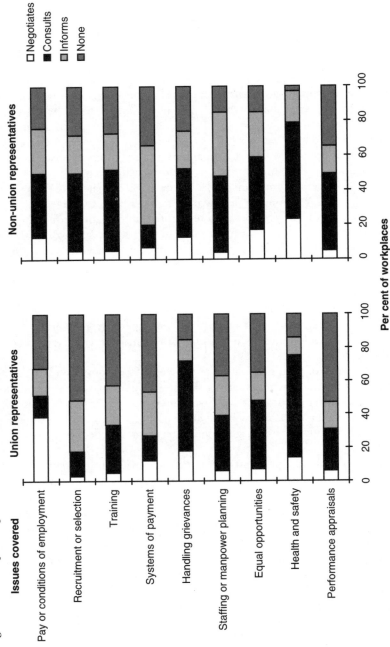

Base: All workplaces with a union or non-union representative and 25 or more employees.
Figures are weighted and based on responses from 920 (union representatives) and 117 (non-union representatives) managers.

Second, the degree of joint regulation is no greater in workplaces with lay union representatives than it is in those with non-union representatives. The average number of issues over which negotiations occurred was similar at 1.1 for union representatives and 0.9 for non-union representatives. Indeed, there was greater consultation with non-union representatives – an average of 3.7 issues compared with 2.9 for union representatives.

Third, and perhaps the most compelling finding of them all, was the extent to which worker representatives were excluded altogether from the province of many workplace issues. Lay union representatives had no involvement in around half of workplaces – not even for the provision of information – on matters such as performance appraisals (53 per cent), recruitment (52 per cent), payment systems (46 per cent) and training (43 per cent). The degree of involvement of non-union representatives was higher, but in around a third of workplaces these representatives had no role in the same issues.

One obvious explanation for the relative lack of joint regulation is that much of it occurs away from the workplace. In Chapter 4 we found there to be little scope for deviating from agreed policies in workplaces where there was a personnel specialist at a higher level in the organisation (see Table 4.3). This transpires to be an important factor. Where workplace managers in 'branch sites' did not have to follow policy on any issues, they were more likely to negotiate with union representatives over both pay and non-pay matters (41 per cent compared with 16 per cent where policies had to be observed on most issues).[19] Yet, even in this former group, where managers had greater autonomy, there were a quarter (24 per cent) of cases where union representatives had no negotiating role and were consulted on just a few matters. On average, managers in relatively autonomous branch sites negotiated or consulted with union representatives over five of the nine issues.

A second factor, for unionised workplaces, might be the strength of the union. Taking union density as a proxy for this, we find the greater the level of union density the more likely management were to consult and negotiate over workplace matters. Those workplaces where at least some negotiations took place with union representatives had a union density of 61 per cent, compared with 56 per cent where there was no negotiation but some consultation, and 42 per cent where there was neither. The difference was enhanced after taking into account managerial autonomy at the workplace. Thus, in branch sites where managers did not have to follow higher-level policies, union density in workplaces where there was negotiation (55 per cent) was double that in those with no negotiation or consultation (27 per cent). Similarly, the greater the union density, the more issues that were negotiated.

To summarise, union recognition cannot be directly equated to joint regulation. Where unions were recognised and lay union representatives were present, their involvement at the workplace was heavily constrained by two factors: first, the locus of decision-making may be away from the workplace (where there is, perhaps, a greater role for full-time union officials); second, even where it is not, management may permit only a modest role, confining joint regulation to a limited agenda of issues. Union strength at the workplace, as measured by union density, was associated with greater joint regulation.

Pay determination

At its heart, the employment relationship is an exchange of effort for earnings. The method and process by which these earnings are determined has historically been the most important source of conflict in the relationship. While economists have tended to focus on skills and qualifications ('human capital') as the root of differences in pay across individuals, others have highlighted the importance of institutions and the scope for variation from one employer to the next for work of a similar kind (Nolan and Brown, 1983; Groshen, 1991). In this section we look at the institutional role, while in Chapter 7 we look at how pay varies from one individual to another.

Discussion of pay determination has centred around the level of collective bargaining. The consistent picture over several decades, from surveys and case studies alike, is of decentralisation. In the latter half of the 1980s, it was estimated that one million employees moved out of the coverage of industry-level agreements (Brown and Walsh, 1991). Most notable was the collapse of the national agreement between the Engineering Employers Federation and the Confederation of Ship-building and Engineering Unions in 1990, which had been the benchmark for many other agreements. Sisson (1987: 13) has argued that decentralisation in Britain has been pursued by employers 'in order to get control in the workplace'. Often missing from these discussions is an attempt to give an adequate account of the process of pay determination in settings where there are no unions and no bargaining takes place. This section gives a brief account of some of the data collected in this area.[20]

We begin by presenting some descriptive findings. It is necessary to broadly qualify the results before we proceed. Many workplace managers experienced difficulties answering questions in this area, especially in the public sector. In large tranches of the public sector, covering jobs as diverse as Members of Parliament and nurses, pay is formally outside the scope of collective bargaining. Alternative mechanisms such as indexation formulae and pay review bodies are in place (Bailey, 1996). And, across all workplaces, the pay-setting process is often handled beyond the workplace and may be opaque to managers at a local level. The patterns of pay determination are, nonetheless, clearly discernible.

Overall, 52 per cent of workplaces did not enter into collective bargaining over pay and conditions.[21] The half of workplaces which did engage in collective bargaining tended to operate it for all or almost all employees. Only 11 per cent of workplaces fell between these two extremes. The distribution of workplaces falling into either camp broadly matches that for union recognition, discussed above, so we will not pursue this any further. Rather, we will look more closely at the detail of pay setting arrangements and its fragmentation within workplaces.

For each occupational group employed at the workplace, managers were asked how pay was set, choosing from a list of seven options. As we know how many employees are in each occupation, we can use this information to calculate the proportion of all employees covered by each of the seven arrangements. Table 5.6 presents the results, for non-managerial employees only, broken down by workplace size and sector. Just under half had their pay (unilaterally) set for them by management, either at a higher level in the organisation or by workplace management. The extent of individual negotiations over pay was very low, covering just 2 per cent of non-managerial employees. Of the 36 per cent of non-managerial employees covered by collective bargaining, most were covered by arrangements that are organisation or workplace-specific. It was still the case, however, that two out of five of these employees were covered by collective bargaining across several employers – these are predominantly in the public sector, and in the private sector this amounted to no more than one in six of the non-managerial employees covered by collective bargaining. Even here, it remains, numerically at least, more important than individual negotiations.

Within the private sector, the coverage of the different methods varied a good deal by workplace size. Larger workplaces were much more likely to have some collective bargaining, though there was no major difference in the extent to which pay was decided at the workplace – that is, the higher proportion of employees covered by workplace collective bargaining in large private sector workplaces was offset by the lower proportion having pay set by workplace management. In the public sector, the role of workplace management in pay setting was negligible. A much higher proportion of employees were covered by 'some other form' of pay determination, most likely (as noted above) by either an indexation formula or a review body.

Shifting the focus back to the workplace, we can see to what extent these various arrangements apply uniformly within a workplace. Table 5.7 shows the proportion of workplaces using each of the methods in isolation (for non-managerial employees) and the overall proportion using any of the main methods. There is a high degree of uniformity in pay-setting arrangements – almost three-quarters of workplaces used only one of the seven methods for each group of non-managerial employees.

Many of the differences between sectors were noted in the analysis of employee coverage, though some further points arise in the summary rows at the bottom of the table. Only one in five private sector workplaces engaged in collective bargaining, whereas four in five had pay set by management and one in ten negotiated on an individual basis with some employees. Two-fifths of public sector workplaces did not engage in collective bargaining, more than offset by those where pay was set in some other way.

Conclusion

This chapter has provided a broad overview of the incidence and character of employee representation. In summarising, we begin with the converse situation, where there is no employee representation. Almost a half of workplaces had no union members. Nearly a tenth of workplaces had some union members, but no

Table 5.6 Determination of pay for non-managerial employees, by workplace size and sector

	Multi-employer collective bargaining	Single employer collective bargaining	Workplace collective bargaining	Management at a higher level	Management at workplace	Individual negotiation	Set by some other method
	% of employees	% of employees	% of employees	% of employees	% of employees	% of employees	% of employees
Private sector							
25–49 employees	4	5	2	39	41	5	3
50–99 employees	4	9	3	30	45	5	4
100–199 employees	10	11	7	29	35	1	6
200–499 employees	5	13	14	29	30	2	6
500 or more employees	2	25	16	17	37	0	2
All private sector workplaces	5	14	9	28	37	2	4
Public sector							
25–49 employees	30	11	0	16	3	0	40
50–99 employees	30	19	0	10	3	1	36
100–199 employees	37	15	1	11	3	0	33
200–499 employees	43	20	1	8	2	2	24
500 or more employees	35	16	6	4	2	0	38
All public sector workplaces	35	16	3	8	3	0	35
All workplaces	14	15	7	22	26	2	14

Base: All workplaces with 25 or more employees.
Figures are weighted and based on responses from 1,273 (private sector) and 586 (public sector) managers.

Table 5.7 Uniformity and fragmentation of pay determination for non-managerial employees, by sector

	Sector		All workplaces
	Private	Public	
	% of workplaces	% of workplaces	% of workplaces
Method of pay determination			
Only multi-employer collective bargaining	2	22	7
Only single employer collective bargaining	6	11	7
Only workplace collective bargaining	1	0	1
Only set by management at higher level	32	9	25
Only set by management at workplace	31	1	23
Only individual negotiation	3	0	3
Only some other method	3	20	8
Mixture of different methods	22	37	26
All workplaces	100	100	100
Any collective bargaining	20	60	31
Any set by management	83	23	66
Any individual negotiation	9	1	7
Any other methods	6	54	19

Base: All workplaces with 25 or more employees.
Figures are weighted and based on responses from 1,863 managers.

recognised unions. Two-thirds of workplaces had no worker representatives. Nearly half of workplaces had no joint consultative committee, either at the workplace or at a higher level in the organisation. Taken together, 32 per cent of workplaces met all of the above conditions – in these workplaces there was an absence of any formal structure representing employees' interests. These workplaces were mostly small and mostly stand-alone sites. They were disproportionately found in certain industries including construction, hotels and restaurants and other business services. It is more difficult for unions to organise in small workplaces and small organisations. We also found, though, that managers in these workplaces held the least favourable views towards unions – 2 per cent were in favour of union membership compared with 42 per cent among managers in all other workplaces. They were also the most likely to agree that they alone were best placed to make decisions, 69 per cent compared with 49 per cent. In Chapter 9 we look, from an employee perspective, at whether there is a 'representation gap', but there is sufficient evidence presented here to suggest that managers in many workplaces are content to operate without any means of independent employee voice (Towers, 1997).

Compare this to the situation in workplaces with recognised unions, which accounted for 45 per cent of all workplaces. The structure of recognition in these workplaces was such that, by design or default, only one union was recognised in

41 per cent of these workplaces. A further 31 per cent of workplaces operated single table bargaining. This left just 28 per cent of recognised workplaces where negotiations were held with separate bargaining units. In most of the private sector bargaining took place at either the company or workplace level. Multi-employer bargaining was mostly a public sector phenomenon, covering one in three employees in this sector.

Three-quarters of workplaces with recognition had worker representatives on site. For the most part, their role in workplace affairs was rather circumscribed. In only one in five cases did management negotiate with them over both pay and non-pay matters. In one in two cases there were no negotiations over any matters, and on many topics including training, a large proportion of union representatives had no involvement of any kind. This was partly related, in larger organisations, to (a lack of) managerial autonomy at the workplace, but it was also related to union strength. Where local managers did not have to follow policies set at a higher level and where union density was high, joint regulation was more common. This evidence points strongly towards a relatively marginal role for unions in many workplaces, but is this also part and parcel of an approach of favouring more direct means of employee participation and other more individualistic means of managing employees?

We address this question by returning to the material presented at the end of Chapter 4 on high commitment management practices (see Table 4.12). For simplicity we adopt a count of these practices, ranging from none to all fifteen. Figure 5.5 compares the number of practices used in workplaces with and without recognised unions. Union recognition is associated with more of these practices being in place. However, this is mostly because these practices were more

Figure 5.5 Number of high commitment management practices, by trade union recognition

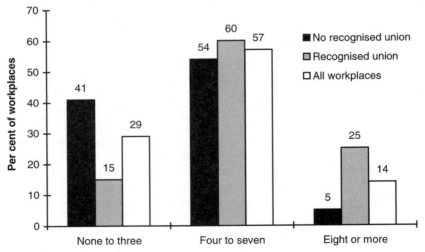

Base: All workplaces with 25 or more employees.
Figures are weighted and based on responses from 1,711 managers.

widespread in large, private sector workplaces and throughout the public sector. For example, in private sector workplaces with 100 or more employees, there were no differences between those that did and did not recognise unions.

Keeping our attention focused on private sector workplaces, we look more closely at the association with unions. Union density was related to the extent of joint regulation at the workplace. It was also related to the spread of high commitment management practices: the more practices there were in place in recognised workplaces, the greater the union density. In particular, where at least half of the practices were in place, union density averaged 47 per cent, compared with 35 per cent where it was below this number. Similarly, where joint negotiations took place with union representatives, these workplaces were slightly more likely to have at least half of the management practices in place, 15 per cent compared with 12 per cent. Taken together, this evidence suggests that an active and strong union presence is compatible with the broad suite of high commitment management practices. The proportion of workplaces, however, which had realised this compatibility was low: only 4 per cent of recognised workplaces had a majority unionised workforce, where local representatives negotiated with managers over some issues and where at least half of these high commitment management practices were in place. They were well out-numbered by recognised workplaces where density was below half, no negotiation took place with unions and less than half of these management practices were in place (36 per cent). And, for the private sector as a whole, it was just as common for workplaces with at least half of these management practices in place to have no recognised unions. To conclude, we find evidence of both 'new unionism' *and* union exclusion, but in different, rather than the same, workplaces.

Notes

1 Note also that, for 75 cases in the sample, union members were present, but managers were unable to provide *any* figures on either membership or density levels. These cases have been excluded from the estimates of union density in this section.

2 We interpret the views of the single respondent as reflecting the overall management view.

3 We did not probe any further, so it is not possible to establish whether these cases were in breach of the law. As Dunn and Wright (1993: 39) point out 'the difference between a live and a defunct closed shop can be ... elusive'.

4 Under the Trade Union Reform and Employment Rights Act, 1993.

5 The differences in density associated with a check-off system do not appear to be explained by better management knowledge of union membership levels. Differences between levels of union density as reported by employees and as reported by management were consistent across workplaces with or without check-off arrangements.

6 The *Fairness at Work* White Paper (Department of Trade and Industry, 1998a) included detailed proposals for a statutory union recognition procedure. These proposals were included within the scope of the 1999 Employment Relations Bill. Prior to this, a statutory recognition procedure had operated for a short period in the latter half of the 1970s (Dickens and Bain, 1986).

7 If collective agreements were negotiated at a level above the workplace, the workplace is still defined as one which recognises trade unions.

8 The concept of recognition, as we defined it, is problematic in some public sector workplaces. About one in three public sector employees – including fire-fighters, police, nurses and teachers – have their pay adjusted by an indexation formula or by independent review (Bailey, 1996). These

workers are not covered by collective bargaining over pay. However, unions represent employees in all of these grades and, for example, make submissions to pay review bodies, and also negotiate at a national and local level about pay-related matters such as grading structures and incentive allowances. In the National Health Service there have also been locally negotiated pay 'top-ups', most recently in the 1996/97 pay round (Thornley, 1998). To further complicate the picture, within a given workplace it is unlikely to be the case that *all* employees are covered by indexation or pay review arrangements. We report the answers as given by respondents, accepting that in a small proportion of cases the responses may contain errors.

9   This obviously implies cases where some, but not all, unions were recognised.

10   Representatives of recognised unions are conferred with certain legal privileges, including the right to time off for trade union activities and disclosure of management information to aid the process of collective bargaining.

11   The Safety Representatives and Safety Committees Regulations 1977.

12   Some of these were specific health and safety committees; otherwise health and safety was one of the issues covered by more general joint consultative arrangements – see following note.

13   The definition we have used excludes single issue committees (such as those dealing with health and safety), which were found in 3 per cent of workplaces.

14   This percentage cannot be directly compared to the figure of 35 per cent in 1990, because there higher level committees were only counted if local workplace representatives attended the meetings (Millward *et al.*, 1992: 151-5).

15   Companies with 1,000 employees or more operating in two or more member states of the European Economic Area, excepting the UK, and with at least 150 employees in two of those states, were covered by the 1994 Directive.

16   This policy was reversed following the change in government in 1997. The current administration has given a commitment to implementing the European Works Council Directive into British law by December 1999.

17   In previous surveys the question was open-ended. This time managers were shown a card with a list of twelve pre-determined responses, and they also had the option of identifying any issues not covered on the card.

18   We have excluded from this analysis the relatively few cases of non-union worker representatives in workplaces with recognised unions.

19   There were too few observations to do a parallel analysis of the situation in branch sites with non-union representatives.

20   The questions in this area have been remodelled, so that only limited comparisons can be made with earlier surveys in the series (see Chapter 10). The purpose of the remodelling was twofold: first, to better reflect the diversity of pay setting arrangements *within* workplaces by asking more questions about different occupational groups; and, second, to better reflect diversity in the composition of pay.

21   In aggregate, this is very close to the 55 per cent of workplaces in which there was no union recognition. There is, however, a discrepancy between the figures on union recognition and those on collective bargaining coverage. Some workplaces without union recognition claimed to have some employees covered by collective bargaining, while a few managers in workplaces with union recognition claimed to have no employees covered by collective bargaining. The first discrepancy might be explained by union recognition at a level higher than the workplace. The second discrepancy could be related to doubts over the status of unions in workplaces where some or all employees were covered by pay review bodies.

6 Measures of workplace performance and well-being

The twentieth century has been a period of relative economic decline in Britain compared to other industrialised nations – the standard of living has risen, but has not kept pace with growth in many other countries. It has been common to attribute part of this decline to the 'British worker question'. This has become 'a jingle so familiar that some people just could not get it out of their heads' – the tune ran 'British workers did not work hard enough'. (Nichols, 1986: xi). The most recent Competitiveness White Paper (DTI, 1998b: 11), however, puts the onus firmly on employers as well as employees: 'skill levels ... are too low across too much of the workforce. Too many British companies have low ambitions. Too few match world best practice.' Given our findings to date, it is apparent that the social relations of production cannot be overlooked. Many researchers have focused on this in the past, but of late there has been heightened interest in the contribution that the character of employment relations makes to workplace performance. The question is not just a narrow economic one, but ranges more widely to encompass equity considerations and the health and well-being of the workforce.

In this chapter our goal is important but modest. It is to look at the overall performance of British workplaces across two broad dimensions, the economic and, otherwise, its general health or well-being. The chapter sets out some of the measures that are given a more detailed statistical treatment in Chapter 12. As a preliminary step to any analysis of the determinants of performance or well-being, it is first necessary to examine how much confidence can be assigned to the specified measures and, second, to examine how they correlate with one another.

Confidence in the measures of performance collected is plainly necessary if plausible models are to be developed. Doubts have been, rightly, raised about the adequacy of performance measures which are subjective and unvalidated. We, therefore, spend some time examining the types of performance measures compiled by workplaces, and whether these appear to be in any way related to the measures themselves. More generally, there is also much interest in the 'regime' of monitoring, and the extent to which it functions as a tool to regulate behaviour.

Correlations are also important as too many studies draw simple links between a facet of employment relations and a single 'outcome' measure. There are complex relationships between measures of economic performance and other indicators of the 'well-being' of a workplace. Fernie and Metcalf (1995) find that workplaces with ideal 'employee involvement' practices are associated with a relatively good economic performance, but a relatively poor performance on other measures like voluntary labour turnover and absenteeism – although the point is not pursued. In short, is good performance on one dimension positively associated with performance on other dimensions, or are there trade-offs?

The measures reported in this chapter are derived solely from the interviews with managers. They include economic measures like financial performance, labour productivity and quality, along with other indicators such as resignations, disciplinary sanctions, dismissals, absenteeism, workplace 'strife' and injury and illness levels. We then explore associations between the different measures and conclude by presenting preliminary descriptive results on how both groups of measures are associated with management practices and employee representation. This sets the scene for the more detailed treatment of these issues in Chapter 12.

Workplace monitoring

Information systems play an important role in management's ability to steer or control the workplace. The collection of this information may be used to predict or forecast likely trends, and afford time in which to make adjustments. The recording of information on employees may serve wider purposes as a monitoring tool. Indeed, in some cases the sophistication of the monitoring system has been likened to a modern-day Panopticon, with management using technology as a surveillance device. In these settings, the 'architectural apparatus' of the monitoring system becomes a device 'for creating and sustaining power relations independent of the person who exercises it' (Foucault, cited in Sewell and Wilkinson, 1992: 109). In this section, we look at how both economic performance and employee behaviour are monitored, and the extent to which management use the information to influence behaviour through the setting of targets.

Performance monitoring and targets

We asked managers about nine areas in which performance records might be kept and targets might be set. The responses are presented in Figure 6.1, and there are two main findings evident from it. First, most workplaces kept records on a variety of matters and also, though to a lesser extent, set a variety of targets. Second, the difference between the proportion of workplaces that kept records and the proportion that set targets in the same area varied a good deal by topic. We will examine both of these findings in more detail.

Less than 1 per cent of managers said no records on any of these topics were kept at their workplace. Most important was capturing both sides of the financial ledger, with nine in ten workplaces holding records on sales (or budgets) as well as costs. Not far behind in the rankings were labour costs, absenteeism and workforce training, where at least four in five workplaces kept records in these

Figure 6.1 Performance records kept and targets set

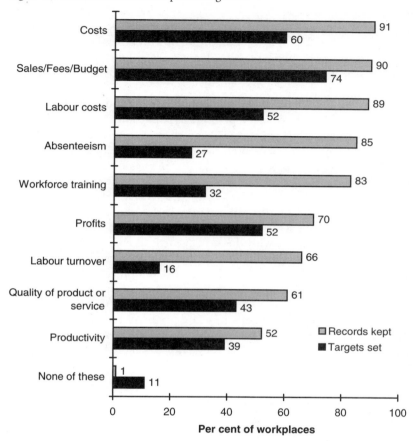

Base: All workplaces with at least 25 employees.
Figures are weighted and based on responses from 1,926 (records) and 1,923 (targets) managers.

areas. Indeed, in all areas, at least half of the workplaces kept records with productivity the least likely to be recorded. Almost nine in ten managers (87 per cent) reported keeping records on five or more of these items.

In contrast, setting targets was not so widespread. Over a tenth (11 per cent) of workplaces did not set them in any areas, and the proportion setting targets in any single area did not exceed three-quarters of workplaces. It was most common to set targets in the area of sales (or budgets), followed by a clustering of between a half and two-thirds of workplaces setting targets in the area of costs, labour costs specifically, and profits. The areas where targets were least likely to be set were labour turnover, absenteeism and workforce training. The typical workplace set targets in four areas with two-fifths (40 per cent) doing so in five or more areas.

Some notable differences emerged between the broad areas of financial data and the management of employees from examining the ranking of areas where records are kept and comparing it with the ranking for setting targets. For example, absenteeism was ranked fourth in the proportion of workplaces keeping records, but eighth in the ranking of target setting. Conversely, productivity was ranked last (i.e. ninth) in the record-keeping stakes, but rose to sixth on the target-setting list.

Another way of characterising this difference in the treatment of financial versus 'people' issues is to look at the percentage point differences between the proportion of workplaces keeping records and those setting targets in a given area. Naturally, the proportion keeping records always exceeded those setting targets, but the difference ranges from just 13 percentage points in productivity, 16 percentage points in sales (or budgets) and 18 percentage points in profits through to 58 percentage points in absenteeism, 51 percentage points in workforce training and 50 percentage points in labour turnover. In short, most workplaces kept records in financial areas and most also set targets in these areas; and most workplaces kept records to do with the management of employees, but only a minority set targets in these areas. It may be that it is not feasible to set targets (i.e. to control) for matters such as absenteeism and labour turnover, but this is at best a partial explanation. We now turn to look at some of the possible explanations.

Table 6.1 illustrates the differences across workplace size and sector. Generally, the patterns found are consistent. As might be expected, they appear to be partly a function of available resources, with larger workplaces more likely to have kept records and set targets. Larger private sector workplaces, for example, were twice

Table 6.1 Performance records held and targets set, by sector and workplace size

	Performance records held in five or more areas*		Targets set in five or more areas*	
	Private sector	Public sector	Private sector	Public sector
	% of workplaces	% of workplaces	% of workplaces	% of workplaces
Workplace size				
25–49 employees	87	72	37	21
50–99 employees	95	77	46	28
100–199 employees	96	84	63	25
200–499 employees	98	89	75	40
500 or more employees	95	87	74	42
All workplaces	91	76	46	25

Base: All workplaces with 25 or more employees.
Figures are weighted and based on responses from 1,926 (columns 1 & 2) and 1,922 (columns 3 & 4) managers.
* Areas covered are as per Figure 6.1.

as likely to set targets in five or more areas as small private workplaces. There was no strong association with organisation size. Small stand-alone sites kept records on as many areas as small workplaces that were part of a wider organisation. This suggests that information is mostly collected and used at source (i.e. the workplace) rather than meeting information requirements from the centre.

Workplaces in the public sector were substantially less likely than those in the private sector to have wide-ranging record keeping and target setting. This may run counter to an expectation that public sector workplaces are more bureaucratic and, therefore, more likely to keep records. Closer investigation shows that these differences largely arose over financial matters, with little or no difference between the sectors in keeping records concerning the management of employees. This hints at a possible underlying explanation: namely, that information is collected and targets are set where commercial pressures dictate. There is a clear association between the degree of competition faced by workplaces (in the trading sector) and the extent of record keeping and target setting. In workplaces where managers reported the degree of competition to be 'very high', 93 per cent kept records and 54 per cent set targets in five or more areas. This compares with 83 per cent and 31 per cent, respectively, in workplaces facing average to low competition. These differences mostly occurred over financial, rather than people management, matters. Thus, there were no differences between workplaces facing very high competition and those facing average to low competition in the extent of record keeping or setting targets on absenteeism; but, in the area of profits, the former were roughly twice as likely to do both.

One final factor which appeared to be important was Investors in People accreditation. A degree of sophistication in record keeping and target setting might be required to satisfy the assessors. In the specific area of workforce training, workplaces with IiP accreditation were substantially more likely to set targets than those without (42 per cent compared to 28 per cent).

Thus far we have considered record keeping and target setting only on the basis of its utility to management. We also need to consider the extent to which such records are open to employees (or their representatives) and also the extent to which targets are made explicit. Open access to all records was reported by managers in just 18 per cent of workplaces. Around half (48 per cent) said that some records were confidential while the remaining 34 per cent said all records were confidential. Information was more likely to be withheld from employees in private sector workplaces (42 per cent compared with 16 per cent in the public sector). Given the associations identified in Table 6.1, these seem most likely to be records of a financial kind.[1] There are a number of issues at play here including ethical ones of honesty and openness, the safeguarding of information deemed liable to help competitors and, perhaps, a wish not to arm employees with the type of information that may advantage them in bargaining situations (Brown, 1997).

Where targets were set, around half (49 per cent) of workplaces set them in consultation with employees or their representatives. A further 35 per cent simply informed employees of the targets set, while 16 per cent of workplaces found it unnecessary to consult or inform employees of the targets. Once more, workplaces in the private sector were less likely to consult or inform employees about targets.

Benchmarking and monitoring of quality

Benchmarking has been seen as a means by which workplaces can learn and adopt so-called 'best practice'. The kernel of the idea is to promote mutual collaboration among like workplaces such as occurs in the much lauded Emilia-Romagna district of northern Italy (Porter, 1990).

In just under half of all workplaces, managers said that a benchmarking exercise had been undertaken by the workplace at some stage during the past five years. Of these, nearly nine in ten had benchmarked against other workplaces within their industry, four-fifths against other workplaces within their organisation[2] and, finally, 15 per cent had benchmarked against workplaces located overseas. Table 6.2 shows how this is related to the reported degree of competition faced by workplaces operating in the trading sector. The greater the degree of competition, the more likely workplaces were to have engaged in benchmarking.

Managers were asked to select, from a range of available options, the way(s) in which the quality of work was monitored. The results are presented in Figure 6.2. By far the most common approach – in nine out of ten workplaces – was for supervisors or other managers to monitor quality. All of the other options presented were used in between a half and two-thirds of workplaces.[3] There were no workplaces in the sample where managers said that quality was not monitored.

Most workplaces had in place a range of methods to monitor the quality of work, with 83 per cent having in place at least two, and 43 per cent four methods or more. A consistent theme among those advocating a quality management

Table 6.2 Benchmarking, by degree of competition

	Workplace had benchmarked in past five years against:			
	Any other workplace	*Other workplaces within industry*	*Other workplaces within organisation*	*Other workplaces located overseas*
	% of workplaces	*% of workplaces*	*% of workplaces*	*% of workplaces*
Degree of competition				
Very high	57	48	49	11
High	43	39	31	6
Average to low	39	36	35	3
All workplaces	48	42	40	7

Base: All workplaces in the trading sector (columns 1, 2 & 4) and all workplaces in the trading sector that are part of a wider organisation (column 3) with 25 or more employees.
Figures are weighted and based on responses from at least 1,403 (columns 1, 2 & 4) and 1,086 (column 3) managers.

Figure 6.2 Workplace quality monitoring practices

Base: All workplaces with at least 25 employees.
Figures are weighted and based on responses from 1,926 managers.

approach is that devolving responsibility for quality away from a separate functional area and directly onto employees will improve the quality of the eventual output (Collinson *et al.*, 1998). Whether or not it does, we have little evidence to suggest that management is prepared to rely *solely* on individual employees as a means of ensuring quality. There were less than 1 per cent of workplaces where employees were given sole responsibility for monitoring the quality of their own work. Moreover, contrary to theories of quality management, self-assessment went hand-in-hand with, rather than being a substitute for, monitoring by inspectors in a separate department.

To summarise, most workplaces were likely to have in place a reasonably sophisticated monitoring regime collecting information on both financial and 'people management' matters. This information was often withheld from, or not fully shared with, employees. Target setting was also extensive, though not as widespread as record keeping. Targets were most commonly set in financial areas, and usually by management alone, rather than in conjunction with employees. A little under half of workplaces had used benchmarking as a tool to monitor current performance, and did so typically against competitors in their industry or within the confines of their organisation. Nearly all workplaces relied on traditional modes of supervision and inspection to ensure the quality of the main product or service, but around half had also allocated some responsibility for quality to individual employees. With all of these, competition appeared to provide an impetus to more focused management action.

Workplace performance

In this section we introduce the measures of workplace economic performance collected in the survey. These are briefly described and then subjected to some scrutiny, in order to leave the reader and future analysts clear about their strengths and limitations.

The first point to note is that we collected no 'hard' financial data that could be used to assess the economic performance of one workplace against another.[4] As it is, a quarter of workplaces did not operate in the trading sector, and for these notions of profit and loss simply do not apply. Similarly, the concept of labour productivity has meaning in all workplaces, but there are no standardised measures in many sectors. For example, there are no conventional measures of value-added which would allow a comparison of the labour productivity of a hospital against a school. Our problem, then, was to collect some measures of workplace economic performance which *do* allow analysts to compare schools with hospitals, along with any other type of workplace. The solution adopted was the same as that for previous surveys in the series; namely, to ask managers to assess the performance of their own workplace in a particular area (e.g. labour productivity) *relative* to other workplaces in the same industry, using a subjective scale ranging from 'a lot above average' to 'a lot below average'.[5]

Figure 6.3 shows the distribution of workplaces in relation to these questions for three separate indicators of economic performance: financial performance, labour productivity and quality of output. It is apparent that, despite the way in which the questions were worded, a sizeable proportion of managers were unable to make an assessment of relative performance, most commonly about financial performance and labour productivity. Workplaces where it was not possible to obtain an assessment on any aspect of performance were most common in public administration, health and education; that is, those where there are no common accounting conventions for measuring performance.

It is also clear, where managers are able to make an assessment, that overall they tend to overstate performance. Across workplaces as a whole, one would expect the largest grouping to be in the category of 'about average' for the industry. What we found, however, was that more managers reported their workplace to be *above* average, rather than around, the industry average. Similarly, less than one in ten managers were prepared to concede that their workplace was performing below average.

Machin and Stewart (1996: 218–19) offer three reasons why – in their case just for the relative financial performance measure – these sorts of measures can still be considered reliable despite the overall bias. The first is that managers' views might be more valid than accounting measures which are, themselves, subject to measurement problems and inconsistency in conventions. Second, the responses in all three previous surveys did not differ systematically across the main workplace characteristics (including union status). Third, the reported measure of financial performance in the 1984 survey was strongly related to the probability of a workplace having closed by 1990 (among sampled workplaces for the 1984–90

Figure 6.3 Managers' assessment of workplace economic performance

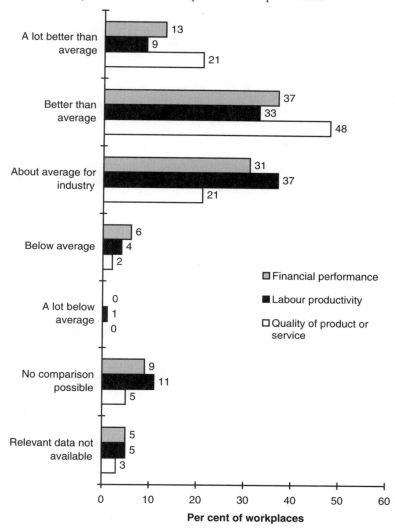

Base: All workplaces with 25 or more employees.
Figures are weighted and based on responses from 1,899 (financial), 1,887 (productivity) and 1,909 (quality) managers.

panel), thereby giving it added validity.[6] Badly-performing workplaces were more than three times as likely to have closed than those performing above average.

In short, if all managers over-state performance in equal measure, then the indicators we use would still be perfectly good as a way of ranking the relative performance of workplaces. We now try to see if there are any systematic differences in the extent of overstatement.

After answering the question on relative financial performance, managers were then asked what financial indicators they had in mind in making their assessment. In 52 per cent of cases they cited profit or value added, 20 per cent mentioned levels of sales, fees or budgets and 19 per cent costs or expenditure. The remainder were split between 3 per cent who mentioned stock market indicators such as share prices, 2 per cent who gave a range of other answers, and 4 per cent who were unable to say. The type of indicator used is not clearly associated with managers' assessment of financial performance.[7] This includes those who could not say what indicators they used to make their assessment.

Extending this argument, none of the three measures of economic performance were associated with the extent of record keeping at the workplace. Similarly, when narrowing this down to the three specific areas – for example, records kept on labour productivity against assessment of relative labour productivity – there were also no differences.

In other words, there is nothing to suggest that those with informed knowledge from records are any more or less likely to be circumspect when asked to make an assessment of this kind. However, there is some evidence that managers do tend to make these assessments on the basis of how well the workplace is doing *generally*, rather than in comparison with other workplaces in the same industry. Among workplaces operating in the trading sector, managers were asked about the state of the market: was it growing, mature, declining or turbulent? As the question related to market circumstances rather than the circumstances of the individual workplace, the responses to the questions on performance *relative to other workplaces in the same industry* should show no association. In fact, on all three dimensions of relative performance, managers in workplaces where the market was said to be growing were much more likely to report above average performance than those where the market was declining – especially for financial performance and labour productivity. For example, on relative financial performance the respective figures were 71 per cent and 43 per cent of workplaces.

Given these results, and this suggested interpretation of the data, it is no surprise that there was reasonably wide variation by industry. Table 6.3 shows the proportion of workplaces in each industry stating their relative performance to be above average for each of the three indicators.[8] In most cases a majority of managers rated their workplace as performing above average. This pattern holds for each dimension of performance and, with only nine exceptions, within each industry. If there was a consistent over-statement across all workplaces, then there should be little variation across industries. This is generally the case, as can be seen from Table 6.3, but there were exceptions. In the area of financial performance, managers in hotels and restaurants and other business services were more likely to say their workplace was performing above average, while those in health and other community services were least likely to say so. The latter industry also had among the lowest proportion of managers reporting above average performance in labour productivity (together with those in construction), while assessments of above average performance were most common in education, wholesale and

Table 6.3 Measures of workplace economic performance, by industry

	Managers reporting above average:		
	Financial performance	Labour productivity	Quality of product or service
	% of workplaces	% of workplaces	% of workplaces
Industry			
Manufacturing	65	47	76
Electricity, gas and water	55	45	68
Construction	55	36	76
Wholesale and retail	62	55	73
Hotels and restaurants	66	50	73
Transport and communications	53	45	84
Financial services	55	51	63
Other business services	64	55	89
Public administration	55	45	47
Education	51	58	68
Health	44	51	82
Other community services	47	37	69
All workplaces	57	50	74

Base: All workplaces where managers were able to make an assessment of performance with 25 or more employees.
Figures are weighted and based on responses from 1,638 (column 1), 1,571 (column 2) and 1,739 (column 3) managers.

retail and other business services. In the area of quality, reports of above average performance were most likely to come from managers in other business services and transport and communication, compared with less than a half in public administration.

In short, across industries, managers appeared to overstate performance fairly consistently, but there were some where industry-specific factors appear to have an effect. For example, the high figure for labour productivity in education may reflect the fact that employees in this industry were most likely to work long hours (see Chapter 7). By way of contrast, managers in transport and communication were more upbeat about quality but relatively sanguine about labour productivity.

In terms of the other main structural features of workplaces, little else was related to managers' assessment of performance. Workplace size was not related to the measures. Organisation size, while providing only very weak levels of association with financial and labour productivity performance, did reveal a significant relationship with managerial perceptions of quality performance. The smaller the organisation to which the workplace belonged, the more likely the manager was to report relatively high quality. Similarly, private sector managers were somewhat more likely to view their financial and labour performance as high, but again it was in the area of quality where the biggest differences were evident. Among private sector workplaces, 74 per cent of managers said that quality was above average, compared with 64 per cent in the public sector.

The final issue to explore in this section is the extent to which these three separate indicators of workplace performance go together. There is a high degree of association between the assessments of financial performance and labour productivity, but less so (though still substantial) between these two and quality.[9] For example, 41 per cent of all workplaces were reported by their managers to have both above average labour productivity and above average quality. Equally, though, 43 per cent of managers either rated their labour productivity to be above average and their quality not, or the other way around. This suggests that while, as might be expected, the elements of performance were positively related overall, managers were able to discriminate between the different elements.

In conclusion, we appear to have collected what might best be thought of as 'confidence' measures. They appear to be sufficiently grounded in three ways: first, as Figure 6.3 shows, there was reasonable variation on each of the measures;[10] second, the results do not appear to be biased in any given way by the amount of information at management's disposal; and, third, while the measures are positively associated, managers appear to be able to discriminate between each of the items. These measures therefore seem more than suitable for the study of economic performance; but this is only one means of judging how well a workplace is doing. It is to these other dimensions that we now turn.

Workplace well-being

The concept of individual well-being is one that has wide currency and is readily understood. At the same time it is recognised that it is not straightforward to measure: there are absolute indicators like healthiness or relative indicators like a 'decent' standard of living. There may also be contradictions, or tensions, in different facets of well-being. For example, as we show in Chapter 8, work can be both stressful and satisfying. In this section we develop a parallel concept to individual well-being and apply it to the workplace.

We treat workplace well-being as conceptually distinct from workplace economic performance, though we examine associations between the two at the end of this chapter. Short-term economic performance may be achieved at the expense of workplace well-being even if, in the long term, this does not prove to be sustainable. Equally, measures that improve workplace well-being may have beneficial effects on economic performance in the longer term. There is, thus, no obvious reason why the two should be correlated at any single time. To give a specific example, labour productivity could be high but this might be a result of recent work intensification which has also led to higher levels of resignations or injuries.

We take a barometer to the workplace looking at eight separate indicators. The indicators we examine are industrial strife; unauthorised absence and voluntary separations; dismissals, other sanctions and resulting Industrial Tribunal applications; and injuries and work-related illness.[11] All of these measures need to be interpreted carefully. Low levels of absenteeism and resignations, for example, are not necessarily indicative of a contented workforce. They may simply reflect the absence of decent alternative employment options in the local labour market. Similarly, workplaces with no experience of industrial action may reflect employees' relative lack of organisation rather than cordial relations with management.

Industrial strife

The first issue we examine is industrial strife; that is, action taken by groups of workers in support of a particular claim. Industrial action is usually taken as a last resort after other means have failed and, as such, it remains an important option for workers pursuing their claims. Figure 6.4 shows the proportion of workplaces where strife, of some sort, was in evidence.

The incidence of industrial action is very low, with only 2 per cent of workplace managers reporting action of any kind in the year preceding the survey.[12] Indeed, the number of workplaces affected by industrial action is so low that we are unable to give a statistically reliable breakdown of the form this action took, other than a crude strike/non-strike distinction.

It has been argued that balloting of union members, a legal prerequisite for any industrial action (if unions are to claim immunity from civil torts), has served to defuse the strike option as it provides a signal to workplace management of the depth of discontent among the workforce: a high proportion voting 'yes', it is said, will bring management back to the bargaining table (Elgar and Simpson, 1993).

In the year preceding the survey, ballots for industrial action had been held in 7 per cent of workplaces, while a further 5 per cent of managers reported being 'threatened' with action (which never eventuated). Where ballots took place, managers said that just half (48 per cent) provided a mandate for action, a proportion considerably lower than available records suggest. Recent figures indicate that around three-quarters of strike ballots produced a vote in favour, as did over nine in ten ballots for non-strike action (Trades Union Congress, 1998). These figures are provided by official balloting agencies and, as such, are likely to be more reliable than reports from managers who may be linking the ballot to whether industrial action then took place.

Of the 2 per cent of workplaces where industrial action had occurred, 52 per cent had experienced strikes, 57 per cent some form of non-strike action, and 9 per cent both. About half of the workplaces with strike action had just the one strike, and the average number of strikes was 2.2. Industrial action was more likely to have taken place in larger workplaces (8 per cent) and in the public sector (4 per cent). Naturally, it was also more likely to have occurred in workplaces where union members were present, though it was higher in recognised workplaces (4 per cent), than in those with no recognition (1 per cent). Where industrial action took place, 14 per cent of managers said that it did so without a sanctioning ballot – in other words, that it was unofficial.[13]

Figure 6.4 Incidence of industrial action

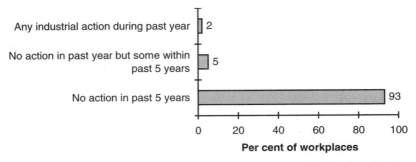

Base: All workplaces (bars 1&2) and all workplaces five or more years old (bars 3 & 4) with at least 25 employees.
Figures are weighted and based on responses from 1,928 (bar 1), and 1,694 (bars 2 & 3) managers.

Finally, as shown in Figure 6.4, 5 per cent of workplaces had experienced no industrial action in the preceding year, but had done so at some stage in the previous five years. Overall, this means that more than nine in ten workplaces had no recent experience of any industrial action.

Absenteeism and voluntary resignations

Both absenteeism and voluntary resignations are often postulated as indicators of individual disaffection with the labour process. Edwards and Scullion (1982), in their study of two clothing factories, found that women on the shop floor were unhappy with a system of discipline which they saw as harsh and arbitrary. Going absent once in a while served as an escape valve while too many warnings about bad work led some women to quit and try their luck elsewhere. Disentangling these manifestations of conflict in the employment relationship from other individual factors, like family circumstances in the case of absence, has proved a difficult task for researchers. One of the reasons why may be that most studies are based on individuals and take little account of factors such as disciplinary procedures. It is instructive to see just how much absenteeism and turnover do vary across workplaces. The wide variation in both suggests that individual factors, like sickness in the case of absenteeism, or local labour market conditions, in the case of turnover, are only part of the story.

Overall, the average daily rate of absenteeism among workplaces with 25 or more employees was 4.1 per cent.[14] All workplaces reported some degree of absenteeism, but those in the lowest tenth of workplaces had a level below 1 per cent, while those in the highest tenth had at least 8.7 per cent of their workforce absent on any given day. What might explain such differences? Table 6.4 shows how the average absence rate varied by sector and workplace size, and it can be seen from this that absenteeism was somewhat higher in the public than the private sector, by about a sixth. VandenHeuvel's (1994) study of Australian workers found absence rates to be 1.6 times higher among public sector workers, after controlling for a variety of other factors. The more modest difference in our sample suggests a need to look to variables other than sector. The table suggests that absence rates within the public sector were largely unrelated to workplace size, but were higher in larger private sector workplaces.

Public sector workplaces were, however, substantially less prone to resignations than workplaces in the private sector. In the year preceding the survey, the average workplace lost 14 per cent of its employees, with the average rate in the public sector just over a third that in the private sector. Again, the average rate in the public sector was not related to workplace size, but among private sector workplaces it was a lot lower in the larger workplaces. Some industries were particularly notable for a very high average rate of resignations (see Table 6.6), especially workplaces in hotels and restaurants where, on average, almost two-fifths of all employees had left their jobs in the preceding twelve months. This was eight times the average rate experienced among workplaces in electricity, gas and water.

If absence from work and resignations were both indicators of disaffection among workers, then they might be expected to be positively related. This was not the case, at least not for the overall picture. Indeed, within the private sector, there was a slight negative association. The smallest workplaces had the highest rate of resignations but the lowest level of absenteeism. There are a number of possible explanations for this finding: management may find it easier to monitor and control absence in smaller workplaces, leaving resignation as the only option for disaffected employees; there could be a connection with job satisfaction, which is higher in small workplaces (see Chapter 8); more prosaically, small workplaces may be less likely to offer generous sick pay entitlements.

Dismissals, sanctions and Industrial Tribunal applications

The three indicators we have looked at thus far are all ones where employees take the initiative. Now we turn to look at action taken *against* employees – to either discipline or dismiss them. Again, as with absenteeism and turnover, high average rates of disciplinary action and dismissals may indicate a dysfunctional employment relationship.

Managers were asked whether, in the past year, any employees had disciplinary sanctions – formal written warnings, suspension with or without pay, and deductions from pay were the three kinds asked about – applied to them. Overall, as shown in Figure 6.5, 60 per cent of workplaces had sanctioned one or more employees in the past year, with the incidence being far more prevalent in larger workplaces (97 per cent) than smaller workplaces (47 per cent).[15] Official warnings are likely to be the first formal means of attempting to alter the behaviour of individual employees, while dismissals represent the end point in attempts to induce conformity to managerial norms. Thus dismissals were much less likely to have occurred, with 39 per cent of workplaces having sacked one or more employees in the previous year.

Table 6.4 Rates of absenteeism and voluntary resignations, by sector and workplace size

	Rate of absenteeism*		Rate of voluntary resignations	
	Private sector	Public sector	Private sector	Public sector
	Average rate per 100 employees	Average rate per 100 employees	Average rate per 100 employees	Average rate per 100 employees
Workplace size				
25–49 employees	3.9	4.3	18.0	6.9
50–99 employees	3.7	4.9	17.3	7.1
100–199 employees	3.8	4.4	16.7	6.9
200–499 employees	4.5	5.0	14.8	7.0
500 or more employees	4.5	4.6	12.5	7.8
All workplaces	3.9	4.5	17.3	7.0

Base: All workplaces with 25 or more employees.
Figures are weighted and based on responses from 1,572 (columns 1 & 2) and 1,815 (columns 3 & 4) managers.
* 19 per cent of managers were unable to provide details on rates of absenteeism.

For both of these matters we know how many employees were affected, so that both measures can be expressed as average rates. This allows us to discriminate between workplaces that apply heavy levels of discipline compared to those where, perhaps, a single employee was affected.

Overall, there were an average of 2.9 disciplinary sanctions per 100 employees and 1.5 dismissals per 100 employees. These are not, it must be said, modest figures, but employees in some workplaces appeared to be far more susceptible than others – see Table 6.6. The average rate of sanctions was highest in workplaces in transport and communication (5.7 per 100 employees) and wholesale and retail (4.8), and was lowest of all in education (0.6). The average workplace in hotels and restaurants dismissed a quite astonishing 5.9 employees in every 100 in the year preceding the survey, a rate over three times higher than that in any other industry.

Workplaces where unions were recognised had much lower average rates of both sanctions (2.0 per 100 employees) and dismissals (0.7 per 100 employees). The ability of unions to defend employees against 'arbitrary' dismissal (eg. by 'wildcat' strikes) was one of the original arguments put forward for individual employment protection rights (Anderman, 1986). Average rates of both sanctions and dismissals were also lower in larger workplaces and in workplaces that were part of larger organisations. There were, however, no differences between workplaces with and without a disciplinary procedure.

Employees do (subject to meeting the qualifying criteria on length of continuous service) have recourse to Industrial Tribunals if they consider themselves to have been dismissed unfairly.[16] Overall, 13 per cent of workplaces had at least one claim made against them in the past year – not just for unfair dismissal, but also

Figure 6.5 Incidence of disciplinary actions and Industrial Tribunal claims, by sector

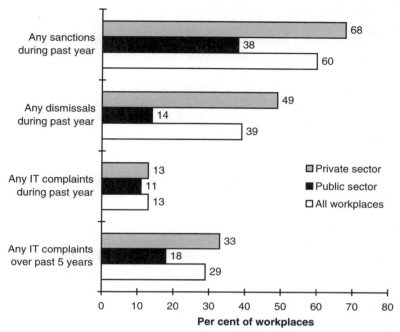

Base: All workplaces (sanctions, dismissals and IT complaints during past year) at least five years old (IT complaints over past five years) with 25 or more employees.
Figures are weighted and based on responses from 1,909 (sanctions), 1,848 (dismissals), 1,914 (IT complaints past year) and 1,642 (IT complaints past five years) managers.

covering other individual employment rights. Again, we also know the number of (ex-) employees in each workplace making claims and overall it equated to an average of 1.7 employees per 1,000; that is, roughly about a tenth of the average rate of dismissals. Once more, the greatest variation was by industry. Among workplaces in transport and communications, an average of 5.8 employees per 1,000 lodged an Industrial Tribunal application, a rate double that in public administration (the second highest). The lowest average rate was in education (0.8 employees per 1,000) but hotels and restaurants (1.5) were below the average, suggesting no straightforward correlation between dismissals and Industrial Tribunal applications.[17] It remains the case, though, that most workplaces have 'clean' recent records with 71 per cent having had no Industrial Tribunal claims made against them in the past five years.

Injuries and work-related illness

Injuries and work-related illness are debilitating and costly, to both the individuals affected and their employer. The Health and Safety Executive (HSE) have estimated the total costs to society of work accidents and work-related illness at some £8–9 billion at 1990 prices (Davies and Teasdale, 1994). The scale of these incidents was, according to our data, very high. Taken together, 61 per cent of all workplaces had seen one or more employees suffer a serious injury or work-related illness in the past year. We examine the two separately.

A third of managers reported that at least one employee in the workplace had experienced a serious injury in the preceding year. The type of injuries asked about were designed to match the reporting requirements placed on employers by the Reporting of Injuries, Diseases and Dangerous Occurrences Regulations 1985.[18] In 15 per cent of workplaces employees had suffered burns, 12 per cent of workplaces had an accident which resulted in broken bones, and 9 per cent of workplaces had seen someone physically assaulted at work (whether by a colleague or customer we do not know).

Overall, an average of 1.5 employees in every 100 had experienced a serious injury in the year preceding the survey. This is broadly in line with figures kept by HSE. In the mid-1990s they found that non-fatal injury rates in manufacturing workplaces ranged from 0.8 per 100 employees in workplaces with 25–49 employees up to 1.5 per 100 employees in workplaces with 200 or more employees (Stevens, 1999). However, this positive association with workplace size is at odds with our own data which suggests that injury rates are lowest in larger workplaces. Nichols *et al.* (1995) analysed the 1990 survey data and verified this association after controlling for a variety of other factors. They argue that injury rates are lower in larger workplaces because they have the wherewithal and resources to deal more effectively with health and safety.

In almost half (45 per cent) of workplaces, managers said that one or more employees had experienced work-related (i.e. induced) illness in the preceding year. Most common of all was stress, reported in 30 per cent of workplaces followed by bone, joint, muscle or limb disorders in 21 per cent of workplaces. The number of employees who suffered from work-related illness averaged 1.8 employees per 100 across all workplaces.

Table 6.5 shows how both average rates varied by sector and workplace size. Workplaces in the private sector had a higher average rate of injuries than those in the public sector, but a lower average rate of work-related illness. Doubtless, this partly reflects physical working conditions. Thus, an average of 5.6 employees per 100 working in hotels and restaurants had experienced a serious injury compared with less than 1 per 100 in financial services; but financial services had more than double the number of employees affected by work-related illness (1.5 per 100 employees compared with 0.7).

Associations between measures of workplace well-being

As we have seen, most of the eight indicators of workplace well-being vary widely, especially across industry, and Table 6.6 uses the average rate-based measure of each indicator to show this. While there are some industries with high average rates on many of the indicators – hotels and restaurants lead on three (resignations, dismissals and injuries) as does transport and communication (industrial action,

Table 6.5 Rates of serious injury and work-related illness, by sector and workplace size

	Serious injury		Work-related illness	
	Private sector	Public sector	Private sector	Public sector
	Average rate per 100 employees	Average rate per 100 employees	Average rate per 100 employees	Average rate per 100 employees
Workplace size				
25–49 employees	1.6	1.6	1.8	3.2
50–99 employees	1.8	1.0	1.1	3.0
100–199 employees	1.1	0.9	1.0	1.9
200–499 employees	1.0	2.3	1.0	2.0
500 or more employees	0.7	1.6	0.9	1.3
All workplaces	1.6	1.4	1.4	2.9

Base: All workplaces with 25 or more employees.
Figures are weighted and based on responses from 1,807 (columns 1 & 2) and 1,744 (columns 3 & 4) managers.

disciplinary sanctions and Industrial Tribunal applications) – there are no obviously discernible patterns across industry.

There might, however, be other patterns which help to explain the differences. One preliminary way of exploring this is to look at the correlations between each of the eight items. Most of the items were positively associated with one another. The only negative association was a slight one between industrial action and resignations.[19] The strongest associations were between resignations and dismissals, and disciplinary sanctions and dismissals.[20] Having said that, most of the associations were quite modest and it would not have been valid to, for example, combine them into some overall measure of workplace well-being. This only takes us so far. As Edwards (1986: 261–2) says, 'to look at correlations of rates of behaviour is to consider only surface phenomena and to miss the underlying mechanisms which explain why the phenomena take place and what ties them together'.

These mechanisms are to do with the social relations of work. Two aspects of this that writers have focused on are performance appraisal systems and individual monitoring of quality. Both have their advocates and critics and it is not apparent how they might be associated with indicators of workplace well-being. Individual monitoring of quality, for example, is thought to empower employees and boost morale and commitment, but may come at the cost of increasing stress. We looked for consistent patterns and let the results speak for themselves. Within private sector workplaces, regular performance appraisals for most non-managerial employees were associated with lower average rates on each of the indicators, bar that for industrial action. Where individual employees had responsibility for monitoring quality, this too was associated with lower average rates on five of the eight indicators (absence, resignations, disciplinary sanctions, Industrial Tribunal

Table 6.6 Indicators of workplace well-being, by industry

	Industrial action	Absenteeism	Voluntary resignations	Formal sanctions	Dismissals	Industrial Tribunal claims	Injury	Illness
	Average number of actions per 100 workplaces	Average rate per 100 employees	Average rate per 100 employees	Average rate per 100 employees	Average rate per 100 employees	Average rate per 1,000 employees	Average rate per 100 employees	Average rate per 100 employees
Industry								
Manufacturing	3.0	4.7	11.4	3.4	1.9	1.3	1.6	1.7
Electricity, gas and water	13.5	3.3	4.6	0.9	0.1	1.1	0.9	2.2
Construction	0.7	2.8	11.5	2.5	1.3	1.6	1.4	0.6
Wholesale and retail	0.2	3.4	19.4	4.8	1.5	1.5	0.4	1.4
Hotels and restaurants	0.0	4.2	38.4	3.6	5.9	1.5	5.6	0.7
Transport and communications	27.6	4.1	10.6	5.7	2.3	5.8	1.8	1.3
Financial services	14.4	4.5	9.4	1.2	0.8	1.1	0.1	1.5
Other business services	0.4	3.0	13.4	2.4	1.4	1.6	0.5	1.0
Public administration	8.3	4.7	6.9	1.9	0.2	2.9	1.5	2.5
Education	4.3	3.5	7.7	0.6	0.2	0.8	1.0	2.9
Health	0.8	5.5	16.6	2.2	1.3	2.0	2.9	2.9
Other community services	2.6	3.7	18.0	2.6	1.7	1.2	1.9	1.4
All workplaces	3.9	4.1	14.4	2.9	1.5	1.7	1.5	1.8

Base: All workplaces with 25 or more employees.
Figures are weighted and based on responses from between 1,572 (absenteeism) and 1,928 (industrial action) managers.

applications, and work-related illness). As with performance appraisals, there was a positive association with industrial action, but also with workplace injuries. There were no consistent patterns within public sector workplaces.

Finally, we turn to the relationship between workplace economic performance and workplace well-being. As noted in the introduction to this chapter, there is no necessary relationship between the two. In general, we find no clear and systematic pattern between any of the measures of economic performance and the eight indicators of workplace well-being. In the private sector, workplaces with above average financial performance had lower rates of labour turnover, and this was also the case where there was above average labour productivity. The one other area where there was some consistency was that injury rates were lower where economic performance was relatively good. In the public sector, a number of the associations were in the opposite direction – for example, injury rates were higher where financial performance was reported to be above average but, again, there was no clear pattern.

Conclusion

This chapter has provided a broad overview of the two main dimensions of workplace performance, economic and other indicators of workplace well-being. The measures of economic performance are all subjective in the sense that they rely on managers to rank their workplace relative to others. Given this caveat, there may be some doubts about their veracity but we believe the evidence suggests that they serve well as general measures of economic performance.

A wide variety of indicators – eight in all – were considered under the rubric of workplace well-being. These showed a variety of things. For most of the indicators, the rates ranged from zero – particularly in industrial action and Industrial Tribunal applications, which are perhaps the two most explicit indicators of conflict – to very high rates, with workplaces in hotels and restaurants, for example, dismissing four times as many workers as the average.

We looked for associations between the various measures of workplace well-being and, besides industrial action, they were on the whole positively, but modestly, related. There was no clear relationship, though, between economic performance and workplace well-being. Most of the discussion in the chapter centred around variations by size, sector and industry, our common touchstones throughout the book. For the findings to have more meaning – to explore the links between employment relations and performance – we need to return to the substance of workplace structures and practices.

At the end of Chapter 4, we looked at the spread of high commitment management practices. In Chapter 5, we found a positive relationship between recognised unions and the spread of these practices. We now take this one stage further, by looking at how the two in combination are associated with workplace performance. Figure 6.6 presents the results for private sector workplaces. On four of these five measures, workplaces with a recognised union and a majority of the high commitment management practices (presented in Table 4.12) did better than the

Figure 6.6 Measures of workplace economic performance and well-being, by trade union recognition and high commitment management practices

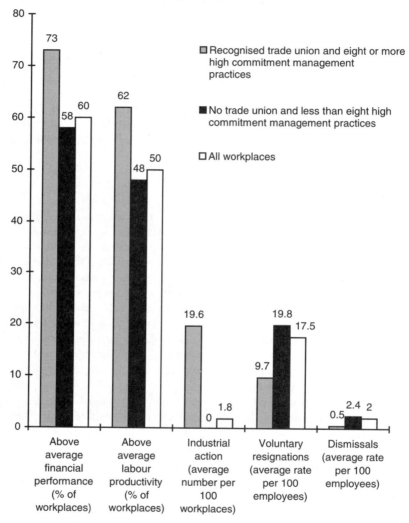

Base: All private sector workplaces with at least 25 employees.
Figures are weighted and based on responses from 1,025 (productivity) to 1,186 (industrial action) managers.

average, and better than workplaces without recognition and a minority of these practices. The one exception was industrial action which, evidently, is almost unique to recognised workplaces. Notwithstanding this, workplaces with union recognition and a majority of the high commitment practices appeared to have more stable workforces and more productive workforces.

These are bald results. They do not allow for alternative 'types' of workplaces, such as those with a majority of the high commitment practices and no union presence. This is because there were so few of these cases in our sample that they have exhausted the limit of conventional tabular analysis. To address these issues in a more systematic and rigorous way we put the issue on hold. One very good reason for doing so is that this and preceding chapters have been exclusively based on management accounts of the employment relationship. Does the same picture hold true when one turns to workers' accounts? This is the focus of the next three chapters.

Notes

1 We did not collect information on which records were kept confidential and which were shared with employees, though a further set of questions asked more generally about information sharing. See Chapter 10 for an analysis of change over time with this data.

2 Whether a workplace had benchmarked against other workplaces within the same organisation was only asked of managers in workplaces that were part of a wider organisation.

3 The category for external auditing or inspections was added at the coding stage on the basis of an 'other, please specify' response.

4 Managers in workplaces in the 'production' sector – manufacturing, the utilities and construction – were, however, asked whether they were willing for the survey data to be matched with recent returns to the Annual Business Enquiry (formerly known as the Census of Production) conducted by the Office for National Statistics (ONS). Nearly all of them (91 per cent) gave their consent. This means, for those workplaces, that it is possible to add 'hard' financial data. We are exploring with ONS how this matched data set can be made available to the research community.

5 In practice, most of the analysis aggregates 'a little below average' and 'a lot below average' responses as there were so few of the latter.

6 However, Machin and Stewart did not draw attention to the fact that, in earlier reported work by Machin (1995: Table A1), this association was not statistically significant in estimated models of the likelihood of plant closures.

7 Workplaces which based their measure on profits or value added were only slightly more likely to report above-average financial performance than those basing it on sales or costs.

8 In this table we only include those workplaces where managers were able to give an assessment of performance.

9 $r = 0.49$ for financial performance and labour productivity, $r = 0.28$ for financial performance and quality of output, and $r = 0.34$ for labour productivity and quality of output.

10 Standard deviation was 0.83 for financial performance, 0.78 for labour productivity and 0.74 for quality of output.

11 The distributions on the rates of absence, resignations, dismissals, sanctions, Industrial Tribunal claims, injuries, and illnesses are all highly skewed and, as such, means are susceptible to outlying values. To moderate this, we have excluded cases with values falling above the 99th percentiles of the distributions.

12 In reporting on past surveys, an alternative measure combining responses of both managers and worker representatives has been used. We use only management accounts for consistency with the other measures in this section.

13   This estimate should be treated with some caution as it is based on a relatively small number of observations. Note that the official statistical estimates of the extent of strike activity make no distinction between official and unofficial action.

14   The actual question asked was: over the last 12 months what percentage of work days was lost through employee sickness or absence at this establishment?

15   The strength of this association is explained by the 'Qantas effect'. If there is an even probability of sanctions being placed, then small workplaces will always have a lower incidence of any sanctions as there are fewer employees who can potentially be sanctioned.

16   From August 1998 these were renamed Employment Tribunals. We use the term which applied at the time of survey fieldwork.

17   Recall that dismissed employees can only submit a Tribunal application for unfair dismissal if they have the required length of continuous service with their employer (two years at the time of the survey). Hotels and restaurants has both a high rate of dismissals and a high rate of turnover more generally. It is quite probable that few workers of the workers dismissed in this industry would be eligible to pursue a Tribunal claim.

18   The list of injuries was an abbreviated version of the 'major injury' categories used under RIDDOR, but the wording may not have implied the same degree of severity. For example, one of the categories was 'acute illness' whereas this is formally listed under RIDDOR as 'acute illness resulting from absorption of any noxious substance or from possible exposure to an organism causing disease'. We believe that our data is more akin to the category of 'non-fatal' injury which implies at least a four-day absence from work as a result of the injury.

19   $r = -0.05$.

20   $r = 0.38$ for resignations and dismissals; $r = 0.33$ for sanctions and dismissals.

7 Employees at work
Attributes and aspects of working life

So far, we have considered the management of employees and the structure and implementation of workplace practices as perceived and described by managers. This chapter and the next change tack and focus on the employment relationship as seen by employees. This chapter covers the substantive elements of people's jobs, while Chapter 8 looks at the attitudes held by employees and examines the extent to which the two are intertwined. The two chapters in combination provide an introduction to some, though not all, of the topics covered in the employee survey. We hope, in doing so, to illustrate the opportunity for further exploration of the data; in particular, to those who have conventionally not been part of the WIRS milieu, such as sociologists and organisational psychologists, as well as to those interested in industrial relations and human resource management.

As with all relationships, the employment relationship is likely to be characterised by a complex set of values, some based on mutual goals, others underpinned by contrasting and sometimes conflicting expectations, agendas and priorities. Brown and Rea (1995) describe the dynamics and flexibility inherent in the employment contract in terms of its 'incompleteness'. The contract, they argue, is characterised by a high degree of interdependency between employers and employees, operating against a context of some conflicting and some shared interests. It is nonetheless open-ended in many respects and it is this 'uncertainty' that makes the employment relationship so complex, and the study of it so fascinating.

These dimensions of the employment relationship have strong parallels in the notion of the 'psychological contract' (Guest *et al.*, 1996; Makin *et al.*, 1996) and its emphasis on the *implicit* contract that prevails between employers and employees, as opposed to more explicit elements defining the terms and conditions of work. Elements of the psychological contract are based on expectations but also upon 'promissory and reciprocal obligations' (Robinson and Rousseau, 1994). These cover fairness, trust and delivery of promises.

How do employees themselves describe the employment relationship? This chapter covers the substantive elements of the relationship, the aim being to create a picture of employees' working lives. After a brief profile describing the main characteristics of employees in Britain, the first section examines the amount of influence and control they have over their work. The following sections then cover aspects of the employment relationship associated with individual access to workplace initiatives such as flexible working, training and participation in workplace decision-making. It is only in the final two sections that we turn to the two basic elements of the employment contract, hours and pay.

Our source for all this material is the employee survey which, as described in Chapter 1, is the major new element to the survey series. The unit of analysis, therefore, shifts from the workplace to employee, but this does not mean that we ignore the workplace; indeed, the main strength of the design of the employee survey is that we are able to match the responses of individual employees with those of the manager interviewed at their workplace. How much the workplace matters in accounting for differences between employees will unfold over this, and the next, chapter.

A profile of the survey population

Chapter 3 looked at the composition of the workforce through information obtained from management.[1] This section presents a brief profile of all employees in workplaces with 25 or more employees, outlining their principal personal and job attributes, drawn this time from the employee survey. In doing so, it provides an introduction to the main classifications used in this and the next chapter. Table 7.1 presents a range of characteristics describing the employee population.[2]

As can be seen from the table, differences in age and household status between employed men and women were relatively slight. The proportion of working men with partners and dependent children was greater than among working women, while women were proportionally more likely to be living with their spouse or partner without any dependent children. Gender differences were much more pronounced in the area of job attributes, especially working hours. We examine working hours in more detail later in this chapter, but here we look briefly at how personal and job attributes interact.

A wide range of factors influence whether people work full or part-time. Individuals may be constrained by the availability of work or may choose to work part-time – evidence suggests most part-time employees do not wish to work full-time (Watson and Fothergill, 1993; Sly 1996). An important influencing factor is likely to be domestic circumstances, with part-time work offering more scope for managing family and household demands (Dex and McCulloch, 1997; Brannen *et al.*, 1997; Humphries and Rubery, 1992). Nine in ten men worked full-time – defined as 30 or more hours per week[3] – compared with six in ten women.

The highest proportion of men working part-time were those who were single, divorced or widowed without dependent children (16 per cent) and they were mostly either at the start or reaching the end of their working lives. By way of contrast, the same category of women were the *least* likely to be working part-time (28 per cent), with the highest proportion among those living with their

Table 7.1 Distribution of employees, by personal and job characteristics

	Male	Female	All employees
	% of employees	% of employees	% of employees
Age			
Less than 20 years	4	5	4
20–29 years	19	21	20
30–39 years	29	27	28
40–49 years	24	25	25
50–59 years	18	20	19
60 years or more	6	3	4
Household status			
Lone parents	5	6	5
Parents living with partner/spouse	39	34	36
No dependent children, living with partner/spouse	31	36	33
Single, widowed or divorced with no dependent children	26	24	25
Total weekly hours			
Less than 10 hours per week	2	6	4
10–29 hours per week	6	35	20
30–48 hours per week	70	55	63
More than 48 hours per week	22	5	13
Occupation			
Managers and administrators	12	5	9
Professional	12	11	11
Associate professional and technical	8	9	9
Clerical and secretarial	8	28	17
Craft and related	17	3	10
Personal and protective service	9	13	11
Sales	5	13	9
Plant and machine operatives	21	7	14
Other occupations	9	11	10
All employees	52	48	100

Base: All employees in workplaces with 25 or more employees.
Figures are weighted and based on responses from 25,931 (age), 25,376 (household), 24,728 (hours) and 25,794 (occupation) employees.

partner or spouse and with dependent children (58 per cent). And, unlike men, it was younger women – those in their twenties – who were least likely to work part-time (24 per cent).

Only a very small proportion of employees – just one in 25 – worked fewer than 10 hours per week. Teenage males made up a third of all men doing so, whereas almost half of women working such low hours were in the prime child-rearing years. With the bulk of their time taken up with unpaid activities such as studying or bringing up children, these people, Hakim (1996) has argued, may have a 'marginal attachment' to work, and thus exhibit different attitudes towards work and their working life. While some attitude surveys exclude altogether people working fewer than 10 hours per week (e.g. the British Social Attitudes Survey), we have retained these employees in our analysis so as to test the significance of this 10-hour threshold.

The situation of lone parents is interesting since it provides further insight into gender differences in working hours.[4] Men who were lone parents mostly worked full-time (91 per cent), but were slightly less likely to work full-time than fathers living with a partner or spouse (96 per cent). For women, this relationship operated the other way – that is single mothers were more likely to work *full-time* than mothers living with a partner or spouse, 55 per cent compared with 42 per cent. However, this still leaves a 36 percentage point gap between the proportion of single fathers and single mothers who worked full-time.

Besides hours of work, occupation is the one other factor which most obviously identifies differences in the types of work done, and may therefore be strongly related to attitudes towards work. As noted in Chapter 3, the occupational classification used in the survey is rather broad but still sufficiently diverse to highlight differences.[5] The spread of employees across occupations was fairly even, but Table 7.1 reveals considerable gender differences. Men predominated in three occupations (managers, craft workers and operative and assembly workers), women in two occupations (clerical workers and sales workers), while the remaining four occupations had a broadly even mix of men and women.

Other factors that we will refer to on occasion throughout this and the next chapter include educational qualifications, the type of employment contract (i.e. permanent, temporary or fixed-term), length of service and union membership. But what we are also able to do, as outlined in Chapter 1, is to incorporate responses from the management interview and examine the extent to which workplace structures and practices appear to affect aspects of employees' jobs and their attitudes towards them.

Job autonomy and influence

One important feature of the employment relationship is the degree of influence and discretion an employee is able to exercise over his or her work (Lincoln and Kalleberg, 1990; Gallie *et al.*, 1998). Later in the chapter employee influence in workplace decision-making is considered, but here the discussion is confined to the degree of control and autonomy employees exercise over their own job. Job control is related to many factors such as the employee's position in the hierarchy, the type of labour process, and the ease or cost involved in monitoring work. One of the key arguments of proponents of post-Fordist forms of work organisation is that employees are empowered by flattening hierarchies and devolving respons-ibility (Legge, 1995). Others contend, however, that devolving control through initiatives such as making employees responsible for assessing quality has the adverse effect of increasing stress (Sewell and Wilkinson, 1992). We will touch briefly on some of these debates, but begin by reporting the descriptive results.

Employees were asked to assess the level of influence they felt they had over three aspects of their work: the range of tasks involved in their job; the pace at which they work; and how they go about doing their job. Figure 7.1 reports the results. Between a quarter and a half of employees said they had a lot of influence over their job, and a further third said they had some influence. Overall, the most widespread area of influence was in relation to how employees carried out their work – of all employees, almost a half reported having a lot of influence and around a third, some influence. The area of least influence related to the range of tasks undertaken in their jobs – a quarter of employees reported having a lot of influence in this area, and two-fifths felt they had some influence.

Figure 7.1 Levels of job influence

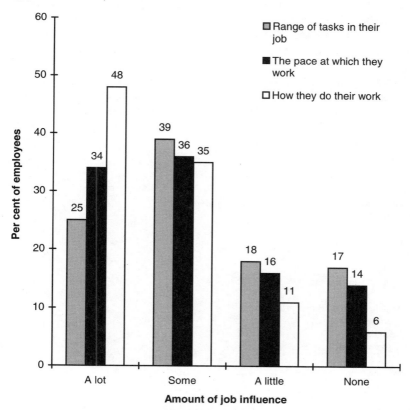

Base: All employees in workplaces with 25 or more employees.
Figures are weighted and based on responses from 25,598 (range of tasks), 25,487 (pace of work) and 25,469 (how they work) employees.

Taking these three spheres of influence – how work is done, pace of work, range of tasks undertaken – we created an overall measure of perceived job influence by summing the answers across the three individual items and scaling back to the original categories.[6] Overall, 30 per cent of employees had a lot of influence over their job, 43 per cent had some influence, while the remaining quarter had little or no influence.

Table 7.2 shows how the level of perceived job influence is related to hours of work and occupation. Greater degrees of perceived influence were associated with longer hours. Of employees working less than 10 hours a week, under a quarter had a lot of job influence, compared to more than a third of employees working in excess of 48 hours. As can also be seen in Table 7.2, by far the highest level of job influence was found among managers, with six in ten having a lot of influence, almost double the proportion in any other occupation. Managers were also more likely to work longer hours than employees in all other occupations (see below), and once account is made of this the positive association between hours and influence was considerably muted.

Chapter 3 considered job influence from the perspective of management where they were asked to say how much influence non-managerial employees in the largest occupational group had across the same three dimensions. The occupational patterns revealed there (see Figure 3.2) were broadly consistent with the portrait

Table 7.2 Job influence, by hours of work and occupation

| | Level of job influence | | | |
| | *A lot* | *Some* | *A little* | *None* |
	% of employees	% of employees	% of employees	% of employees
Total weekly hours				
Less than 10 hours per week	23	40	29	9
10–29 hours per week	25	42	24	9
30–48 hours per week	31	44	20	5
More than 48 hours per week	36	41	18	5
Occupation				
Managers and administrators	58	35	6	0
Professional	33	49	16	1
Associate professional and technical	30	50	17	2
Clerical and secretarial	28	45	21	6
Craft and related	28	45	21	6
Personal and protective service	26	43	25	6
Sales	26	40	25	9
Plant and machine operatives	22	39	27	12
Other occupations	27	39	24	10
All employees	30	43	21	6

Base: All employees in workplaces with 25 or more employees.
Figures are weighted and based on responses from 24,077 (hours) and 25,069 (occupation) employees.

provided by employees themselves.[7] That is, professional employees exercised the greatest degree of job control, and operative and assembly workers the least. By incorporating answers from the management interview we can explore further this link between occupation and job influence. Where an employee was in a job that was the most common at the workplace, their perceived job influence was likely to be lower. Across all (non-managerial) employees, 24 per cent of those that were in the largest occupational group at their workplace had a lot of job influence, compared with 30 per cent where they were not.[8] This difference was consistent for all occupational groups, bar personal service workers and operative and assembly workers, where there was no gap. This (admittedly modest) job influence gap suggests that workplace management were less willing to devolve responsibility to those in the core workforce (that is, the largest occupational group).

It is also consistent with the argument that job influence is related to the ease or cost of job monitoring; employees working together in sufficient numbers are likely to be less costly on average to monitor than employees in other groups. As in Chapter 3, we also find (for employees in the largest occupational group) that where employees had greater levels of job influence, their job responsibilities were more likely to be conveyed by the setting of individual objectives and targets. This association held for employees in five of the eight non-managerial occupational groups. Broadening this out, employees were asked whether, over the preceding year, they had discussed with their supervisor or line manager how they were getting on in their job. Overall, those who had were more likely to rate themselves as having a lot of job influence, 33 per cent compared with 26 per cent. A difference of around this magnitude was found for employees in all occupational groups, except managers who were more likely to rate themselves as having a lot of influence when they had *not* had such discussions.

Flexible working arrangements

One of the most striking labour market developments of the post-war era has been the growth in female participation in the labour force, with the 1980s in particular seeing rapid growth in employment among women with children. This change in the configuration of the labour market, as well as a range of other factors including competitive pressures, labour shortages and the need to retain employees, coupled with a recognition of the challenges of reconciling work and family life, has led to an increased interest in the notion of 'flexible working' arrangements and in so-called 'family friendly policies'. The two concepts are easily blurred. Flexible working including part-time work, flexi-time, job sharing and homeworking may be of benefit to employees with and without children, while family friendly policies including the implementation and extension of statutory maternity rights, parental leave, help with child care, career breaks and so on, are geared specifically to managing work and family life.

Chapters 3 and 4 provided data on the provision of flexible working arrangements, as described by workplace management. This section considers employees' perceptions of such provisions in their workplaces. Respondents were asked about their *personal* access to five different kinds of flexible and family friendly working provisions, including two areas geared specifically towards meeting the needs of dependent children:

- flexible working hours (flexi-time);
- sharing a full-time job with someone else (job sharing);
- working at or from home in normal working hours (homeworking);
- parental leave; and
- a workplace nursery or help with the cost of child care.

Access to these working arrangements is likely to be influenced by a wide range of factors. Independent of actual provision, an individual's personal circumstances may affect their *awareness* of particular facilities – for example, employees without children may be less informed about the availability of child-care provisions. Other research has highlighted that both awareness and take-up of arrangements may be available only to a limited number or narrow range of employees, at management's discretion (Metcalf, 1990). Equally, some forms of flexible working – such as flexi-time, or homeworking – may be more subject to negotiation than others.

Both flexible working and family friendly policies form an important element of current social and political thinking on the workplace and working life.[9] Such arrangements are by no means widely, or equally, available. Just over half of employees (54 per cent) reported that one or more of the five provisions was available to them if needed: of these, well over half (56 per cent) cited only the one provision, a quarter gave two options and the remaining fifth, three or more.

Across all employees a third (32 per cent) said they could work flexi-time if needs be. More women (37 per cent) and part-time workers (37 per cent) said they could work flexi-time than did men (28 per cent) and full-time employees (30 per cent). Flexi-time was much more widely available to some occupational groups than others. Of operative and assembly workers, just 19 per cent said they had access to flexi-time, compared with half (49 per cent) of clerical and secretarial staff.

Other types of flexible working – job sharing and homeworking – were available to fewer employees than flexi-time: 16 per cent said they could job share if needed, and 9 per cent that they could work from or at home. Again, more women than men (23 per cent compared with 10 per cent) said job sharing was open to them, though the reverse was true of homeworking, which 11 per cent of men and 7 per cent of women identified as an option open to them. Occupation was also related to whether or not employees were able to work from home. Around a third (35 per cent) of managers and 22 per cent of professionals said they could work at home if needed. This compared with figures of 3 per cent for employees in personal and protective services, and 1 per cent of those working in operative and assembly work.

Formal employer assistance in meeting or assisting with child care was reported as available by a small minority of employees: just 4 per cent said that help was available to them, either in the form of a workplace nursery or with meeting child-care costs. We will discuss this in more detail below. Access to parental leave was perceived to be more widely available. Just over a quarter (28 per cent) of all employees said they could take parental leave; 31 per cent of women said they had access to this, compared to 25 per cent of men.

All five provisions were perceived as more widely available by public sector employees – a finding supported by management accounts in Chapter 4, as well as other studies on flexible working and family friendly policies (Berry-Lound, 1990; Bridgewood and Savage, 1993; Forth *et al.*, 1997).[10] Of all public sector employees, 64 per cent said that at least one of the provisions was personally available to them, compared to 49 per cent of employees in the private sector. Employees from larger workplaces in the private sector were also more likely to report access to each of the five provisions.

Significant differences have been noted so far in men's and women's perceptions of their personal access to these working provisions. With the exception of homeworking, women were more likely than men to report that each of the provisions was available to them. Part of this is explained by gender segregation: the greater the proportion of women employed at the workplace, the greater the perceived access – for *both* men and women. However, except in workplaces where relatively few men were employed (i.e. they made up less than a quarter of the workforce) differences, albeit small, remained between men and women. It may be that the way employees perceive their entitlements is fashioned by their own need to accommodate work and family life, a dual responsibility which may be felt more acutely by some women employees than men. In addition, it may also be that, within the workplace, traditional notions of male and female responsibilities still hold with employers perceiving a greater need to gear flexible working and family policies towards women.

Taking sector and gender together, Table 7.3 summarises access to the five working provisions among women and men according to whether they work in the private or public sector. All were more prevalent in the public sector, but also *within* sectors women generally perceived themselves to have greater access to such arrangements.

Behind this general result are some further, more subtle, findings which point to possible underlying motivations for employers making these arrangements available. The better the educational qualifications held, the more likely were employees to have access to these working provisions, ranging from 41 per cent of those with no school level qualifications having access to one or more arrangements, to 71 per cent of those with post-graduate qualifications. Indeed, there was a clear positive association between educational qualifications and access to each of the five arrangements examined. This association was generally independent of occupation, holding for seven of the nine occupations. Moreover, this difference also holds within both the private and public sectors. Highly-educated employees may be more adept at securing access to these types of working arrangements. Alternatively employers may target access to these schemes towards higher-skilled employees who may be more difficult, and therefore costly, to

Table 7.3 Flexible and family friendly working arrangements, by gender and sector

	Sector				All employees
	Private		Public		
	Male	Female	Male	Female	
	% of employees	% of employees	% of employees	% of employees	% of employees
Flexi-time	24	36	37	39	32
Parental leave	21	30	35	33	28
Job sharing scheme	6	15	23	34	16
Working at or from home	10	6	13	9	9
Workplace nursery/child care subsidy	2	3	6	9	4
None of these	57	42	40	34	46

Base: All employees in workplaces with 25 or more employees.
Figures are weighted and based on responses from 25,457 employees.

replace. A similar story holds for job influence. Those employees who reported a lot of job influence had substantially greater access to one or more flexible working arrangements. In the public sector two in three employees (68 per cent) with a lot of influence reported access to at least one of the provisions compared with two in five (41 per cent) of those with no job influence. A difference of a similar scale also applied in the private sector.

To sum up, access to flexible and family friendly working provisions appears to be driven by at least three main factors: first, the willingness of employers to provide such schemes; second, the breadth of availability within workplaces; and, third, the ability of individual employees to acquire information and make use of these provisions. On the first of these, it is clear that provision was greater in the public sector, and in larger private sector workplaces. Second, we have provided some suggestive evidence that where these schemes operated they were more likely to be targeted towards high skill employees. And, on the last, on most counts women report greater access than men – this may be explained by differences in men's and women's experiences of managing work and family responsibilities, to which we now turn.

Parents' experience of family friendly working arrangements

Of the two provisions which can clearly be labelled 'family friendly', namely parental leave and some form of assistance with child care, 28 per cent of all employees considered they had access to the former, and just 4 per cent the latter. Both of these were strongly associated with domestic circumstances, with the greatest perceived provision among those with pre-school-age children. Around two in five parents with (only) pre-school-age children had access to parental leave, with 8 per cent having access to child care assistance. Similar, but somewhat lower, proportions of parents with both pre-school and school-age children reported access to these arrangements, and lowest of all were employees without any dependent children – here, only one in four reported having access to parental leave and 3 per cent had access to child-care assistance if needed.

Parents working in the public sector reported better provision than those working in the private sector on both parental leave and child care, and mothers more so than fathers. However, a large part of the difference between mothers and fathers arises because working mothers are much more likely to work in the public sector than working fathers. Thus, as Table 7.3 shows, fathers working in the public sector were somewhat more likely than mothers to report access to parental leave.

Employee access to these working arrangements provides one indicator of their ability to reconcile family and work responsibilities. Another is the options open to them for responding to short-term emergencies that occur in family life. Respondents to the employee survey were asked what action they would normally take 'if they need to take a day off work, at short notice, for example to care for a sick family member'. The vast majority said that they would be able to take time off, one way or another, in order to cope with this kind of situation, as shown in Figure 7.2. Of the various options presented, arguably the most flexible is the opportunity to take time off and make up the working hours at a later stage. Overall, 15 per cent of employees gave this option, and it did not vary a great deal across different types of employees or workplaces. The main divide between employees was whether the time off was paid or unpaid, with almost half of employees saying such time off would be paid and a fifth saying it would be unpaid. Among those who said it was paid we are unable to distinguish whether this meant they used up part of their annual leave entitlements, or there was some type of special paid leave scheme for such circumstances, or, indeed, they rang in sick. Employees working in the public sector were more likely to take paid leave, 54 per cent compared with 45 per cent among employees working in the private sector. This is consistent with evidence from management of special paid leave schemes being more prevalent in the public sector (see Table 4.10). Use of paid leave was also more common for full-time employees than part-time employees; indeed, part-time employees are the group most likely to take unpaid leave (34 per cent).

To summarise, looking across all employees, women were more likely than men to report access to both flexible and family friendly working arrangements. It may be that the demands faced by women in balancing work and family life make them more likely than their male counterparts to enquire about, or negotiate, access to flexible working and family friendly policies at their workplace. Alternatively, the networks of information on such initiatives may be more prevalent among women employees than men. Part of the difference between men and women is explained by the employers they work for, in particular the high representation of working mothers in the public sector, where provision is

Figure 7.2 How employees take time off work at short notice

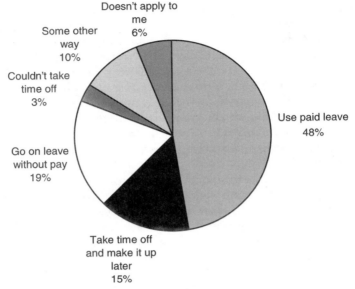

Base: All employees in workplaces with 25 or more employees.
Figures are weighted and based on responses from 25,381 employees.

more widespread: it may be that working mothers are more likely to seek jobs in the public sector because such jobs give them greater flexibility to accommodate family responsibilities.

Training

The presence of structures facilitating the progression of individual job skills and careers may be seen as an indicator of the extent to which employees' needs are met within the employment relationship. Equally, training and skills development can potentially be regarded as inducements to garner employee commitment. Employees were asked how many days training they had received in the last 12 months. The question related solely to training paid for by the employer, and located away from the normal place of work (though either on or off the workplace premises). It is, therefore, parallel to the measure of formal training discussed in Chapter 4.

Six in ten (60 per cent) of all employees had received some training in the year prior to the survey, with two in ten (18 per cent) getting at least five days. Before exploring how this is associated with individual employee characteristics, we need to briefly reprise some of the issues explored in Chapter 4. First, there was a strong association between employer reports of training provision (for experienced employees in the largest occupational group) and individual employee accounts, though employers appear to have somewhat overstated the amount of training relative to employees.[11] Second, in accord with management accounts, training provision was greater among employees in workplaces with Investors in People accreditation and where unions were recognised, though the differences were less pronounced. Thus, 64 per cent of employees in workplaces with IiP had received training compared with 58 per cent in other workplaces, while there was a slightly greater difference depending on whether the workplace had recognised unions or not, 63 per cent compared with 55 per cent. An even more substantial difference remains across sectors, with 70 per cent of public sector employees getting some training in the past year compared with 55 per cent of private sector employees. However, according to management accounts, the greatest differences in training provision were across occupational groups, and it is that to which we now turn.

Table 7.4 shows the level of training provision – any training at all in the past year and, a sub-set of these, those with five days or more training – across employees of different occupations taking into account whether they work full or part-time. As can be seen from the table there is a very clear divide (also shown in Table 4.5) between occupations that are clearly 'blue-collar' and those that are either 'pink' or 'white-collar'. Indeed, less than half of craft workers, operative and assembly workers and those in routine, unskilled jobs received any training at all in the year preceding the survey, irrespective of whether they worked full or part-time. The other clear finding from Table 7.4 is that part-time workers were trained less than their counterparts in full-time jobs. This holds true for employees of *all* occupations, both for whether any training is received and those receiving at least five days. Furthermore, the differences highlighted above with IiP and union recognition only applied to full-time workers in these workplaces. Part-time employees in these workplaces did not have any better provision than those in other workplaces. While, overall, men were more likely to have been trained than women, this was because most part-time employees were women. Looking just at part-time employees, there was no difference between men and women.

Besides occupation and hours of work, there were some other pronounced patterns of training provision which indicate a high level of targeting in access to training. In particular, there was a clear bias in favour of younger workers and against older workers. Setting aside managers, and focusing on full-time employees only, once workers turn 50 years old half no longer had any training and only one in ten had five or more days' training. By way of contrast, over two-thirds (66 per cent) of employees under 20 years old had been trained in the past year with over a third (35 per cent) getting five or more days. Part of this is accounted for by enhanced levels of training for recent recruits so as to make them fully proficient – for example, twice as many full-time non-managerial employees with less than one year's service had five or more days' training compared with the longest serving employees (10 or more years' service). However, even after taking account of this, an age bias remains.

While training is paid for by the employer and, as shown above, is targeted by occupation, length of service and age, it is also the case that training was more likely to take place where training needs were identified. Thus, we find a positive association between job influence and training, and an even more pronounced

Table 7.4 Training in past year, by occupation and full-time/part-time status

	Full-time employees		Part-time employees	
	Any training in past year	5 days or more	Any training in past year	5 days or more
	% of employees	% of employees	% of employees	% of employees
Occupation				
Managers and administrators	77	27	62	22
Professional	79	26	62	9
Associate professional and technical	76	29	66	17
Clerical and secretarial	67	18	55	10
Craft and related	43	16	17	1
Personal and protective service	78	36	54	9
Sales	68	21	65	8
Plant and machine operatives	41	12	28	4
Other occupations	44	10	35	4
All employees	62	21	52	8

Base: All employees in workplaces with 25 or more employees.
Figures are weighted and based on responses from 26,640 employees.

association between individual discussions with line managers or supervisors about training needs and the level of training provision.

Taking these in turn, employees who considered themselves to have little or no job influence had lower levels of training than other employees. Differences remain after taking account of occupation, so it is possible to conclude that employees with greater job responsibility were either more adept at securing training provision, or employers needed to ensure these employees were fully equipped to handle their responsibilities. The opportunity to express training needs was clearly of some importance in securing opportunities. Employees were almost equally split among those who had held discussions with line managers or supervisors on training needs, 48 per cent, compared with 52 per cent where they had not. Where discussions had taken place, 80 per cent of employees had been trained in the past year and 28 per cent for at least five days, while the comparative figures where discussions had not taken place were 41 per cent and 8 per cent. Moreover, differences of this magnitude were found across all occupational groups even after taking into account hours worked. For example, Table 7.4 showed that two-thirds of full-time sales workers were trained in the past year, and about a fifth got five or more days training. Within this group of workers, 79 per cent of those who held discussions with their supervisors were trained and 30 per cent got at least five days' training, compared with respective figures of 53 per cent and 9 per cent for their colleagues who had no such discussions. The holding of such discussions was only slightly associated with whether or not the workplace was IiP accredited – indeed, 48 per cent of employees in workplaces with the IiP award said they had *not* had discussions with managers over their training needs.

Overall, there is widespread variation in access to training across several employee and workplace characteristics. Employees most likely to receive training were younger workers, who were new to the job, employed full-time in a clerical or professional occupation in the public sector. Those least likely to do so were older workers in 'blue-collar' jobs, especially if they happened to be working part-time. Over and above all of these differences, the best way of securing access to training was for employees to have identified their individual training needs with their line manager or supervisor. Formal systems like IiP do not guarantee that such discussions will be held. This leads us more broadly into the issue of consultation.

Consultation with employees

Chapters 4 and 5 considered the prevalence of formal schemes by which managers sought to involve or consult employees, either directly or through representative structures. Here we examine employee perceptions of their involvement in workplace decision-making. In questioning employees about this area we adopted a different approach to that used with management. It was recognised that simply presenting employees with a list of formal schemes would be inappropriate since individuals would be likely to bring their own, often varied, interpretations of what particular initiatives involved. Instead employees were asked to consider how often they were asked by managers for their views on five separate issues of relevance to them and to the workplace as a whole. These were:

- future plans for the workplace;
- staffing issues, including redundancy;
- changes to work practices;
- pay issues; and
- health and safety at work.

The propensity for employees to report *frequent* participation in workplace decision-making was low on all five issues.[12] The most widespread consultation related to health and safety issues – 23 per cent of employees reported frequent contact on this issue. This varied widely by industry: it was lowest in financial services (12 per cent of employees) and public administration (17 per cent), and greatest in hotels and restaurants (35 per cent), electricity, gas and water (33 per cent), health (31 per cent), and construction (30 per cent). The most likely explanation for these differences is that most workplaces not consulting employees directly over health and safety matters had alternative arrangements in place – joint health and safety committees or elected safety representatives – as discussed in Chapter 5. As there are at any rate statutory requirements in this field, we exclude direct consultation over health and safety from further consideration.

Less than a fifth of employees reported frequent consultation regarding workplace change: 17 per cent said they were asked their views on changes to future work practices, and 14 per cent on future plans for the workplace. The lowest levels of frequent participation in decision-making related to staffing issues, such as redundancy (8 per cent) and pay (5 per cent). All in all, three-quarters (77 per cent) of employees said they were not frequently consulted on *any* of the four issues. The remaining quarter of employees were frequently consulted on one issue only (11 per cent), two issues (6 per cent) or three or more (6 per cent). This relatively low level of direct participation in workplace decision-making was consistent across most types of employees, and in different types of workplaces. For example, the percentage of employees reporting that they were frequently consulted on at least one of the four issues did not differ by more than a few percentage points, irrespective of workplace size, organisation size, sector or whether the workplace was a stand-alone site or part of a wider organisation. What, if any, features of the workplace then might account for greater consultation? We address this further below, but first look at differences across individual employee characteristics.

A number of strong differences were found. First, consistent with much else in this chapter, hours worked appeared to matter. Among those working fewer than ten hours a week, only 17 per cent said they were frequently consulted on at least one issue, compared with 31 per cent of those usually working more than 48 hours per week. Part of this is explained by the fact that managers themselves report the highest levels of consultation and they also work the longest hours, but even confining our attention to non-managerial employees, a 7 percentage point difference remains between those working the fewest and the most hours. Second, as indicated above, there were substantial differences across employees in different occupational groups. Managers were the only group where a majority (51 per cent) claimed to be frequently consulted – by other managers? – on one or more issues. Thereafter the gap between employees in other occupations is fairly narrow, ranging from 29 per cent among professional employees through to craft workers where 15 per cent reported frequent consultation. Some of this is issue-dependent; thus, professional employees were most likely to say they were frequently consulted over future workplace plans (22 per cent) and changes to work practices (21 per cent), while sales workers were most likely to be frequently consulted over pay (5 per cent). Third, there was a very strong association between job influence and participation in workplace decision-making, as demonstrated in Table 7.5. This association persists within *all* of the occupational groups. In fact, the proportion reporting frequent consultation on more than one issue was between two and nine times as great among those with a lot of influence as among those with no influence.

In opening this section we noted that employees were not asked about specific forms of consultation. An exception was a general question asking employees to rate the helpfulness of meetings between managers and employees in keeping up to date about workplace matters. As well as a scale indicating degrees of helpfulness, there was also an option to indicate that such meetings did not take place. This question proved to be the one indicator that had the strongest

Table 7.5 Number of issues where frequent consultation occurs, by level of job influence

	Number of issues			
	None	*One*	*Two*	*Three or more*
	% of employees	% of employees	% of employees	% of employees
Level of job influence				
A lot	64	15	9	12
Some	79	11	5	5
A little	88	7	3	2
None	93	4	1	1
All employees	77	11	6	6

Base: All employees in workplaces with 25 or more employees.
Figures are weighted and based on responses from 24,350 employees.

association of all with the degree of consultation. Among the 15 per cent of employees who thought such meetings very helpful, half (53 per cent) said they were frequently consulted over one or more issues, and one in five were frequently consulted over at least three of the four issues. Contrast this with the 15 per cent of employees saying such meetings did not take place at their workplace – here, just 6 per cent said they were frequently consulted over one or more issues, and just 1 per cent mentioned three or more issues.

This returns us to the question posed earlier: which types of workplace level initiatives matter in giving workers a real sense of active participation in decision-making? We have shown that meetings of some kind appear to count for something. By incorporating information on employee involvement practices from the management interview we can see which forms of communication resonate most with employees. In general, employees working in workplaces where there were team briefings or problem-solving groups, or any of the other employee involvement practices discussed in Chapter 4, were more likely to say that they were frequently consulted on one or more of the four issues. However, the differences were very modest indeed, amounting to no more than 4 per cent of employees. This leaves something of a conundrum: what is it about the character of workplace initiatives to involve employees that leads some to consider themselves to be frequently consulted about workplace affairs? This would be a fruitful area for further analysis of the data.

Working hours and overtime

Much of the preceding discussion has highlighted the importance of differences in working hours. There appears to be rather different treatment or status accorded to those working part-time, compared to those working full-time, on issues such as job influence, access to flexible and family friendly working arrangements, and the degree of participation in workplace decision-making. We now extend the discussion of working hours from the opening section of this chapter, paying most attention to those working long hours, focusing on why they do so and what rewards, if any, follow.

Long hours culture

Long working hours are known to be a feature of the working lives of a sizeable proportion of employees, and many commentators have suggested that a 'long hours culture' operates in certain industries and certain types of workplaces. British male employees, on average, work more hours than men elsewhere in the European Union and many would prefer to work fewer hours (Stewart and Swaffield, 1996). The total number of hours worked by employees has become an important issue with the advent of the Working Time Regulations which came into force in October 1998 (after the survey fieldwork had been completed). The Working Time Regulations were introduced – consequent to the European Working Time Directive – as a response to health and safety concerns about the long hours culture and the absence of adequate rest breaks in some industries. They introduce, among other things, a 48-hour limit on the 'average' working week (including overtime) for most employees.[13] The survey data provides a benchmark for future research.

As identified in Table 7.1, one in eight of all employees said they usually worked more than 48 hours per week, including extra hours or overtime.[14] We will use this as the benchmark indicator of 'long hours', though it is also worth noting that a third of employees reported that they usually worked over 40 hours per week. There was a strong gender bias among employees working long hours, with one in five men falling into this group, compared with one in 20 women. A more detailed breakdown is given in Table 7.6.

No occupational group or industry is immune to long hours, but they were clearly more prevalent in some jobs and some workplaces than others. Long hours working was most common among managers, professional workers, and operative and assembly workers. It was also prevalent among employees working in construction, and transport and communications. In each occupation, and in each industry, it was overwhelmingly men who worked long hours. Only among female managers and professionals, and among women employed in education – many of whom would be managers or professionals (e.g. teachers) – were more than one in ten women working over 48 hours per week. By contrast, with the narrow exception of clerical workers, more than one in ten men in all walks of life were working more than 48 hours per week. Among managers and among those employed in construction, the situation can be considered chronic with one in three men working long hours.

Men in their forties were most likely to work long hours (25 per cent), while for women it was those in their thirties (6 per cent). However, after taking parental status into account, working fathers were *more* likely than other men of a similar

Table 7.6 Employees working over 48 hours per week, by occupation, industry and gender

	Male	Female	All employees
	% of employees	% of employees	% of employees
Occupation			
Managers and administrators	37	21	32
Professional	24	17	21
Associate professional and technical	12	3	7
Clerical and secretarial	9	1	3
Craft and related	20	5	19
Personal and protective service	20	2	10
Sales	15	1	5
Plant and machine operatives	25	5	20
Other occupations	17	1	9
Industry			
Manufacturing	23	4	18
Electricity, gas and water	13	6	11
Construction	32	3	28
Wholesale and retail	18	2	9
Hotels and restaurants	19	7	12
Transport and communications	29	5	24
Financial services	22	3	10
Other business services	27	7	17
Public administration	11	3	8
Education	27	10	15
Health	13	2	4
Other community services	15	5	10
All employees	22	5	13

Base: All employees working in excess of 48 hours per week in workplaces with 25 or more employees.
Figures are weighted and based on responses from 24,728 employees.

age to work long hours, while working mothers were *less* likely to do so than other women of a similar age. For example, among men in their forties, 28 per cent of fathers worked long hours compared with 21 per cent of those without dependent children. Among women in their thirties this was reversed, 2 per cent of working mothers had long hours compared with 12 per cent of other women in the same age band.

Besides the patterns of working identified in Table 7.6, other types of workplaces where long hours were somewhat more prevalent were those in the private sector (15 per cent), in stand-alone sites (16 per cent), and in workplaces with no union members (18 per cent). There was no clearly discernible pattern by workplace size, but the proportion of employees working long hours fell with organisation size from 20 per cent in small organisations (fewer than 100 employees) to 10 per cent in the largest organisations (10,000 employees or more).

Overtime: rationale and rewards

As noted earlier, one in three employees worked longer than 40 hours per week, which in most cases would be above the 'standard' or contracted hours for a full-time working week. Rather than entering into complex definitions in the questionnaire about contracted hours, we simply asked employees how many overtime hours, if any, they usually worked each week.[15] More than half (53 per cent) said they usually did overtime work, with a quarter doing up to 5 hours per week, 17 per cent doing between 6 and 10 hours, and 11 per cent in excess of 10 hours. It is, of course, possible for part-time employees to work overtime and, in fact, a third (32 per cent) did, about half the proportion of full-time employees working overtime (60 per cent). In most other respects, the pattern of overtime working was very similar to that for employees working in excess of 48 hours per week, so we will not discuss it further. Rather we will focus on why employees work overtime.[16]

What can be learned about employees' attitudes to the employment relationship by examining their rationale for working overtime? It may be that employees feel motivated by a sense of commitment to the tasks involved in their job, or to their colleagues, or to the organisation. As Lincoln and Kalleberg (1990) argue, it is important to maintain the distinction between commitments which reflect group and personal pressures, or prevailing norms, and those which represent the subjective feelings of the individual. In addition, employees may be motivated purely by instrumental reasons, if they gain financially from extending their working week.

Employees were asked to specify their *main* reason for working extra hours or overtime.[17] Table 7.7 presents the results, demonstrating that employees differed widely in their explanation for working extra hours. Three responses each accounted for about a quarter of employees working overtime. The most commonly advanced reason was for money, closely followed by those who, in effect, are compelled to work overtime as a requirement of their job. The third most common reason was where employees themselves shoulder the responsibility for completing

Table 7.7 Main reasons for working overtime, by gender

	Male	Female	All employees
	% of employees	% of employees	% of employees
Main reason for working overtime			
Need the money	34	23	29
Required as part of my job	28	21	25
To get the work done	21	26	23
Don't want to let colleagues down	8	16	12
Some other reason	5	8	6
Enjoy the work	4	6	5

Base: All employees who sometimes or always work overtime in workplaces with 25 or more employees. Figures are weighted and based on responses from 21,179 employees.

work tasks, followed by those who did not want to let colleagues down. In order these reasons might best be categorised as instrumental, compulsory, commitment to the job, and commitment to the workgroup.

Men and women presented quite different rationales for working overtime. Women were more likely to indicate they did overtime because they were committed to the job or the workgroup, while men were more likely to do overtime for instrumental reasons or because it was compulsory.

Across occupational groups there were very substantial differences in the motivation for working overtime, with a broad divide between 'blue collar' and 'white collar' jobs. A substantial proportion of employees engaged in 'blue collar' work did overtime for instrumental reasons: this was the case for 62 per cent of operative and assembly workers, 53 per cent of craft workers and 46 per cent of those doing routine, unskilled manual work. Very few managers or professionals did overtime mainly for the money – just 2 per cent and 4 per cent, respectively – mostly because they were rarely paid for it (see below). They were much more likely to do overtime out of commitment to the job – in both groups 47 per cent of employees said this. Other 'white collar' workers were also most likely to give this as the reason, 39 per cent for clerical workers, and 32 per cent for technicians. Again, by way of contrast, in none of the other five occupational groups was a job commitment rationale offered by more than one in ten employees.

This broad division between instrumental reasons and job commitment was strongly associated with job influence. Overall, among those with a lot of job influence, 29 per cent worked overtime out of job commitment and 19 per cent for instrumental reasons. At the other end of the scale, among employees with no job influence 7 per cent worked overtime for job commitment reasons compared with 55 per cent for instrumental reasons. These associations remain after taking account of occupation.

There was considerably less difference between occupations across the other reasons. Sales workers were the most likely to do overtime out of commitment to the work group (19 per cent), managers and professionals the least (6 per cent). Personal and protective service workers were the most likely to report that they did overtime because they enjoyed the work (10 per cent), and operative and assembly workers were the least likely to say this (2 per cent). Finally, between a fifth and a third of employees in all occupations said they did overtime because it was required.

Some of the broad differences between men and women identified above persisted after taking occupation into account. Thus, in seven out of nine occupations, men were more likely than women to say they were compelled to work overtime, while in six of the nine occupations women were more likely than men to indicate commitment to the work group. There was, however, no discernible pattern for instrumental reasons or job commitment between men and women after controlling for occupation.

As well as asking reasons for working overtime, employees were asked whether the overtime was paid, whether they were given time off in lieu, or neither of these. Over half (54 per cent) were normally paid for their overtime hours, 13 per cent ordinarily took time off in lieu, and 10 per cent were sometimes paid and sometimes took time off. This leaves a fifth (22 per cent) of workers who were neither paid nor given time off in lieu. That is not to say that this does not eventually yield its own rewards, either through wage increases or advancement. We assume this form of implicit deal provides much of the underlying logic for a 'long hours culture'.

The proportion of employees in different occupational groups who were normally paid for their overtime hours varied enormously from, at one extreme, a very low proportion among managers (13 per cent) and professionals (15 per cent), to one where nearly all operative and assembly workers (91 per cent) and craft workers (87 per cent) were paid. Time off in lieu, rather than pay, was most common for clerks (27 per cent) and technicians (24 per cent). These two groups also had the highest proportion of overtime workers who were sometimes paid and sometimes given time off (18 per cent and 19 per cent, respectively). Around two-thirds of managers and professionals did not receive any form of reimbursement for their extra hours. In all other occupations, no more than a quarter were neither paid nor given time off in lieu.

As might be inferred from the above discussion, there was a close association between the reasons for working overtime and the reward. Expressed as a percentage of all those working overtime, just over a quarter of employees (26 per cent) worked overtime for instrumental reasons *and* were normally paid for those hours. Of those putting forward instrumental reasons nine in ten were normally paid for their efforts, with only 4 per cent in the apparently contradictory position of doing it for the money but never getting paid. There were two further substantial clusters, each accounting for about a tenth of all employees doing overtime. The first is those who were required to work overtime and were normally paid for these extra hours. The second is those who cited job commitment and who get no reimbursement for their overtime hours.

Almost half (44 per cent) of those working overtime because it was required as part of their job were paid for the hours, but around a third (29 per cent) got no reimbursement. These proportions were reversed among those doing overtime out of commitment to the job, with 22 per cent being paid and 43 per cent receiving no pay. This may be because the requirement to work overtime is often an explicit part of the employment contract, while the notion of commitment is more a tacit element of the employment relationship.

This section has provided a measure of overtime working among employees, and examined what lies behind their work efforts. Across employees as a whole, over half (53 per cent) usually worked some overtime, one in three (31 per cent) worked more than 40 hours per week, and more than one in ten (13 per cent) worked over 48 hours per week. Male employees were much more likely to work very long hours than women, and this applied across all occupations. Such long hours must, inevitably, have consequences for life outside work and it was notable that working fathers were more likely to work long hours than other men.

Half of all employees regularly worked overtime. They did so for a variety of reasons. By far the biggest group – over a quarter of those doing overtime – had a very straightforward arrangement: they worked overtime for the money and they were normally paid for it. For many other employees the story was a good deal more complicated. Most managers and professionals worked overtime out of commitment to their job or because it was required of them, and got no direct reward.

Pay

As we observe daily in our lives, pay differs widely from one individual to the next. Uncovering the reasons why it does so is one of the most well-researched areas in economics and sociology, and a whole host of potential factors have been identified covering individual, job and workplace characteristics. The most important explanatory factors are known to be hours of work and occupation. Cross-sectional data, such as ours, is known to have some limitations in exploring the determinants of pay – what is more important is being able to look at lifetime earnings, and movements between jobs (Abowd *et al.* 1998). Nonetheless, what we are able to do, unlike many other surveys of employees, is match information from employees and managers, so that the full range of possible explanatory factors might be taken into account.

All employees, full- and part-time, were asked how much they were paid each week before tax and other deductions, by choosing one of twelve ranges.[18] At the two extremes, 6 per cent of employees said they were paid less than £50 per week, while 3 per cent were paid more than £680 per week. The median worker was paid somewhere between £221 and £260 per week. Because we have used bands to collect the information, it is not possible to show differences in average pay among different types of employees. Rather, what we do to illustrate the differences is to look at who falls into the bottom and top quartiles of the earnings distribution.

Across all employees, the bottom quarter of earners were paid less than £140 per week, while the top quarter were paid over £360 per week. When looking at particular groups of workers, the proportion falling into the bottom and top quarters of the distribution indicates the degree of association between the grouping and pay. If it is greater than a quarter then employees in that group are disproportionately low (or high) paid. For example, among those working fewer than ten hours per week, 89 per cent were in the bottom quarter of earners and just 3 per cent were in the top. By the time we get to those working over 48 hours per week, the proportion in the bottom quarter was only 2 per cent, while around half were in the top quarter of earners. These numbers confirm the importance of working hours, and from here onwards we separate full-time from part-time employees, so as to partially control for hours.

As expected, occupation is the other main determinant of pay. Figure 7.3 shows, for full-time employees, the proportion in each occupational group in the *top* quarter of earners; and, for part-time employees, the proportion in the *bottom* quarter of earners. There is a striking, near hierarchical pattern to the results. Four out of five full-time managers were in the top quarter of earners, compared with just one in 20 full-time employees in routine unskilled work. This divergence

Figure 7.3 Proportion of full-time employees in the top quarter and part-time employees in the bottom quarter of earners, by occupation

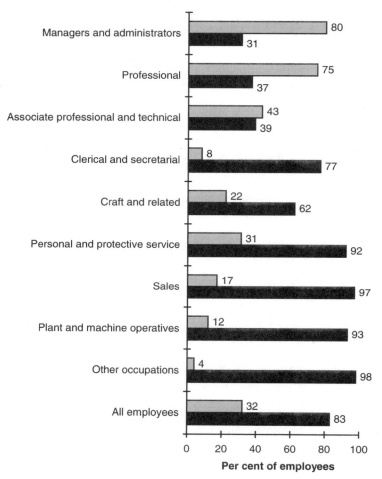

□ Full-time employees in top quarter of earners (£361 or more per week)
■ Part-time employees in bottom quarter of earners (£140 or less per week)

Base: All employees in workplaces with 25 or more employees.
Figures are weighted and based on responses from 24,381 employees.

was equally marked among part-time workers. Nearly all part-time routine unskilled workers fell into the bottom quarter of earners, compared with a third of part-time managers.

Most analytical treatments of pay are partly hamstrung by the absence of some of the relevant information in the data source used. Typically, individual level data has patchy contextual information on the workplace, while workplace-level data compresses the variation found in individual data. It is rare for researchers to be able to address both 'human capital' arguments and those which credit the employer with an important role, such as 'efficiency wage' theories. The linked nature of our data set permits this kind of approach.

We illustrate the importance of both individual and workplace level factors by focusing on gender differentials. It is a well-known observation that women earn less than men. Most of this is accounted for by differences in the duration of the working week and the types of job done. However, studies show that, even with the most elaborate of controls, there remains an 'unexplained' differential between women and men (Zabalza and Tzannatos, 1985). One of the commonly advanced explanations for this is sex discrimination. Equal pay legislation is designed to counter sex discrimination in earnings by giving legal force to the proposition that there should be equal pay for work of equal value. However, the legislation only applies to employees within an organisation; it is not possible for female employees in one organisation to demand equal pay with men doing the same kind of work in a different organisation. This means that a potential source of gender differentials in earnings is gender segregation across employers. We will explore whether this appears to matter.

First, we establish the basic differences in earnings between women and men. Among full-time employees, 21 per cent of women were in the top quarter of earners, about half the comparable figure for men (39 per cent). For part-time employees there was also a disparity, though small – 84 per cent of women were in the bottom quarter of earners, compared with 81 per cent of men. Within occupational groups, some of these differences became narrower, some greater. Taking full-time personal and protective service workers as an example, the difference was large – 8 per cent of women in this group were in the top quarter of earners, compared with 46 per cent of men. For part-time professionals, though, there was no difference – just over a third of both women and men were in the bottom quarter of earners. While the differences may have varied, the pattern was consistent and unambiguous: women doing broadly comparable hours and broadly comparable work earned less than their male counterparts.

Turning now to workplace factors, does gender segregation matter? The overall figures suggest that it does. Among part-time employees, 65 per cent of those in workplaces where at least three-quarters of the workforce was male ('male-dominated') were in the bottom quarter of earners, compared with 84 per cent of those in workplaces that were 'female-dominated'. A large difference also applied for full-time employees – in male-dominated workplaces 33 per cent were in the top quarter of earners, compared with 24 per cent of those in female-dominated workplaces. These differences may apply because men and women are in different jobs within those workplaces. Table 7.8 takes this into account by showing the extent of occupational differences. Many of the comparisons cannot be made for part-time employees because there were so few part-timers in male-dominated workplaces. For full-time employees, however, those working in female-dominated workplaces are less well paid than those in male-dominated workplaces after taking into account like work and working hours.

Table 7.8 Proportion of full-time employees in the top quarter and part-time employees in the bottom quarter of earners, by gender concentration and occupation

	Full-time employees in top quarter of earners (£361 or more per week)			Part-time employees in bottom quarter of earners (£140 or less per week)		
	Male dominated workplace	Mixed workplace	Female dominated workplace	Male dominated workplace	Mixed workplace	Female dominated workplace
	% of employees	% of employees	% of employees	% of employees	% of employees	% of employees
Occupation						
Managers and administrators	88	78	70	*	(27)	*
Professional	75	77	68	*	40	33
Associate professional and technical	56	43	30	*	41	39
Clerical and secretarial	8	8	3	74	77	76
Craft and related	28	13	3	*	(79)	*
Personal and protective service	48	38	1	*	94	90
Sales	32	17	2	*	98	97
Plant and machine operatives	18	3	0	*	98	*
Other occupations	9	1	0	(82)	98	100

Base: All employees in workplaces with 25 or more employees.
Figures are weighted and based on responses from 24,264 employees.

Having established that the gender of the employee and the gender mix of the workplace both appear to account for differences in earnings, the final stage is to see how the two effects interact – were both important, or was the individual's gender more important than whether they worked mostly with men or women? To test this adequately would require a more sophisticated treatment than we can give in this book. We also encounter the constraint of too few part-time employees in the sample to produce a comprehensive four-way table. However, for full-time employees, we can explore the interaction. In seven of the nine occupational groups, those most likely to be in the top quarter of earners were men working in male-dominated workplaces while the least well-paid were women working in female-dominated workplaces. This provides strong evidence that, for pay as well as occupation, working hours and gender, it also matters *where* employees work.

This analysis has provided much of interest for those concerned about the position of women employees relative to men. Its main purpose, however, was to illustrate ways in which material from the employee survey can be used to enhance understanding, by drawing on both individual and workplace level factors. The opportunities for further work in the area of earnings, but much else besides, are tremendous.

Conclusion

This chapter has ranged widely across the substantive content of people's jobs. Just as the effects of workplace size, sector and activity appeared pervasive in explaining differences in management practices and employee representation, so too did we find consistently recurring features of individual characteristics and jobs that explained much of the variation throughout. The principal ones were gender, hours of work and occupation. As with the workplace factors they are all inter-related and, where we could, we sought to disentangle one from the other to highlight the factor of greatest significance. For example, we found that women got less training than men, but this was because women were far more likely to be part-time employees. In this case, working hours appears the more significant factor. By contrast, it was clearly the case that women reported greater access than men to flexible and family friendly working arrangements. While this was generally higher for public sector than private sector workers, it was also higher for women than men working in the public sector.

One other factor also counted for much throughout the chapter: job influence. Most managers considered themselves to have a lot of job influence. In all other occupational groups, however, no more than a third and no less than a fifth of workers had a lot of influence. Discounting managers' influence was only slightly related to hours of work and was not related to gender. Unlike these factors, job influence is not an innate attribute of the individual or of the formal job character-istics; rather, it is one of those aspects of the employment contract that cannot be written down and is determined within the day-to-day workings of the employment relationship. This is important because we found consistently throughout the chapter that job influence was a factor which appeared to explain differences independent of innate attributes. For example, employees with job influence in all occupations were more likely to say they were frequently consulted over some workplace issues. It was equally important in explaining motives for working overtime. Indeed, the scale of the differences hints at job influence as a possible explanatory factor in general work motivation. That is the subject of the next chapter.

In closing this chapter, it is worth briefly reiterating the novelty of the material we have presented. What distinguishes this employee survey from most others is the facility to match individual employee responses with the detailed information obtained in the management interview. We demonstrated in the case of pay how both individual and workplace-level factors are important, and there were other illustrations throughout the chapter. Some of these results might easily be obtained from any employee survey – for example, that training provision was higher for public sector than private sector employees. Others, though, clearly show how matching management and employee accounts adds to the complexity of the story and extends our understanding of how the employment relationship functions. For example, job influence was related to occupation, with managers and, to a lesser extent, professionals having the most job influence. Other studies, like Gallie *et al.* (1998), also show this. The novel finding was that influence tended to be lower where employees formed part of the largest occupational group at the workplace. Why management might be less willing to allow employees in the core workforce the same amount of influence as other employees is a question we are unable to answer, but it is a question which might not have been posed without matched data such as these.

Notes

1 We use a subtle distinction in labelling to try and minimise confusion throughout this chapter. By 'management' we mean the workplace managers with day-to-day responsibility for employee relations matters who took part in the face-to-face interviews. This is a different group from 'managers', who are employees of managerial rank who were randomly selected and took part in the employee element of the survey.

2 Data gathered from the completed questionnaires have been weighted to control for non-response among sub-groups of the population. A short description of the weighting procedure is found in the Technical Appendix. The survey data are fully representative of all employees working in workplaces with 25 employees or more.

3 This conforms with the European Union wide statistical convention.

4 Employees were not asked whether they were lone parents. They were identified as such if they said they were single, widowed or divorced and had dependent children. While this definition encompasses lone parents, it potentially includes a number of absentee parents.

5 As with all items in the employee survey, occupation is self-reported. Employees were asked to tick the box which best described their job with several examples given of each. They were then asked to describe the main tasks undertaken in their job. Coders from SCPR highlighted potential discrepancies between the written account and the reported occupation. Where there was a discrepancy we have used the revised code. This occurred in 13 per cent of cases. In aggregate, most occupational groups altered by just 1 or 2 per cent. The greatest discrepancies occurred with personal and protective service workers, which went up from 7 per cent to 10 per cent of employees after the revision. Both the original and revised codes will be available in the data sets deposited with the Data Archive.

6 In constructing the scale, each item is compared with other items to assess how well they relate to one another. A summary measure of the overall reliability of the scale is provided by the Cronbach alpha statistic. The widely accepted minimum standard for internal consistency is 0.70. In creating the scale on job influence, alpha = 0.79. For further information on scale preparation generally, see de Vaus (1996).

7 Although, the correlation between *individual* employees in the largest occupational group and the management account was modest. The figures are $r = 0.07$ for range of tasks, $r = 0.07$ for pace of work, and $r = 0.10$ for how work is done. Management credited employees with relatively greater influence over the range of tasks, but employees rated themselves as having more influence over the other two dimensions than management did.

8 The largest occupational group was the one with the greatest number of *non-managerial* employees at the workplace. Thus, employees taking part in the survey who are managers are excluded from these figures.

9 A number of proposals on flexible working have been made by the current government, set out for example in the *Fairness at Work* White Paper (Department of Trade and Industry, 1998a) and the National Child Care Strategy (Department for Education and Employment, 1998) which seek to support working families and reinforce a family friendly culture at work.

10 There was a high degree of correspondence between management's accounts of flexible working schemes available for non-managerial employees and individual employee perceptions with correlations ranging from $r = 0.15$ for parental leave to $r = 0.35$ for workplace nursery or help with child care.

11 $r = 0.16$. The degree of exact correspondence is only small (kappa = 0.06), when limited to employees with more than one year's service in the largest occupational group.

12 Due to a typographical error in the employee questionnaire, it is only possible to distinguish between employees reporting 'frequent' consultation or not, rather than the four category classification intended – the other three categories being 'sometimes', 'hardly ever' and 'never'. The questionnaire mistakenly ordered these other categories. With this qualification in mind, the data is nonetheless robust and amenable to analysis. For example, a reliability analysis on the five issues re-coded to frequent/not frequent produces an alpha of 0.77.

13 See Working Time Regulations 1998 (Statutory Instruments 1998, No. 1833). The 48-hour limit is the average over a 17-week period. The regulations allow employers and employees to enter into agreements to exempt themselves from this limit.

14 This is identical to figures from the Spring 1998 Labour Force Survey where 13 per cent of employees said they worked over 48 hours per week in their main job. The question on working hours in the employee survey has a high level of missing response (5 per cent) which we believe may slightly underestimate the number working in excess of 48 hours per week. Most of these people gave an answer covering a range, rather than a single figure for usual hours.

15 As with the question on the usual duration of the working week, this question generated a high level of missing responses, 10 per cent in this case, around half of whom left the question blank. Some may have done so because they did not work overtime and, if this is the case, then our results may overstate levels of overtime.

16 Just over a quarter of the employees who did not usually work overtime (28 per cent, or 13 per cent of all employees) said that they *never* did so – these employees have been excluded from the analysis below.

17 A small percentage (3 per cent) of them gave more than one answer. One approach would have been to apportion their answers depending upon how many responses they gave, but as the overall frequencies did not alter we excluded them altogether from the analysis.

18 The ranges were chosen to approximate decile bands and the top and bottom 5 per cent of the earnings distribution as estimated from the 1996 New Earnings Survey. Where pay varied from week to week employees were asked to give an average figure. The level of missing responses to this question was low, just 1 per cent.

8 Employee attitudes to work

In this chapter we move into the realm of organisational psychology, trying to relate the substantive content of people's jobs to what they think of their work and their workplace. People's subjective assessments of their well-being at work may be affected by a variety of factors. Gallie *et al.* (1998) identify four: the nature of the work task; social integration in the workplace; participation in decision-making; and job security. Guest and Conway (1998) have an alternative list of 'antecedents' of motivation. In their model, how the workplace is managed and the organisational climate, together with individuals' experience of employment, help to determine the three elements of the 'psychological contract': fairness, trust, and delivery on promises made. These, in turn, shape people's attitudes to their work.

Common to both explanations is a recognition that people have different 'work orientations', the underlying values they bring to their work. It may be that these values differ systematically across particular types of workers so that, when we observe differences in attitudes, they are set against a varied tapestry of values. If, for example, part-timers have higher levels of job satisfaction than full-timers, is this because their jobs are 'better' in some objective sense, or part-timers are more easily satisfied? Differences in work orientations have also been explored across occupations, for example between professional and manual workers. We alluded to some of these differences in the last chapter when exploring reasons for working overtime.

It is most important to note that we did not attempt to define or measure employees' work orientations. This is an area where sociologists of work have been unable to agree on reliable measures, and one which is certainly not within the scope of a relatively short questionnaire. Can patterns in the attitudes of employees, identified in our results, be attributed to aspects of their employment relationship rather than differences in personal, underlying values? Our approach is to establish whether general patterns found in the data are consistent within sub-groups whose work orientation, we might anticipate, may be similar. If such patterns are found to persist, then they are likely to be independent of work orientation. The main employee characteristics we focus on are gender, occupation and the four-way division of working hours used in the last chapter.

Our end point in this chapter is a measure of job satisfaction. Evidence is built up cumulatively, on matters such as job security, job intensity, work-related stress and fair treatment to explain why some employees have higher levels of job satisfaction than others. In concluding, we explore the interaction between job satisfaction and organisational commitment, and make some preliminary observations about how these relate to management practice.

Job security

The issue of job security has been one of the most discussed issues of the 1990s, despite little objective evidence that jobs are much less secure now than in the recent past. Economists, for example, have looked closely at job tenure and found a small fall in the median duration of jobs for men, but not for women (Gregg and Wadsworth, 1995). It may be, however, that people *perceive* themselves to be less secure. Evidence from pollsters International Survey Research (1997) suggests this to be the case, with the proportion of UK employees feeling secure in their job falling each year in the 1990s. Whether their perceptions are accurate or not may not matter. Insecurity is thought to be associated with lower morale and lower commitment among employees and may, therefore, have deleterious consequences for workplace performance (Gallie *et al.*, 1998). We explore perceptions of security from the individual perspective, but also examine the environment in which people work and whether this too has any bearing.

Felstead *et al.* (1998) distinguish between two different elements of insecurity: the chances of losing the current job, and the anticipated difficulty in obtaining another. Our measure is based on a single indicator: employees were asked the extent to which they agreed or disagreed with the statement that 'I feel my job is secure in this workplace'. As we shall see, some of the patterns identified suggest that both elements identified by Felstead *et al.* were captured in this measure.

The overall picture is one of relative security, not insecurity – 60 per cent of employees agreed or strongly agreed with the statement and just 20 per cent disagreed. Women were slightly more likely than men to say they felt secure in their jobs, 63 per cent compared with 56 per cent. Similarly, part-time workers were more likely than full-timers to feel secure, 67 per cent compared with 57 per cent. Disentangling these two effects, we find that gender was slightly more important than hours of work. But of even greater importance was age, where the most secure were those aged under 20 (72 per cent) and those in their sixties (73 per cent). One explanation for this might be that the cost of losing a job at either end of one's career is relatively low, so feelings of security are partly contingent upon the consequences, as well as the risk, of job loss. Consistent with this argument, we find the U-shaped pattern to be similar for full and part-time workers, but part-time workers always felt more secure than full-time workers, irrespective of age. This means that the least secure of all were full-time workers in the prime of their careers – it is these who, arguably, have the most to lose from job loss – where around half (53 per cent) said they felt secure in their jobs. To reinforce this, among full-time workers, it was parents who reported lower levels of job security.

As might be expected, employees in non-permanent jobs felt substantially less secure than those in permanent jobs – 36 per cent of temporary workers and 39 per cent of those on fixed-term contracts felt secure, compared with 61 per cent of permanent employees. However, permanent workers who worked *alongside* non-permanent workers also felt less secure.[1] Among permanent employees in workplaces which used temporary agency workers ('temps'), 56 per cent felt that their job was secure. This compared with two-thirds (66 per cent) of permanent employees in workplaces where no temps were used. There was a much less pronounced difference where permanent employees worked together with those on fixed-term contracts, 60 per cent compared with 63 per cent, but the association was still a negative one. This suggests that one of the consequences for employers of engaging staff on fixed-term contracts, or using temps, may be a heightened sense of job insecurity among the permanent workforce.

There were also substantial differences in job security according to occupation; however, unlike many of the associations that we observed in the previous chapter, there was no clear hierarchical pattern. The highest levels of job security were found among sales workers (73 per cent) and personal service workers (68 per cent), while technical workers were the least secure (52 per cent). Managers, themselves, were among the least secure with only 56 per cent saying they felt secure in their jobs.

The single factor most clearly related to a sense of job security was job influence, as Figure 8.1 shows. Over two-thirds of those with a lot of job influence felt secure, compared with well under half of those with no influence. Moreover, for each occupational group, the percentage of employees who felt secure in their job was higher where job influence was higher. For example, we saw above that technical workers had the lowest level of job security, but those who had a lot of job influence felt much more secure than those with no influence over their jobs, 63 per cent compared with 36 per cent.

Factors such as age, occupation and job influence all vary across employees within a workplace. What, though, of the broader work environment – were there some workplaces in which workers *as a whole* felt more or less secure? In the management interview, managers were asked whether they agreed or disagreed with the statement that 'employees are led to expect long-term employment in this organisation'. In workplaces where management agreed with this statement, 63 per cent of employees said they felt secure in their jobs, compared with 44 per cent of those in workplaces where management disagreed. On the face of it, this suggests that workplace environment is important. Of course, it may be that management were reflecting the prevailing circumstances of the workplace rather than any deliberate policy. One way of examining this more closely is to examine practice and policy on job security as discussed in Chapter 4.

Table 8.1 shows how perceived job security was associated with various indicators of workplace practice and policy. In Chapter 4 we showed that workplaces with a policy of guaranteed job security or no compulsory redundancies

Figure 8.1 Perceived job security, by level of job influence

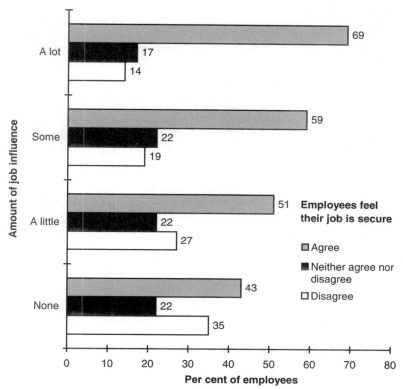

Base: All employees in workplaces with 25 or more employees.
Figures are weighted and based on responses from 23,894 employees.

were equally likely to have experienced workforce reductions in the preceding year. It was these reductions which appeared to weigh more with employees. There was no difference at all between employees in workplaces with a guaranteed job security policy and those without; but, where there had been workforce reductions, job security was lower – especially if these took the form of redundancies.

Seeing *jobs* disappear seems important, unlike the disappearance of individual employees through dismissal. It may be that employees perceive the risk of job loss through dismissal to be less random than workforce reductions (i.e. should they not step out of line their job will be secure), though it may surprise some that such an association does not hold given the wide disparities in dismissal rates seen in Chapter 6. Finally, these patterns were consistent whether or not management believed that long-term employment was to be expected; but, in all cases, perceived job security among employees was higher in workplaces where management agreed with this statement. This suggests that it may be possible for management to foster a general culture of relative job security.

Table 8.1 Perceived job security, by workplace level indicators

	Management view on: 'Employees are led to expect long-term employment in this organisation'		
	Agree	Neither agree nor disagree	Disagree
	% of employees agreeing job is secure	% of employees agreeing job is secure	% of employees agreeing job is secure
Guaranteed job security			
Yes	61	48	43
No	63	56	44
Method of workforce reduction			
No workforce reductions	67	58	54
No redundancies	59	53	39
Redundancies	55	51	34
Number of redundancies in past year			
None	66	55	50
1–9	59	59	40
10–19	53	52	41
More than 20	52	41	32
Number of dismissals in past year			
None	63	52	42
One only	65	57	55
2–5	62	58	45
6–10	62	58	47
More than 10	62	54	25
All employees	63	55	44

Base: All employees in workplaces with 25 or more employees.
Figures are weighted and based on responses from 24,280 (security), 24,345 (method), 23,759 (redundancies) 23,644 (dismissals) employees.

Perceptions of work intensity and work-related stress

As well as heightened job insecurity, another condition of contemporary work often highlighted by commentators is stress. Indeed, the two are popularly intertwined, although organisational psychologists point to a whole host of factors which can induce stress – many originating outside the work environment – and job security (or changes in it) is only one of these (Warr, 1998). Sometimes work intensity serves as a mediating factor, the so-called 'fear' factor whereby employees work harder to minimise the risk of job loss, thereby leading to work-related stress.

In the employee survey, we collected three separate measures of work intensity and work-related stress. The overall frequencies are presented in Figure 8.2. Three

Figure 8.2 Indicators of work intensity and work-related stress

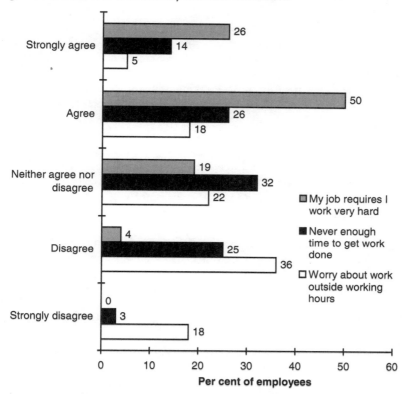

Base: All employees in workplaces with 25 or more employees.
Figures are weighted and based on responses from 25,560 (work hard), 25,298 (no time) and 25,261 (worry about work) employees.

in four employees felt their job required them to work very hard; four in ten thought they never had enough time to get their work done; and one in four worried a lot about their work outside working hours. The first two items are more to do with work intensity, whereas the third is more to do with work-related stress. While distinct, the remarks above suggest they may well be associated. This was quite evidently the case – in one direction. Of those employees who said they worried about work outside working hours, 89 per cent also agreed that they worked very hard, and 69 per cent said they never had enough time to get their work done. Put another way, among those who agreed with the two statements on work intensity, two-fifths then went on to agree that their work was stressful. We continue to look at the three indicators as a block as, by and large, the patterns of association are consistent across each of the measures.

On each of the three measures, the proportion of employees who agreed with the statements increased substantially with hours worked. Among those working fewer than 10 hours per week, 60 per cent said they worked very hard, 16 per cent claimed to be short of time and just 9 per cent worried about work outside working hours. For those working over 48 hours per week, these percentages were 82 per cent, 52 per cent and 34 per cent respectively.

Somewhat deceptively, the proportions of men and women agreeing with each of these statements were broadly similar. However, as women worked far fewer hours than men overall, this suggests that some gender differences are masked when looking at aggregate figures. After taking hours of work into account, two consistent differences arise. First, on each measure, women were more likely than men doing similar hours to agree that their jobs were intense and stressful. Take as an example women and men working 30 to 48 hours per week. In this group, 83 per cent of women claimed to be working very hard compared with 71 per cent of men, and there were also differences in those agreeing they had a lack of time to get work done (46 per cent of women and 39 per cent of men), and worrying a lot about their work (27 per cent of women and 22 per cent of men).

These differences may reflect the fact that women working full-time absorb a greater burden of domestic work than male full-timers (Wajcman, 1998). This also fits with our second consistent finding. Parents, both men and women alike, were more likely to report intense and stressful jobs than those without dependants. Especially notable were mothers working over 48 hours per week (of which, it must be said, there were relatively few), among whom over nine-tenths (93 per cent) said their job required them to work hard, four-fifths (79 per cent) had insufficient time to complete their work, and almost three-fifths (56 per cent) worried about their work outside working hours.

There were, as might be expected, substantial differences across occupational groups. On each measure, managers and professionals were more likely than other groups to agree that their jobs were intense and stressful, while the lowest proportions were found further down the occupational 'hierarchy' – though, it is worth noting that over two-thirds of employees in every occupation claimed that

Table 8.2 Indicators of job intensity and work-related stress, by perceived job security

	My job requires I work hard	Never enough time to get work done	Worry about work outside working hours
	% of employees who agree	% of employees who agree	% of employees who agree
Employees feel their job is secure			
Agree	77	37	19
Neither agree nor disagree	77	44	25
Disagree	73	47	34
All employees	76	41	23

Base: All employees in workplaces with 25 or more employees.
Figures are weighted and based on responses from 24,072 employees.

their job required them to work very hard. Public sector workers were more likely than private sector workers to agree with each of the measures, notably a lack of time to get work done, 49 per cent compared with 36 per cent. Workers in education reported the highest levels on each measure: 82 per cent said they had to work very hard, 56 per cent complained of insufficient time to get work done, and 37 per cent worried a lot about their work outside working hours. After taking account of occupation, it does appear that public sector workers are in jobs where they feel greater pressure and greater stress, with six of the nine occupations showing a significant difference in this area. Although more women than men worked in the public sector, this did not alter the general finding that women were more likely to say they had intense and stressful work.

Unlike perceptions of job security, the level of job intensity was not associated with recent job losses (where there is only a slight negative association), but what of the impact of job security itself? As noted at the start of this section, many commentators have claimed that heightened job insecurity will lead to greater levels of job intensity and stress, as workers work harder to stave off the prospect of job loss or, more directly, worry about the consequences of job loss. We were able to examine whether such associations exist, bearing in mind the limitations of cross-sectional data for this purpose. The results are shown in Table 8.2.

There was no clear link between perceived job security and how hard employees reported that they had to work. Given that there are equally plausible explanations for a positive or a negative association (e.g. 'I work hard because my job is insecure', or 'Because I work so hard I feel my job is secure') this should come as no surprise. However, on the other two measures, there were negative associations with perceived job security, the most substantial to do with our stress-related item: worrying about work outside working hours. The proportion of workers feeling insecure who worried about their work was almost double that of workers who felt secure in their jobs. This negative association was found across all occupational groups, and it therefore seems reasonable to conclude that job insecurity leads to greater levels of work-related stress. We will examine later in this chapter what other consequences there may be for the employment relationship.

Views about workplace managers

In the previous chapter, we examined provision and access for individual employees to flexible and family friendly working arrangements, off-the-job training and participation in workplace decision-making. Employees were also asked corresponding questions seeking their views on the management approach in each of these three areas. These can, therefore, be examined in relation to the substantive level of provision. Employees also provided an overall rating of fair treatment from managers. As the views of managers (as employees) are likely to be influenced by their own role in determining access we have excluded them from this section.

Management support for balancing work and family responsibilities

Just over half of all employees (52 per cent) agreed that managers at their workplace were 'understanding about employees having to meet family responsibilities', a quarter (26 per cent) neither agreed nor disagreed, and the remaining 22 per cent disagreed. The proportion of employees agreeing with the statement was higher where they had access to one of the five flexible and family friendly working arrangements discussed in the previous chapter (see Table 7.3), ranging from 67 per cent among employees who were able to work from home during normal working hours to, curiously, just 56 per cent where some form of assistance with child care was available. Where employees did not have access to any of these working arrangements, the proportion rating managers as being understanding about balancing both work and family dimensions fell to 42 per cent.

Women were more likely than men to agree, as were people working fewer hours. We know, from Chapter 7, that women generally reported greater access than men to flexible and family friendly working arrangements, but it was also the case that part-timers had less access than full-time employees. Over half (53 per cent) of part-time workers who had no access to the specified working arrangements agreed that managers were understanding about balancing work and family responsibilities. This was nearly identical to the proportion of full-time employees who *did* have access to one or more of these arrangements with the same view. It was parents who were at the polar extremes. Perceived management support was lowest among full-time employees with dependent children who had no access to any flexible or family friendly working arrangements (37 per cent), while it was greatest among parents working part-time who did (71 per cent). Nonetheless, *irrespective* of parental status and personal access to these working arrangements, part-timers were more positive. It may be that part-timers have more control over their own working hours, which allows them to balance both work and family responsibilities. Some might still consider it puzzling, however, that part-timers without dependants and with no access to flexible or family friendly working arrangements were as likely as full-timers in the opposite situation to find management supportive.[2]

Management support for skill development

Following the pattern of the previous question around half (49 per cent) of all non-managerial employees felt that, at their workplace, people were 'encouraged to develop their skills', a quarter (26 per cent) neither agreed nor disagreed, and the remaining 25 per cent felt they were not encouraged. Among employees who had received off-the-job training in the past 12 months, not surprisingly, levels of satisfaction with this aspect of their employment were more widespread. Just a third (35 per cent) of those who had no training in the past year thought they were encouraged to develop their skills, and the proportion reporting this rose steadily with the extent of training provision to reach 70 per cent among those who had received 10 or more days' training.

Women were more likely than men to think that workplace managers encouraged skill development, 54 per cent compared with 45 per cent, as too were part-time employees compared with full-time employees, though the difference was not as pronounced. This latter difference was, if anything, amplified after taking hours into account. For example, 43 per cent of employees working fewer than 10 hours per week who had received no training in the past year said that skill development was encouraged, compared with 29 per cent of employees working more than 48 hours per week in the same position. Given the number of hours these employees are devoting to work, it is perhaps understandable that relatively few agreed with the statement. As before, even where some training had been provided (and is, we assume, measured in equal units: days of working time) part-time employees were more positive about management's stance than full-timers.

Employees at workplaces with IiP accreditation were marginally more likely to believe that management encouraged skill development – 52 per cent compared with 48 per cent of workplaces without accreditation – and this difference persisted irrespective of the level of training provision. This might suggest that employees are more inclined to take at face value the IiP award (assuming they were aware of it) and the cultural change it is intended to engender, even though they may not have personally benefited (in the past year) from any training. However, a far more substantial influence was whether line managers helped to identify training needs; 62 per cent of employees agreed that skill development is encouraged where such discussions took place, compared with 37 per cent where they did not. And it was these discussions, rather than the formal IiP award, which accounted for the aggregate difference between employees working in workplaces with IiP or not.

Management support for employee participation

In Chapter 7 we looked at the incidence of employee involvement in workplace decision-making, finding that only a quarter of employees were frequently consulted on one or more of four issues we asked about. As well as this, employees were asked to rate how good they thought managers were over three different dimensions of employee involvement:

- keeping everyone up to date about proposed changes;
- providing everyone with the chance to comment on proposed changes; and,
- responding to suggestions from employees.

The proportion of (non-managerial) employees rating management as good or poor in each of these areas is shown in Figure 8.3, together with an overall summary measure of management support for employee involvement.[3] When compared with the previous two areas we have examined, the overall picture is much less favourable here. Managers do best, according to employees, at keeping them informed of proposed changes; but when it comes to consulting with them or

Figure 8.3 Employee views on management support for employee participation

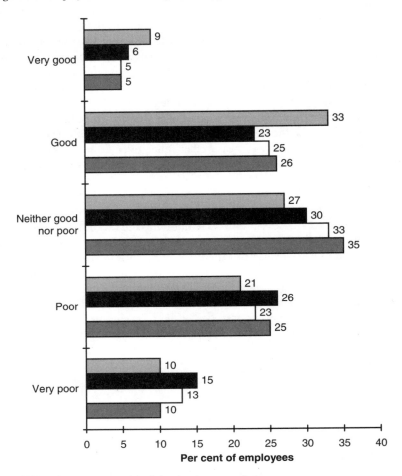

Keeping everyone up to date about proposed changes
Providing everyone with the chance to comment on proposed changes
Responding to suggestions from employees
Involving employees – overall scale

Base: All non-management employees in workplaces with 25 or more employees.
Figures are weighted and based on responses from 22,463 (keeping everyone up to date), 22,099 (chance to comment), 21,703 (responding to suggestions) and 21,352 (involving employees), employees.

taking on board their views, more employees rate management as poor than good. This was also the case for our overall scale of management support for employee involvement.

These aggregate level indicators mask a very high degree of variability across a range of employee characteristics. Once again, in common with the two previous areas, both women and part-time employees were more likely to rate management as good than either men or full-time employees. For example, 41 per cent of employees working fewer than 10 hours per week rated management as good at employee involvement, compared with just over a quarter (28 per cent) of those working over 48 hours per week. This is despite the relatively low level of consultation of part-time workers (see the account presented in Chapter 7). We return to this theme below, but first look at the association with the incidence of frequent consultation (see Table 7.5). Where there was no frequent consultation, just 22 per cent of employees rated management as good at consulting (and 41 per cent rated them poor), compared with 84 per cent among those (admittedly few) non-managerial employees who were frequently consulted on all four of the issues asked about.

There was also wide variability across workers of different occupations. However, unlike many of the associations identified in Chapter 7, there is no discernible 'hierarchical' pattern. Of all non-managerial groups, personal and protective service workers, and sales workers were most likely to rate management as good at employee involvement (both groups 38 per cent) while craft workers, and operative and assembly workers were least likely to rate them good (both groups 21 per cent).

A marked association was also evident with years of service: the longer employees have been at the workplace, the more likely they were to rate management poor. Nearly half of new recruits (44 per cent) rated management good at employee involvement and 21 per cent rated them poor. These proportions were reversed among those who had been at the same workplace for ten years or more, 25 per cent and 41 per cent respectively. Among those who reported no frequent consultation, 35 per cent of new recruits rated management good at consulting. This compares with just 17 per cent of those with ten or more years' service (among whom 48 per cent rated management poor at employee involvement). Contrast this with employees who said they were frequently consulted over one or more issues. Here, irrespective of the length of service, the number of employees rating management as good at employee involvement exceeds those rating it poor. This suggests that, in the long term, sustained non-involvement leads to disillusion with workplace management.

It also leads to disillusion among those who give the most to the workplace, in terms of working hours. Where there had been no frequent consultation, there was a large gulf between those working few and those working long hours. Among non-managerial employees in this position and who were working less than 10 hours per week, the proportion rating management as good at employee involvement was 31 per cent, roughly equal to the number rating them poor. Among those similarly not consulted and working over 48 hours per week, just 17 per cent rated management good and 50 per cent rated them poor at employee involvement. It seems that where the obligation of intense work is placed on employees, and there is no reciprocity in the form of employee involvement, disenchantment may result. We now turn to this more broadly through a summary measure of fairness.

Fair treatment

Thus far we have covered employee views on workplace managers' disposition towards balancing work and family responsibilities, skill development, and employee involvement. All of these, conceivably, might be issues employees take into account when they reflect on the essential fairness of the employment relationship. We asked employees to say whether or not they thought managers treated employees fairly, and we relate this to the three issues already covered in this section. The case for these three issues forming the basis of views on fair treatment is overwhelmingly supported by the data, as Figure 8.4 illustrates, where the associations are substantial and consistent. Where employees agreed that

Figure 8.4 Fairness in the employment relationship

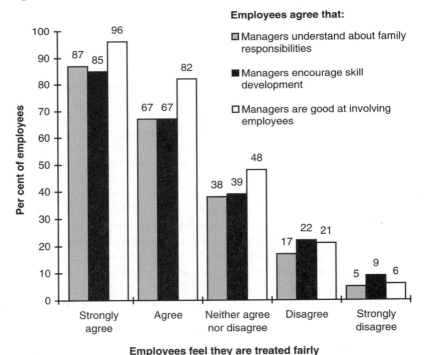

Base: All non-management employees in workplaces with 25 or more employees.
Figures are weighted and based on responses from 21,432 (bar 1), 21,731 (bar 2) and 21,091 (bar 3) employees.

managers were understanding about them meeting their family responsibilities, where they agreed that they were encouraged to develop their skills and where they rated management as good at employee involvement, then they thought themselves to be fairly treated. The associations were also symmetrical: where these things did not apply, employees did not think they were fairly treated.

We have already seen, elsewhere in this section, the types of individual and job characteristics most closely associated with fair treatment. It might also be that there are features of the workplace which are associated with employees' assessment of fair treatment. Table 8.3 looks at how it was related to workplace size, sector and industry. Employees were more likely to regard themselves as fairly treated where they worked in small workplaces. Perceptions of fair treatment also tended to be somewhat higher in the public sector. The two effects worked in combination, such that employees in large, private sector workplaces were the least likely to consider themselves fairly treated, whereas employees in small, public sector workplaces were the most likely to do so. There were also notable industry differences. Perceptions of fair treatment were more common in hotels and restaurants, and in education workplaces, while the lowest proportion of employees reporting fair treatment were found in manufacturing, and in transport and communication.

In workplaces with recognised unions, perceptions of fair treatment were lower – here, 47 per cent of employees said there was fair treatment at the workplace, compared with 53 per cent in workplaces with no recognised unions. A somewhat larger difference was evident depending upon whether the employee was a union member, with 43 per cent reporting fair treatment compared with 54 per cent of those who were not members. This difference persisted within workplaces with recognised unions. In fact, there was far greater similarity among union members, and among non-union members, irrespective of *where* they worked. Yet the question was explicitly couched in terms of the fairness of the employer. There are two possible ways of accounting for this difference. One is that, within workplaces, employers *do* treat union members less fairly than those who are not members. The other, perhaps more plausible interpretation, is that union members have different perceptions of what constitutes fair treatment. For example, union members might have an enhanced level of awareness – through contacts with worker representatives, union newsletters and the like – about the types of conditions that prevail in other workplaces. In short, their standards of fairness may be greater and consequently their reported attitudes are more tenuated despite what is, probably, equivalent treatment to that experienced by those who are not union members. Indirectly, this resonates with the broad issue raised in the introduction to this chapter: to what extent are attitudes conditioned by expectations and, more broadly, work orientations?

A further illustration is provided by part-time workers. By all the objective measures reported in the last chapter, they fared less well than full-timers. Part-timers were less likely to have access to flexible and family friendly working arrangements, less likely to have had off-the-job training in the past year, and less likely to have been frequently consulted on any issue. Yet, despite this, they were

Table 8.3 Fairness in the employment relationship, by workplace characteristics

	Non-managerial employees who say managers are good at treating them fairly		All employees
	Sector		
	Private	Public	
	% of employees	% of employees	% of employees
Workplace size			
25–49 employees	53	64	57
50–99 employees	52	51	52
100–199 employees	48	52	49
200–499 employees	46	49	47
500 or more employees	43	49	45
Industry			
Manufacturing	39	(14)	39
Electricity, gas and water	45	40	45
Construction	47	45	46
Wholesale and retail	53	(33)	53
Hotels and restaurants	61	57	60
Transport and communications	39	39	39
Financial services	54	–	54
Other business services	57	38	55
Public administration	–	49	49
Education	64	59	59
Health	58	53	54
Other community services	55	55	55
All employees	48	52	49

Base: All non-managerial employees in workplaces with 25 or more employees.
Figures are weighted and based on responses from 22,276 employees.

more likely to regard themselves as fairly treated than full-timers, and by a hefty margin – 61 per cent compared with 45 per cent.

Our employee questionnaire was never intended to measure expectations, and it would require a very different study to do so effectively, but attitudes to work do seem to be conditioned by expectations; and these expectations may be determined outside as well as inside the work environment. That is not to say that searching for associations across attitudinal items, or between attitudes and circumstances, is a pointless venture. On the contrary, we have identified systematic associations between these circumstances and attitudes. It is simply that one cannot afford to forget the interplay with expectations lurking in the background. This is a sound warning as we move into the final section on organisational commitment and job satisfaction.

Job satisfaction and employee commitment

If, as discussed at the outset of Chapter 7, the contemporary employment contract is essentially open-ended and includes implicit or psychological conditions, what dimensions of the relationship 'work best' for employees in encouraging commitment and enhancing job satisfaction? Employee commitment is a concept typically defined in terms of 'the strength of an individual's identification with and involvement in a particular organisation' (Mowday *et al.*, 1982). This notion of commitment is taken as embracing a wider role for the employee where his or her stake goes beyond income and the satisfaction of personal interests. The concept of job satisfaction is underpinned by a constellation of related attitudes about various aspects of an employee's job and facets of his or her working life: the challenges presented by work, by learning, and by levels of autonomy and control over job; the sense of achievement from work; the recognition received for work effort and work quality; and also earnings and other rewards obtained (Locke, 1976; Spector, 1997). The two are inter-related but, nonetheless, distinct measures and were measured distinctly in the survey. We begin by looking at job satisfaction, relating it to the other attitudinal items explored in this chapter, then turn to examine employee commitment and the extent to which it is a corollary of job satisfaction. Finally, we then relate employee commitment to 'high commitment' management practices and present some initial results on whether it is associated with superior workplace performance.

Job satisfaction

As Clark (1996) argues, job satisfaction is of interest for a range of reasons. As a measure of people's feelings about their working lives, it provides an important indicator of individual well-being. It may also provide insight into employees' decisions about the extent of their participation in the workplace, how hard they work, and whether or not they stay with their job. Employees were asked how satisfied or dissatisfied they were with four aspects of their working lives:

- the amount of influence they have over their job;
- the amount of pay they receive;
- the sense of achievement they get from their work; and
- the respect they get from their managers.

The results of each aspect of job satisfaction are presented for all employees in Figure 8.5, together with a job satisfaction scale which has been created to give a global picture.[4] On three of the individual measures – job influence, sense of achievement, and respect from managers – around three in five employees expressed a degree of job satisfaction with a significant minority (though no more than 15 per cent) saying that they were very satisfied with this aspect of their job. The lowest area of job satisfaction related to pay, with a third of employees feeling content but a higher proportion feeling dissatisfied. On each aspect, around a

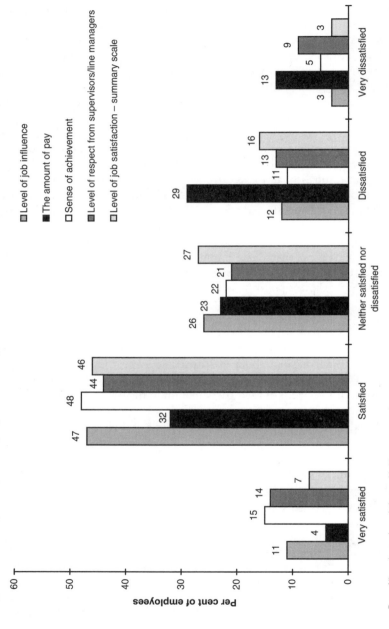

Figure 8.5 Level of job satisfaction, by aspects of working life

- Level of job influence
- The amount of pay
- Sense of achievement
- Level of respect from supervisors/line managers
- Level of job satisfaction – summary scale

Base: All employees in workplaces with 25 or more employees.
Figures are weighted and based on responses ranging from 25,031 (satisfaction) to 25,691 (pay) employees.

quarter of employees felt undecided about their feelings, or were unable to commit themselves either way, reporting that they were neither satisfied nor dissatisfied.

On the summary measure, fewer than one in ten employees were very satisfied with their jobs, almost half were satisfied, three in ten were neither satisfied nor dissatisfied, and the remaining two in ten said they were dissatisfied or very dissatisfied. While relations between gender and job satisfaction have been extremely inconsistent across studies (Spector, 1997), we find more women expressing positive views (58 per cent satisfied) than men (49 per cent), and almost a quarter of men (23 per cent) being dissatisfied with their job, compared to 15 per cent of women. Relative dissatisfaction among men was most pointed in relation to pay with 45 per cent unhappy with this aspect of their job, compared to 37 per cent of women.

In common with findings from other studies (Clark, 1996; Spector, 1997), significant differences in job satisfaction were also found in relation to the age of employees, the hours they worked and their occupation. The proportion of employees expressing positive views about work increased in line with age. Of younger employees, a half were satisfied with their job, compared with three-quarters of those aged 60 years and over.[5] This contrasts with length of service, where the longer an employee has been at the workplace, the *less* satisfied they are. Thus the most satisfied were older workers new to the job, and the least satisfied were younger workers who had not moved on since commencing work.

Part-time employees were more likely than full-time employees to be satisfied (62 per cent compared with 51 per cent) and the most widespread satisfaction was found among those working less than ten hours a week (66 per cent). Of all occupational groups, job satisfaction was far more evident among managers (71 per cent) than other occupational groups. In general, variation across other occupations was less pronounced; less than half of those employed in operative and assembly work, and craft and skilled services were satisfied with their jobs (40 per cent and 47 per cent, respectively).

So far this analysis has examined differences according to the principal individual and job characteristics. If job satisfaction is to have any salience in understanding and, in the longer term, enhancing the employment relationship, there must be demonstrated associations between levels of job satisfaction and other dimensions of the employment contract. This chapter has explored several of the more implicit aspects of the employment contract: job security, work intensity, work-related stress, and fair treatment. We show how each of these are associated with job satisfaction in Table 8.4. The table is restricted to non-managerial employees because, as noted above, managers are able to shape a number of the implicit aspects of the employment contract. On every single dimension, part-time employees were more likely to be satisfied than full-timers, with the order of difference for the most part around about 10 percentage points. Taking these dimensions in order, job influence (as was apparent in Chapter 7) appears to be a critical factor in explaining job satisfaction. Those with a lot of job influence were five times more likely to be satisfied with their job than those with no job influence. This is important because we showed that job influence

Table 8.4 Job satisfaction, by non-managerial employee attitudes to work and full-time/part-time status

	Employees expressing a high level of job satisfaction (summary measure)		
	Part-time (less than 30 hours per week)	Full-time (30 or more hours per week)	All employees
	% of employees	% of employees	% of employees
Level of job influence			
A lot	82	69	72
Some	64	51	54
A little	47	26	32
None	27	10	15
Employees feel their job is secure			
Agree	70	59	62
Neither agree nor disagree	47	41	43
Disagree	40	28	31
My job requires I work hard			
Agree	61	49	52
Neither agree nor disagree	60	46	50
Disagree	59	43	48
Never enough time to get work done			
Agree	52	44	45
Neither agree nor disagree	58	49	51
Disagree	69	55	59
Worry about work outside working hours			
Agree	50	43	44
Neither agree nor disagree	57	51	52
Disagree	64	50	54
Managers understand about family responsibilities			
Agree	75	65	68
Neither agree nor disagree	50	44	45
Disagree	25	19	20
Managers encourage skill development			
Agree	77	68	71
Neither agree nor disagree	52	42	44
Disagree	29	19	21
Managers are good at involving employees			
Agree	84	77	79
Neither agree nor disagree	55	50	51
Disagree	32	25	26
Managers treat employees fairly			
Agree	78	72	74
Neither agree nor disagree	42	40	40
Disagree	26	17	19
All employees	61	48	52

Base: All non-managerial employees in workplaces with 25 or more employees.
Figures are weighted and based on responses from 19,838 (fair treatment) to 20,939 (family responsibilities) employees.

was largely independent of gender and working hours and (for non-managerial employees) only slightly related to occupation.

Differences were not so wide-ranging when it came to job security, but were still substantial. Across all employees, the proportion who were satisfied with their job roughly doubled comparing those who felt insecure about their job with those who said they were secure. However, the various measures of work intensity and work-related stress we explored were nowhere near as strongly related. Indeed, the findings here show clearly that work intensity has a quite different consequence for job satisfaction than stress-related measures – satisfaction levels were marginally higher among those who said they were required to work hard, whereas they were considerably lower among employees who complained of a shortage of time and who were worried about their work outside working hours.

The four measures we explored in the section on views about workplace managers were all strongly and positively associated with job satisfaction. Indeed, the pattern is nearly identical across each measure. Where employees thought that management showed understanding about balancing work and family responsibilities, encouraged skill development, involved them and treated them fairly, they were much more likely to be satisfied. This is not just a matter of employees ticking all the 'agree' boxes throughout the questionnaire. As we have shown, employees' views on all of these matters were strongly related to their actual experience. The findings show unequivocally the circumstances under which some employees feel more content about their jobs – does this, then, translate into higher commitment?

Employee commitment

In the last chapter, when examining the motivation for working overtime, commitment was explored indirectly. We now turn to a *direct* measure of employees' views from a series of questions about the extent to which they shared the goals and values of their organisation.[6] Employees were asked the extent to which they agreed or disagreed with a series of statements as follows:

- I share many of the values of my organisation;
- I feel loyal to my organisation; and,
- I am proud to tell people who I work for.

Across employees as a whole, a majority were in agreement with all three statements relating to workplace commitment, the most widespread display being a sense of loyalty (see Figure 8.6). In general, men and women did not differ in relation to these measures with both showing virtually equal levels of agreement, although women were more likely to express a sense of loyalty than men (69 per cent compared to 61 per cent).

Strong differences were, however, evident across occupations, with managers and professionals demonstrating the most widespread commitment. Of managers, 81 per cent said they felt loyal to their organisation, 76 per cent shared many of

Figure 8.6 Indicators of employee commitment

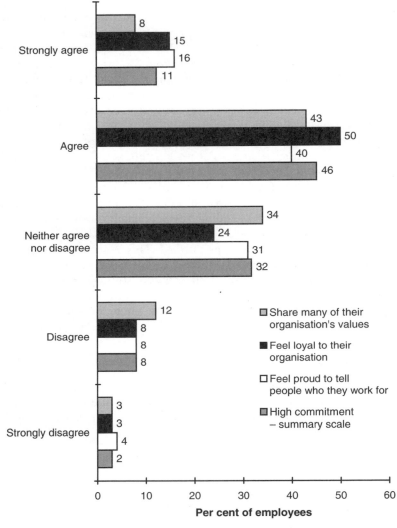

Base: All employees in workplaces with 25 or more employees.
Figures are weighted and based on responses from 24,466 (share values), 25,404 (feel loyal),
25,417 (feel proud) and 24,070 (high commitment) employees.

the organisation's values, and 72 per cent felt proud to tell people who they work for. This level of attachment was simply not shared among other occupational groups. While in most occupations a majority of employees were committed on each of the dimensions, significantly lower levels of commitment were found among craft and skilled workers, and those engaged in operative and assembly work. Among these groups, commitment levels were as much as 20 percentage points lower than among employees as a whole.

Taking these measures as a whole it has been possible to create a single workplace commitment scale, also shown in Figure 8.6.[7] Across all employees, well over half (57 per cent) had an overall high commitment score, with 11 per cent scoring very high. Just one in ten employees demonstrated a low commitment to their workplace, and the remaining third (32 per cent) fall into the middle band of neither high nor low commitment. Taking this umbrella measure, which categories of employees were most clearly associated with high and low levels of employee commitment?

As suggested above, occupation was closely associated with commitment. It followed a similar pattern on the summary scale as on the individual measures; high commitment was more widespread among managers and professionals, but far less evident among craft and skilled workers and operative and assembly workers. In all occupational groups, bar the latter, part-time employees were more likely to report high commitment than full-timers. In fact, there was a slight U-shaped association between hours of work and commitment, with the highest levels found among those working the fewest hours (68 per cent) and those working the longest (63 per cent). Excluding managers, the U-shape remains: those displaying high commitment among employees working long hours fell to 57 per cent, though it remained lowest of all among (non-managerial) employees working between 30 and 48 hours per week (52 per cent).

The fact that many of those working over 48 hours per week were not directly reimbursed for doing so might be taken as an indicator of high commitment, but we can explore this more concretely by relating back to the reason for working overtime (see Table 7.7). The results are presented in Figure 8.7. The two extremes are represented by the employees who said they worked overtime because they enjoyed their work, of whom nine in ten expressed a sense of commitment, compared with just four in ten of those who worked overtime because they needed the money. Those who did not want to let colleagues down evinced somewhat higher commitment than those who worked overtime to get the job done.

Finally, there was a very high degree of association between commitment and job satisfaction. Of those employees who voiced very high levels of commitment to the workplace, 88 per cent were satisfied with their job overall, compared with just 5 per cent where employees had very low commitment.

Employee commitment, high commitment management practices and workplace performance

Thus far we have neglected possible workplace factors in exploring differences in job satisfaction and employee commitment. Employees in smaller workplaces (62 per cent), smaller organisations (60 per cent) and the public sector (60 per cent) were all more likely to have high commitment. Among employees working in education (70 per cent) and health (64 per cent), high commitment was even more evident, while workers in transport and communication had the lowest

Figure 8.7 Employees with high commitment, by main reasons for working overtime

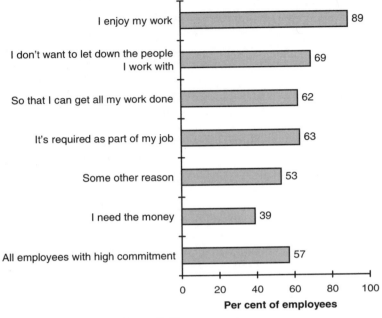

Base: All employees in workplaces with 25 or more employees.
Figures are weighted and based on responses from 23,386 employees.

proportion of highly-committed employees (48 per cent). Given the very high correlation with job satisfaction it is not surprising that we found the same workplace patterns accounting for the major differences between satisfied and dissatisfied workers.

While of some contextual interest, these figures do not shed much light on how management practices at the workplace might be related to employee commitment. In Chapters 3 and 4 we looked at a raft of management initiatives, many of which are thought to engender commitment among employees. There is insufficient space to discuss associations between particular management practices and commitment; and, at any rate, the received wisdom is that it is the way such practices operate in tandem that matters. Our most simple measure of this is the count of the number of 'high commitment' management practices presented in Table 4.12. There was a strong positive association between employee commitment and the number of these practices in place. Across all employees, 61 per cent of those in workplaces where a majority of the practices were in place were highly committed, compared with 47 per cent where no more than a few of the practices were in place. The most substantial differences were among full-time employees in the largest occupational group, where the respective figures were 58 per cent and 38 per cent. This suggests a clear connection between management initiatives to promote commitment and how employees respond to these initiatives.

We have already shown, in the conclusion to Chapter 6, that high commitment management practices are related to measures of workplace economic performance and well-being. Table 8.5 examines how a selection of these measures are related to employee commitment. The findings are consistent, though the scale of the differences is quite modest. Employees who were highly committed to their job were more likely to be working in better-performing workplaces than those who had low commitment. For instance, 14 per cent of employees with very high levels of commitment were employed in workplaces with above average financial performance, compared with just 8 per cent of employees with very low commitment.

This is not an ideal approach to such analyses. What matters more, for determining workplace performance, is whether employees *as a whole* at a given workplace are committed or not. Within workplaces, it was rare for all employees to be highly committed – in just 3 per cent of workplaces was this the case – but there was a reasonable spread on the average commitment score. What Table 8.5 appears to suggest is an overall commitment 'effect'. To examine this adequately requires a shift in the unit of analysis to the workplace and a more elaborate statistical treatment – this is the subject of Chapter 12.

Conclusion

Employee accounts of the employment relationship have a very high degree of internal consistency. The associations found between all the different aspects of the implicit contract all make good sense. This is heartening in one respect, but also raises an issue of fundamental importance. On the one hand, practitioners reading this are provided with robust evidence that the route by which to promote job satisfaction and employee commitment is to give employees secure jobs, that are not too stressful, and to treat them fairly by acknowledging their life outside of work, encourage skill development and involve them in changes to the workplace. None of this is new, but the scale of the associations we have found provide compelling evidence of their force. On the other hand, we are discussing attitudinal measures, and the associations between these and the grit and substance of workplace-level initiatives was sometimes only slight – for example, employees felt no more secure in their jobs if they were covered by a policy of guaranteed job security or no compulsory redundancies. In some areas, though, management actions mattered – taking the example of job security once more, employees felt less secure where there had been recent redundancies.

Throughout the chapter we have had to contend with findings which, at first glance, appear to be at odds with objective circumstances. These were most evident when comparing part-time with full-time employees. In all of the areas examined in Chapter 7, part-timers fared worse than full-timers on substantive job content, having less training, were less likely to be consulted, less well-paid and so on. In the attitudinal items examined in this chapter, though, part-timers have uniformly been more positive than full-timers. Once working hours were taken into account, it was apparent that objective circumstances *were* related to attitudes in expected

Table 8.5 Workplace performance and well-being, by employee commitment

	Workplace performance			
	Above average financial performance	*Above average labour productivity*	*Rate of voluntary resignations*	*Rate of dismissals*
	% of employees	*% of employees*	*Average rate per 100 employees*	*Average rate per 100 employees*
Level of employee commitment				
Very high	14	11	11.7	1.1
High	15	10	11.4	1.0
Neither high nor low	14	9	12.5	1.2
Low	10	6	12.3	1.4
Very low	8	7	12.6	1.7
All employees	14	9	11.9	1.1

Base: All employees in workplaces with 25 or more employees.
Figures are weighted and based on responses from 23,710 (column 1), 23,556 (column 2), 23,081 (column 3) and 23,285 (column 4) employees.

ways, but there was no eroding the broad gap in the disposition of part-timers compared with full-timers.

As stated at the outset of the chapter, one possible explanation for these differences is that of work orientations. Yet it would be a mistake to reduce this to a blunt statement, for example, that part-timers have a marginal attachment to work and hence have lower expectations of it. We illustrate with two examples.

Among part-time employees, there were three distinct clusters of employees: those less than thirty years old without dependants; mothers working part-time; and people in their fifties who never had or no longer had dependants. Together they accounted for nearly all part-timers. We identified, at the start of the chapter, that older and younger part-time workers were the most likely to feel secure. Similar proportions of all three groups said they were fairly treated by management, but thereafter the picture differed. Young part-timers had substantially lower levels of commitment and job satisfaction than older part-timers. Mothers working part-time fell midway between these two groups.

A further example is the very large differences in commitment shown by those with differing motives for working overtime. Those who did it for the money were far less likely than other groups to be highly committed, even though they usually worked long hours. If we regard these people as broadly 'instrumental' in their approach to work, and contrast them with those who were not directly rewarded for working overtime, further stark differences emerged. While broadly equal proportions thought their jobs were secure, the 'instrumentalists' were about half as likely to worry about work outside working hours, regard themselves as fairly treated, and to consider themselves to have satisfying jobs.

In both cases these differences went beyond occupation, working hours and gender being related to a host of aspects of employee's working lives and their experience of the employment contract. They were, in fact, most closely related to job influence. This has been a recurring theme throughout the past two chapters. More than any other indicator, job influence appears to have captured the essence of the implicit aspects of the employment contract. Not only this, the implicit contract also appears to count in determining employee commitment, which was more in evidence in workplaces with a greater number of high commitment management practices.

Notes

1 'Alongside' is defined as there being some non-permanent employees working at the workplace, as captured in the management interview (see Chapter 3).
2 Unless part-time workers regard the very fact that they are able to work part-time as an indicator of an understanding attitude on the part of management.
3 The scores for each of the three items were summed, then scaled back to the original categories. The scale was found to be highly reliable (Cronbach alpha = 0.88).
4 Scale created as described above, with alpha = 0.73
5 Clark (1996) found a slightly different pattern when examining age in relation to overall job satisfaction noting a U-shaped relationship, with those in their early working years expressing some satisfaction, reducing among those in their mid-thirties, and then becoming more widespread among those at the end of their working lives. With our data, this relationship only holds for male full-timers.
6 After cognitive testing, the term 'organisation' was used in preference to 'workplace', given that so many people worked for large organisations with many sites and this, rather than the specific workplace, was the main way in which they identified with their employer.
7 Scale created as described above (alpha = 0.83).

9 The role and activities of worker representatives

The third group of respondents in WERS 98 were worker representatives. They have been a permanent feature of the survey series. The primary role of a worker representative is to act as an intermediary between employees and management. Where a representative is present as a result of a union being recognised, their duties will also cover matters related to union organisation. Their role will be shaped by the concerns and needs of the employees they represent; but, as secondary agents, their 'existence and operation are conditioned by the employing organizations of those represented' (Hyman, 1997: 309). The purpose of this chapter is to unpick these two and, in doing so, to describe the activities of worker representatives in Britain.

As if to symbolise the conditional nature of their role, our access to worker representatives was through the avenue of workplace managers. There were two types of worker representatives potentially identified in the course of the management interview, who were then selected for interview themselves. The first, and by far the most common type, were those formally representing recognised trade unions, who we refer to as lay union representatives.[1] The selected respondent was the most senior representative of whichever recognised union had the most members at the workplace. They had to be either an employee of the workplace, or an employee of another workplace in the same organisation with responsibility for representing union members at the sampled workplace.[2] Interviews were never conducted with full-time union officials, that is, employees of the union. In workplaces without union recognition, a second type of worker representative was potentially selected for interview. These 'non-union representatives' were the most senior employee sitting on a workplace-based joint consultative committee. Overall, 860 interviews were conducted and are used in this analysis, 815 with lay union representatives and 45 with non-union representatives.[3]

The object of including non-union representatives was to see whether, and how, their role and activities differed from union representatives. Our attempts to do so were hindered by the small numbers of these representatives. Apart from their small numbers, an additional problem was the high proportion of managers within this group (29 per cent), which raises some doubts about the independence of these representatives. The bulk of this chapter, therefore, concentrates on the activities of union representatives.

British trade unions have long been characterised by extensive systems of workplace representation that give employees direct access to a collective voice at work. The closeness of this relationship, defined in a wider sense than just physical location – someone who shares common traits and values – is meant to ensure that members' concerns are relayed to management both promptly and with a greater understanding of the issues. This contrasts with many European systems where members are represented by officials from within the union's organisation (Terry, 1995). Questions remain, however, about the modern role of worker representatives – these reprise many of the issues raised in Chapter 5 about the purpose and character of workplace trade unions.

The worker representative sample is not a general sample of worker representatives, but of senior representatives (in cases where managers gave authority for the interview to proceed).[4] It is, therefore, not possible to claim that our analysis is representative of *all* worker representatives. Rather, what we have is a representative sub-sample of workplaces where we are able to present a portrait of the character of workplace employment relations from the perspective of the most senior (and, presumably, the most informed) worker representative at the workplace.

The chapter commences by describing how the representative function is structured across organisations, drawing on management data. For the reasons described above, the focus then narrows to union representatives, where we examine their characteristics and activities. Finally, we evaluate the relationships that representatives have with both managers and employees.

Where are the representatives?

In Chapter 5 we saw that two-fifths (40 per cent) of workplaces had worker representatives, mostly lay union representatives. The majority of non-union representatives were in workplaces where they were the only form of representation available to employees. The number of workplaces with 'dual channels' of employee representation was small. In 4 per cent of all workplaces (or in 13 per cent of workplaces with a union representative present at the workplace), dual channels were found.

Fewer than half of all workplaces with a representative relied on just one employee to fulfil this role. In Chapter 5 we showed that the average number of representatives per workplace was 4.3. A better measure of the depth and importance of representation at the workplace is the number of employees per representative. The character of representation is likely to be very different, for example, in cases where one representative covers a workforce of 1,000 compared with one covering 100 workers. Starting with lay union representatives, each one on average represented 28 union members. This figure may underestimate the actual number they represent given the possibility that some non-union members may be 'free-riders', benefiting from the activities of the representative. If it was assumed that all employees in a workplace, union members or not, were covered by representative activities, then each lay union representative covered 53 employees – this constitutes an upper bound.

We would expect to see variation in the ratio of union members to representatives according to the number of employees at each workplace.[5] With more employees to select from, larger workplaces should generate more union representatives, which, other things being equal, would tend to make the ratio smaller (Brown *et al.*, 1978). Offsetting this are economies of scale that arise once a 'critical mass' of representatives exists. For example, ten representatives in a large workplace may be able to do the same job as well as eleven. Past evidence has shown that the second factor outweighs the first, and this is confirmed in Table 9.1. The ratio of union members to union representatives in the largest workplaces was a little over three times that in the smallest. There was little difference in the ratio between the private and public sectors, but differences were much more pronounced across industries. For example, in financial services the average number of union members per union representative (43:1) was more than twice that in education (18:1). Most of the industry differences arose from variations in the size of workplaces across industries.

The ratio might be expected to differ depending upon the number of recognised unions at the workplace. Overall, there was little difference in the ratio in workplaces where there was a single recognised union (27:1), compared with workplaces with multiple unions (29:1). This is largely because the increased number of representatives that arises from more unions at the workplace is almost exactly offset by a higher average workplace size and union density in these workplaces.

For non-union representatives, it is less straightforward to identify their 'constituency'. If we assume that they acted on behalf of *all* employees at the workplace, there were 44 employees per non-union representative. Among workplaces with no union presence, the ratio fell to 24 employees for every non-

Table 9.1 Number of employees per representative, by workplace size

	Union members per union representative	Employees per non-union representative
	Mean	Mean
Workplace size		
25–49 employees	17	(19)
50–99 employees	28	(26)
100–199 employees	34	40
200–499 employees	42	92
500 or more employees	53	289
All workplaces	28	44

Base: All workplaces with a union representative (column 1) and all workplaces with a non-union representative (column 2) and 25 or more employees.
Figures are weighted and based on responses from 932 (column 1) and 290 (column 2) managers.

union representative. In the 4 per cent of workplaces where there were dual channels of representation, there were 27 employees for every (lay union and non-union) representative. As with union representatives, workplace size was closely related to the ratio of employees to non-union representatives – see Table 9.1. In small- and medium-sized workplaces the ratio was broadly equivalent to the union representative to union members ratio, but in larger workplaces it was much higher.

Who are the representatives?

The preceding section was based on information provided in the course of the management interview. For the detail on the characteristics and activities of worker representatives, we turn to the interviews conducted with them. As noted in the introduction to this chapter, given the low number of non-union representatives in our sample, together with doubts about their overall independence from management, we exclude them from the remainder of the analysis and look simply at union representatives.

Characteristics of union representatives

The typical (senior) union representative was male (65 per cent), and had been employed at his workplace for 11 years, six of those years as a representative. He was formally elected into the position and had at some time received training on how to perform his duties. He did not hold an official position with his union either at a national, regional or district level.

Notwithstanding the caveats given in the introduction, it is instructive to see how far this typical union representative differs from the typical union member in terms of personal and job characteristics. Table 9.2 shows the composition of union representatives by occupation and gender, and compares this with the composition of union members in the same workplaces.[6] The latter data is taken from the employee survey. Union representatives were employed across all nine occupational categories, with professionals being, by far, the largest single group. The proportion of union representatives employed as professionals was more than double that of union members in the same workplaces. By contrast, the proportion of union representatives who were operative and assembly workers was almost half that of union members.

Recent work by the Labour Research Department (1998) suggests there is a disparity between the gender mix of union members and that of union officials.[7] Table 9.2 shows a similar (but slight) imbalance between union representatives and members. Two-thirds of union representatives in our sample were men, and this was about 3 percentage points higher than the proportion of union members in the same workplaces who were men. A further way of capturing this is to look at the gender mix of union members *within* workplaces and see how this is associated with the gender of their representatives. In workplaces where half or more of union members were women, 59 per cent of the union representatives

Table 9.2 Gender of union representatives and union members, by occupation

	Union representatives			Union members		
	Male	Female	All representatives	Male	Female	All members
	% of representatives	% of representatives	% of representatives	% of employees	% of employees	% of employees
Occupation						
Managers and administrators	6	3	10	2	6	13
Professional	16	17	33	6	7	11
Associate professional and technical	6	1	6	4	7	14
Clerical and secretarial	4	5	10	4	10	14
Craft and related	11	1	12	13	1	14
Personal and protective service	6	4	10	5	4	9
Sales	2	2	4	1	3	3
Plant and machine operatives	10	1	11	18	3	21
Other occupations	3	1	4	5	3	8
All workplaces	64	36	100	61	39	100

Base: All workplaces with a union representative where SEQ's were successfully placed and 25 or more employees.
Figures are weighted and based on responses from 747 (columns 1–3) union representatives and 7,625 (columns 4–6) employees.

we interviewed were also women. In contrast, 96 per cent of the workplaces with a majority of male union members had male union representatives.

It might be thought that this pattern simply reflects differences in the gender composition of employment (rather than union membership), but when examining this the pattern is almost exactly replicated. Moreover, examining each industry separately, the patterns are similar if somewhat less pronounced. For example, in education and health – both industries with very high proportions of female employment – the proportion of workplaces where half or more of union members were women and where a female union representative was interviewed were 63 and 62 per cent respectively, only slightly higher than the average for all workplaces.

The evidence presented above clearly points to imbalances in the occupational composition, less so in the gender mix, of union representatives when compared with their members. Hyman (1997: 310) argues that we should not necessarily expect representatives to share the characteristics of their members 'if only because they normally require a distinctive set of motivational qualities'. This argument suggests that the more pertinent question is whether the union representative legitimately represents the interests of his or her members. Where they have been directly elected by the members, this is more likely to be the case. Overall, 58 per cent of union representatives were elected by the members, 30 per cent were volunteers, and 12 per cent became a representative through some other means. Male representatives were much more likely than female representatives to be elected, and professionals and associate professionals were the most likely to have volunteered. Elected representatives had been carrying out representative duties longer than other representatives, an average of 8.9 years compared with 5.5 for volunteers.

Training for representative duties

As already noted, the typical representative had received some training for their role – in fact, the exact proportion was 70 per cent. The three in ten union representatives who had not been trained were more likely to be found in small workplaces, and this applied to both public sector and private sector workplaces. Not surprisingly, there was a strong association between the proportion of representatives with training and how long they had been performing these duties. Around nine in ten (91 per cent) of those who had been representatives for ten or more years had been trained at some stage compared with under half (44 per cent) of those in this role for one year or less. Elected representatives (83 per cent) were also much more likely to have been trained than volunteers (49 per cent), even after taking into account the number of years spent as a representative.

Just under a third of all union representatives had received training in the year preceding the survey. They were asked what this training entailed and Figure 9.1 gives a breakdown of the responses. About three in ten representatives mentioned a course that covered a wide variety of matters, or was too specific to be grouped, or lacked detail as to its content. We have put these into the 'other' category.

Figure 9.1 Types of training received by union representatives

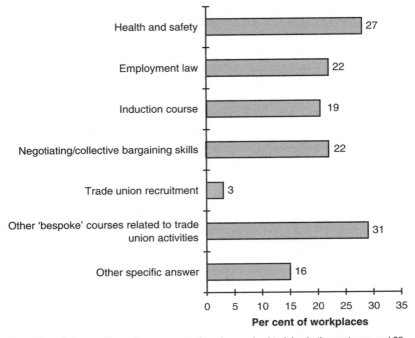

Base: All workplaces with a union representative who received training in the past year and 25
or more employees.
Figures are weighted and based on responses from 274 union representatives.

Where it was possible to identify the course content from the responses given, there was an even spread across most topics covered, with one in four receiving training in health and safety, and one in five having taken part in an induction course. Very few union representatives in their first year in the role received training other than the induction course. What may surprise some was the very small number who had attended dedicated courses on recruitment of union members, especially given the declining membership faced by most unions. It may be that induction courses and the 'other' courses covered recruitment, but the scale of the difference when compared with, say, employment law does suggest less emphasis is given to training in this area.

What do the representatives do?

Relatively little detailed research has been undertaken into the activities of union representatives since the seminal work of Batstone *et al.* (1977) two decades ago. Godfrey and Marchington (1996) is a recent exception. Their study, based on interviews with 76 'shop stewards',[8] concluded that 'the stewards of the 1990s are remarkably similar to those described in earlier studies' with 'remarkable stability in their influence and role' (1996: 343). Much of our questioning of worker representatives was designed to explore the issues of influence and role, and this section looks directly at their activities.

A union representative's role can be split into two functions: as an agent of their union; and as a spokesperson for employees at their workplace. The balance between these functions is unlikely to be constant. It may vary over time, by the characteristics of the representative, or according to workplace characteristics. Before exploring that, we need to put firm parameters around the concept of union representatives activities by looking at the amount of time they devote to the role.

Time spent on representative activities

Representatives were asked how much time they spent each week on representative activities, both at the workplace *and* outside working hours. The results are reported in Figure 9.2. A majority of (senior) union representatives spent less than two hours per week on representative activities; indeed, it was most common of all to spend less than one hour per week. Around one in five spent more than ten hours per week, and they were much more likely to do this if they represented union members from another site within the organisation (37 per cent).

Those representatives who spent more hours were much more likely to be employed in large workplaces, as shown in Table 9.3. For example, six in ten union representatives in the largest workplaces carried out their duties for more than ten hours per week, six times the proportion in the smallest workplaces. Similarly, those doing the fewest hours were most likely to be in the smallest workplaces. There were no major differences in time spent when comparing private

Figure 9.2 Time spent representing union members

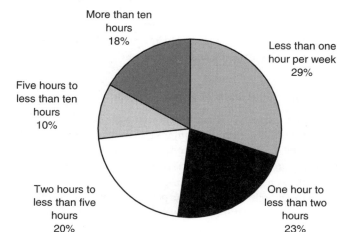

Base: All workplaces with a union representative and 25 or more employees.
Figures are weighted and based on responses from 811 union representatives.

Table 9.3 Time spent on representative duties, by workplace size

	Time spent on duties by union representatives		
	Less than one hour per week	One to less than 10 hours per week	More than 10 hours per week
	% of workplaces	% of workplaces	% of workplaces
Workplace size			
25–49 employees	51	39	10
50–99 employees	20	69	11
100–199 employees	15	66	19
200–499 employees	7	53	40
500 or more employees	3	37	60
All workplaces	29	52	18

Base: All workplaces with a union representative and 25 or more employees.
Figures are weighted and based on responses from 811 union representatives.

or public sector union representatives; however, in the private sector, there was a strong positive association between union density and the number of hours spent representing employees.[9] For example, where union density was at least half, 27 per cent of union representatives in the private sector spent more than ten hours per week on union activities, whereas where density was below half only 13 per cent spent an equivalent amount of time.

Over four-fifths (82 per cent) of union representatives were paid by their employer for time spent on representative duties while at work. Being paid was less likely the fewer hours spent – two-thirds (65 per cent) of those spending less than an hour per week were paid, compared with 95 per cent of those spending over ten hours. A slightly higher proportion of union representatives in private sector workplaces (87 per cent) said they were paid than those in the public sector (79 per cent). This reflected the relatively low proportion of education workplaces that had paid union representatives (59 per cent).

Communicating information to union members

One of the main functions of a union representative is to act as a channel through which information flows between members and management, or between members and the union itself. The most common way in which representatives conveyed information to members was via a general meeting. Just under two-thirds (62 per cent) of workplaces held general meetings and, of these, 72 per cent had held one at least twice in the past year with 16 per cent having meetings as regularly as once a month. The larger the workplace, the more likely were meetings to have been held, with fewer than half (48 per cent) having done so in workplaces with 25–49 employees compared with over four-fifths (84 per cent) in those with more than 500 employees. Where no meetings were held, almost all of the representatives (94 per cent) spent less than ten hours a week on union activities, with over half (55 per cent) having spent less than an hour. There was also a relationship with union density – just under half (46 per cent) of workplaces with density below half had not held any general meetings of members in the preceding year, compared with 32 per cent where union density was half or more.

While meetings were the most common means of communicating with members, other means, such as notice boards and newsletters, were also widely used. Just under three-fifths (59 per cent) of union representatives used workplace notice boards, and a similar proportion used newsletters (56 per cent). About half of all representatives (44 per cent) said they used personal contact to convey information to members. Among those not working at the same site as the membership, distance did not seem to hinder access, as this proportion was the same. Finally, around one in ten representatives (8 per cent) used e-mail to contact members, and this figure was much higher in workplaces with at least 500 employees (23 per cent).

Union representative activities

During the course of the interview, worker representatives were presented with a list of six issues they might be involved in, and asked whether they had spent any time dealing with them in the preceding year. They were then asked which of these issues they considered the most important. The results are summarised in Figure 9.3. Just over one in ten representatives said there was nothing on the list that corresponded with their activities. Of the remainder, issues surrounding the health and safety of employees and their treatment by management were the most commonly mentioned, with almost two-thirds saying they did either of these. Around a third said that they had worked with managers to improve performance.

Of particular note was the relative lack of importance given to that most traditional of trade union activities – maintaining wages and benefits – and the high level of activity and importance attached to dealing with problems raised by the treatment of employees by management, and to resolving disputes. Part of the explanation for this may be that collective bargaining over pay was removed from the workplace, making the main task of union representatives in this situation dealing with issues on the ground as they arose.

All issues were more commonly dealt with in larger workplaces and, as a corollary, worker representatives in these workplaces involved themselves in a wider range of issues. For example, almost a third (29 per cent) of representatives in workplaces with 500 or more employees said they dealt with all six issues and three-quarters (74 per cent) with four or more. By comparison, only 3 per cent dealt with all six in workplaces with fewer than 50 employees and 15 per cent with four issues or more.

The one factor dominating all others, not surprisingly, was the amount of time union representatives spent on union activities. Of those that spent less than an hour a week on representative duties, 39 per cent found none of the

Figure 9.3 Issues union representatives involved with in the past year

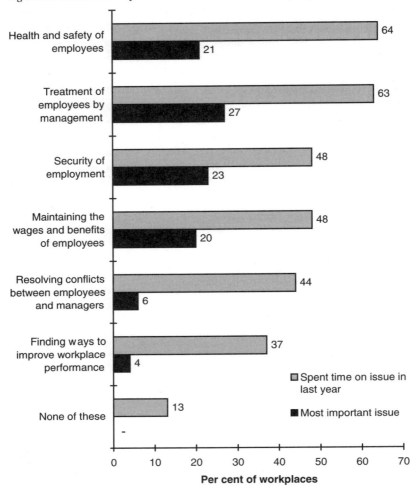

Base: All workplaces with a union representative and 25 or more employees.
Figures are weighted and based on responses from 813 (spent time on) and 774 (most important) union representatives.

issues to be relevant, while just 5 per cent of all other representatives responded similarly. At the opposite end of the scale, over four-fifths (86 per cent) of union representatives who spent more than ten hours per week on union activities mentioned four or more issues, with just under half (45 per cent) mentioning all six. Just 5 per cent of those who spent less than one hour per week on union activities said they occupied themselves on four or more of the issues.

These time-driven differences carried over into differences in the activities of male and female union representatives. Women were much more likely to say that none of the issues were relevant for their role, 25 per cent compared with 7 per cent of men. In addition, on each of the issues, fewer women said they dealt with them. However, male representatives in workplaces with a mainly female union membership were not greatly different from other male representatives.

A closer look at the data revealed the way in which certain issues went together. Where the maintenance of wages and benefits was important, security of employment was often also an issue. Likewise, many representatives mentioned together the treatment of employees by management, health and safety issues, and the resolution of disputes. The concerns of representatives appear to loosely divide into those who are mostly concerned with union representatives' 'bread and butter' issues, and those which relate to resolving problems at the workplace as they flare up.

Trade union organisation

In discussing the activities undertaken by union representatives, we have explored their role as representatives, but have paid no attention to the second function, their organising role. Somewhere within most union representative's duties is the recruitment of new members. The need to recruit reflects the realities faced by all union officials, given that average annual membership turnover has been estimated to be 12 per cent (Cully and Woodland, 1998). Its importance is best illustrated by the fact that nearly four-fifths (79 per cent) said they had attempted to recruit new members in the past year, and of these only 7 per cent had done so without success.

The likelihood of having recruited in the past year was higher in larger workplaces, and the extent of the difference is shown in Table 9.4. There were new recruits in just over half (53 per cent) of workplaces with fewer than 50 employees compared with 96 per cent in those with more than 500 employees. Recruitment was also more likely to have taken place in workplaces that were part of a larger organisation. There was little difference in the pattern of recruitment according to the level of union density. Only in workplaces where fewer than a quarter of employees were union members were attempts at recruitment substantially above average (87 per cent), though, so too was the relative lack of success (12 per cent, compared with 5 per cent overall).

Of the union representatives who made no effort to recruit new members, over half worked less than an hour per week on representative activities (57 per cent). Approaching it from the other direction, of those spending less than an hour per week on union activities, 55 per cent had not recruited any new members, compared with under a fifth (18 per cent) of those that spent at least an hour per week.

The fact that managers informed union representatives of the presence of a new employee appeared to have little effect on their ability to recruit new members. Where this occurred (as it did in 44 per cent of cases), just over three-quarters (77 per cent) said they had successfully recruited in the past 12 months, compared with 71 per cent where this information was not made available.

Table 9.4 Successful recruitment of new trade union members, by time spent and workplace size

	Less than 10 hours per week	10 or more hours per week	All union representatives
	% of workplaces	% of workplaces	% of workplaces
Workplace size			
25–49 employees	51	*	53
50–99 employees	76	*	76
100–199 employees	91	(96)	92
200–499 employees	92	95	93
500 or more employees	93	98	96
All workplaces	70	89	73

Base: All workplaces with a union representative and 25 or more employees.
Figures are weighted and based on responses from 800 union representatives.

Membership losses

About two-thirds (69 per cent) of union representatives said they had lost union members at their workplace in the preceding year. A variety of reasons were offered, the main ones were that it was due to members leaving the workplace, either voluntarily (83 per cent) or not (39 per cent). There were relatively few reports of members leaving to join another union (9 per cent). A fifth (21 per cent) of union representatives said members were lost as a result of failures to renew union subscriptions; this was unrelated to how subscriptions were paid.

Contact with trade union officials

Most representatives had been in contact with their union in the past year, though a substantial minority (27 per cent) had not. Just over a quarter (28 per cent) had met union officials at least once a month, with a similar proportion (27 per cent) reporting contact at least once every three months. Those who held official positions within their trade union reported more regular contact with half (48 per cent) saying they had meetings at least once a month, compared with 19 per cent of other union representatives.

The most common reason for contacting officials was to obtain assistance in handling individual grievance cases, with almost two-thirds (64 per cent) reporting in this way. It was also common to contact officials for legal advice and this went hand-in-hand with seeking help on grievance cases, nearly half (46 per cent) reporting this. The least common reason for contacting union officials was to do with industrial action (19 per cent). Union representatives in workplaces where there was industrial action, either threatened or actual, were more than twice as likely to ask for help in the conduct of an industrial action.

Meetings with other union representatives

Union representatives might also meet with representatives from their own union or from another union, assuming there are other representatives at the workplace. Where there were, meetings were held to discuss workplace matters in almost three-quarters of cases (70 per cent). The likelihood of these taking place varied according to the structure of lay representation, with meetings held most commonly where there was more than one representative from a single union at the workplace. Here, 96 per cent of representatives said a meeting was held, whereas in workplaces with multiple unions (and representatives), 62 per cent reported joint union meetings. More important was the overall number of representatives: the more union representatives there were, either from their own or another union, the greater the chance of a meeting being held.

Union representatives' relationship with management

Most of the preceding analysis has implicitly assumed that union representatives are carrying out the functions required of them by the workers they represent. Yet how they exercise their representative role may be shaped and constrained by management. To begin with, Figure 9.4 reports the results of three questions where union representatives were asked to judge the type of support they received from workplace management. On each of these, more union representatives agreed with the statement than disagreed. About a third felt they did not work closely with managers, a fifth said managers didn't value their opinions and a tenth felt that managers didn't support them in their role.[10]

These questions were then combined to form an overall measure of the union representative's relationship with management.[11] This can then be related to the more concrete provision of facilities and so forth. On the overall measure, 11 per cent of worker representatives got 'very strong' support from management and 42 per cent 'strong' support, with 17 per cent getting either 'weak' or 'very weak' support; the remaining 30 per cent fell in between.

An obvious way for managers to provide support is through the provision of facilities, and the extent of this is shown in Figure 9.5. A quarter of the representatives had an office specifically set aside to conduct their duties, and two-fifths said they had access to some type of office (which may have been their own), leaving many in the difficult position of working without access to a private space. It was far more widespread, however, for meeting rooms to be made available, with four-fifths having access to this facility. Of the other facilities we asked about, most union representatives had access to a telephone or a photocopier, but considerably fewer said they were able to use a computer at their place of work. Just under a third of workplaces made all the facilities available and only 7 per cent of union representatives had none of these facilities available to them. Workplaces where management were in favour of union membership were somewhat more likely to provide offices and computing facilities.

Figure 9.4 Union representatives' views on their relationship with management

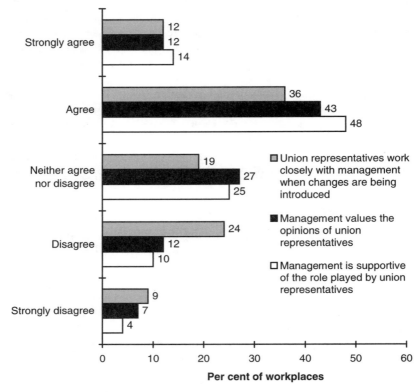

Base: All workplaces with a union representative and 25 or more employees.
Figures are weighted and based on responses from 814 (bars 1 & 2) and 813 (bar 3) union representatives.

Apart from the provision of facilities, we measured concrete management support for the role of union representatives in several other ways. These are related to the overall indicator of management support for the role and activities of worker representatives in Table 9.5. There was considerable variation across the various indicators. For example, four in five representatives (82 per cent) were paid for the time they spent on union activities, but only one in five (23 per cent) were paid when they went on union training courses.

The association with the union representatives' overall assessment of management support produced a consistent U-shaped pattern. Those who thought management were strongly supportive of their role had some justification in their view when compared with those who thought that management support was neither strong nor weak. However, those who thought management support weak were as likely as those who thought it strong to be paid for representative activities and for trade union training, except for the perhaps critical issue of being informed of potential new recruits. It is clear that the wider question of management support taps into something deeper than the type of facilities provided.

Figure 9.5 Facilities available to union representatives

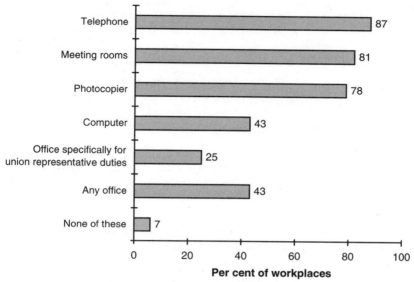

Base: All workplaces with a union representative and 25 or more employees.
Figures are weighted and based on responses from 780 union representatives.

Joint regulation of the employment relationship

In Chapter 5 we examined the pattern of negotiation, consultation and information-sharing with lay union representatives as portrayed by management. In
most workplaces, the management account suggested a relatively limited role for
representatives in workplace affairs (see Figure 5.4). Identical questions were also
asked in the course of the interview with union representatives. For seven of the
nine issues asked about, the most common response on the part of union
representatives was to say they had no involvement in the matter. Where negotiations did occur, these were most likely to have been over pay, handling of grievances
and health and safety. Broadly, then, the account provided by union representatives
concurs with that provided by management and we will not discuss it further in
this section. Instead, we look in a little more detail at union representatives'
involvement in pay determination and industrial disputes.

Pay bargaining

Just under a quarter of all union representatives said that they were personally
involved in pay bargaining. Figure 9.6 shows how this varied across industry.
Manufacturing, and electricity, gas and water supply stand out as industries with
a high incidence of union representative involvement. More broadly, involvement
was largely dependent on how the management of employment relations, and

Table 9.5 Managerial support for union representatives

	Management support for union representatives – overall scale		
	Strong	*Neither strong nor weak*	*Weak*
	% of workplaces	*% of workplaces*	*% of workplaces*
All facilities (as in Figure 9.5)	36	24	25
Managers pay for training	22	19	32
Notified of new employee	52	39	22
Check-off used to collect dues	70	58	75
Paid for representative activities	84	78	83

Base: All workplaces with a union representative and 25 or more employees.
Figures are weighted and based on responses from 813 union representatives.

pay bargaining specifically, was structured within the organisation. In common with many of the patterns identified in Chapters 4 and 5, the personal involvement of the local union representative was more likely in larger workplaces, and less likely in workplaces that were part of a wider organisation.

When involved in negotiations, almost all representatives said they entered these talks accompanied by someone else (92 per cent). In most cases this was another union representative (78 per cent), but a majority also said they were assisted by a full-time official from their trade union (57 per cent). It was extremely rare – only 6 per cent of workplaces – for non-union employee representatives to be involved in these negotiations.

When a union representative was directly involved in negotiations with management, almost nine out of ten (85 per cent) consulted the employees they represented before commencing negotiations. A similar proportion (90 per cent) also consulted members on whether the offer should be accepted before any agreement had been reached. Where union representatives were not directly involved in pay bargaining, consultation with members was far less common. Two out of three representatives (67 per cent) said that members were consulted before negotiations commenced, but only one in three (32 per cent) said that members were asked to ratify the deal.

Involvement in collective disputes

A quarter (23 per cent) of union representatives said there had been some form of collective dispute over pay or conditions in the past year. Of these, just over half (57 per cent) led to industrial action, the remainder not escalating beyond a threat. There is a significant discrepancy in the incidence of industrial action between the accounts of worker representatives and managers. For the same set of workplaces, 5 per cent of managers recorded industrial action on one or more occasions in the preceding year, compared with 13 per cent of worker representatives.

Figure 9.6 Whether union representative was directly involved in determining or negotiating pay, by industry

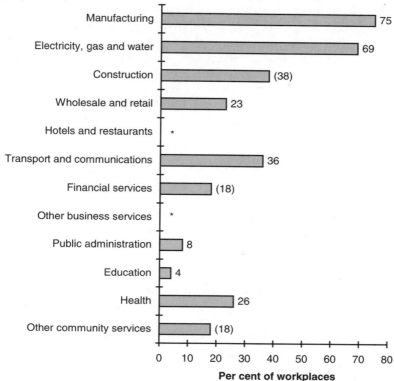

Base: All workplaces with a union representative and 25 or more employees.
Figures are weighted and based on responses from 814 union representatives.

When industrial action occurred it took on a variety of forms. Union representatives were given a list of nine types of industrial action and were asked to say whether any had occurred in the past year, and if so, on how many occasions. Strike activity was the most common activity (27 per cent) closely followed by work to rule (26 per cent) and overtime bans (21 per cent). Three-quarters said that only one of these forms had occurred, and only 9 per cent said three or more. Some of the nine forms of actions were more common in some sectors, for example, overtime bans happened more often in the private than the public sector (39 per cent compared with 11 per cent) whereas work to rule was more commonly a public sector phenomenon (31 per cent compared with 18 per cent).

It appears that on most occasions union representatives organise industrial action themselves, as only a third (28 per cent) said they had been in contact with union officials asking for assistance in proceeding with industrial action. Assistance may not have been taken as help with the conduct of ballots, or it may be that help with this was not sought because ballots were not held. Where there had been any form of industrial action reported by union representatives in the past year, over half (54 per cent) took place without a ballot to establish the level of support for action. The implication of this is a much higher level of non-official action than reported by management (where the respective figure was 14 per cent). This might account for some of the overall difference in the reported incidence of industrial action between managers and worker representatives. Where ballots were held, representatives were asked to state the proportion of eligible employees who voted. The pattern across workplaces varied. Around 40 per cent said all or almost all participated, whereas a fifth said that only some employees voted, and the remainder fell somewhere in between.

Employee views of representation

The chapter ends by taking a look at how union members view their representatives and, more generally, at employee views on the role of unions at the workplace. Drawing on the survey of employees, we can evaluate attitudes to representation and situate them in the context of the structure of representation at the workplace.

Contact with representatives

We start by looking at employee awareness of the representative function, by matching responses from a question which asked employees about their contact with worker representatives.[12] Overall, 19 per cent of union members in workplaces with representatives said they frequently contacted a representative and a further half (53 per cent) reported occasional contact. The rest were split between those that knew of a representative but did not make contact (21 per cent) and those who did not know any representatives (6 per cent). Where the representative was not based at the workplace, contact with employees was far less. In these workplaces almost a quarter (23 per cent) of union members said they did not know any union representatives. Non-union members also had a lower awareness of the presence of union representatives, with just over a third (36 per cent) saying they did not know of one in workplaces where they were present.

Forms of representation

All employees were asked a series of hypothetical questions dealing with various workplace matters. The preamble said 'Ideally, who do you think would best represent you in dealing with managers here about the following issues?', those issues being: pay increases; making a complaint about work; and disciplinary situations. Table 9.6 presents the results, showing how they varied according to union membership and union recognition. Only in the area of pay increases did more employees prefer trade unions to represent them than either of the other options of representing themselves or of being represented by somebody else. On both the other issues, employees generally preferred to deal directly with managers rather than go through a third party – this was especially the case for dealing with work problems.

Hypothetical questions are problematic because some people may not have the experience to draw upon to contemplate alternatives to their present circumstances. This is evidently the case for many non-union members who may have no experience of what a union is able to offer. We deal with this as best we can, by controlling for whether or not an employee is a union member and whether or not they work in workplaces with a recognised union.

Understandably, union members mostly preferred to be represented by a trade union, though a substantial minority did not. On the issue of dealing with a problem at work, they were equally split between seeking support from the union or dealing with it themselves. While this type of event may well call for a more individualistic solution, it is likely to be disconcerting reading for trade unions to note that 14 per cent of members in recognised workplaces believe they could achieve a superior pay outcome through individual negotiations rather than through the collective settlement.

Non-union members generally said they would prefer to represent themselves on each of these issues, though on pay matters one in five would prefer to have

Table 9.6 Employee attitudes towards representation at the workplace, by employee and workplace characteristics

	Who best represents employee in dealings with management:		
	Myself	*Trade union*	*Somebody else*
	% of employees	*% of employees*	*% of employees*
Increases in pay			
Union member in recognised workplace	14	79	6
Union member in non-recognised workplace	43	41	15
Non-union member in recognised workplace	49	31	19
Non-union member in non-recognised workplace	68	14	17
Dealing with complaints about work			
Union member in recognised workplace	47	46	7
Union member in non-recognised workplace	70	23	6
Non-union member in recognised workplace	74	12	13
Non-union member in non-recognised workplace	78	9	12
Disciplinary cases			
Union member in recognised workplace	21	73	5
Union member in non-recognised workplace	43	46	11
Non-union member in recognised workplace	60	19	21
Non-union member in non-recognised workplace	71	11	17

Base: All employees in workplaces with 25 or more employees.
Figures are weighted and based on responses from 21,121 (pay), 21,224 (complaints) and 21,224 (discipline) employees.

union representation. The proportion saying this was twice as high among non-union members in workplaces with recognised unions than those without.

More generally, these results show how responses to hypothetical questions are conditioned by circumstances. In workplaces where unions were recognised, both union members and non-union members were more likely than their counterparts in workplaces with no recognised unions to prefer union representation. The differences between the two groups of non-union members were, however, smaller than those between the two groups of union members.

General views about the role of unions

We also examined how employees view representation through a set of general questions asked of all employees where a trade union was present at the workplace.[13] These questions covered three dimensions of unionism: unions' ability to take notice of their members' problems and complaints; how seriously they are taken by management; and whether they make a difference to what it is like at work. Figure 9.7 shows the proportions of employees who agreed with each of these statements, according to their membership status. Unions were rated best at dealing with members' problems and complaints, where a majority of members and non-members agreed with this statement. Employees, in general, also thought that unions were taken seriously by management with all groups more likely to agree than disagree with this statement. On the broader question of whether unions actually made a difference, the results were more ambiguous. Union members were inclined to agree, but around half of non-union members were unable to agree or disagree and roughly equal numbers placed themselves in either camp.

We were able to sub-divide non-union members into those who had been a member at some stage in the past and those who had never been a member. While union members were more positive on each issue than non-union members, ex-union members were less positive than those who had never been members. The differences were generally small, but their consistency suggests that some ex-members have a residue of cynicism about their experience.

The extent to which unions were seen as being taken seriously by management was related to the level of union density. The proportion of union members who agreed with the statement being around two-fifths (43 per cent) when density was below a quarter, compared with three-fifths (58 per cent) when density was above 90 per cent. A similar relationship was also found on the question of whether unions made a difference to what it is like at work, with the respective figures being 33 per cent and 53 per cent.

Conclusion

This chapter has provided a fairly rare account of the role and activities of contemporary union representatives, drawing for the most part on the detailed interview with them. It considerably enriches the account provided by management in Chapter 5.

Figure 9.7 Employee attitudes towards representation at the workplace

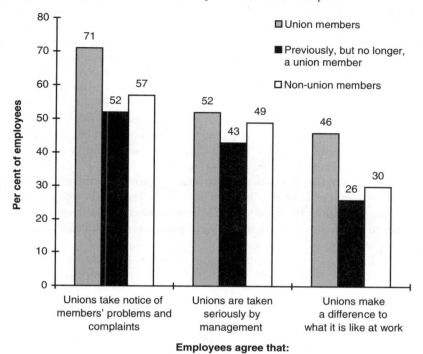

Base: All workplaces with 25 or more employees where employees say there is a union present. Figures are weighted and based on responses from 12,279 (take notice), 12,226 (taken seriously) and 12,219 (make a difference) employees.

It also provides cumulative evidence, which buttresses the conclusions to Chapter 5, that while management may shape or constrain the role and activities of worker representatives, much of the variation is to do with the strength and depth of union organisation at the workplace. Where union representatives were elected rather than volunteering, where they had been trained in their role, and crucially where they spent more hours per week on union activities, their role was more significant. More hours was associated with active recruitment of new members.

This interacted with union strength at the workplace, as measured by union density. Where this was higher, union representatives spent more time on their union activities, were more likely to have general meetings with their members, and the members in turn were more likely to say that unions were taken seriously by management.

It is also clear that these two aspects – union strength and depth, and management support – are mutually intertwined. The more hours union representatives spent on their activities the more likely were these hours to be paid, and the greater the number of facilities provided to assist them in their role.

At the end of the chapter, we looked more broadly at what employees thought of representation and the role of unions at the workplace. Bearing in mind the weaknesses of hypothetical and subjective questions, the results did not appear to support the argument that a 'representation gap' (Towers, 1997) can simply be inferred from an absence of representative structures. Non-union members in recognised workplaces did not differ substantially from their counterparts in workplaces without recognised unions in wanting to represent themselves in matters affecting their terms and conditions of employment, even though they had the wherewithal to join a union if they wished. Similarly, ex-union members were more sceptical than those who had never been union members about the role that unions played at the workplace. By contrast, union members were more positive, especially where union density was high.

Taken together with the evidence provided by union representatives themselves, and of management in Chapter 5, it is apparent, if an all too obvious point, that representation is more highly regarded and at its most effective where unions are well organised and, perhaps, have a more legitimate role as a partner in workplace employment relations.

Notes

1 Union representatives are often referred to as shop stewards, especially among blue-collar workers, and sometimes have other titles (e.g. convenor, Father of the Chapel). In local or central government they often have the title of Chair or Secretary of the union side of a negotiating committee. Whatever their title, their distinguishing feature is that they are acknowledged by management to be a representative for their union at a given workplace.

2 This situation is analogous to that of the management interviews, where a number were undertaken away from the sampled address, typically with a manager at a head or regional office. Just 8 per cent of the interviews with lay union representatives were with a representative from another workplace.

3 There were, in fact, 882 interviews conducted, but 22 cases have been discarded because of doubts over whether the respondent was correctly selected.

4 In 210 cases (18 per cent) a worker representative was identified to be interviewed in the course of the management interview but, subsequently, did not take part in the survey. It is reckoned, by SCPR interviewers, that in 117 cases this was a result of management refusing access to the worker representative (Airey *et al.*, 1999: 60).

5 Of course, mathematically it will vary since the maximum that the ratio can take differs across each of the size bands – 49:1 in the smallest band, 99:1 in the second and so on.

6 Figures on the composition of union members are taken from the employee survey in those workplaces where union representatives were surveyed.

7 The research examined the ten largest trade unions and found the proportion of women who were full-time regional officers was, at best, half that of women's share in total membership, and in most cases, closer to a quarter. While we might expect the gender bias to diminish the further we go down the union organisational hierarchy, this figure provides a useful benchmark.

8 As already noted, we avoided use of this term, in part because of its overt connotations with manufacturing and manual work. In fact, 40 of the 76 representatives interviewed by Godfrey and Marchington worked in the public sector, and 46 were 'white collar' workers.

9 Gamma = 0.43 for the relationship between the number of hours spent on representative activities and union density in the private sector. Gamma = 0.15 for the public sector.

10 A further question was asked in this block, but couched in a negative rather than a positive way as with the other three items. The distribution of the responses to this item appeared to be biased because of the wording and we have excluded it from this analysis.

11 The measure is a simple summary scale, whereby responses are summed and scaled back to the original (Cronbach alpha = 0.85).

12 We have excluded employees who said they were union representatives.

13 Trade union presence at the workplace is as defined by employees themselves.

10 Changes in employment relations, 1980–1998

Neil Millward, John Forth and
Alex Bryson[†]

In this chapter we shift focus – from the detailed snapshot of current employment relations which the previous chapters have provided, to the moving picture of how employment relations have changed since the beginning of the 1980s. No one can doubt that change occurred. But there are few sources of systematic information that can be used to demonstrate the extent and amount of change, the nature of the changes and some of the reasons for them. Our survey series is well suited to these tasks. Although the first survey in 1980 was only dimly seen as the first of a series, its successors have always been designed to provide substantial scope for analysing change.

We use a variety of evidence from the series to describe and illuminate the changes in employment relations that have occurred since 1980, treating the material in similar order to the topics of Chapters 2 to 6. First we look at changes in the profile of workplaces and the workforces they deploy. We then turn to how management is organised to deal with employment relations. Then we examine the changing use of a number of practices that management use to inform and consult directly with employees and to reward their performance. We go on to look at employee representation, principally by trade unions, and at other formal consultative structures. The chapter ends with a brief discussion of industrial conflict and some broad conclusions.

Analysing change using the survey series

The foundation for our ability to analyse change over the period 1980 to 1998 is the maintenance of certain core features of the survey design. These are:

- the workplace as the unit of sampling and data collection;
- a consistent definition of our primary respondents;

† This chapter is an initial analysis of change over the course of the WIRS series, which is given an extended treatment in our forthcoming volume, *All Change at Work?* Neil Millward and John Forth are at the National Institute of Economic and Social Research and Alex Bryson is at the Policy Studies Institute. Funding from the Leverhulme Trust is gratefully acknowledged.

- minimal changes in the scope and design of our samples;
- minimal changes in a core set of questions in our interviews; and
- the maintenance of high quality in fieldwork and data preparation.

The first and last of these requirements have been maintained throughout. The second has been maintained in relation to our principal management respondent, the most senior person at the sampled workplace responsible for personnel or employee relations matters.[1] The sample scope has had minor variations. Broadly speaking, it has succeeded in covering all manufacturing and service industries, both publicly and privately owned.[2] Smaller workplaces, below the former threshold of 25 employees, were included in the 1998 survey for the first time, but these have been excluded from all the analyses presented in this chapter in order to maintain a consistent basis for comparisons. Minor variations have been made in the sample design and weighting schemes, but not of sufficient scale to threaten the comparability of the results.[3]

On question wording, matters are more complex. In each successive survey, some questions have been dropped from earlier questionnaires and replaced by more useful or salient questions. Changes of this nature were most widespread between the 1990 and 1998 surveys. In other cases, minor alterations in question wording or format have been introduced at one point or another. For some of these, the changes mean that ostensibly comparable questions cannot be compared with confidence. Nonetheless the survey series contains a core of some 200 or so questions which can be used to construct identical, or broadly comparable, variables for 1998 and at least one earlier survey.

This time-series dataset provides successive cross-section estimates, or 'snapshots', of employment relations at the time of each survey. In the first instance, the time-series data enable us to look at the aggregate picture, tracing the degree of change or stability that is evident among the whole population of workplaces over the period. We are then able to look at change within particular sectors of the economy, such as the private sector, manufacturing industries or smaller workplaces. However, the changes thus revealed from one survey to another, say between 1990 and 1998, are 'net' changes in the sense that they arise from three different sources of change that cannot be separately identified in the cross-section data. First, among workplaces that continue in operation, there may be changes in behaviour, such as the derecognition of unions. This may or may not be linked to a change in some of those workplace characteristics that are associated with the behaviour in question, such as a move from public to private sector ownership. Second, comparing workplaces that leave the population with those that join it, similar types of workplace may differ in terms of their behaviour. For example, large manufacturing plants that close down may invariably have recognised unions, whereas new large manufacturing plants might be less likely to do so. Third, those that leave the population may differ from those that join it in respect of characteristics associated with the behaviour of interest, such as union recognition. For example, leavers may be mostly in manufacturing, while joiners may be mostly in private sector services. If being in manufacturing is associated with recognising trade unions, the shift from manufacturing to services might produce a net change in the aggregate level of union recognition, even if workplaces with similar characteristics continue to behave in the same way.

In cases where the time-series results show stability from one survey to another it may be tempting to conclude that there has been no change of any sort. However, there may have been counteracting changes that offset each other. In some instances these may be substantial, but this fact would be unknowable from the cross-section survey results.[4]

Change within continuing units is best measured by a panel survey, where the same units are interviewed at two (or more) successive points in time. Following the largely successful panel elements in earlier stages of the survey series, this element of the 1998 project was elaborated and expanded to include the public sector. As a consequence, we have the results of a large-scale panel survey that repeated many of the questions asked at the same workplace eight years earlier in the 1990 survey. When used in combination with the survey data from units that left the population after 1990 (which include roughly equal numbers of closures and workplaces that dropped below our 25 employee threshold) and from units that joined the population since 1990 (which include roughly equal numbers of entirely new workplaces and workplaces that grew above our 25 employee threshold), the data from the panel survey enable us to identify the differing contributions made to the aggregate picture by the three types of change discussed above. This greatly enriches what can be learned from the time-series data. We discuss such analyses to a limited extent in the remainder of this chapter, but more extensively in our companion volume.

The context of change in employment relations

Before looking at the degree of change in employment relations over the survey series, it is useful to consider the backdrop against which such change has taken place. Substantial developments have occurred in the economy, in the labour market and in the political and legal spheres over the past 18 years: all are relevant to our discussion of the trends in workplace employment relations. Adding a historic dimension to the discussion in Chapter 1, what follows is but a brief overview of some of those contextual developments.

The political, legal and social context

Few will fail to recognise the significance of the timing of the WIRS series in terms of its political context. Spanning a total of 18 years, the series extends across almost the whole of the recent era of Conservative government. The first survey, in 1980, was undertaken before the incoming Conservative government had brought in any of their initial reforms, while the fourth survey, in 1998, took place before the new Labour government had enacted its first legislative provisions. This fortunate coincidence leaves us with a time series that covers a discrete political era and provides a benchmark for subsequent eras of a different complexion.

The election of the Conservative government in 1979 signalled the beginning of a period of policy reform that was to change the face of the British labour market. The overriding concern was to promote the free play of market forces. By restricting the activities of trade unions and weakening some parts of the framework of statutory employment protection, successive Conservative governments aimed to bolster employers' 'right to manage' and increase the degree of flexibility in the labour market, in the expectation that this would increase the competitiveness of British business and promote employment growth. The public sector was transformed by a wave of privatisations, the contracting-out of many services from local and central government and the movement of many functions from core departments to agencies.

All this took place within a wider social programme through which the government aimed to promote self-reliance, entrepreneurship and 'acquisitive individualism' (Phelps Brown, 1990: 1). Within this new context, and in an environment characterised by increasingly competitive product markets, a number of employers took the opportunity to achieve a greater degree of control over the work process and reassert managerial authority. The example was set by managers appointed by government to revitalise state enterprises such as British Leyland, the British Steel Corporation and British Coal. Much academic debate in the 1980s then focused on the extent to which 'macho management' and anti-union strategies had percolated through the private sector. Observers noted that managers were moving away from the pluralism of the post-war decades towards a more unitarist approach (Poole and Mansfield, 1993), and it was clear that employers were beginning to reject long-held assumptions of joint regulation in favour of greater freedom of action (Kessler and Bayliss, 1998: 130).

Attention turned to management practices that embodied the new spirit of individualism: methods of direct communication and employee involvement, appraisal systems and performance-related pay. Some argued that this formed part of a new style of management which, in some cases, amounted to a more integrated, strategic and people-centred approach labelled 'human resource management' (Guest, 1987). Others said that, in practice, developments were more in keeping with the cost-reduction or 'macho management' approach seen in the early 1980s (Sisson, 1994: 15).

To the extent that managers were employing methods that focused more on the individual than the collective, they were aided by a comprehensive programme of employment legislation designed to strengthen the hand of employers and weaken the hands of employees and their trade unions (Dickens and Hall, 1995; Brown *et al.*, 1997). The period between our 1980 and 1984 surveys saw the first phase of this 'step-by-step' programme. Support for trade union representation and collective bargaining was substantially withdrawn by repealing the provisions for the statutory recognition of unions, and the extension of union-negotiated terms and conditions to other workers. Restrictions were placed on secondary industrial action and the enforceability of the closed shop, while unions were also made liable for unlawful industrial action. Employees, for their part, became more vulnerable to selective dismissal when on strike and saw the protection afforded to them against unfair dismissal also weakened. Between the second and third surveys in the series, protection against unfair dismissal was further weakened by extending the qualifying period for legal redress to two years. All industrial action became unlawful unless preceded by a secret ballot and unions were prohibited from taking disciplinary action against members not participating in industrial action.

The programme of legislative change was continued in the 1990s. The period between the latest two surveys in the series saw the final outlawing of the closed shop; an increase in balloting and notice requirements over industrial action; the extension of union liability to cover unlawful industrial action called by shop stewards and other union officials; the abolition of the vestiges of minimum wage protection through the Wages Councils; and increased requirements for the administration of check-off procedures.

However, it is also important to remember the countervailing trends over the period, many of which originated within European law. Enhanced protection for employees and increased rights of consultation during business transfers, the extension of sex discrimination and equal pay legislation, and the extension of regulations governing health and safety consultation were all prompted, at least in part, by legal rulings or Directives at a European level.

The WIRS series contains information that is relevant to all of these legislative changes; on some of them the series provides the most valuable evidence available for assessing the impact of the changes in government policy and the legal framework of employment.

The economic and labour market context

Employment legislation was only one of many influences on the nature and distribution of employment during the Conservatives' period of office. Many sectors, including financial services, transportation, telecommunications and broadcasting, were exposed to increased competition through deregulation. Competitive conditions in many industries were also radically changed by the liberalisation of trade, both within the European Union and elsewhere, and by the changing economics of transportation and the ease of communication on a global scale.

In terms of economic growth, Britain experienced what amounted to two full cycles during the period covered by the WIRS series. Broadly speaking, the survey series was preceded by a period of growth during the second half of the 1970s, albeit with some turbulence as governments attempted to rein in inflation. The 1980s then began with a severe recession, followed by a prolonged period of growth through the remainder of the decade. A similar pattern has emerged in the 1990s, with the economy having spent the early part of the decade back in recession, but having since recovered to a position of sustained growth. In terms of comparability, the conditions under which the 1990 survey was undertaken bore a broad resemblance to those at the time of the first survey in 1980, both having taken place against the backdrop of an emerging recession. However, the latter recession also extended to service industries, which had been much less affected around the time of the first survey. Conditions for the fourth survey in 1998 were closer to those seen in 1984. The 1998 fieldwork took place after a period of steady growth, but there were concerns about future prospects, especially in the manufacturing sector.

The changing composition of the economy and labour force

The effects of the two recessions on manufacturing industry and the comparative growth of services over the last 18 years are clearly evident in our surveys, as can be seen in Table 10.1. At the time of the first and second surveys in 1980 and 1984, workplaces engaged in service industries outnumbered those in manufacturing and extraction by a ratio of around two to one. However, the 1990 and 1998 surveys have shown how the dominance of service industries has increased, with workplaces in this sector now outnumbering those in manufacturing by a factor of three to one. The share of employment in private sector services overtook that in private sector manufacturing between the first and second surveys, and has risen further since then. Private sector service industries now account for over two-fifths of all employees covered by the survey. Having employed a majority of private sector employees in 1980, workplaces engaged in manufacturing and extraction now account for just 37 per cent of private sector employment and 25 per cent of all employees covered by the survey series.

At the same time, the period since 1984 has also seen a substantial contraction of the public sector, brought about by successive waves of privatisation and the contracting-out of a wide range of public sector services. In 1984, almost two-

Table 10.1 Distribution of workplaces and employees, by broad sector, 1980 to 1998

	1980	1984	1990	1998
	% of workplaces	% of workplaces	% of workplaces	% of workplaces
Private sector manufacturing/extraction	25	21	21	18
Private sector services	43	42	49	54
Public sector workplaces	32	37	30	28
	% of employees	% of employees	% of employees	% of employees
Private sector manufacturing/extraction	38	27	27	25
Private sector services	26	29	38	44
Public sector workplaces	36	43	35	32

Base: All workplaces with 25 or more employees.
Figures are weighted and based on responses from 2,040 (1980), 2,019 (1984), 2,061 (1990) and 1,929 (1998) managers.

fifths of all workplaces covered by the survey were located within the public sector. One in eight of these (13 per cent, or 5 per cent of all workplaces) were to be found in one of the nationalised industries (at that time including electricity, gas and water supply, railways and telecommunications, among others). By 1998, privatisation had left the Post Office and London Transport as the only major employers in industry or commerce under state ownership, with the share of all workplaces accounted for by nationalised industries having fallen to only 1 per cent (4 per cent of all workplaces in the public sector).[5] The proportion of workplaces in the public sector as a whole had fallen by a quarter to 28 per cent. Similarly, while the public sector accounted for 43 per cent of all employees in workplaces with 25 or more employees in 1984, by the time of the most recent survey in 1998 this figure stood at just 32 per cent.

Another commonly-cited development, often associated with the growth of the service sector, is the trend towards smaller workplaces. This trend is undoubtedly apparent across the population of workplaces of all sizes, but our survey series covers only those with 25 or more employees. In fact, the size distribution of this sub-population has remained extremely stable over the past two decades. In 1998 workplaces with between 25 and 49 employees continued to account for around a half of all workplaces covered by the survey, as they did in 1980, while those with between 50 and 99 employees continued to account for a quarter. At the other extreme, the proportion of workplaces with 500 or more employees has remained steady at around 3 per cent in each of the four surveys. Private sector service workplaces are now less concentrated at the lower end of the size distribution. However, in direct contrast to the situation in 1980, the majority of large private sector workplaces are now found in the service sector rather than in manufacturing.

While there may have been no overall trend towards smaller workplaces in the population covered by our series, there has been an increase in the proportion of stand-alone sites in which the workplace and the organisation are one and the same. These accounted for around a fifth (21 per cent) of all workplaces in each of the first three surveys. In the 1990s, however, they increased in prominence and by 1998 accounted for just over a quarter (27 per cent) of workplaces with 25 or more employees. At the same time there has been a slight decrease in the proportion of workplaces that belong to very large organisations with 10,000 or more employees (30 per cent in 1980, compared with 26 per cent in 1998). Within the private sector, there has also been a recent increase in the proportion of workplaces under foreign ownership or control. Representing just 6 per cent of all private sector workplaces in 1980, foreign-owned workplaces now account for around one in eight workplaces (13 per cent) in the private sector.

Alongside changes in the industrial and ownership composition of our survey population, equally significant changes have clearly taken place in the character of the labour force in Britain. Increases in the labour market participation of women and in the incidence of part-time working are perhaps the most notable developments. Both are apparent from our survey data.

In Table 10.2, workplaces are classified as having either a low, medium or high percentage of female employees within their workforce. The table shows that there was little change between 1980 and 1984. Since then, the proportion of workplaces in which women comprise only a low percentage (less than 25 per cent) of all employees has fallen from around a third in 1984 to around a quarter in 1998. The corresponding increase has occurred, not in the adjacent category where workplaces have a medium percentage of female employees, but in the category having a high percentage (75 per cent or more) of women among their workforce. The proportion of workplaces with a high percentage of female employees rose from 22 per cent in 1984 to 29 per cent in 1998.

The increasing incidence of part-time working within workplaces is shown in Table 10.3. Although there was little change in the 1980s, the overall trend since 1990 has been unambiguously towards an increased presence of part-time employees at workplace level. The overall proportion of workplaces without any part-time employees remained approximately the same in the last two surveys, although among manufacturing workplaces this situation became more common. However, where at least some part-time workers are present they are now found in greater proportions than ever before. The proportion of workplaces in which at least a quarter of all employees work part-time has grown substantially since 1990, from 32 per cent to 44 per cent in 1998.

Across the population of workplaces covered by the series, a quarter of employees now work part-time. In 1990 the figure stood at less than a fifth (18 per cent). These aggregate figures show a net increase of seven percentage points over the eight-year period. However, such time-series data cannot tell us whether this increase arose primarily from a greater utilisation of part-time workers within workplaces that survived through the period or from a greater incidence of part-time work among workplaces entering the survey population since 1990 than among those leaving it. Our panel survey and our datasets of leavers and joiners do provide this added detail, giving us a unique insight into the origins of this increase in part-time working.

The utilisation of part-time workers within continuing workplaces did not increase significantly between 1990 and 1998. Some 19 per cent of the employees

Table 10.2 Proportions of employees within workplaces who are female, 1980 to 1998

	1980	1984	1990	1998
	% of workplaces	*% of workplaces*	*% of workplaces*	*% of workplaces*
Female share of employment				
Low (less than 25%)	36	35	33	27
Medium (25% to less than 75%)	42	44	43	44
High (75% or more)	22	22	24	29

Base: All workplaces with 25 or more employees.
Figures are weighted and based on responses from 1,983 (1980), 1,854 (1984), 1,772 (1990) and 1,914 (1998) managers.

Table 10.3 Proportions of employees within workplaces who work part-time, 1980 to 1998

	1980	1984	1990	1998
	% of workplaces	% of workplaces	% of workplaces	% of workplaces
Part-time share of employment				
No part-time employees	13	18	14	16
Less than 25%	55	51	54	40
25% or more	32	31	32	44

Base: All workplaces with 25 or more employees.
Figures are weighted and based on responses from 2,012 (1980), 2,002 (1984), 2,008 (1990) and 1,914 (1998) managers.

of continuing workplaces worked part-time in 1990, compared with 21 per cent in 1998. However, among workplaces that joined the survey population from 1990 onwards (those beginning their operations between 1990 and 1998, or those who moved above the 25 employee threshold in that time), over a quarter (27 per cent) of employees were working part-time at the time of the 1998 survey. By comparison, part-time employees formed only a sixth (16 per cent) of employment among workplaces that dropped out of the survey population in this period (workplaces that closed down or moved below the 25 employee threshold between 1990 and 1998). Further investigations revealed that around two-fifths of this difference was accounted for by the growth in private service industries, where part-time employment was already more common. A greater proportion (around three-fifths) was accounted for by the greater use of part-time work among service sector workplaces that joined the population when compared with service sector workplaces that left it.

In summary, there were a number of substantial changes in the composition of employment within workplaces across the different sectors of the economy during the 1980s and 1990s, as well as in the economic, social and legal contexts in which employment relationships were conducted. But how did those relationships themselves change? Did managements organise themselves differently to deal with the changing character of employment relations? It is to address such questions that we now turn.

The management of employees

The presence of specialists at the workplace

The existence of an on-site specialist is a good indicator that a workplace is devoting substantial resources to dealing with employee relations issues. We define personnel specialists as managers whose job titles contain any of the terms 'personnel, human resources or industrial, employee or staff relations' *and* who spend at least a quarter of their time on such matters.[6]

The proportion of workplaces with personnel specialists, defined in this way, rose by a third during the 1990s, having remained roughly constant during the second half of the 1980s. This recent upward trend was despite the moves towards increasing line management responsibility for employee relations matters that others have observed (Institute of Personnel and Development, 1995; Colling and Ferner, 1992), and the encroachment of general managers and other specialists on the traditional territory of personnel managers (Storey, 1992). By 1998, a fifth (20 per cent) of workplaces employed a personnel specialist, up from 14 per cent in 1984 and 15 per cent in 1990.[7] The increase was apparent throughout the economy, in both the public and private sectors, in manufacturing and services, in UK- and foreign-owned workplaces and in all but the largest workplaces (where specialists were already almost universal).

In stand-alone sites – often overlooked in the literature, which has tended to focus on large, complex organisations – the incidence of personnel specialists doubled between 1990 and 1998 (from 5 per cent to 11 per cent). Even so, by 1998, branch sites were still twice as likely to employ specialists as stand-alone workplaces: 23 per cent did so, up from 17 per cent in 1990.

Employee relations management in complex organisations

Other studies have shown that employee relations considerations are more likely to feature in the formulation of business strategy in organisations where the function is represented at board level (Marginson *et al.*, 1993) and where personnel specialists are located in head offices. However, our results show that fewer head offices employed such specialists in 1998 than before: the proportion doing so fell sharply between 1990 and 1998, from nearly half (47 per cent) to just over a third (36 per cent). Indeed, personnel representation at board level fell in the private sector as a whole from 1984 onwards, as can be seen in Table 10.4.[8] This trend accelerated in the 1990s. It was particularly marked in smaller organisations

Table 10.4 Representation of the personnel function on the board of directors within private sector organisations, by broad industry, 1980 to 1998

	1980	1984	1990	1998
	% of workplaces	*% of workplaces*	*% of workplaces*	*% of workplaces*
Private sector manufacturing/extraction	73	73	64	44
Private sector services	73	77	74	69
All private sector workplaces	73	76	71	64

Base: All private sector workplaces with 25 or more employees that are part of a larger organisation with a UK head office.
Figures are weighted and based on responses from 867 (1980), 808 (1984), 991 (1990) and 846 (1998) managers.

with fewer than 1,000 employees and in private manufacturing generally. By 1998, around two-thirds of private sector service workplaces reported board-level representation for employee relations, but in manufacturing the figure was under a half.

Has the role of the employee relations manager changed?

Throughout our survey series, our main management respondents have been shown a list of job responsibilities and asked: 'Can you tell me for each one whether or not it forms part of your job or the job of someone responsible to you?'[9] The list has varied across the years, reflecting contemporary interest, but most items have been ever-present, allowing us to map change over time.[10]

Table 10.5 shows that specialists continued to perform somewhat different roles from those undertaken by non-specialists. In 1998, as earlier, they were substantially more likely to deal with pay or conditions of employment, and rather less likely to have responsibility for training.

There has been little change in the functions performed by specialists since 1984, at least for the six responsibilities for which we have time-series data. The only enduring change was the reduced responsibility for systems of payment between 1984 and 1990. However, although the average number of tasks that they performed remained virtually unchanged, personnel specialists were spending

Table 10.5 Job responsibilities of management respondent, by personnel specialist/non-specialist status, 1984 to 1998

	1984	1990	1998
	% of workplaces	% of workplaces	% of workplaces
Personnel specialists			
Handling grievances	94	93	96
Pay or conditions of employment	92	90	90
Recruitment or selection of employees	90	96	93
Staffing or manpower planning	86	83	81
Training of employees	78	71	78
Systems of payment	69	62	62
Non-specialists			
Handling grievances	83	87	91
Pay or conditions of employment	64	69	73
Recruitment or selection of employees	89	91	92
Staffing or manpower planning	85	84	90
Training of employees	83	82	88
Systems of payment	50	60	54

Base: All private sector workplaces with 25 or more employees.
Figures are weighted and based on responses from 781 specialists and 1,013 non-specialists (1984); 798 specialists and 899 non-specialists (1990); and 723 specialists and 1,017 non-specialists (1998).
Note: Excludes interviews not held at the workplace.

less time on them in 1998 than in earlier years. In 1984 they were spending an average of 86 per cent of their time on employee relations activities; by 1998, this had fallen to 69 per cent of their time. This change was largely because fewer specialists were spending *all* of their time on employee relations matters: a sixth (17 per cent) were doing so in 1998, compared to over half (55 per cent) in 1984.

In contrast, the portfolio of employee relations responsibilities falling to non-specialists grew. In 1984, they performed an average of 4.5 of the six tasks listed; by 1998, they were performing an average of 4.9 of them. Each of the six tasks had rather more non-specialists dealing with them than earlier, but on two matters the increase was particularly clear. One was the perennial issue of pay and conditions of employment which, as we see later, became more subject to unilateral management control than previously. The other was the handling of grievances. As we note later in the chapter, the incidence of grievances that gave rise to legal proceedings also increased over the same period. General managers, it appears, have become drawn more often into the handling of grievances, as well as the bread-and-butter issues of pay and conditions.

The collection and interpretation of information is one of the basic tasks of management, who can be expected to collect a range of information about the nature and behaviour of the employees within their workplace. In the 1990 survey managers were asked whether certain items of information were 'collected and used by management, here or at a higher level, to review performance and policies on an annual or more frequent basis?' In 1998 respondents were asked a less specific question in relation to many of the same items: 'Are any of the following records kept for this establishment?' Even accounting for the fact that the less specific 1998 question may have elicited more positive responses, there appears to have been an increase in information collection by workplace managers on the six items common to both surveys, as reported in Table 10.6. The mean number of items for which information was collected rose substantially from 3.0 to 3.7

Table 10.6 Information collected by management, 1990 and 1998

	1990	1998
	% of workplaces	*% of workplaces*
Information collected on:		
Labour costs	69	89
Productivity	44	53
Absenteeism	71	85
Workforce training	61	83
Ethnic mix of workforce	24	33
Gender mix of workforce	26	30
None of these	11	2

Base: All workplaces with 25 or more employees.
Figures are weighted and based on responses from 1,697 (1990) and 1,740 (1998) managers.
Note: Excludes interviews not held at the workplace.

and, whereas a tenth of managers said none of these items were collected in 1990, only 2 per cent did so in 1998.

While there must remain doubts about how much of this apparent increase in information collection is an artefact of the change in question wording, no such doubts need be entertained when the relative prominence of the various items is considered. Labour costs, absence and training were the three most frequently cited items in 1998, as they were in 1990. Details of the ethnic and gender mix of the workforce remained the least likely to be recorded.

Managers in workplaces that were part of a wider organisation collected more information on their workforces than managers in stand-alone sites, even when workplaces of similar size were compared. This may well reflect the demands for information from managers higher up in the organisation. During the 1990s, head offices became more reliant on their branches for workplace-level inform-ation. Head offices had been collecting more information than branches in 1990, but by 1998 branches were collecting more than head offices, suggesting that the monitoring of policies and performance was being devolved to workplace managers.

Employers' association membership and multi-employer bargaining

Employers' associations are one of many sources of advice and information that local employee relations managers, whether specialists or not, may turn to. At the start of our series they also constituted the employers' side of industry-wide or regional negotiating bodies on a substantial scale. In both these roles, employers' associations diminished in importance during the 1980s, indicating that 'more and more managements seem to be assuming responsibility for their own industrial relations' (Sisson, 1993: 205). Employers' association membership in industry and commerce fell during the 1980s from 22 per cent of workplaces in 1984 to 13 per cent in 1990.[11] The latest results suggest a modest recovery, with 18 per cent of workplaces reporting membership in 1998.[12] The recovery was complete among the largest workplaces with 500 or more employees, among whom membership levels in 1998 returned to the level of 1984.

Multi-employer bargaining, which had greatly diminished in importance in the 1980s, became even more of a rarity in the 1990s. Among workplaces with recognised trade unions, multi-employer negotiations affected the pay of some or all employees in 68 per cent of workplaces in 1980. In 1990 this had fallen to 60 per cent, but in 1998 it was down to 34 per cent. In all three broad sectors of the economy the fall over the whole period 1980 to 1998 was substantial: in public services the drop was from 81 to 47 per cent; in private manufacturing it was from 57 to 25 per cent; and, most dramatically, in private services, from 54 to just 12 per cent.

When the falling proportion of workplaces with recognised unions is taken into account, the demise of multi-employer bargaining is even more apparent. Among all workplaces with 25 or more employees, multi-employer bargaining directly affected 43 per cent of workplaces in 1980, 31 per cent in 1990 and just

14 per cent in 1998. The public sector emerged as the only major sector of the economy where multi-employer bargaining remained common in 1998; 41 per cent of public sector workplaces were affected by it. In the private sector the proportion in 1998 was a mere 4 per cent of workplaces, down from over a quarter in 1980. Private sector employers had effectively abandoned acting jointly to regulate the terms and conditions of employment.

Communication with the workforce

One of the elements of the employment relationship that has received increasing attention during the course of the survey series is the methods management use to communicate with employees. In 1980 our focus was very much on the formal representative structures through which this communication occurred, but in our 1984 survey we began investigating the broader picture and have included a number of comparable questions in subsequent surveys. Some of these questions refer to methods or channels of communication that are clearly one-way; others may provide opportunities for genuine two-way communication between management and other employees, although we cannot always be clear that this is the case.

Channels of communication

In our interviews, after a series of questions about consultation through employee committees or groups, managers were asked if they used any from a list of other methods to communicate or consult with the workforce. Table 10.7 reports the results. The one most commonly mentioned in both 1984 and 1990 was 'systematic use of the management chain for communicating with all employees', which approximately 60 per cent of respondents endorsed in both years. In 1998 it was again the most commonly reported method, with 60 per cent reporting its use.[13] As in previous years, there was little variation across the broad sectors of the

Table 10.7 Methods other than consultative committees used by management to communicate or consult with employees, 1984 to 1998

	1984	1990	1998
	% of workplaces	% of workplaces	% of workplaces
Systematic use of the management chain	62	60	60
Regular newsletters distributed to all employees	34	41	50
Regular meetings between management and workforce	34	41	48*
Suggestion scheme	25	28	33

Base: All workplaces with 25 or more employees.
Figures are weighted and based on responses from 2,019 (1984), 2,061 (1990) and 1,929 (1998) managers.
* Imputed from panel data.

economy in the extent of use of the management chain for communicating with employees. However, it was naturally more common in larger workplaces than smaller ones, and this tendency remained at similar levels from 1984 through to 1998.

The second most commonly reported method in 1998 was regular newsletters distributed to all employees. The extent of the use of newsletters had increased substantially in the second half of the 1980s, from 34 per cent of workplaces in 1984 to 41 per cent in 1990. In 1998 the figure reached 50 per cent. As was the case in earlier years, the use of newsletters in 1998 was most common in the public sector, rather less common in private services and least common in private manufacturing.

Although the increase in the use of newsletters from 1990 to 1998 was widespread, it was particularly marked in manufacturing industry, rising from 22 per cent to 34 per cent of workplaces. There was also a substantial increase from 1984 to 1998 in the use of newsletters in small organisations with fewer than 1,000 employees. Here, mention of newsletters rose from 13 per cent in 1984 to 32 per cent in 1998; the comparable figures for workplaces belonging to the largest organisations (those with over 10,000 employees) were 59 and 69 per cent respectively. It seems likely the falling real cost of printing, spurred by new technology, made regular newsletters a more accessible form of communication to employees. However, they were not the only form of communication to have become more widely used during the late 1980s and 1990s.

Regular meetings (at least once a year) between senior management and all sections of the workforce (either altogether or section by section) were also a form of communication that became more widely used in the late 1980s; they were reported in 34 and 41 per cent of workplaces in 1984 and 1990 respectively. This trend continued in the 1990s such that, by 1998, half of all workplaces reported such meetings.[14] The incidence of such meetings had increased among workplaces of all sizes between 1984 and 1990. Since 1990, however, change has been registered primarily among smaller workplaces. Two-fifths of workplaces with less than 100 employees mentioned regular workforce meetings in 1990; by 1998, the proportion had risen to a half. This brought the proportion close to that seen among the largest workplaces (those with 500 or more employees) which, in contrast, had changed little over the same period.

A fourth specific channel of communication investigated in the survey series, in this case predominantly between employees and management, was the use of suggestion schemes. In 1998 the questioning on suggestion schemes was more elaborate than in earlier surveys and raises some doubts about the comparability of the results. One question asked if management had any other channels, besides quality circles or problem-solving groups, through which employees could make suggestions for improving working methods; suggestion schemes were among the coded responses. Later, respondents were asked if management communicates or consults with employees by using, *inter alia*, suggestion schemes. Combining these two questions gives the result that 33 per cent of workplaces in 1998 operated a suggestion scheme, an increase from the 1990 figure of 28 per cent.

Extent of information given to employees

Since 1984 the survey series has tried to capture something of the extent to which management inform employees or their representatives about a range of matters that might be expected to be of general interest. There have been some changes in the items inquired about, but four items have consistently featured in our management interviews. Three concerned financial matters; the fourth concerned employment levels.

The first of the questions asked managers if they gave employees or their representatives any information about the financial position of their workplace. In 1998 the question included the word 'regularly'. Despite this change, which would tend to produce fewer positive responses, the proportion of workplaces where management answered in the affirmative rose from 60 per cent in 1990 to 66 per cent in 1998, continuing the upward trend from 1984, as shown in Table 10.8. In the private sector, both manufacturing and services, the increase between 1990 and 1998 was slight. However, in the public sector it was more substantial, increasing from 70 per cent of workplaces in 1990 to 79 per cent in 1998. The most marked changes were in small- and medium-sized workplaces (those with fewer than 500 employees), especially in the public sector.

The second question (not asked in stand-alone sites) was about the financial position of the organisation to which the workplace belonged. Here there was little change in the aggregate figure, the proportion responding affirmatively being 61 per cent in 1990 and 63 per cent in 1998. In the private sector, there appeared to be an increase between 1990 and 1998 in the provision of this type of information among workplaces with union members, but not in those without.

The third question on giving information about investment plans to employees was modified in both 1990 and 1998, necessitating some caution in the interpretation of the substantial increases shown in Table 10.8.[15] It seems likely that there was a substantial increase in information-sharing about investment plans between 1990 and 1998, possibly greater than the change from 41 to 53 per cent shown in the table. Disaggregating the figures by broad sector suggests the increase in the

Table 10.8 Provision of information by management to employees or their representatives, 1984 to 1998

	1984	1990	1998
	% of workplaces	*% of workplaces*	*% of workplaces*
Information about:			
Financial position of workplace	55	60	66
Financial position of organisation*	60	61	63
Investment plans	27†	41†	53
Staffing/manpower plans	67†	60	61

Base: All workplaces with 25 or more employees.
Figures are weighted and based on responses from 1,943 (1984), 2,028 (1990) and 1,926 (1998) managers.
* Part of a wider organisation only (Bases: 1,780, 1,736 and 1,549 respectively).
† Question wording includes the additional phrase ' ... before the implementation of any changes.'

private sector, both manufacturing and services, was modest. But there clearly was a substantial change among public sector workplaces, the proportions being 33 per cent in 1990 and 61 per cent in 1998. This seems plausible because many of the changes among the public sector over the period – such as the moves to agency operation in much of central government, to trust status in the National Health Service and the devolution of budgeting in many spheres – would have involved more transparent financial planning.

The fourth question about information given to employees concerned managements' staffing plans.[16] The aggregate results showed a decline from 1984 to 60 per cent of workplaces in 1990 and no significant change from this in 1998. Again, however, there were changes within sectors during the recent period. Fewer manufacturing workplaces provided information about staffing plans in 1998 than in 1990 (from 52 per cent down to 37 per cent), but this was offset by small rises in both private and public services. The patterns identified in previous years remained: information was more commonly provided in the public sector and, within the private sector, in larger workplaces and those with recognised trade unions.

A comprehensive assessment of the provision of information by management to employees would cover further topics besides the ones discussed above, which are the only ones for which we have even roughly comparable data for more than one survey. However, an overall impression can be gained from combining the three topics covered by our four questions (two on financial performance, one on investment, one on staffing plans) into a single measure that counts the number of topics on which a particular workplace management gave their employees information. The results of this summary measure suggest an increasing polarization regarding the breadth of information given by management to employees. The proportion of workplaces where management gave employees no information on any of these stayed more or less constant over the period 1984 to 1998 at around 16 per cent. But the proportion of workplaces where management provided information on all three topics rose progressively from 20 per cent in 1980 to 36 per cent in 1998. So while there remained a substantial minority of managements divulging little information to their workforces, an increasing number gave out information on a range of issues. This increase was more rapid amongst unionised workplaces who, by 1998, were roughly twice as likely as non-union workplaces to provide employees with a broad range of information.

Financial participation

Profit sharing and employee share ownership are two forms of financial participation by employees in the operation of their employing organisation that have attracted increasing attention during the course of our survey series – and at various junctures attracted favourable treatment by government through tax exemptions.

We first asked about profit sharing in our 1984 survey and found that 19 per cent of workplaces in industry and commerce had such a scheme. By 1990, as

Table 10.9 shows, this proportion had risen to 44 per cent. In 1998 the comparable figure was little changed at 46 per cent.[17] There were, however, changes below the aggregate level between 1990 and 1998, with an increase in manufacturing industry (from 33 per cent to 50 per cent) and a small drop in private sector services (from 50 per cent to 46 per cent). There was an increase in workplaces belonging to larger organisations, but no change among stand-alone sites. The increasing number of foreign-owned workplaces showed an increased use of profit sharing, while their domestically-owned counterparts did not. Workplaces with recognised trade unions became slightly more likely to have profit sharing, in contrast to the situation in 1990 when they were indistinguishable from non-union workplaces in this respect.

Our survey data enable us to look at the incidence of share ownership schemes over the full duration of the series. In 1980, 13 per cent of all workplaces in industry and commerce had employees who were participating in a share ownership scheme operated by their employer, reflecting a rapid growth in such schemes in the late 1970s. This figure rose to 22 per cent in 1984 and 30 per cent in 1990. The latest survey, however, shows a drop in the incidence of share ownership schemes, to 24 per cent.[18] The recent trend is therefore somewhat different to that seen in respect of profit-sharing arrangements.

The incidence of share ownership schemes in the private sector fell only slightly among manufacturing industries between 1990 and 1998 (from 25 per cent to 22 per cent). A much greater fall was evident within private sector services (from 34 per cent in 1990 to 25 per cent in 1998). As a result, by 1998, the two industry sectors had almost reached a position of parity, having come from a position in 1980 and 1984 in which services were twice as likely to have share ownership schemes as manufacturing. A similar pattern was apparent among domestic and foreign-owned workplaces in the private sector. In the 1980s, foreign-owned workplaces had been less likely to report share ownership schemes than their domestically-owned counterparts. However, whilst the incidence of schemes among domestically-owned workplaces dropped back between 1990 and 1998 (from 33 per cent to 25 per cent), the incidence among those that were foreign-owned showed a notable increase (from 13 per cent to 21 per cent).

Table 10.9 Incidence of profit-sharing arrangements and share ownership schemes, 1980 to 1998

	1980	1984	1990	1998
	% of workplaces	*% of workplaces*	*% of workplaces*	*% of workplaces*
Profit-sharing arrangements	–	19	44	46
Share ownership schemes	13	22	30	24

Base: All trading sector workplaces with 25 or more employees.
Figures are weighted and based on responses from 1,389 (1980), 1,333 (1984), 1,497 (1990) and 1,377 (1998) managers.

Share ownership schemes became slightly more common over the 1990s among workplaces that were part of medium-sized organisations (100–999 employees). This was in contrast to the pattern within organisations having 1,000 employees or more, where 1998 saw a fall in the incidence of share ownership schemes when compared with 1990. There continued to be a very small amount of employee share ownership – around 3 per cent – among workplaces that were part of smaller organisations (those having less than 100 employees), as there had been throughout the series.

So far our analysis of employee relations has largely concerned managerial practices. But management are not the sole actors in the relationship. We now turn to consider facets of the relationship that stem largely from the initiatives of employees.

Trade union membership and recognition

The representation of employees by trade unions or staff associations was regarded as a central feature of the system of industrial relations in Britain when our survey series started in 1980. At that time unions represented employees in a decisive majority of workplaces and through numerous channels, often taking the place of direct communication between management and employees. Between 1980 and 1990, 'so great were the changes that … the traditional, distinctive system of British industrial relations no longer characterised the economy as a whole' (Millward *et al.*, 1992: 350). Changes since 1990 have seen a further diminution of the role of trade unions in representing employees at workplace level. We examine these changes below.

Union presence

The presence of one or more union members is a crude indicator of whether a workplace has employee representation based on trade unions. We base our indicator on the reports of managers.[19]

Having held steady from 1980 to 1984, union presence at workplace level fell sharply from 1984 to 1990 and did so again between 1990 and 1998. From 73 per cent of workplaces in 1980 and 1984, the proportion fell to 64 per cent in 1990 and then to 54 per cent in 1998. While slight changes in question format between 1984 and 1990 qualified the precise amount of the decline for that period,[20] there is no such difficulty with the 1990–98 comparison. The fall between 1990 and 1998 brought the proportion of workplaces with union members down by almost a third over the whole of the period from 1980 to 1998.

Union presence has always differed markedly across the broad sectors of the economy and these differences have become more pronounced since 1980. In each of the three previous surveys, the public sector had union members in virtually every workplace, with private manufacturing industry having high proportions and private service industries having the lowest proportions. This ordering persisted in 1998. However, while union presence in the public sector has remained almost ubiquitous throughout the WIRS series, in private services it dropped from 50 per cent of workplaces in 1980 to 35 per cent in 1998. In private manufacturing it fell more sharply, from 77 per cent of workplaces in 1980 to 42 per cent in 1998, with the fall accelerating over the 1990s.

Union membership density

A more widely used measure of the extent of trade unionism is membership density, the percentage of employees who are union members.[21] Figure 10.1 shows that this fell from 65 per cent in 1980 to 58 per cent in 1984 and to 47 per cent in 1990. By 1998 it was down to 36 per cent.

Each of the broad sectors of the economy had registered falling aggregate union density up to 1990 and each showed further falls from 1990 to 1998. However, the pattern of change between the two periods was different. In the earlier period, union density fell by roughly a quarter in private sector manufacturing and private sector services, but much less so in the public sector. Since 1990, however, the fall was much greater in private services than in the other two sectors – over a third, compared with around a fifth. As a result, the contrast grew between the low

Figure 10.1 Aggregate union membership density, by broad sector, 1980 to 1998

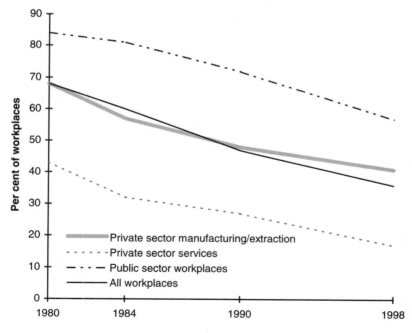

Base: All workplaces with 25 or more employees.
Figures are weighted and based on responses from 1,801 (1980), 1,685 (1984), 1,850 (1990) and 1,853 (1998) managers.

levels of union membership in private sector services and the relatively high levels in private manufacturing and the public sector.

This aggregate picture obscures important detail about the changing way in which union membership density has varied across workplaces, shown in Table 10.10. This classifies workplaces into bands, based on union density: 1–24 per cent, 25–49 per cent and so on. Separate categories are given for the extreme cases of no members and 100 per cent membership. We have already noted the steep increase since 1984 in the proportion having no members.[22] Even more striking is the decline in the proportion of cases with 100 per cent membership. This dropped successively from 18 per cent in 1980 to 7 per cent in 1990 and still further to just 2 per cent in 1998. There was also a fall in cases with very high densities of between 90 and 99 per cent from 1984 onwards.

This major fall in the incidence of workplaces with very high membership densities affected both the public and private sectors and workplaces of different sizes. Much of the fall can be attributed to the virtual disappearance of the closed shop. The proportion of all workplaces in which at least some employees had to be union members in order to get or keep their jobs fell from 23 per cent in 1980 to just 4 per cent in 1990 and 1 per cent in 1998.

While cases with very high union density are an important part of the picture of declining membership, other aspects are more readily understood by returning to look in more detail at aggregate membership density. We do this in Table 10.11, confining it to the private sector of the economy, where the variation was greatest.

The trend of declining membership in the private sector during the 1980s accelerated from 1990 onwards. The rate of decrease moved from 2.7 per cent per year in the late 1980s to 3.5 per cent per year in the 1990s.[23]

The pattern of decline is particularly striking in relation to trade union recognition, by which we mean management's recognition of trade unions for collective

Table 10.10 Union density, 1980 to 1998

	1980*	*1984*	*1990*	*1998*
	% of workplaces	*% of workplaces*	*% of workplaces*	*% of workplaces*
No union members	30	30	39	47
1–24%	8	10	10	14
25–49%	7	10	9	11
50–74%	13	15	16	14
75–89%	13	12	11	7
90–99%	12	12	8	5
100% membership	18	12	7	2

Base: All workplaces with 25 or more employees.
Figures are weighted and based on responses from 1,801 (1980), 1,685 (1984), 1,850 (1990) and 1,853 (1998) managers.
* 1980 figures refer to full-time employees only.

Table 10.11 Aggregate union density in the private sector, by workplace characteristics, 1980 to 1998

	Aggregate density				Average annual change	
	1980*	*1984*	*1990*	*1998*	*1984–90*	*1990–98*
	% of employees who are union members				%	%
Union recognition						
Yes	75	68	66	53	−0.3	−2.6
No	6	5	4	4	−2.6	−0.2
Workplace size						
25–49 employees	36	26	19	8	−4.0	−7.5
50–99 employees	39	30	25	14	−2.9	−5.7
100–199 employees	47	39	32	21	−2.9	−4.7
200–499 employees	59	47	49	32	0.7	−4.4
500 or more employees	77	68	53	45	−3.5	−2.1
Organisation size						
Less than 100 employees	27	20	14	6	−5.0	−7.1
100–999 employees	46	31	24	17	−3.9	−3.4
1,000–9,999 employees	60	50	39	28	−3.5	−3.6
10,000 employees or more	70	56	48	40	−2.5	−2.0
Organisational status						
Stand-alone workplace	34	27	19	11	−4.6	−5.8
Part of a wider organisation	61	46	40	30	−2.4	−3.0
Workplace age††						
Less than 5 years	42	30	23	19	–	–
5–9 years	43	37	19	14	–	–
10–24 years	49	37	32†	16	–	–
25 or more years	62	48	44†	38	–	–
Proportion of part-time employees						
No part-time employees	52	49	45	31	−1.3	−4.0
Less than 25%	58	45	38	31	−2.7	−2.1
25% or more	42	28	20	14	−4.5	−3.9
All private sector workplaces	56	43	36	26	−2.7	−3.5

Base: All private sector workplaces with 25 or more employees.
Figures are weighted and based on responses from 1,212 (1980), 1,043 (1984), 1,321 (1990) and 1,283 (1998) managers.
* 1980 figures refer to full-time employees only.
† 1990 figures refer to workplaces aged 10–20 years and 21 years or more.
†† 1990 figures are for years at current address only.

bargaining over pay. In the decade up to 1990, union membership in private sector workplaces with recognised unions had drifted slowly downwards from three-quarters to two-thirds of employees. But between 1990 and 1998 it dropped more rapidly from two-thirds to just over half. Where unions were not recognised by management, membership remained low throughout the 1980s and 1990s. Overall, the increasing proportion of workplaces with no recognition, which we discuss later in this chapter, had the effect of reducing aggregate union density throughout the period since 1980. Falling union density among workplaces with recognition added to this, most noticeably from 1990 onwards.

The falls in membership in the private sector since 1980 affected all sizes of workplace and all sizes of enterprise. Since 1990, however, smaller workplaces have shown a more rapid rate of decline in density than the largest workplaces with 500 or more employees. Similarly it was the smallest enterprises that showed the sharpest falls in recent times.

Older workplaces tended to have higher union membership than younger workplaces throughout the 1980s. This association persisted in 1998. But, whereas in the earlier surveys union density increased relatively smoothly with the age of workplaces, in 1998 higher levels of density were only apparent in the oldest workplaces. In 1998, even workplaces between 10 and 24 years old had an aggregate union density of only 16 per cent, compared with the 38 per cent for workplaces at least 25 years old. This suggests that workplaces established since the 1970s, when union membership was at its historical peak, have been less likely to acquire union members than their forerunners. The very steep drop in union density in the youngest private sector workplaces (those less than five years old) from 42 per cent in 1980 to 19 per cent in 1998 is perhaps the strongest single indicator of the difficulties facing the trade union movement in its attempts to retain and rebuild its membership base.

Besides those discussed above, other workplace characteristics such as workforce composition and industrial activity continued to be associated with union membership density in 1998. The fall in membership affected all types of workplace in the private sector. It affected the types of workplace where unions have always found it more difficult to recruit and retain members, as well as those where membership was the norm.

Trade union recognition

Management's willingness to allow trade unions to represent employees has most clearly been expressed in Britain by recognising unions for negotiating pay and conditions of employment, whether at the workplace or some higher level. This key indicator of joint regulation and the role of unions has been a fundamental question in the survey series since its inception.

After remaining stable in the early 1980s at roughly 65 per cent, the proportion of workplaces with recognised unions declined substantially from 1984 to 1990, a trend that continued through to 1998. The figure fell from 53 to 42 per cent in the most recent period, as shown in Figure 10.2.[24] The pace of change was very

Figure 10.2 Trade union recognition, by broad sector, 1980 to 1998

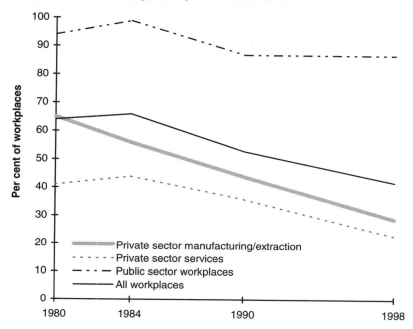

Base: All workplaces with 25 or more employees.
Figures are weighted and based on responses from 2,040 (1980), 2,019 (1984), 2,061 (1990) and 1,929 (1998).

similar, with the result that by 1998 substantially fewer than half of workplaces with 25 or more employees had recognised unions.

In the public sector, union recognition for at least some employees at each workplace remained very much the norm. The survey results show no change from 1990 to 1998, remaining at 87 per cent. Pay determination by review bodies rather than by direct employer/union bargaining largely accounts for the small proportion of public sector workplaces where no unions are recognised for pay bargaining. The continuing decline in the extent of recognition in the 1990s was therefore a private sector phenomenon. Manufacturing and services showed similar rates of decline, with each losing about a third between 1990 and 1998.

Within the private sector, almost all types of workplace showed a lower incidence of union recognition in 1998 than in 1990. All of the broad industrial sectors exhibited this trend, except for the energy and water supply industries, where former public utilities predominated. Engineering and metal goods showed a particularly sharp fall from 37 per cent to 19 per cent of workplaces having recognised unions, continuing a trend that began with the collapse of the industry-wide negotiating machinery in 1990.

All sizes of workplace exhibited the declining incidence of union recognition in the 1990s – see Table 10.12 – but the smallest workplaces had a greater rate of

Table 10.12 Trade union recognition, by size and age of private sector workplaces, 1980 to 1998

	1980	1984	1990	1998
	% of workplaces	% of workplaces	% of workplaces	% of workplaces
Workplace size				
25–49 employees	41	40	30	16
50–99 employees	49	49	40	23
100–199 employees	65	62	48	39
200–499 employees	75	66	69	54
500 or more employees	92	86	75	64
Workplace age[††]				
Less than 10 years	43	41	23	18
10–24 years	47	42	31[†]	22
25 or more years	53	52	52[†]	32

Base: All private sector workplaces with 25 or more employees.
Figures are weighted and based on responses from 1,330 (1980), 1,189 (1984), 1,429 (1990) and 1,317 (1998) managers.
[†] 1990 figures refer to workplaces aged 10 to 20 years and 21 years or more.
[††] 1990 figures are for years at current address only.

fall than larger ones. In workplaces with 25 to 49 employees the incidence of union recognition in the private sector fell by half, from 30 per cent to 16 per cent, whereas for workplaces with 500 or more employees it fell from 75 per cent to 64 per cent.

Enterprise size also had a bearing on the declining incidence of recognition in the private sector. Between 1984 and 1998, union recognition amongst workplaces belonging to enterprises of less than 1,000 employees more than halved, from 35 per cent to 15 per cent. By comparison, for workplaces belonging to enterprises with 10,000 or more UK employees the incidence of recognition dropped from 70 per cent to 50 per cent.

Earlier work on previous surveys showed that the age of workplaces was associated more strongly with recognition at the end of the 1980s than at the start (Millward, 1994). Further, more detailed analysis demonstrated that, with other relevant variables controlled for, the rate of recognition among new workplaces was lower in the 1980s than in earlier decades (Disney *et al.*, 1995). Table 10.12 indicates that this lower rate of recognition among young workplaces in the private sector persisted in the 1990s. Less than a fifth of private sector workplaces under ten years old in 1998 had recognised unions, compared with around two-fifths in the early 1980s. As with our analysis of union density, it is this historically low rate of recognition among new workplaces that has the most profound implications for the trade union movement.

In summary, the decline in the incidence of union recognition that we identified from our 1990 survey results persisted through to 1998. It was a widespread phenomenon in the private sector, but it particularly affected smaller workplaces and newer workplaces. However, these results are from cross-section surveys that cannot show whether particular workplaces changed their recognition arrangements over the period. Our 1990–98 panel survey was designed to address such questions.

Changes in union recognition, 1990–98

Using identical questions in the 1990 and 1998 panel interviews, our panel of over 800 continuing workplaces showed very little net change in recognition between 1990 and 1998. In 1990, 56 per cent of panel workplaces recognised one or more trade unions; in 1998, 55 per cent of these same workplaces did so. New recognition cases amounting to 4 per cent of the panel sample were outnumbered by the 6 per cent of cases where there was derecognition. In short, changes in recognition among continuing workplaces roughly balanced out; they account for hardly any of the net fall recorded by the corresponding cross-section surveys between 1990 and 1998.

Nor, indeed, did the fall occur because workplaces that either closed after 1990 or dropped below our 25 employee threshold were more likely to have recognised unions than those that survived: our sample of 'leavers' had an incidence of recognition of 51 per cent, fairly close to the figure for continuing workplaces in 1990 of 56 per cent. The net fall in recognition between 1990 and 1998 arose because the workplaces that replaced the leavers in the population were much less likely to recognise unions: only 30 per cent of them did so. The lower rate of recognition among these newer workplaces was unquestionably the principal reason for the fall in recognition among the generality of workplaces between 1990 and 1998.

We can, in fact, be more precise than this. By using the technique of shift-share analysis on workplaces that left the WIRS population and those that joined it we are able to discount the amount of the change that is attributable to the differing composition of these groups and reveal how much arises from changed behaviour among similar types of workplace.[25] Virtually none of the change arose from the fact that the joiners were more likely to be in the private services sector and employed more part-time workers. Almost all of the change arose because workplaces that joined the WIRS population between 1990 and 1998, even controlling for their sector and employment of part-time workers, were less likely to recognise unions than similar workplaces that had dropped out of the population.

The coverage of collective bargaining

Union recognition at a workplace does not imply that all employees there are directly affected by collective bargaining agreements. Further questions have been used in the survey series to establish the proportion of employees in workplaces with recognised unions that are indeed covered by collective bargaining.[26] The results have been aggregated across all workplaces to give an overall figure. The figure fell from 70 per cent of all employees in 1984 to 54 per cent in 1990. By 1998 it had fallen further to 41 per cent of employees.

The pattern of declining coverage naturally mirrored the pattern of falling recognition. It was apparent in each of the three major sectors of the economy. In the public sector, where pay review bodies replaced joint regulation for some major occupational groups and some derecognition had also occurred, aggregate coverage fell from 80 per cent in 1990 to 63 per cent in 1998. In private manufacturing the fall was slight, from 51 per cent to 46 per cent of employees. Private services was the sector with the largest proportionate fall: from 33 per cent to 22 per cent.

Employee representation at the workplace

Employees may be represented in their dealings with management in a number of different ways. Traditionally, trade unions have provided the most common vehicle for collective representation. But the decline in the extent of union membership and recognition over the period of our survey series has led increasingly to questions as to whether other forms of collective representation have emerged. First, however, we examine how the extent of workplace representation by recognised trade unions has developed over the period.

Workplace representatives of recognised unions

Within unionised workplaces, the extent of on-site representation by shop stewards or other lay union representatives fell during the 1980s, but there was no further decline between 1990 and 1998.[27] In broad terms, around 80 per cent of workplaces with recognition in both 1980 and 1984 had a union representative on site; by 1990 this proportion fell to around 70 per cent and stayed roughly at the 1990 level in 1998, as can be seen in Figure 10.3. Stability in this measure of the extent of local representation was apparent in both the public and private sectors from 1990 onwards.

Of course, the continuous decline in the extent of recognition in the private sector meant that many fewer private sector workplaces had a local union representative in 1998 than in 1980. The figure fell from 38 per cent of all private sector workplaces in 1980 to 26 per cent in 1990 and further still to 17 per cent in 1998.

Full-time lay union representatives – not to be confused with full-time union officials – are an indication that management regards the role of trade unions at the workplace as of central importance. Such representatives remained rare among workplaces with recognised unions. The change from 2 per cent in 1990 to 4 per cent in 1998 is on the margin of statistical significance and the results are perhaps best interpreted as showing that full-time lay representatives became no rarer in the 1990s in unionised workplaces in either the public or private sectors.

Figure 10.3 Presence of union representatives in workplaces with a recognised union, 1980 to 1998

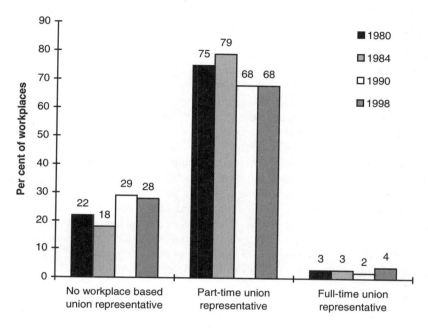

Base: All workplaces with a recognised trade union and 25 or more employees.
Figures are weighted and based on responses from 1,575 (1980), 1,593 (1984), 1,416 (1990) and 1,116 (1998) managers.

Other workplace representatives

While representatives of recognised unions have provided by far the most common examples of employee representative, other forms have existed and continue to do so. Here we restrict our attention to non-union representatives, excluding those dealing solely with health and safety matters. For simplicity we consider only non-union representatives in workplaces where there are no union members present and, because of data limitations, to the situation in 1990 and 1998.[28] Since workplaces without union members were very rare in the public sector we consider only private sector workplaces.

In the private sector, non-union representatives were uncommon in workplaces without union members. In 1990, 11 per cent of non-union workplaces had individual employee representatives. In 1998 the proportion was almost the same (12 per cent). However, while there was no change over this period in the private sector as a whole, such representatives became somewhat more common in private sector services (rising from 7 per cent in 1990 to 11 per cent in 1998) and somewhat less common in manufacturing (falling from 20 per cent to 15 per cent). As might be expected, non-union representatives were more common in larger workplaces and this remained the case.

Consultative committees

Joint consultative committees with members of management and employee representatives have been part of the institutional framework of employment relations in Britain for decades. Our first two surveys showed that around a third of all workplaces had a consultative committee, but the proportion fell to 29 per cent in 1990, largely because of a substantial fall in manufacturing. There was no further fall by 1998, the proportion remaining at 29 per cent, as shown in Table 10.13. However, workplace consultative committees became somewhat less common in the public sector, falling from 49 per cent to 39 per cent between 1990 and 1998. They became more common in the private sector, the proportion of workplaces with them rising from 20 per cent to 25 per cent since 1990. This slight resurgence in the private sector, following the steady decline in the 1980s, was confined to small and medium-sized workplaces and was more apparent where unions were recognised than where they were not.

The bulk of the foregoing analysis has focused on the practices and arrangements used at workplace level that govern relations between management and employees. These are a central concern of our survey series. But what of the quality of those relations? We end this summary of the changes over the period 1980–98 with a brief examination of some indicators of conflict at workplace level.

Table 10.13 Presence of workplace-level joint consultative committees, by workplace characteristics, 1980 to 1998

	1980	1984	1990	1998
	% of workplaces	% of workplaces	% of workplaces	% of workplaces
Sector				
Private	30	26	20	25
Public	43	48	49	39
Workplace size (private sector)				
25–99 employees	25	21	16	19
100–499 employees	44	45	34	42
500 or more employees	66	68	57	54
Union recognition (private sector)				
Yes	40	32	23	32
No	20	21	18	22
All workplaces	34	34	29	29

Base: All workplaces with 25 or more employees.
Figures are weighted and based on responses from 2,031 (1980), 2,017 (1984), 2,057 (1990) and 1,926 (1998) managers.

Workplace conflict

Collective industrial conflict was one of the major concerns of government, researchers and practitioners at the time when the first of our series of surveys was being designed. Its salience diminished during the course of the 1980s, such that the proportion of workplaces where any respondents reported any type of collective industrial action had halved by 1990. Officially-recorded strikes, a more limited measure, fell even more substantially. Indeed, recent years have had fewer officially-recorded strikes than any year since records began in the late nineteenth century. The declining prevalence of union representation and the legal restrictions on industrial action imposed by successive Conservative governments are widely believed to be major causes of the virtual disappearance of the strike as a feature of British employment relations. The rise of various forms of individual conflict between employee and employer might be seen as a corollary. Leaving a more extended discussion to further research, here we briefly describe how our 1998 survey results update the changing picture of collective and individual conflict revealed by the survey series. We focus on just two measures: the incidence of any form of strike or industrial action at workplaces in the past year; and the number of Industrial Tribunal cases initiated by employees or ex-employees of the workplace in the past year. Both of these measures rely on the reports of managers.[29]

The incidence of industrial action tumbled between 1990 and 1998, falling from 13 to just 2 per cent of workplaces. Strike action fell the most dramatically, from 11 per cent to just 1 per cent of workplaces. Non-strike action dropped from 5 per cent to 1 per cent of workplaces. Overtime bans and work-to-rules were the most common forms of non-strike action, as they were throughout the 1980s and 1990s. Collective industrial action of any kind has thus virtually disappeared from British workplaces, a far cry from the situation at the start of our series, when around a quarter of workplaces experienced it in the course of a year. Only a small portion of the drop can be attributed to the fall in the extent of trade union representation. Union recognition has dropped by a third; industrial action by nine-tenths. Clearly workers in unionised workplaces are now far less likely to take industrial action than was the case in the early 1980s, for a host of reasons which lie beyond the scope of this chapter to explore.

Industrial Tribunal actions continued their rapid growth in the 1990s, in small part because of the extension of the jurisdictions covered by the tribunals. Whereas 9 per cent of workplaces had been the object of such litigation in 1990, 13 per cent were in 1998. In most workplaces where this had occurred a single case had been instigated, generally regarding unfair dismissal by an ex-employee; this continued the pattern of previous surveys. The aggregate number of cases per thousand employees rose from 1.4 in 1990 to 2.0 in 1998, continuing the upward trend established in the 1980s.[30] The increase was greatest in workplaces where there were union members but where unions lacked recognition by management. In short, individual conflict between employers and employees rose during the course of our series at the same time that collective conflict all but disappeared.

Conclusion

The Workplace Industrial Relation Survey series was initiated at a major turning-point in the history of management–employee relations in Britain. At the end of the 1970s, a struggle between the collective forces of employers on the one hand, and employees and their trade unions on the other hand culminated, in a wave of industrial conflict and the election of a government committed to radical reforms. There has been a metamorphosis in the discourse and the practice of industrial relations in Britain since that time. The term 'industrial relations' has itself been replaced in common parlance by 'employee relations', 'employment relations' and a range of other terms, none of which carry the collectivist overtones of the phrase that came so naturally to mind when we were designing our 1980 survey. Our renaming of the survey in 1998 and, more fundamentally, our redesigning of it, acknowledged the sea change that took place in relations between employers and employees over the intervening 18 years. But our redesign retained enough from the earlier surveys to track many of the major phenomena over the whole period. In this chapter we aimed to give a broad picture of how these practices and arrangements have changed.

Our survey series is at its most authoritative in documenting the decline in the institutions that exemplified the system of joint regulation that existed at the end of the 1970s. In 1998, the workplace coverage of multi-employer bargaining, was half what it was in 1980. Trade union membership had nearly halved, while the recognition of trade unions by management for negotiating terms of employment had fallen by a third. Compulsory union membership arrangements had all but disappeared.

But while trade union representation was disappearing at an accelerating rate, not all of the indicators of union presence and activity suggest increasing weakness. Union representatives maintained their presence from 1990 onwards and the decline of full-time representatives that had occurred in the 1980s did not continue. Union representation continued to be associated with the existence of other channels of communication between employees and management, including general consultative councils and health and safety committees.

Other, more direct, methods of communicating with the workforce became more commonly used by management – and there were more workplaces where information was shared on a significant scale – but there remained substantial numbers of workplaces where, by managers' own accounts, very little information was shared with employees. Comprehensive managerial communication practices designed to engender 'employee involvement' may have become more common, but are by no means widespread. Profit sharing and employee share ownership – other means of increasing employee involvement – became more widely used in industry and commerce in the 1980s, but remained stable or suffered a decline in the 1990s.

It would be hard to interpret the changes that we have documented in this chapter as firm indications of the adoption of a new model of employee relations. More plausible is the notion that a number of alternative approaches to employee relations are being adopted in different types of workplace and in different parts of the economy.

But while there clearly has been a substantial amount of change, the nature and processes of change have yet to be fully understood. At the beginning of this chapter we outlined a range of contextual developments – political, legal, social and economic – that have each arguably played their own part. Yet such influences work through into changes at workplace level in a number of different ways: behavioural change within continuing workplaces; different behaviour by new workplaces from similar ones that they replaced; and the changing composition of the population of workplaces, such as the shift from manufacturing to services. The interlocking elements of our survey design allow us to pinpoint how important these three different routes have been.

Two examples serve to illustrate the value and the potential of separately identifying and assessing the different possible explanations for any particular net change observed over time. Early in the chapter we presented evidence of the increased use of part-time workers at workplace level. Our analysis showed that continuing workplaces hardly changed their use of part-time workers. Change therefore arose as a result of differences between workplaces that left the population and those that joined it. The growth in private service industries, where part-time employment was already more common, played a substantial part in the process. More important, however, was the greater number of part-time jobs available in workplaces that joined the population compared with the number available in similar workplaces that had left it.

Our second example concerns trade union representation. We showed that the decline in trade union representation after 1990 was not primarily because derecognition was widespread in continuing workplaces. Nor was it because the population of workplaces had shifted towards those that were less likely in the past to have recognised unions. The overriding reason for the decline in union representation was that new workplaces were much less likely to recognise unions than similar workplaces that they replaced in the population. It is notable that the new workplaces of the 1990s were also less likely to recognise unions than similar new workplaces in earlier decades.

These examples illustrate the broader point that changes in employment relations at the aggregate level, as depicted by our survey series, may arrive through a variety of routes. Within the confines of a single chapter, we have been able to report results for just some of the main questions asked in the series and to apply these detailed forms of analysis to just a small selection of those. For our more extensive treatment – and hence to a more detailed understanding of the changes in British employment relations during the 1980s and 1990s – we refer the reader to our companion volume, *All Change at Work?*

Notes

1   In each of the surveys such a role-holder has not always been present or available and a substitute at a higher organisational level has been found. A minority of cases thus have 'proxy informants'. The incidence of such cases was lowest (8 per cent) in 1980 and highest (18 per cent) in 1990.

2   The geographical coverage has been constant: England, Wales and Scotland. Industrial coverage was constant for the first three surveys. In 1998 the industrial scope excluded certain extractive industries which were included within the scope of earlier surveys. The number of cases affected by this variation in scope is no greater than 15 in any of the earlier surveys. We have found very few results affected by excluding these cases from the earlier surveys and have retained them in the results presented in this volume.

3   Differential sampling by employment size has been used throughout the series, as has weighting to compensate for it. Some modest differential sampling by industry was introduced in 1990 and this principle was extended in 1998. Again, differential weighting was introduced to compensate. Additional weighting was included for the first three surveys to compensate for the age of the sampling frame and its consequent under-inclusion of smaller workplaces near the threshold of 25 employees. In 1998 the new sampling frame was considered sufficiently up to date to make this unnecessary. However, the 1998 weighting scheme involved trimming the extreme weights, a practice not previously adopted.

4   Changes over time can, of course, be measured using retrospective questions, but these are likely to be highly unreliable for a period as long as eight years.

5   In the absence of a question in the 1998 survey that identified workplaces in nationalised industries, this figure was arrived at by first identifying the industry classifications of all cases under state ownership within the 1990 survey. Public sector cases in the 1998 survey with equivalent industry classifications were then identified as being part of nationalised industries.

6   An alternative definition is used in Chapter 4.

7   These figures are based on interviews undertaken solely at the sampled workplace: as are all person-related data in this section, so that they can be accurately matched with the characteristics of the sampled workplace.

8   To retain consistency across years, the time-series is confined to workplaces in the private sector with a UK head office. Some of the decline may be accounted for by the fact that the 1998 survey question did not include representation on the 'top governing body', but any discrepancy is minimised by confining the time-series to workplaces in the private sector.

9   The 1980 data are not strictly comparable because the question did not include '... or the job of someone responsible to you'. We therefore focus on the period 1984–1998.

10   Equal opportunities, health and safety and performance appraisal were only listed in 1998. Job evaluation/grading was asked for every year except 1998. Staffing or manpower planning was not included in 1980. In 1998 the list included 'handling of grievances', rather than the broader 'grievances, discipline, disputes' which had appeared in previous years.

11   The 1980 data are not considered to be comparable.

12   The 1998 measure is broader than the measure used in earlier surveys because the 1998 question omits reference to the employers' association negotiating on behalf of its members to regulate pay or terms of employment. One might therefore expect to see some increase in employers' association membership arising from the changed wording. However, the figures are given credence by a separate question which asked respondents whether they had taken advice on employee relations matters from outside bodies, including employers' associations. The list simply included employers' associations without a definition. The results show a similar revival in fortunes for employers' associations during the 1990s.

13   The show-card wording in 1998 was 'Systematic use of the management chain/cascading of information'.

14   The 1998 figures are imputed from panel data. Detailed analysis, discussed in our companion volume, demonstrates that the data provide more direct estimates for our time series than the new question contained in the 1998 cross-section survey.

15   The 1984 question read, 'Can you tell me whether management here gives employees or their representatives information about investment plans before the implementation of any changes in them?' The 1990 question dropped the last phrase 'before the implementation ...' and added the word 'internal' before 'investment plans'. The 1998 question was, 'Does management regularly give employees or their representatives information about internal investment plans?' The wording

change in 1990 would tend to increase the number of positive responses in that year compared with 1984. On the other hand, the 1998 wording change would tend to reduce positive responses in 1998 compared with 1990.

16 The phrase in 1984 and 1990 was 'staffing or manpower plans', but this change seems trivial. However, the question wording was also changed in line with some of the other items mentioned above and notably with the insertion of the word 'regularly' in 1998.

17 In 1998, respondents were asked if 'any employees at the workplace received payments or dividends' from a list of five types of arrangement, the first two being 'profit-related payments or bonuses' and a 'deferred profit-sharing scheme' (see Chapter 4). In previous years, the question was broader, asking whether 'the employing organisation operated any of the schemes for employees here'. The effect of the change in wording between 1990 and 1998 is likely, if anything, to have led to an understatement of the increase in profit sharing over the period.

18 As noted above the incidence of such schemes in previous years was derived from a broader question asking whether 'the employing organisation operated any of the schemes for employees here'. To promote comparability between years, cases from 1980–90 have been restricted to those where at least some employees at the workplace were actually participating in the scheme. Nonetheless, it should be noted that only the 1984 and 1990 questions made specific reference to share option schemes. At least some of the observed drop between 1990 and 1998 may result from these changes in question wording.

19 This is largely because these are more complete in the WIRS series as a whole; we have worker representatives' reports of union membership only for sub-samples in all four surveys and employee reports only in 1998.

20 In the 1980 and 1984 results, other answers, don't know and not answered were treated as having no members. In both 1990 and 1998 every productive case has a 'yes' or 'no' answer.

21 Here, as in the earlier WIRS source books, the estimates presented comprise the aggregate union density across the population of workplaces covered by the survey, as estimated by management respondents, not a mean of the union density for each workplace. Figures for 1980 refer to full-time employees only; union membership numbers were not collected for part-time employees in the 1980 survey. Figures may vary slightly from those in earlier source books because of different treatment of some missing values and minor computational differences between the present and earlier analyses.

22 The figures for 'zero membership density' and 'no members present' are not the same because cases which had some members, but where precise numbers were unknown, are excluded from the density estimates.

23 For calculating rates of change we have taken the interval between the 1990 and 1998 surveys as seven and three-quarter years. The first three surveys were separated by whole years. In making these comparisons we have ignored the 1980 figures which only refer to full-time employees.

24 Data from both the 1990 and 1998 surveys have been amended in the course of our analysis for some public sector workplaces engaged in primary or secondary education to remove measurement error arising from the misreporting of union recognition, as strictly defined in the questionnaire to mean for the purposes of collective bargaining over pay and conditions. In 1990, 2 per cent of such workplaces reported recognised unions although the only unions present came under the remit of the Pay Review Body for schoolteachers in England and Wales; these workplaces were therefore not party to collective bargaining over pay. Recoding such workplaces to having no recognised unions lowered the proportion of all public sector primary and secondary schools that had recognised unions in 1990 from 70 per cent to 67 per cent. The scale of the adjustment was not sufficient to alter the proportion of recognised workplaces in the public sector as a whole.

    In 1998, cases of this type were much more common and amounted to 20 per cent of all workplaces in this sector. Recoding these workplaces to having no recognised unions lowered the proportion with recognised unions from 93 per cent to 73 per cent. Accordingly, the proportion of recognised workplaces in the public sector was reduced from 94 per cent to 87 per cent, and from 44 per cent to 42 per cent in the sample as a whole. These changes were made to enable exact comparisons with earlier years. Elsewhere in this volume, union recognition is measured as reported by respondents – see endnote 8 in Chapter 5.

25   To perform this analysis we divided the sample into five categories representing types of workplace that differ markedly in their incidence of recognition, as identified by previous research (Millward, 1994; Disney *et al.*, 1995). These categories were: public sector; private manufacturing, no part-time employees; private manufacturing, some part-time employees; private services, less than a quarter of employees part-time; and private services, more than a quarter of employees part-time.

26   In 1990 the question asked directly what proportion of employees were covered by negotiations between management and recognised unions or groups of unions. In 1998 there were up to nine questions asking how pay was determined for each major occupational group at the workplace. Responses that referred to collective bargaining have been summed in relation to the number of employees in the relevant occupational group to provide the number covered at each workplace. There were some cases where this measure was inconsistent with the response to the question on union recognition. The inconsistencies have been resolved as far as possible, but there remain cases with reported recognition but no coverage. The 1998 coverage estimate should therefore be viewed with some caution and probably regarded as a lower bound.

27   In 1990 and 1998 the question referred to representatives of recognised unions. In the earlier surveys the question did not explicitly refer to the recognised unions, although it was only asked where they existed. There are some doubts over the comparability of the results between 1984 and 1990.

28   The survey questions on employee representatives, other than those of recognised unions, have changed during the course of the series, making comparisons difficult. The closest comparison is between a 1998 survey question, 'Are there any employees here who act as representatives of other employees in dealings with management?' and a similar question in 1990 which referred to *non-union* representatives. To make them comparable we restrict the analysis to workplaces with no union members. Both questions exclude representatives concerned only with health and safety matters.

29   Earlier surveys suggested some under-reporting of industrial action by managers, and so combined them with those of worker representatives. Here we rely on managers' reports for all four surveys in order to be consistent with the results presented in Chapter 6.

30   The figure represents the aggregate rate of tribunal cases across all employees in the survey population, which is why it differs from the figure reported in Chapter 6, this being a mean of the rate of applications in each workplace. After examination, a very small number of cases reporting more than 100 tribunal actions in the year have been excluded from the calculation.

11 Small business employment relations

Chapter 1 explained how and why the employment size threshold for the survey had been dropped from 25 employees in previous surveys to 10 employees in WERS 98. For reasons noted in that chapter, the analysis so far has excluded the smallest workplaces, those with between 10 and 24 employees. This allowed us to present comparable data with other surveys in the series and to avoid these smallest (and most numerous) workplaces dominating the overall results. In this chapter we draw in part on the data collected in these small workplaces to present a separate account of *small business* employment relations. Small businesses occupy a distinct part of the lexicon in academic and policy debates. There are separate academic departments wholly devoted to studying small business and separate associations representing their interests. They even have their own Minister at government level.

In presenting results for these smaller workplaces, there are various ways in which we could have analysed the results. One would have simply been to focus on the issue of workplace size: how do employment relations in workplaces with 10 to 24 employees differ from those with 25 or more? The results presented so far often show that workplace size is a significant influence on workplace practices; do these relationships extend down to smaller workplaces? In particular we might expect to see less formality and bureaucracy in smaller workplaces.

This chapter provides a slightly different, and arguably more sophisticated, comparison. It is to illustrate the distinctiveness, or not, of small businesses by contrasting them with otherwise similar small workplaces that were part of a wider organisation ('small multiples').

Before describing the nature or extent of the employment relationship within small businesses, we first need to define exactly what we mean by small businesses and small multiples. We restricted our attention to private sector workplaces with fewer than 100 employees (i.e. with between 10 and 99 employees). We then divided these into two groups. The first, 'small businesses', are stand-alone sites. The second are workplaces that are part of a wider organisation, where total employment in the *organisation* exceeds 100 employees.[1] These we call 'small multiples'. Thus, the workplaces in our comparison are directly comparable in terms of the number of employees, but had quite distinct ownership and control structures. A typical example from the retail sector would be an independent grocer compared with a store from one of the national supermarket chains. Both are engaged in the same activity, both had fewer than 100 employees, but the structures of ownership and control could not have been more diverse. Additionally, we use the term 'small workplaces' to refer to both small businesses and small multiples.

Hence, in this chapter, we are focusing on generally smaller workplaces within the sample, but otherwise holding workplace size constant. This allows us to explore another potentially significant source of variation between workplaces: the degree of alignment between the ownership of an enterprise and day-to-day control at the workplace level. Our sample of small private sector workplaces divides into three categories: small multiples, small businesses with an owner-manager present and small businesses where there was no owner-manager present. We would expect small businesses with owner-managers present to differ from those without, because the principal–agent issues typically involved in reconciling the interests of owners and managers do not arise. However, even where the ownership of the business is separate from its management, we might expect management practices in stand-alone workplaces to differ from those that are part of a wider organisation.

The main difference we expected to observe between small businesses and multiples was the degree of formality used in regulating the employment relationship. Typically, small businesses are thought to see little need to pre-plan relations with employees. They are content to adopt a minimalist management style, where management are content provided 'workers are working' (Scott *et al.*, 1989).

Throughout this chapter we rely on data from the management interview only. It would have been possible to incorporate a worker representative and employee perspective but, for reasons of brevity, we have not done so.[2] Broadly, the chapter follows the format and themes of Chapters 2 to 6 of the book, making occasional references, where appropriate, to those findings.

Although there may have been good arguments for developing a dedicated survey of small businesses,[3] we instead designed the research instruments to be both flexible and diverse enough to allow for investigation of the formal practices likely to be found in the largest workplaces – those with over 500 employees – and the informal phenomena likely to be prevalent in the smallest workplaces – those with at least 10 employees. For example, we used open-ended questions to investigate methods used to resolve individual and collective disputes where there were no formal procedures, knowing that these were less likely to be in place in small businesses, but unsure of the processes that would be in place. This approach allowed the respondent to answer as they thought best, while allowing the analyst to decide on groupings after the event.

Small business in context

As with Chapter 2, we commence by looking at the profile of all small workplaces. It was the smallest workplaces (i.e. those with between 10 and 24 employees) that predominate, as shown in Table 11.1. The size distribution of small businesses and small multiples was very similar, but there were marked differences in industrial composition. The former were found largely in manufacturing, health and other business services, while the latter figured heavily in wholesale and retail trade. Here, the presence of large retail chains explains much of this difference. In fact, of small multiples, a third (35 per cent) belonged to an organisation with at least 10,000 employees in the UK. Similarly, 45 per cent were part of an organisation with over 100 other workplaces nationally.

A little over half of all small businesses were family-run, in the sense that a single individual or family had a controlling interest in the company. In most of these cases, at least one of the controlling owners was actively involved in day-to-day management of the business on a full-time basis. Overall, this means that a little over two-fifths of small businesses had a working owner present, more than ten times the proportion of small multiples that had a working owner present. The latter were mostly characterised by having no individual or family with a controlling interest. Indeed, 63 per cent of small multiples were part of publicly-listed companies and 20 per cent were at least partly foreign-owned.

Table 11.1 Characteristics of small businesses and small multiples

	Small businesses	Small multiples
	% of workplaces	% of workplaces
Workplace size		
10–24 employees	60	56
25–49 employees	28	27
50–99 employees	11	17
Industry		
Manufacturing	20	9
Electricity, gas and water	0	0
Construction	8	5
Wholesale and retail	14	37
Hotels and restaurants	5	14
Transport and communications	3	4
Financial services	2	7
Other business services	15	12
Public administration	0	1
Education	3	2
Health	20	6
Other community services	8	2
Ownership		
Controlling interest and full-time working owner	43	4
Controlling interest, but no full-time working owner	10	9
No controlling interest / public limited company	47	87

Base: All small businesses (private stand-alone sites) and all small multiples (private sites that are part of a wider organisation totalling 100 or more employees) with 10–99 employees.
Figures are weighted and based on responses from 250 (column 1) and 403 (column 2) managers.

In short, while the like-for-like comparison largely holds with workplace size, there were some notable differences in the industry distribution, but the major differences are (by definition) in the ownership structures.

Employment structures in small businesses

Chapter 3 noted the extensive debate on the changing nature of work and, in particular, the shift away from the 'standard' full-time permanent job. Small businesses have not been immune to these developments. For example, a study undertaken for the Institute of Personnel and Development (1998) showed that small firms were increasingly reducing the number of people who have a contract of employment with the workplace. We are unable to address rates of change in the use of non-standard forms of labour, but we can address its incidence. The findings show that, across both small businesses and small multiples, there was a significant variety and level of sophistication in the types of labour deployed.

Workforce composition

Commencing with the individual characteristics of those who made up the workforce, we find broadly similar breakdowns of men (52 per cent) and women (48 per cent) in all small workplaces as a whole.

There were differences in the age composition of the workforces, with small businesses much more likely than small multiples to have made use of older workers and somewhat less likely to use young workers. But it was small multiples which were the workplaces 'out of step' with the broader picture of workplaces as a whole (see Table 3.2). Young workers made up a tenth or more of the workforce in 39 per cent of small multiples and older workers in 43 per cent of cases; comparable figures for small businesses were 32 per cent and 70 per cent respectively. This probably reflects the disproportionate use of younger workers in wholesale and retail.

Small businesses employ less people from ethnic minorities than small multiples. Around a quarter (27 per cent) employ some, while in just 7 per cent of cases people from an ethnic minority group made up at least a tenth of the workforce. In small multiples the respective figures were 43 per cent and 17 per cent.

Small businesses and small multiples had broadly similar occupational profiles, with the former making somewhat greater use of professionals and clerical workers, while the latter were twice as likely to employ sales workers. These differences are probably accounted for by the type of work done at the workplace. This probably also explains the greater use of part-time workers in small multiples where they made up at least half the workforce in just over a third (35 per cent) of cases compared with a quarter of small businesses.

Use of contracting-out and other non-standard labour

Most workplaces used contractors for one or more workplace activities. Table 11.2 shows that the use of either contractors and/or other forms of non-standard labour, was substantial across all small workplaces. It was lowest among small businesses with working owners which were most likely, if anything, to have just used contractors (48 per cent) rather than contractors and any other form of non-standard labour (27 per cent). However, their use was still substantial, with small businesses with working owners using contractors for an average (median) of three specified services. By way of contrast, small businesses without a working owner also contracted out an average of three services, while small multiples did so for four. Where small workplaces as a whole used contractors, they were most likely to have done so for cleaning (51 per cent) and building maintenance (57 per cent), with the incidence of both of these being substantially higher among small multiples. A fifth (22 per cent) of all small workplaces had, over the past five years, contracted out some services that had been previously undertaken by employees either at the workplace or within the organisation.

The use of the five different forms of non-standard labour varied substantially depending on the type of workplace, but compared with larger workplaces their use was generally lower (see Table 3.6). Among small businesses, especially those without a working owner present, there was a relatively high incidence of both homeworkers and freelance workers. Small multiples made the greatest use of temporary agency workers.

Each of these different forms of non-standard labour can be conceived of as a way of achieving numerical flexibility; that is, the ability to adjust the size of the workforce in line with short-term variations in the demand for labour. Overall, small businesses without working owners were more likely than both those with working owners and small multiples to rely on numerical flexibility.

Due to the small number of cases, we were unable to provide a breakdown between small businesses and small multiples of the motivation for using contractors and non-standard labour. In Chapter 3, we suggested that the primary

Table 11.2 Sub-contracting and use of non-standard labour, by small businesses and small multiples

	Small businesses		Small multiples
	Full-time working owner	*No full-time working owner*	
	% of workplaces	*% of workplaces*	*% of workplaces*
Sub-contract one or more services	75	82	90
Temporary agency employees	9	12	19
Fixed-term contract employees	13	32	26
Freelance workers	19	25	5
Homeworkers	8	23	5
Zero-hour contract employees	0	4	8

Base: All small businesses and all small multiples with 10–99 employees (see Table 11.1 for definition). Figures are weighted and based on responses from 116 (column 1), 134 (column 2) and 401 (column 3) managers.

motivation was to seek a reduction in direct labour costs. There was some evidence that their use lowers the incidence of low pay among direct employees. For example, around two-thirds (65 per cent) of small businesses that undertook all specified activities in house without any use of non-standard labour had some low-paid employees (that is earning less than £3.50 per hour), compared with 42 per cent of small businesses that had contracted-out services or used non-standard labour.

Apart from having some choice over how to structure employment, managers can also offer employees flexibility in terms of when their labour is delivered. Employees in small workplaces are no less likely than those in larger workplaces to have demands that at times conflict with their working life. The question was whether such demands were met through the provision of flexible and family friendly working arrangements. Table 11.3 shows that over half of small businesses did not have any of the six practices listed under this heading. In comparison, around two-fifths of small multiples had none, a proportion broadly consistent with larger workplaces.[4] Overall, small multiples were twice as likely to offer four of the six practices listed in Table 11.3 than were small businesses. The only practices more prevalent in small businesses were flexi-time and working from home. Among small businesses we found no differences according to the presence of a working owner.[5]

The incidence of each of these six practices differed considerably according to the proportion of the workforce that were women. In both small businesses and small multiples, the higher the proportion of females in total employment, the more likely the workplace was to have had any of the practices. Where more than half of the workforce was female, around two-thirds (63 per cent) of all small workplaces had at least one of these practices compared with just under half (48 per cent) where the proportion of women was half or less.

Of all small workplaces with at least one of these arrangements, a majority of managers said they were associated with either no or minimal additional costs and just under 90 per cent said they resulted in benefits to the workplace, usually in terms of happier staff. There was no difference between small businesses and small multiples in terms of managers' assessment of the worth of the schemes; however, more small businesses reported at least some costs from their implementation.

To summarise, our findings in this section show that small businesses and small multiples compose their workforce somewhat differently. Small businesses were more likely to have made use of older workers, while small multiples disproportionately employed younger people, those from an ethnic minority and part-timers. Most small businesses and small multiples alike attained at least some degree of numerical flexibility, primarily through the use of contractors while, overall, small businesses without working owners were significantly more likely to engage a greater variety of non-standard forms of labour than either small multiples or small businesses with working owners. Generally, small multiples were significantly more likely than small businesses to offer formal arrangements that allowed their employees to better balance any domestic or personal responsibilities with those they had at work. Finally, as noted in the opening to this section,

Table 11.3 Presence of flexible and family friendly working arrangements, by small businesses and small multiples

	Small businesses	Small multiples
	% of workplaces	% of workplaces
Switching from full to part-time	25	52
Flexi-time	16	10
Working at or from home	9	8
Job sharing scheme	7	24
Term-time only contract	6	12
Workplace nursery/child care subsidy	3	5
None of these	57	40

Base: All small businesses and all small multiples with 10–99 employees (see Table 11.1 for definition). Figures are weighted and based on responses from 250 (column 1) and 402 (column 2) managers.

although we cannot directly inform the debate on the *changing* nature of 'traditional' employment structures, the evidence suggests a rich variety and degree of complexity in the types of labour used and deployed in both small multiples and small businesses.

The management of employees

It is often argued that managers in small businesses have a distinct perspective on how best to manage employees. Some portray small business managers, especially owners, as following autocratic, fraternal or paternalistic styles of managing their employees (Lockwood, 1975; Newby, 1977; and Scase, 1995). However, although such ideal types are worthy areas of small business research, we were unable to test them without a dedicated instrument and, as such, restricted our analysis to a straightforward appraisal of the practices used to recruit, train and manage employees.

Most small workplaces had no personnel specialist on site, but they were much rarer among small businesses (9 per cent) than in small multiples (29 per cent). For the purposes of our survey then, the respondents were those 'at the top';[6] how, then, did they view their role? Figure 11.1 shows the results. In around three-quarters of small businesses the manager said that 'those at the top are best placed to make decisions about this workplace', compared with about half of managers in small multiples. Small businesses with working owners were the most likely to strongly agree with this statement (74 per cent).

This provides a useful backdrop to this section. It indicates that small businesses were more likely to favour direct control, whereas small multiples may be more likely to rely on formal practices, that is to say, bureaucratic control. First, we briefly describe the patterns of recruitment and the means used to make employees aware of their job responsibilities. We then look at the organisation of work and

Figure 11.1 Management attitudes on decision making, by small businesses and small multiples

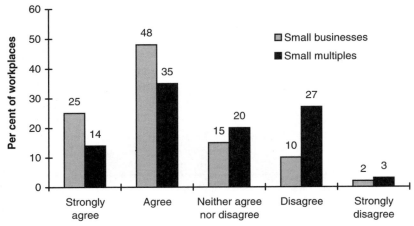

Those at the top are best placed to make decisions about this workplace

Base: All small businesses and all small multiples with 10–99 employees (see Table 11.1 for definition).
Figures are weighted and based on responses from 250 (small businesses) and 403 (small multiples) managers.

direct employee participation and see whether small businesses were more or less innovative in having in place high commitment management practices. Finally, we look at procedural regulation of the employment relationship.

Recruitment

In Chapter 4, we argued that the means used by managers to recruit employees gave an indication of the degree of formality in workplace procedures. Virtually all small workplaces (95 per cent) had a vacancy in the year prior to the survey. When it comes to hiring new employees, both small businesses and small multiples ranked motivation, experience and skills as the three most important factors taken into account – all being mentioned in at least three-quarters of cases. For the most part, differences in the incidence of the various recruitment practices were fairly narrow, but small businesses were more likely to take the age of recruits into account (33 per cent) than small multiples (21 per cent).

One factor that might be an indicator of an informal approach to recruitment is reliance on recommendations from other employees. Small businesses with working owners were much more likely to take recommendations from other employees, with over half (53 per cent) doing so. The comparable figures for both small businesses without working owners and small multiples were 37 per cent and 36 per cent respectively.

Conveying job responsibilities

Once small workplace managers have their new employees, they need to ensure they know exactly what is required of them. Consistent with Chapter 3, direct supervision was the most common means of controlling the activities of individual employees, with 81 per cent using this method. In each of the nine possible ways of conveying job responsibilities to employees that we asked about, small multiples were more likely than small businesses to have had them in place for the largest occupational group. Thus, small multiples were twice as likely to have used staff handbooks or manuals than small businesses (61 per cent compared with 30 per cent); equally there were differences of a similar magnitude over setting individual objectives and targets (52 per cent compared with 23 per cent). In other words, small multiples had a wider range of practices in place to convey responsibilities.

Work organisation

Overall, 72 per cent of managers in all small workplaces said that at least some employees in the largest occupational group worked in formally designated teams, with the proportion being higher in small multiples (79 per cent) than in small businesses (65 per cent), and in particular, those where a full-time working owner was present (58 per cent). Approximately a third of all small workplaces (34 per cent) said that all employees in the largest occupational group worked in teams. Having all or almost all employees in teams was no more likely in the very smallest of workplaces (those with 10 to 24 employees), which suggests that managers had been able to make the distinction between teamworking and more traditional notions of the workforce being 'one big happy family'.

As we showed in Chapter 3, however, considerably fewer workplaces conform to a more stringent definition of teamworking. Less than a third (28 per cent) of small businesses and small multiples met our definition of fully-autonomous or semi-autonomous teamworking. It was not surprising that an even lower proportion of small businesses with a full-time working owner on site (24 per cent) organise work in such strictly defined teams, particularly since the definition implies that control is diluted or even diverted from the owner to the team itself.

Training

In the 12 months prior to the survey, around four-fifths (79 per cent) of small multiples provided formal off-the-job training for at least some experienced employees in the largest occupational group, compared with just over half (55 per cent) of small businesses. The proportions that provided training for most of their employees were substantially less, the respective figures being 30 and 17 per cent. Small businesses may be less likely to possess the financial resources to provide a significant amount of off-the-job training.[7] Alternatively, they may in general, judge the benefits of training to be less attractive relative to the costs incurred (Storey and Westhead, 1997).

Chapter 4 showed that the incidence of training was related to the amount of job-specific skills required by employees in the largest occupational group, and the same relationship was found here. The greater the job-specific skills, the greater the likelihood of managers saying they invested in the skills of their employees. This relationship held for both small businesses and small multiples.[8]

Apart from the incidence of training we were also able to look at the skills in which employees were trained. Managers were shown a list of ten items ranging from computing skills to improvement of communication techniques. From this list over three-fifths (62 per cent) of all small workplace managers said employees had received training in matters related to health and safety, with the next most common form of training being in the operation of new equipment (46 per cent). There was no difference between small businesses and small multiples in the proportion providing training in these two issues, however; differences were apparent in less technical areas of training. For example, around a quarter of small businesses said they trained employees in teamworking (26 per cent), improving communication skills (25 per cent) or in customer service (25 per cent), whereas comparable figures for small multiples were around half (50 per cent, 45 per cent and 54 per cent respectively).

Incentive pay schemes

Small businesses and small multiples look particularly distinct from one another in terms of their use of various forms of incentive pay. Figure 11.2 shows that around four-fifths of small multiples operate a form of incentive pay, compared with less than a half of small businesses. There were also distinct differences in the types of schemes used, although in part this is explained by the nature of these workplaces; for example, the relative absence of employee share ownership schemes in small businesses is to be expected. Small multiples were almost three times more likely to have had profit-related pay schemes than small businesses, with a difference of about two to one in terms of performance-related pay.

Cash bonuses are somewhat different from the other forms of incentive pay, because they are not clearly based on formal criteria. So we might expect them to be more prevalent among small businesses. In fact, the overall incidence of cash bonuses was higher in small multiples than small businesses. However, if any form of incentive pay was in operation, cash bonuses were more likely to be used by small businesses (48 per cent), with 34 per cent relying solely on this mechanism. In contrast, two-fifths (39 per cent) of small multiples operating some form of incentive pay distributed cash bonuses, but only 10 per cent did so in isolation from other schemes. Indeed a majority of small multiples (63 per cent) operate two or more of these incentive pay schemes whereas most small businesses (78 per cent) prefer to rely on just one. Taken together, this suggests that small businesses were more inclined than small multiples to use less complicated means of rewarding their employees.

Figure 11.2 Incidence of incentive pay, by small businesses and small multiples

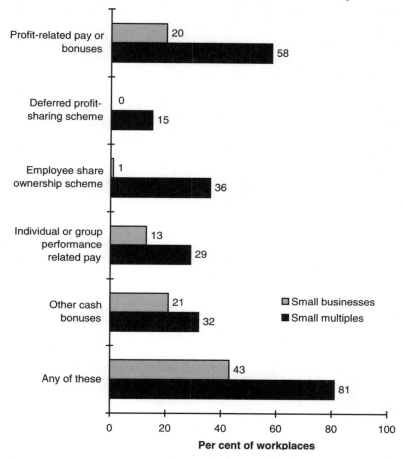

Base: All small businesses and all small multiples with 10–99 employees (see Table 11.1 for definition).
Figures are weighted and based on responses from 250 (small businesses) and 403 (small multiples) managers.

Communicating with employees

Workplaces that have relatively small numbers of employees conjure a range of images about the way information is conveyed from managers to employees. One thinks of managers walking the floor, delivering their message on a personal level, removing the need for formal mechanisms of communication. In reality, however, it was common for even small workplaces to have had at least one of the following formal means of communicating with employees: team briefings; regular meetings with the entire workforce present; systematic use of the management chain; and newsletters. Only a tenth (13 per cent) of all small workplaces had none of these, the proportion higher among small businesses (22 per cent) than small multiples

(5 per cent). Small business managers with less than 25 employees were even more likely to have reported none of these (27 per cent). We found no significant difference, though, according to whether a working owner was present.

Regular meetings with the entire workforce present were the most often used formal method of communicating with employees in both small businesses (44 per cent) and small multiples (64 per cent). However, the picture was not the same for all workplaces within these groups. We found larger workplaces were more likely to split their discussions with employees into smaller groups.

Fewer small businesses (32 per cent) than small multiples (54 per cent) said they used the management chain to disseminate information to employees. However, again we found that, the larger the workplace size within small businesses as a whole, the more likely were managers to report its use; 42 per cent of those with 25 or more employees did so, compared to 26 per cent of those with 10 to 24 employees. Similarly, newsletters were more common in small businesses with 25 or more employees (17 per cent) than those with less than 25 employees (9 per cent). Among small multiples, staff newsletters were more widely used (54 per cent). Thus there was fairly strong evidence that the methods used to communicate information were tailored to the size of the workplace. Here, workplace size would appear a stronger explanatory factor than the structure of ownership and control.

Employee involvement

There are a variety of ways of giving employees the chance to participate in the day-to-day operation of the workplace. Some might be more formal than others. In line with Chapter 4, we can compare the use of problem-solving groups – which encompass quality circles and continuous improvement groups – with the use of suggestion schemes.

Less than a third (26 per cent) of all small workplaces currently involve their non-managerial employees in problem-solving groups, with the proportion being marginally higher in small multiples (28 per cent) than in small businesses (23 per cent). Considerably fewer small businesses where there was a full-time working owner present had these groups, the number being around a fifth (17 per cent). Additionally, we found small businesses were less likely to reward these employees for outstanding performance either in terms of financial or non-financial rewards.

Approximately a third (30 per cent) of all small workplaces operated a suggestion scheme, with very little difference apparent between small businesses and small multiples. Just over a third of all small workplaces used a suggestion scheme or a problem solving group (34 per cent), with 10 per cent using both and 55 per cent using neither. Across both small businesses and small multiples the use of either of these practices was very similar. The assumed absence of formality within small businesses, at least here, does not translate into a greater reliance on the more informal methods of involving employees.

Procedural regulation of the employment relationship

The degree of formality at the workplace is sharply indicated by the presence or absence of formal procedures designed to regulate the employment relationship. In this section we look at four such procedures – regular performance appraisals, grievance procedures, disciplinary procedures and equal opportunities policies – to see whether small businesses were less likely to utilise them and, if so, to explore the reasons why this might be so. Table 11.4 summarises the position for each of these practices.

Small businesses were considerably less likely than small multiples to formally appraise employees. In approximately three-fifths (63 per cent) of small businesses, there were no appraisals of any form, with about a third reporting that most (60 per cent or more) of their non-managerial employees were appraised on an annual or more regular basis. In contrast, 75 per cent of small multiples appraise at least some employees, with two-thirds doing so for at least 60 per cent of their non-managerial employees. There are also differences in the way appraisals were conducted. In small multiples appraisals were mostly performed by an employee's line manager (79 per cent), whereas only 57 per cent of small businesses responded similarly, with 57 per cent reporting that it could be carried out by another manager. The rationale for using an appraisal system also differed. While both types of workplace said that the main purpose was to give feedback on an employee's performance (88 per cent of small businesses and 97 per cent of small multiples), significantly more managers in small multiples said they were also used for the following: assessing suitability for promotion; discussing career moves; setting personal objectives; evaluating training needs; and promotion of behavioural change.

The majority of all small workplaces reported formal procedures for dealing with individual grievances and disciplinary cases. Table 11.4 shows that, while there was almost universal application of both in small multiples, they were less widespread in small businesses; around two-thirds reporting the presence of either.

Table 11.4 Incidence of appraisals, formal procedures for dealing with individual disputes and equal opportunities policies, by small businesses and small multiples

	Small businesses	Small multiples
	% of workplaces	% of workplaces
Formal appraisals for most (at least 60%) of non-managerial employees	32	66
Formal individual grievance procedure	68	95
Formal disciplinary and dismissals procedure	70	96
Equal opportunities policy	19	70

Base: All small businesses and all small multiples with 10–99 employees (see Table 11.1 for definition). Figures are weighted and based on responses from 250 and 402 (rows 1 & 2), 250 and 403 (row 3) and 247 and 391 (row 4) managers.

Moreover, around a tenth of small business managers said that grievance and disciplinary procedures were conveyed by word of mouth rather than existing in a written form. If we exclude this tenth as evidence of informal rather than formal regulation, we are left with 61 per cent of small businesses which had a 'strict' formal procedure covering employee grievances and 60 per cent with a 'strict' formal disciplinary procedure.

Rather few small businesses had a formal written policy on equal opportunities when compared with small multiples. In trying to look for reasons why they may be less likely to have such a policy, we found little evidence to suggest that structural reasons – such as the presence of a working owner – were responsible. We were able, though, to look at responses to a question which asked specifically why there was no policy. Just over two-fifths (42 per cent) of small business managers where there was no policy said it was unnecessary, while a further fifth (18 per cent) said that they had not thought of implementing one. Of the remainder, about a third said they either had a policy but it wasn't formalised (19 per cent); or that it was in the process of being formalised (5 per cent); or that they aimed to be an equal opportunities employer regardless of having a policy (12 per cent).

In Chapter 3 we noted the apparent importance of equal opportunities policies in accounting for some of the differences in employment patterns. Were similar associations evident in small businesses? On average, workplaces with an equal opportunities policy in place employed more women and more people from an ethnic minority, but there was no real difference in terms of age. As noted earlier, the employment of people from an ethnic minority was lower in small businesses and it was lowest of all where there was no equal opportunities policy in place (2 per cent of the workforce). It was two-and-a-half times greater among small multiples with a policy in place (5 per cent of the workforce).

Employee representation

We now turn to look at the institutional structures that might give rise to joint negotiation or consultation over the terms of the employment relationship. Generally, small business managers have been described as having no conscious notion of internal communications as a matter needing attention, with most communication being of the one way downward variety (Scott *et al.*, 1989). As with the previous section, we will be looking for evidence of formality (or not), but also the degree of influence employees have in their dealings with management.

Indicators of union presence

As demonstrated in Chapter 5, the various indicators of union presence at the workplace were strongly associated with workplace employment size. We would therefore expect them to feature less strongly among all small workplaces. But it is, nevertheless, instructive to compare small businesses with small multiples, because the former it has been argued are more likely to be anti-union (Rainnie, 1989). This is a stance arguably consistent with either an autocratic or paternalistic approach to management, where managers (particularly owner managers) perceive little need for union interference. For small multiples, we explore whether it is workplace or organisation size which is more closely related to union presence.

Just over a quarter (28 per cent) of all small workplaces had one or more union member(s) in the workforce (according to managers), with an 11 percentage point difference between small businesses and small multiples as shown in Table 11.5. If a working owner was present at the workplace, union presence was even less likely. These differences were paralleled in levels of aggregate union density. Across all small businesses, 5 per cent of employees were union members while density was about three times greater in small multiples (14 per cent).

As found in Chapter 5, management attitudes towards trade union membership were strongly associated with union presence and density, though with some interesting nuances. First, very few managers in small businesses said they were in favour of union membership at their workplace (7 per cent) and it was negligible among small businesses with a working owner (1 per cent). Yet the association between management's views and workplace union density was much more pronounced for small multiples than it was for small businesses. This was mainly because there were so few union members in small businesses and so few managers who were in favour of membership.

It therefore comes as no surprise to find that the level of union recognition in all small workplaces was correspondingly low. It ranged from just 7 per cent in small businesses with a working owner present to 25 per cent of small multiples. Again, this latter figure was consistent with that found in the private sector overall. The 'recognition gap' – that is, the difference in the percentage of workplaces with union members present and those recognising unions – was fairly similar for both small businesses (10 per cent) and small multiples (8 per cent). The non-recognition rate, however, was much higher in small businesses.

These figures suggest that the pattern for small multiples was broadly consistent with that found in the private sector generally, where union presence was more closely related to organisation size rather than workplace size. Among small businesses a union presence was mostly absent. These two findings are consistent with an analysis of union presence which is related to the resources required to organise and recruit members. In addition, there does appear to be a distinct working owner effect, with managers here the least in favour of unions and the least likely to have to engage with them.

Worker representatives

Given the above indicators of union presence, together with the findings from Chapter 5, having a worker representative on site might be expected to be something of a rarity. So it proves, though again with some nuance.

Of small businesses with union recognition, less than a fifth (19 per cent) – or 2 per cent of all small businesses – had a lay union representative on site. This proportion was substantially lower than found generally in larger private sector workplaces. Of small multiples with union recognition, the proportion was

Table 11.5 Indicators of union presence among small businesses and small multiples, by workplace characteristics

	At least one union member at the workplace			Union recognition		
	Small business with a full-time working owner	All small businesses	Small multiples	Small business with a full-time working owner	All small businesses	Small multiples
	% of workplaces	% of workplaces	% of workplaces	% of workplaces	% of workplaces	% of workplaces
Workplace size						
10–24 employees	(7)	20	32	(3)	11	25
25–49 employees	21	22	31	16	14	22
50–99 employees	(26)	34	42	(9)	10	30
Broad industry						
Production industries	19	35	37	15	23	24
Service industries	11	17	33	4	7	25
All workplaces	14	22	33	7	12	25

Base: All small businesses and all small multiples with 10–99 employees (see Table 11.1 for definition).
Figures are weighted and based on responses from 116 (column 1), 250 (column 2), 403 (column3), 115 (column 4), 246 (column 5) and 399 (column 6) managers.

considerably higher (43 per cent), but still well below that found in larger workplaces. There was, though, among these workplaces, greater recourse to union representatives based at another workplace in the organisation (24 per cent overall). Hence union members in over a half (67 per cent) of small multiples with union recognition had access to a union representative. The absence of any lay union representative was not associated with the presence of non-union worker representatives. These were found in less than one in ten of both small businesses (7 per cent) and small multiples (9 per cent). This means that, overall, there were no worker representatives of any kind in 91 per cent of small businesses and 77 per cent of small multiples.

Joint consultative committees

Clearly, trade unions and their representatives were not the medium that most managers in small workplaces used to communicate with their employees. What then of joint consultative committees: do they substitute for a union presence, or as found in Chapter 5, do they complement it?

There was a multi-issue workplace-based joint consultative committee in 17 per cent of small businesses and 11 per cent of small multiples. In addition, a further 43 per cent of small multiples were covered by a joint consultative committee at a higher level in the organisation. Small businesses with working owners were the least likely to have had any committee representation (9 per cent).

There were too few observations in our sample to give an adequate account of the operation of these committees, as we did in Chapter 5. Broadly speaking, however, in around two-fifths (44 per cent) of small businesses with committees, the employees who sat on the committee were appointed by management, compared with around a quarter (25 per cent) of small multiples.

In Chapter 5 we found a strong association between a union presence and the incidence of a joint consultative committee (at either a workplace or a higher level). Figure 11.3 looks at the situation for small businesses and small multiples. The association was confirmed for small multiples. Of the quarter of small multiples with union recognition, 77 per cent also had a multi-issue committee in place, compared with 46 per cent of those without recognition. Among small businesses, though, there was no similar association. Overall, the best way to characterise small businesses was by an absence of both recognised unions and consultative committees – three-quarters had neither. For small businesses with a working owner present the proportion was even greater (84 per cent).

Pay determination

The final part of this section examines the process of pay determination. Given the absence of representative structures it was evident that management would play the dominant role in pay setting, but there were some subtleties behind this general picture. Figure 11.4 shows the method used to determine pay levels at small businesses and small multiples for all non-managerial employees.

Figure 11.3 Types of employee representation, by small businesses and small multiples

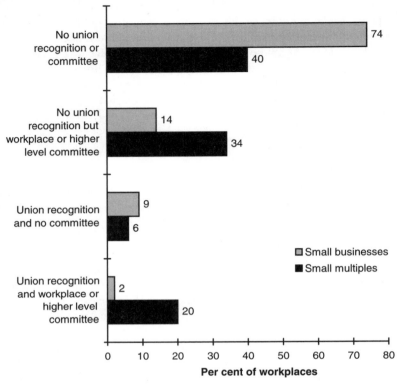

Base: All small businesses and all small multiples with 10–99 employees (see Table 11.1 for definition).
Figures are weighted and based on responses from 246 (small businesses) and 391 (small multiples) managers.

There was little collective bargaining taking place in small businesses – just 1 per cent had all non-managerial employees covered by collective bargaining at any level, while a further 4 per cent had at least some covered. Unlike larger workplaces, where they were covered by collective bargaining, it was most common for this to be at a multi-employer level. By way of contrast, 19 per cent of small multiples engaged in collective bargaining and in 14 per cent of them all non-managerial employees had their pay set this way. For small multiples, the main level of bargaining was the organisation (and the workplace was the least important).

The most common way of setting pay in small businesses was unilaterally by management. Two-thirds used this method for all non-managerial employees in the business and an additional 12 per cent used it for some employees. It was particularly noteworthy, however, that a relatively high proportion (over a tenth) of small businesses negotiated individually over pay. This was a substantially higher proportion than found in small multiples or, more generally, in larger workplaces

Figure 11.4 Uniformity and fragmentation of pay determination for non-managerial employees, by small businesses and small multiples

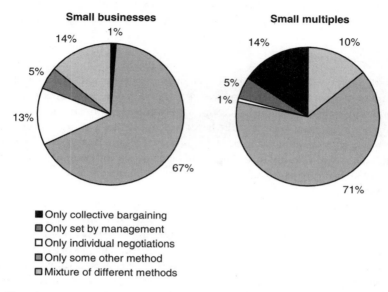

Base: All small businesses and all small multiples with 10–99 employees (see Table 11.1 for definition). Figures are weighted and based on responses from 246 (small businesses) and 393 (small multiples) managers.

(see Table 5.7). A further 7 per cent of small businesses held individual negotiations over pay with some employees, giving a total of 20 per cent. This compares with just 4 per cent of small multiples.

This section lends considerable weight to the argument that working owners see little need to involve others in decisions about their business. By their own account they are best placed to make decisions about the workplace and an 'independent' employee voice – either in the form of trade unions or joint consultative committees – was notably absent for over eight in ten of these businesses. Whether such managers were autocratic or paternalistic in their style of management we cannot say. In contrast, the incidence of representative structures was significantly greater in small businesses without a working owner, and even greater within small multiples.

Measures of workplace performance and well-being

Non-union workplaces were somewhat tarnished on the state of their overall performance and well-being by analysts using the 1990 survey. Sisson (1993) portrayed them as 'bleak houses' and Guest (1995) as 'black holes'. A simple extrapolation was made to suggest that small private sector workplaces were likely to be the least 'healthy' of all. Using a comparison between small businesses and small multiples we now examine whether these labels had any resonance for small workplaces. Owing to limitations in space, we are unable to cover material in the same depth as Chapter 6, so instead we provide a short descriptive account of the main measures, beginning with a brief overview of the monitoring of performance.

Monitoring performance

As with larger workplaces, keeping records on performance was extremely widespread among all small workplaces, with only 1 per cent keeping no records. Significantly, there were no differences between small businesses and small multiples on financial areas, but the latter were more likely to keep records in all areas to do with the management of employees. Despite this, record keeping in these areas was still extensive among small businesses – for example, seven in ten (70 per cent) kept records on absenteeism and six in ten (57 per cent) on labour turnover.

Small businesses were, however, substantially less likely to set performance targets. A third (34 per cent) had no targets, compared with just 3 per cent of small multiples. Overall, the patterns of target setting were broadly similar to those found among larger workplaces (see Figure 6.1). Over half (56 per cent) of small businesses kept whatever performance records they collected fully confidential and did not share them with employees or their representatives. Small businesses with a full-time working owner were the most likely to do this with 59 per cent making all records confidential, 35 per cent sharing some information and 6 per cent allowing full access. By way of contrast, only around a quarter (28 per cent) of small multiples kept all records confidential and 16 per cent allowed full access.

Workplace economic performance

In Chapter 6 we discussed the adequacy of the three economic performance measures – financial performance, labour productivity and quality of product or service – and suggested they were robust enough to be used for further analysis. There is little point in reiterating any of this, except to say that, on these measures, near identical patterns were found among small workplaces when compared with larger ones. Thus 48 per cent of small businesses and 55 per cent of small multiples rated their financial performance above average; 42 per cent of both thought labour productivity above average; and the figures for quality being above average were 77 per cent and 71 per cent respectively (see Figure 6.3 for a comparison against larger workplaces). Managers in small businesses were, however, more likely to say that no comparison was possible or that the relevant data was not available.

Workplace well-being

Four broad areas of workplace well-being were examined in Chapter 6 – industrial 'strife'; absenteeism and voluntary redundancies; dismissals and other individual disputes; and injuries and work-related illness – and we look at each in turn. The measures are all summarised in Table 11.6.

Given the low levels of industrial action found in larger workplaces and its association with union presence, it comes as no surprise to find that 99 per cent of all small workplaces had not experienced any form of industrial action in the past year. The same proportion of small businesses had not experienced any in the past five years and the respective figure for small multiples barely differed at 97 per cent.[9]

The low levels of industrial action in all small workplaces might suggest that employees working there had a low proclivity towards taking such action, but another interpretation might be that they had no recourse to collective action because of the general absence of representative structures. In these cases, conflicts in the employment relationship may manifest themselves in more individualistic ways, namely by unapproved absence or quitting the job. The level of absenteeism shown in Table 11.6 was largely on a par with the rate found in larger private sector workplaces (see Table 6.4) and was slightly higher in small multiples than small businesses. Voluntary resignations, though, were slightly higher in small workplaces than in larger private sector ones, and higher in small multiples than small businesses.

Having looked at a couple of key ways in which employees might signal a breakdown in the employment relationship, we now take a look at the opposite case where managers were unhappy with some aspect of their workers' behaviour. Disciplinary sanctions – formal written warnings, suspensions with or without pay and deductions from pay – represent the first formal weapon in any manager's arsenal, while dismissals are largely a last resort when all else fails. The typical small workplace had seen none of these in the past year: 48 per cent of small businesses and 46 per cent of small multiples had sanctioned one or more of their employees during the 12 months prior to the survey, while 34 per cent of both

Table 11.6 Indicators of workplace well-being, by small businesses and small multiples

		Small businesses	Small multiples
Industrial action	Average number of actions per 100 workplaces	1.1	5.8
Absenteeism	Average rate per 100 employees	3.8	4.6
Voluntary resignations	Average rate per 100 employees	17.2	20.6
Formal sanctions	Average rate per 100 employees	3.5	3.8
Dismissals	Average rate per 100 employees	2.3	2.5
Industrial Tribunal claims	Average rate per 1,000 employees	1.5	0.6
Injury	Average rate per 100 employees	1.2	2.8
Illness	Average rate per 100 employees	1.4	1.4

Base: All small businesses and all small multiples with 10–99 employees (see Table 11.1 for definition). Figures are weighted and based on responses from between 222 and 250 (column 1) and between 314 and 402 (column 2) managers.

types of workplace had dismissed at least one employee. Yet the rates of dismissals were higher than those in larger workplaces (see Table 6.6) and highest of all in small businesses.

Employees with the necessary length of service have recourse to Industrial Tribunals if they feel their employment rights have been breached, including the right not to be unfairly dismissed. Overall, 5 per cent of small businesses and 3 per cent of small multiples had been the subject of a Tribunal application in the year preceding the survey. The rate for small businesses was about double that in small multiples. However, the rate of claims in small businesses was slightly lower than that in larger workplaces (see Table 6.6).

The final area we examined was accidents at work and work-related illness. As with several other of these event-based outcomes, the typical small workplace was most likely to have experienced neither in the previous year. In around a fifth (21 per cent) of all small workplaces, an employee had been seriously injured and 23 per cent of managers reported a work-related illness. However, in 63 per cent of these workplaces, neither had been reported. Small multiples had higher injury rates than small businesses (which were also in excess of those found in larger private sector workplaces – Table 6.5). This was not true for work-related illness, where parity existed between small multiples, small businesses and larger private sector workplaces.

Conclusion

Although we have, for the first time, rich quantitative data telling us about the ways in which the employment relationship is formally regulated within all small workplaces, this does not detract from the fertile sources of qualitative data available from case studies and the like. Rather we see the two as complementary methods of unravelling the nature of small business employee relations, the former painting broad brush strokes and the latter revealing the nuances and informal conventions integral to understanding any picture in its entirety. Generally speaking, we believe the picture provided is one where small workplaces do not operate in a purely informal manner.

The definition used at the outset produced two distinct groupings – directly comparable in terms of workplace size, but with distinct ownership and organis-ational structures. All small multiples within our sample belonged to organisations with more than 100 employees – 35 per cent of which belonged to organisations with 10,000 or more employees – and by design 'small businesses' never had more than 99 employees. Small businesses and small multiples had quite distinct ownership structures. Over half of small businesses were individually or family owned, while around two-fifths had a full-time working owner on site – more than ten times the proportion of small multiples. The latter were mostly characterised by having no individual or family with a controlling interest, with over three-fifths being publicly-listed companies.

The introduction to this chapter suggested that formalisation and bureaucracy were as much a function of distancing owner-managers from production as a logistic of organisational size. The greater use of formal procedures in regulating the employment relationship within small multiples is born from two distinct circumstances. First, owners divorced from the workplace still need to maintain control but are unable to directly supervise 'what is going on'. Second, as organisation size increases, management problems often develop. People no longer know everyone else and it is at this stage that there is the need to develop formal procedures and practices (Hendry *et al.*, 1991). Thus delegation of general decision making increases. Specialists will be brought in, with recruitment, performance, negotiations, working practices, training and discipline advancing from *ad hoc* processes to institutionalised practices (Atkinson and Meager, 1994).

The body of evidence presented here supports these arguments. Organisational size and patterns of ownership proved to be clearly associated with the incidence of formal structures and practices within small workplaces. Overall, small businesses – especially those with working owners – had a *less* formal approach than small multiples to the regulation of the employment relationship. Compared to other small workplaces, they were less likely to have significant personnel expertise in-house, or the more sophisticated personnel systems such as performance appraisal, incentive pay systems, or family friendly working practices. Combined with this – and especially when a working owner was present – these businesses tended to lack representative structures. Owner-managers generally took the view that they were there to take the decisions, and this was reflected in the way they ran their businesses.

At the same time, it would be over-simplisitic to conclude that the small business approach to organising work is totally unstructured. The evidence suggests the difference is generally one of degree – a relative rather than absolute absence of structure. For example, the majority of small businesses did have grievance and disciplinary procedures, but they were less likely to be written down.

Finally, what of employees in small businesses? This chapter has relied exclusively on the management account. Employees in small businesses were less likely to be involved in decision-making than employees in other workplaces, yet a significantly higher proportion of employees in small businesses express high or very high levels of job satisfaction.[10] Further analysis of the employee data may illuminate this apparent paradox – a task we leave to others.

Notes

1 For consistency in the analysis and so as to avoid double counting, we have excluded 53 private sector workplaces which are part of a larger organisation that, in total, employed fewer than 100 people.

2 Additionally, the small numbers of eligible worker representatives within all small workplaces, but especially within small businesses, preclude any robust in-depth account of their perspective.

3 This was the approach adopted in the most recent Australian survey. See Chapter 13 of Morehead *et al.* (1997).

4 The practices included in Chapter 4 are slightly different. We were unable to use the same set of practices for all small workplaces due to a lack of observations in some categories.

5   Although we are confident that our research instruments are significantly tuned into informal practices, it may be that to some extent small businesses are just more informal places where managers and employees make deals that are family friendly, but do not call them 'entitlements' or 'policies'.

6   Certainly the case for owner managers, but arguably so for all managers at the workplace level. Although we accept that, for example, managers at particularly small workplaces that are part of large organisations such as food/retail outlets may perceive the 'top' to be some distance removed from their own position.

7   We cannot, of course, judge whether this was compensated for through greater provision of less formal on-the-job training.

8   Job-specific skills were measured by the amount of time taken for a new recruit to perform their job as well as an experienced employee. When the time was a week or less, 46 per cent of small businesses trained employees, compared with 60 per cent when it took more than a week. The equivalent proportions for small multiples were 63 and 85 per cent.

9   Among small businesses there was only one workplace where industrial action had taken place in the year preceding the survey (only five small multiple cases) and no other small businesses in our sample had any experience of it over the full five-year period.

10   Relevant data are set out in Figure 6 and Table 10 of the *First Findings* booklet (Cully *et al.*, 1998).

12 The climate of employment relations

A three-way analysis

One of the most widely researched issues in contemporary employment relations is the link that might exist between the nature of employment relations and performance. This is sometimes reduced to quite narrow prescriptive investigations into 'what works at work', the search for which often proves illusive – 'there are no one or two "magic bullets" that are *the* work practices that will stimulate worker and business performance' (Ichniowski *et al.*, 1996: 322). Recently, a body of research has emerged from the United States and from Britain which, cumulatively, suggests that bundles of innovative management practices yield realisable gains. It follows in the wake of earlier work which examined the impact that unions might have on economic performance (Freeman and Medoff, 1984).

For those interested in the broad canvas of employment relations, a focus on performance can seem somewhat reductivist – 'bottom-line' performance is obviously important, but, as we showed in Chapter 6, there are a host of indicators which fall into the wider rubric of workplace well-being. Additionally, Chapter 8 showed very wide variation in employee well-being. These might best be thought of as pointers towards the overall climate of employment relations. Industrial action was rare, affecting just 2 per cent of workplaces. Other indicators of workplace well-being were less clear cut – labour turnover was relatively high in many workplaces, as too were rates of disciplinary action taken against employees, and there were many workplaces where serious injuries and work-related illness had occurred. Many of these indicators were associated with one another, but generally the associations were weak. From employee accounts, we found that more employees were satisfied with their jobs than dissatisfied, but there were more who thought management poor at involving employees than thought them good at doing so. Worker representatives generally regarded themselves as working closely with management, and most employees believed that representatives were taken seriously by management (though non-union members less so).

Plainly, as implied, perceptions of climate are multi-faceted, and a more direct measure is required. All three groups of respondents were asked to provide an overall rating of relations between management and employees at the workplace. It is these assessments which we take as the best single indicator of 'climate' and which form the basis of the discussion throughout this chapter. We choose to focus on climate, rather than economic performance or workplace well-being, because it is a more general measure of the overall character of employment relations. As we go on to show, the use of it as a general measure is validated through the close association it has with the various other measures of economic performance, workplace well-being and workforce well-being.

The approach adopted in this chapter is distinct from earlier ones – little descriptive material is presented; instead, multi-variate statistical techniques are used to estimate some of the determinants of workplace performance (as reported by management) and the climate of employment relations (as reported by all three groups of respondents). We are able to take advantage of the features of the survey design in this analysis in two ways: first, by applying the same set of variables against the alternative perspective of each group of respondents; and, second, by matching data from management and employees at both an individual and a workplace level. The more consistent the account provided under such circumstances, the more robust the findings are likely to be.

The opening part of the chapter presents the descriptive results on climate and demonstrates its usefulness as a general measure of the character of employment relations. This is followed by a section which relates management accounts of the employment relationship with various measures of workplace performance and climate. The final section then uses matched data to establish whether, from all three perspectives, a common tale can be told about the determinants of climate.

Three perspectives on climate

Towards the end of the management and worker representative interviews, respondents were asked 'Looking at this scale, how would you rate the relationship between management and employees generally at this workplace?'. The scale ranged from 'very good' through to 'very poor'. The employee questionnaire included a nearly identical question.[1] The patterns of responses to the climate question from each of the relevant actors in the employment relationship are shown in Figure 12.1. It is immediately obvious that both union representatives and (non-managerial) employees have, on the whole, very different views of climate from those of managers. Managers are far more positive than either of the other groups, whose responses look very similar. We explore below the degree of concordance between the three different accounts by comparing matched pairs, but, prior to that, we examine more closely the answers from each group of respondents.

Management view of climate

Managers were overwhelmingly positive in their assessment of climate, with nine in ten rating it good or very good, and one in 50 rating it poor. There were only two managers in the sample who thought the climate was very poor. This pattern of response is very similar to that in past surveys in the WIRS series, which led McCarthy (1994) to suggest that managers were apparently complacent, or the measure itself was faulty. The other criticism that might be levelled at the data is

Figure 12.1 Management, union representative and employee perspectives on the climate of employment relations at the workplace

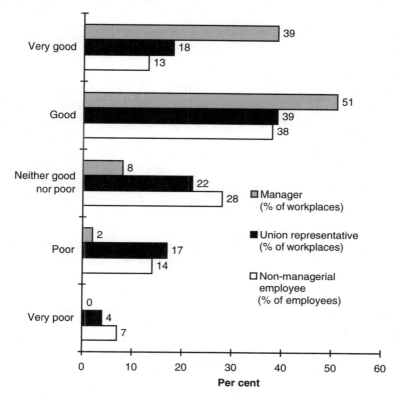

Base: All workplaces with 25 or more employees (managers), all workplaces with 25 or more employees and a union representative (unions), and all non-managerial employees in workplaces with 25 or more employees.
Figures are weighted and based on responses from 1,927 managers, 813 union representatives and 22,604 employees.

whether it is valid to make a distinction between the 'very good' and 'good' categories.

Table 12.1 shows how management responses to the climate question were associated with measures of economic performance and workplace well-being (as reported in Chapter 6). Disregarding the 'poor' category, where there were too few respondents to produce reliable results, a clear pattern is apparent. Those rating climate as very good had the highest proportion of workplaces where managers said that financial performance and labour productivity were above the average for their industry. In the same workplaces, the average rate of labour turnover was the lowest, the rate of dismissals was the highest and industrial action was near non-existent. Conversely, among workplaces where managers thought climate was neither good nor poor, indicators of economic performance and workplace well-being were generally worse. Notably, the proportion where relative labour productivity was above average was below half that of workplaces where management rated climate very good. All of these differences became slightly more pronounced when the analysis was restricted to private sector workplaces.

Union representatives' view of climate

A majority of union representatives rated climate at their workplace as good or very good, but a substantial minority were less positive, including one in five who thought climate poor or very poor. Once again, we can relate union representatives' assessment of climate against other measures to see the extent to which climate serves as a useful summary measure of the nature of workplace employment relations. The results are presented in Table 12.2. Climate, according to union representatives, is very closely related to the position and role afforded them by management at the workplace. Where union representatives were positive about climate, they were also far more likely to say that management were supportive and unions given a role in negotiating change. In workplaces where union representatives thought the climate was very good, around three-quarters or more thought they worked closely with management on introducing change, that their opinions were valued by management, and that their role was supported

Table 12.1 Managers' assessment of climate, by workplace economic performance and well-being

	Climate of employment relations:				
	Very good	*Good*	*Neither good nor poor*	*Poor*	*Very poor*
	% better than average	*% better than average*	*% better than average*	*% better than average*	*% better than average*
Financial performance	62	55	43	(70)	*
Labour productivity	63	45	27	(62)	*
	Average rate per 100 employees	*Average rate per 100 employees*	*Average rate per 100 employees*	*Average rate per 100 employees*	*Average rate per 100 employees*
Dismissals	1.6	1.6	1.3	(0.6)	*
Voluntary resignations	12.7	15.4	15.2	(17.8)	*
	Average rate per 100 workplaces	*Average rate per 100 workplaces*	*Average rate per 100 workplaces*	*Average rate per 100 workplaces*	*Average rate per 100 workplaces*
Industrial action	0.8	5.3	8.2	(14)	*

Base: All workplaces with 25 or more employees.
Figures are weighted and based on responses from 1,638 (row 1) 1,571 (row 2), 1,841 (row 3), 1,813 (row 4) and 1,927 (row 5) managers.

Table 12.2 Union representatives' assessment of climate, by their attitudes to the employment relationship

	Climate of employment relations:					
	Very good	*Good*	*Neither good nor poor*	*Poor*	*Very poor*	
	% of workplaces	% of workplaces	% of workplaces	% of workplaces	% of workplaces	
Union representatives work closely with management when changes are being introduced:						
Agree	73	61	32	22	21	
Neither agree nor disagree	19	21	18	20	4	
Disagree	8	18	50	58	75	
Management values the opinions of union representatives:						
Agree	82	70	38	17	29	
Neither agree nor disagree	16	23	40	36	7	
Disagree	2	7	22	47	64	
Management supportive of union representatives' role:						
Agree	86	81	40	25	34	
Neither agree nor disagree	14	11	46	44	16	
Disagree	0	8	15	31	50	
Industrial action						
Average number of actions per 100 workplaces	12	21	20	49	(57)	

Base: All workplaces with union representatives and 25 or more employees.
Figures are weighted and based on responses from 813 (panels 1–3) and 772 (panel 4) union representatives.

by management. By contrast, where union representatives thought climate was poor, no more than a quarter agreed with these statements. On the more concrete measure of industrial action – as reported by union representatives – the differences were also substantial. Those who rated climate as very good were in workplaces where the average number of incidents of industrial action in the preceding year was 12 per 100 workplaces, compared with 49 incidents per 100 workplaces where union representatives thought climate poor.

When examined against the same set of performance measures reported by management (i.e. as in Table 12.1) the associations with climate were far weaker or non-existent. For example, in workplaces where union representatives rated climate as very good, 59 per cent of managers said that financial performance was above average compared with 52 per cent of managers in workplaces where union representatives rated climate as poor. The respective figures for the rates of labour turnover in the same workplaces were 8.5 per 100 employees and 9.2 per 100 employees. In short, the indicators were in a consistent direction with the management account but considerably muted.

Employees' view of climate

As with union representatives, a (bare) majority of non-managerial employees rated climate as good or very good. If managerial respondents to the employee questionnaire were included, the number who thought climate good or very good across all employees rises by 3 percentage points. Indeed, the distribution of these managerial respondents was very similar to those who completed the management interview and they are excluded from any further analysis.

Replicating the pattern shown for management and union representatives, employee views on climate were systematically and strongly related to their responses on other questions, as can be seen from Table 12.3. As we saw in Chapter 8, the implicit aspects of the employment contract play a very strong role in determining employee well-being at work. It is no surprise that they also figure prominently in employees' assessment of climate. All of the differences are very substantial. Employees who thought the climate of employment relations at their workplace was very good or good were much more likely to also have a lot of job influence, think that their jobs were secure, believe that employees were treated fairly by managers, be satisfied with their jobs and have a high level of commitment. The association with fair treatment is extremely strong – nearly all employees who thought climate was very good believed that employees were treated fairly by management, while nine in ten of those who thought it very poor believed they were treated unfairly. Conversely, just one in 50 employees who rated climate to be very poor thought that managers treated them fairly.

As with union representatives, we also compared employees' views on climate with the same set of performance measures reported by management respondents. Again, a number of associations consistent with the management account were found, but more muted. On the economic measures of workplace performance, there was no association at all between employees' assessment of climate and

Table 12.3 Non-managerial employees' assessment of climate, by their attitudes to the employment relationship

	Climate of employment relations:				
	Very good	*Good*	*Neither good nor poor*	*Poor*	*Very poor*
	% of employees	*% of employees*	*% of employees*	*% of employees*	*% of employees*
Level of job influence:					
A lot	40	30	23	21	16
Some	41	47	44	40	33
A little	15	19	25	28	30
None	3	4	8	10	20
Employees feel their job is secure:					
Agree	81	68	52	46	34
Neither agree nor disagree	11	19	26	20	19
Disagree	7	13	22	34	47
Level of fair treatment:					
Good	95	75	23	10	2
Neither good nor bad	4	20	52	30	9
Poor	1	5	25	60	89
Level of job satisfaction:					
High	88	68	38	22	8
Neither high nor low	10	25	39	32	21
Low	2	7	23	46	71
Level of employee commitment:					
High	89	71	41	26	14
Neither high nor low	10	27	48	48	33
Low	1	2	10	26	53

Base: All non-managerial employees in workplaces with 25 or more employees.
Figures are weighted and based on responses from 20,915 employees.

management reports on relative financial performance. However, employees did rate climate as better in those workplaces where management said that labour productivity was above average. Over half of employees (56 per cent) who rated climate as very good worked in workplaces with above average labour productivity, compared with around two-fifths of employees (43 per cent) who rated climate as very poor. On the measures of workplace well-being, employees did not appear to take into account the number of dismissals at the workplace, but did so with the level of labour turnover and the rate of industrial action. Labour turnover, however, was associated in the opposite direction to that found when exploring management accounts – that is, it was higher where employees were more positive about climate. With industrial action, though, the pattern was consistent with management accounts, with a greater number of incidents found in workplaces where employees thought the climate poor.

In just 4 per cent of all workplaces did all surveyed employees rate climate as being good or very good. Conversely, in only 1 per cent of workplaces did all surveyed employees think climate was worse than this. In other words, there was a great deal of variation *within* workplaces, with nearly all workplaces having some employees who thought climate was good and some who thought it was poor.

Comparing management, union representative and employee accounts

While Figure 12.1 plainly shows substantial differences in the views of workplace management when compared with those of union representatives and employees, this type of comparison is somewhat misleading. There are two reasons for this. First, responses from union representatives and employees are only available in a sub-set of workplaces, whereas a management response was obtained in all workplaces. It may be that, when comparing responses in the same set of workplaces, there are no differences. This is *not* the case. For example, restricting attention just to those workplaces where union representatives were interviewed, the distribution of management responses was virtually identical to that shown for all managers in Figure 12.1 – 36 per cent rating climate as very good and 51 per cent good.

The second reason why the comparison may be misleading is because there may be a large proportion of workplaces where management, union representatives and employees are in accord, and the aggregate differences arise because of very sharp disagreements in other workplaces. This is also *not* the case, as can be seen from Table 12.4, which compares matched pairs of respondents. Comparing management and union representative responses, there was agreement in just over a third of matched cases, which was somewhat greater than the extent of agreement between matched pairs of union representatives and employees, where the overall distributions were very similar. Statistical tests also showed that the extent of agreement for each of the three lots of matched pairs was little more than would be generated by chance.[2]

There are two conclusions which can be drawn from this analysis. First, the three separate measures of climate appear to be valid assessments of the overall character of employment relations for each set of respondents, given the strong associations with other measures provided by the *same* respondent. Second, each set of respondents has a distinct perspective on the climate of employment relations, such that the extent of actual agreement – around a third of cases for each combination of matched pairs – is quite modest. What this means, as we proceed into the multi-variate analysis, is that we cannot rely on the account provided by a single set of respondents as Fernie *et al.* (1994) did in their analysis using the 1990 WIRS; rather, a three-way analysis is required.

Table 12.4 Agreement on the climate of employment relations

	Managers versus union representatives	Managers versus employees	Union representatives versus employees
	% of workplaces	% of employees	% of employees
Both parties agree	37	31	30
Manager's rating worse by one point	11	11	–
Manager's rating worse by more than one point	1	1	–
Union representative's rating worse by one point	27	–	20
Union representative's rating worse by more than one point	24	–	12
Employee's rating worse by one point	–	32	23
Employee's rating worse by more than one point	–	25	15

Base: All workplaces (column 2) with union representatives (column 1 & 3) and 25 or more employees.
Figures are weighted and based on responses from 813 (column 1) union representatives, 22,590 (column 2) employees and 11,587 (column 3) employees.

Management practices, workplace performance and climate

The conclusion to Chapter 4 grouped together a range of contemporary management practices which we, following the literature, labelled 'high commitment' management practices. These practices were more prevalent where there was a personnel specialist either at the workplace or at a higher level in the organisation and were even more prevalent where there was also an integrated employee development plan. At the end of Chapter 5 it was shown that private sector workplaces with recognised unions had more of these practices in place. Chapter 6 concluded by showing that workplaces with a majority of the high commitment management practices and a recognised union performed better on four separate measures of performance. These analyses set the scene for this section – the evidence presented in them was cross-tabular and open to the criticism that other, intervening, factors may account for the patterns observed. For example, as recognised unions are predominantly found in larger workplaces, it is often difficult to disentangle through two or three-way tables whether it is union presence or employment size which is the dominant factor in explaining the prevalence of many features of workplace employment relations.

Multi-variate analysis allows for the suggestive associations presented in Chapters 4–6 to be more robustly examined. As outlined in the introduction to this chapter, the debate centres around whether high commitment management practices yield realisable benefits to the workplace, either by enriching the jobs of workers and/or by improving performance. Ichniowski *et al.* (1996) have provided the most thorough overview of the debates. Crudely speaking, the model is that workplace performance is, among other things, a function of innovative work practices. This is a term which has 'no settled meaning', but which generally refers to the type of practices we have labelled as 'high commitment'. These practices may lead to employees working harder or working smarter, or may simply be more efficient ways of doing things. There is the further issue, generally treated as a subsidiary one in the various studies, of the role of trade unions.

We follow the treatment of previous studies in confining attention to private sector workplaces, as it is here that cost and incentive structures are more overt. In Table 12.5 we summarise the results of a series of multi-variate models for private sector workplaces which are all commonly structured. Each of the 15 high commitment management practices was individually tested to see whether, after controlling for a range of structural features,[3] the null hypothesis of no association with measures of workplace economic performance and well-being could be rejected.[4] As with all cross-section data, identifying significant associations does not infer causality. Rather than presenting the size of the coefficients (to avoid them being interpreted as additive effects), we simply identify whether the practice is positively associated (+) with the performance measure, negatively associated (–) or not associated. Each highlighted association is statistically significant, at conventional thresholds.

The results of this multi-variate analysis are strongly consistent. Looking at them first by practices, only one of the 75 possible combinations was associated

Table 12.5 Measures of workplace performance in the private sector, by high commitment work practices: estimated probabilities

	Financial performance	Labour productivity	Rate of voluntary resignations	Dismissals rate	Climate of employee relations
Largest occupational group has/have:					
Temporary agency workers			+*		
Employees on fixed-term contracts			_***	_***	
Personality tests					+***
Performance tests	+*				
Formal off-the-job training for most employees	+**		_***		+***
Profit-related pay				_**	+
Employee share ownership scheme	+***				
Regular appraisals	+***			_***	+**
Fully-autonomous or semi-autonomous teams		+**	_*	_**	+***
Single status for managers and other employees				_**	+
Guaranteed job security	+**		_***	_*	+***
Workplace has:					
Formal disciplinary and grievance procedure			_***	_**	
Group-based team briefings with feedback					
Non-managerial employees participating in problem-solving groups	+***	+**	_***		+***
Two or more family friendly practices or special leave schemes	+**	+***	_**	_**	

Base: All private sector workplaces with 25 or more employees.

Figures are weighted and based on responses between 1,087 (column 1), 1,050 (column 2), 1,166 (column 3), 1,186 (column 4), and 1,215 (column 5) managers.

*** significant at the 0.01 level; ** significant at the 0.05 level; * significant at the 0.10 level.

Note: Ordered probit regressions. The full model includes the following controls: workplace size; part-time and female proportions – both dichotomous variables (more than 50%); whether the workplace is a single site; and industry.

with worse performance – that between the use of temporary agency workers in the largest occupational group and the rate of labour turnover (which was significantly higher) – while 30 were associated with better performance. Two of the management practices – employee share ownership schemes and group-based team briefings encompassing employee feedback – were not associated with any of the performance measures. The former of these may be due to the low take-up of share ownership even where most non-managerial employees were eligible to own shares (see Figure 4.6). Each of the remaining 12 management practices were associated with either better economic performance, workplace well-being (i.e. *lower* rates of labour turnover or dismissals) or better climate. A number of the practices were associated with several of these, notably off-the-job training, regular performance appraisals, fully-autonomous or semi-autonomous team-working, guaranteed job security or no compulsory redundancies, problem-solving groups and the provision of family friendly working arrangements.

Approached the other way, by measures of performance, it is apparent that these management practices were more closely associated with measures of workplace well-being than with measures of economic performance. Six of the 15 practices were associated with relatively good financial performance and just three of the 15 with relatively good labour productivity. By contrast, eight of the 15 practices were associated with lower rates of dismissals and seven with lower rates of labour turnover. Six of the practices were associated with a better employment relations climate, five of these being very strong associations.

All in all, this provides compelling evidence of the link between high commitment management practices and better performance. What is particularly striking is the consistency of the associations, with nearly half of the possible combinations being associated with better performance, and also the commonality of a number of the practices across different dimensions of performance. The validity of climate as a general indicator is also reinforced with these results as five of the six management practices associated with better climate were those that were most commonly associated with the other measures of performance. The final section concentrates on this dimension.

Determinants of climate

The findings reported in the previous section are consistent with a number of recent studies, both in Britain and in the United States, which have found associations between management practices and measures of performance. Only one of those studies uses a data set which matches answers from two groups of respondents (Patterson *et al.*, 1997). In this study, Patterson and his colleagues show job satisfaction as reported by employees is, when averaged for each workplace, positively and strongly associated with improved profitability and productivity as obtained from management records. We attempt to extend this approach below, by grouping data from all three sets of respondents.

For each set of respondents the answers to the question on climate was regressed against a count of the number of high commitment management practices, indicators of union presence and strength, and the proportion of employees at the workplace who were highly committed, plus a range of control variables as before.[5] The source for all of the data is management, except for the dependent variable (i.e. climate) and the proportion of highly-committed employees, which comes from the employee survey (see Chapter 8). As with the previous section, the focus of attention is on the private sector.[6]

One way of presenting the results would have been to produce tables showing the estimated coefficients and standard errors for each of the regressions. Such tables can be awkward to interpret, especially when trying to draw inferences about the scale of the effects for workplaces. Instead, we present the estimated probabilities of an 'average' workplace having very good, good, average or poor climate,[7] by plugging-in the values of the coefficients into the distribution of workplaces.

The first account of climate comes from management. One of the potential problems here is the lack of variation in the responses with nine out of ten managers rating climate as very good or good. However, Table 12.1 suggested that it *was* meaningful to distinguish between these two categories. There were two clear findings which emerged from the regressions and these are evident in Table 12.6. The number of high commitment management practices in place is positively associated with better climate – this would have been expected given our results when looking at the practices on an individual basis. Thus an average workplace with a majority of the practices in place had an estimated 39 per cent chance of its manager rating climate as very good, compared with 25 per cent where there were three or fewer of the practices in place. Even more stark, though, was the effect of the proportion of highly-committed employees at the workplace. In workplaces where three-quarters or more of the employees were highly-committed, the estimated probability of management rating climate very good (after controlling for a wide range of other variables) was two-and-a-half times that in workplaces where less than a quarter were highly-committed.

The presence of a recognised union had no measurable effect, with the estimated probabilities being no different from the average workplace. In Chapters 5 and 6 we suggested that it was not unionism *per se* that was associated with better performance, but an active union presence in tandem with high commitment management. These associations did not persist in the multi-variate analysis or, more strictly, were not significant. In part, this arises from the fact that most workplaces with a majority of high commitment management practices in place also recognised unions, so that there was insufficient variation to adequately test the interaction between the two.

From the structural controls some other findings of interest emerged, but are not reported in the table. As employment size increased climate tended to worsen, while it was significantly higher if the workforce was made up of at least half women or the workplace was a stand-alone site.

Our second informant on climate is the union representative. Along with employees they were far less positive than management, but their accounts only accorded with employees in the same workplaces in less than a third of cases.

Table 12.6 Management's perspective on the climate of employment relations in private sector workplaces: estimated probabilities

	Climate of employment relations:			
	Very good	Good	Average	Poor or very poor
	% of workplaces	% of workplaces	% of workplaces	% of workplaces
Number of high commitment management practices				
Fewer than 4	25	63	10	2
4 to 7	30	60	8	1
8 or more	39	55	5	1
Proportion of employees who are highly committed				
Less than a quarter	21	65	12	2
Between a quarter and a half	21	65	12	2
Between a half and three-quarters	31	61	7	1
Three-quarters or more	51	46	3	0
Recognised union	31	60	8	1
Average workplace climate	30	60	8	1

Base: All private sector workplaces with 25 or more employees.
Figures are weighted and based on responses from 918 managers.
Note: Ordered probit regressions. The full model includes the following controls: workplace size; part-time and female proportions – both dichotomous variables (more than 50%); whether the workplace is a single site; and industry.

Taking their responses and regressing them against an identical set of variables as before, we can begin to see to whether a common picture is emerging from alternative sources.[8] The results are presented in Table 12.7. The evidence of high commitment management practices feeding through into better climate is not supported by worker representatives. The second half of the table, however, is entirely in line with the management account: namely, the greater the proportion of highly-committed employees at the workplace (as reported by employees), the better the climate (as reported by worker representatives) after controlling for a wide range of structural features (as reported by management).

Our final informant is the (non-managerial) employee. These were the least positive of the three groups of respondents. The correct unit of analysis for exploring variation in the employee data is the employee, not the workplace. Unlike the management and union representative regressions, the link between climate and employee commitment is a direct one, so we use the employee commitment scale as reported in Chapter 8. The regressions included both workplace and employee characteristics, including gender, working hours and

Table 12.7 Union representative's perspective on the climate of employment relations in private sector workplaces: estimated probabilities

	Climate of employment relations:			
	Very good	Good	Average	Poor or very poor
	% of workplaces	% of workplaces	% of workplaces	% of workplaces
Number of high commitment management practices				
Fewer than 4	8	45	25	22
4 to 7	9	47	24	20
8 or more	7	44	25	24
Proportion of employees who are highly committed				
Less than a quarter	3	31	28	37
Between a quarter and a half	6	42	27	24
Between a half and three quarters	12	50	23	15
Three quarters or more	16	53	20	11
Average workplace climate	8	46	24	21

Base: All private sector workplaces with union representatives and 25 or more employees.
Figures are weighted and based on responses from 363 union representatives.
Note: Ordered probit regressions. The full model includes the following controls: workplace size; part-time and female proportions - both dichotomous variables (more than 50%); whether the workplace is a single site; and industry.

union membership. The results are reported in Table 12.8. Dealing with the management practices first, the estimated probability of an 'average' employee rating climate as good or very good was highest in workplaces with the most practices in place. Unlike the account provided by the union representative, this is consistent with the management account, though the scale of the differences are not great. Much more stark, and flagged in Table 12.3, was the association between the individual employee's commitment and climate. Controlling for other variables which might be intervening in this relationship has hardly altered the scale of the association, particularly that between low commitment and poor climate. There was an 80 per cent chance that an average employee with very low commitment would report a poor or very poor climate after taking a wide range of factors into account.

In common with the analysis of the management view on climate, employees were more likely to report climate as worse in larger workplaces. More important, though, were various individual characteristics. Men were more likely than women to think climate poor, as were full-timers compared with part-timers. More union members thought climate poor than non-members.

Table 12.8 Employees' perspective on the climate of employment relations in private sector workplaces: estimated probabilities

	Climate of employment relations:			
	Very good	Good	Average	Poor or very poor
	% of workplaces	% of workplaces	% of workplaces	% of workplaces
Number of high commitment management practices				
Fewer than 4	11	40	29	20
4 to 7	12	41	28	20
8 or more	15	44	26	15
Level of employee commitment:				
Very high	38	49	11	2
High	16	52	24	8
Neither high nor low	4	34	36	25
Low	1	13	31	56
Very low	0	3	16	80
Average workplace climate	12	41	28	19

Base: All private sector workplaces with 25 or more employees.
Figures are weighted and based on responses from 11,763 employees.
Note: Ordered probit regressions. The full model includes the following controls: workplace size; part-time proportions – dichotomous variable (more than 50%); whether the workplace is a single site; industry; whether the employee works full-time; their gender; and whether they are a union member.

It is important to be clear about what has been done here. Each of the parties to the employment relationship – management, union representatives and employees – provided an assessment of the employment relations climate at their workplace. On all three scores, climate was considered, generally, to be good. The three sets of assessments differed, particularly that of management who were far more positive. But even though union representatives' and employees' assessments were similarly distributed, the level of agreement between the two at the workplace was only modest. Given this background, it might reasonably be expected that any multi-variate analysis would be unlikely to yield consistent results. Not only were the results broadly consistent, but the pooling of management data with employee data showed that at both the workplace level and the individual employee level the results were substantiated.

Employee commitment was strongly and positively related to all three groups' assessments of climate. The greater the proportion of highly committed employees at the workplace, the more likely were managers and worker representatives to think climate good or very good. The more committed the employee, the greater the probability that they were positive about climate. Likewise, the count of high commitment management practices was positively associated with climate whether we take the management perspective or the individual employee perspective.

Conclusion

This chapter has differed from most of the preceding ones in that it has adopted a quite different mode of analysis to investigate what is, in some senses, the narrow issue of the climate of employment relations. Too far removed from 'bottom line' performance for some, too woolly for others, it is nonetheless perhaps the single best summary indicator of the state of employment relations in the workplace. This was amply demonstrated in the opening section where we showed that distinctions along a five point scale of climate did capture variation along other dimensions of the employment relationship. For management, it was related to both workplace performance and measures of workplace well-being. For worker representatives, it was strongly related to their evaluations of their own role and function at the workplace. For employees, it was most closely related to whether they considered workers to be fairly treated at the workplace. It is fitting, then, that it gets such an extended treatment in this chapter.

The nature of that treatment is also worthy of comment. For the most part throughout this book, we have viewed employment relations through the eyes of a single group of respondents: management, or worker representatives, or employees. It was only in the middle chapters devoted to the employee survey and worker representative interviews that any matching of the three data sources was made. This chapter has, in the final section, made highly effective use of the novelty of the survey design which allows for three-way comparisons through the common setting of the workplace. It has produced results which are broadly in line with a body of other recent evidence, but has done so in a way that is unlike any other studies of which we are aware: by using a large-scale nationally representative data source with independent sources of information.

The substantive findings of these results are also of considerable note. The workplaces doing best on a number of dimensions were those where high commitment management practices were well embedded in the labour process and where a high proportion of employees in the workplace said they felt committed to the organisation. The consistency of this finding from both management and employees is persuasive evidence of its force.

Milkman (1998), discussing changes in the American workplace from where much of this debate stems, sounds a word of caution. While not disputing the findings of other research which shows that there is a 'high road' that yields benefits to workers and employers alike, she highlights the relatively poor diffusion of the high road approach in American workplaces. This is broadly similar to our own conclusion for British workplaces based on the analysis in this chapter. High commitment management practices are associated with better economic performance, better workplace well-being and a better climate of employment relations, but just 14 per cent of all workplaces have a majority of them in place.

Notes

1   The precise wording was 'In general, how would you describe relations between managers and employees here?', with the same scale as used in the questions asked of managers and worker representatives.

2   Kappa (K) is a statistic used to measure the degree of concordance, with values lying between 1 (perfect concordance) and 0 (any agreement is by chance). For the three matched pairs, $K = 0.12$ (management and worker representatives), $K = 0.03$ (management and non-managerial employees), and $K = 0.04$ (worker representatives and non-managerial employees).

3   These are workplace employment size (banded), organisational status, industrial activity, and whether a majority of the workforce are either part-time or female.

4   Each of the variables that identify a management practice have a number of missing observations, which were usually different for different workplaces, and therefore accumulate for the entire range of 15 practices. Since each equation is estimated on the same set of workplaces, the final set of workplaces is considerably lower than the entire sample of workplaces with 25 or more employees.

5   The estimating technique was ordered probit, which is more suitable than other methods when the dependent variable is ordinal and categorical.

6   Separate regressions were run for all workplaces and fitted less well, due to a generally poor fit in public sector workplaces.

7   The categories of poor and very poor were grouped for union representatives and employees for consistency with management respondents, none of whom rated climate as very poor.

8   We could not, of course, examine for any union effects as the base is only workplaces with recognised unions.

13 Conclusions
Overview and assessment

In 1980, when the first survey in this series was conducted, it was possible to talk of a British system of industrial relations, one characterised by robust trade unions and individual employers or employers' associations who engaged in 'free' collective bargaining to set the terms and conditions of employment for the majority of the workforce. By 1990, when the third survey was undertaken, that system had fragmented to such a degree that one could no longer characterise it as a single entity. Indeed, some went so far as to foresee 'the end of institutional industrial relations' (Purcell, 1993). There may have been insufficient homogeneity with which to characterise a new system of industrial relations (Millward, 1994), but a secular shift seemed to have occurred.[1]

As we came to draw up our plans for the 1998 survey, all indications were that the 'traditional' system had unravelled even further since 1990.[2] Official statistics showed that union density fell from 39 per cent of employees in 1990 to 30 per cent in 1997, and the coverage of major national agreements fell over the same period from 35 per cent of employees to 21 per cent.[3] Case study evidence pointed to growing interest in direct employee participation and management practices originating in the United States and Japan. And, whereas unions and others in the labour movement had once actively opposed using regulatory channels to establish minimum employment standards – seen to be potentially corrosive in a system of free collective bargaining – union policy at the peak level now called for minimum wages and a floor of rights for all employees. In short, the issues at the forefront of academic and policy debates in the late 1990s were very different from those 20 years earlier. British employment relations might still be 'muddling through' (Edwards *et al.*, 1992) but to where, and to what effect?

That is what we set out to discover, our first step being to re-cast the survey design: by adding new questions and removing now less salient others; surveying employees for the first time; and lowering the workplace size threshold to 10 employees. This, inevitably, has had consequences for how we report the survey findings. Thus, this volume has given most weight to the newer areas seeking to give a full account of the breadth of the 1998 survey. It is accompanied by a volume on changes in British employment relations covering the period of the entire series 1980–98, written by other members of the research team (Millward *et al.*, 2000).

In our approach to analysis we have put our own interpretation on the survey findings: having altered the survey design it is incumbent upon us to reflect on and interpret the findings rather than simply report the results. We anticipate that some of the interpretations will be challenged, something we welcome. Indeed, it is one of the chief virtues of surveys that the findings are open to re-assessment and validation because of the transparency of the method. That is also one of the purposes in making the survey data publicly available for other researchers to use.

This concluding chapter will touch on three particular areas, highlighting some of the more important findings for each of the three kinds of survey respondents. First, we look at how best to characterise the contemporary approach to managing employees. Second, we examine the state of employee representation, commenting on whether the downward trend evident since the second survey in 1984 might be reversed. Third, we ask what all this means for employees, focusing on the level of job satisfaction. We end with some pointers to the future.

Management strategy and structure

Management or managing is an uncertain and often contradictory undertaking – they are 'both co-ordinator of a complex and often baffling productive operation, and simultaneously a vehicle of discipline' (Hyman, 1987: 35). How this uncertainty is itself managed, or handled, is what lies behind most contemporary discussions of the management of employees. Is it the case that strategic behaviour can be detected, or is management largely 'pragmatic and opportunistic' (Purcell and Sisson, 1983: 116) as it has often been characterised? In recent times, commencing with writers in the United States (Kochan *et al.*, 1986), analysts have suggested that a strategic approach to management – one where human resource management is integrated with business aims and objectives – is both feasible and observable. Others, however, suggest that management choices are constrained or even determined by the structures in which they operate.

Chapters 3 to 6 presented a full account of contemporary management practice in the field of employment relations. Chapter 4, in particular, looked at the organisation of the management function and the broad approach to managing employees from the time of recruitment through to the termination of the employment contract. Throughout, there was much evidence of managerial discretion. There were wide-ranging differences in the deployment of labour, with numerical flexibility pursued in many workplaces, often associated with low pay. A more fine-tuned approach to flexibility, involving the use of non-standard forms of labour within the core workforce, was also identified. There was also considerable evidence of union exclusion on the part of employers, which was usually effective; but, again, contrary to many popular accounts, the survey evidence was more complex, pointing to high commitment management practices going hand-in-hand with an active union presence.

This raises the question of whether these management practices, when examined as a set, constitute a strategic approach. In two-thirds of workplaces, managers claimed to have a formal strategic plan in place that encompassed an employee component. In four-fifths of these cases, someone on the employment relations side was involved in drawing up the plan, such that 57 per cent of workplaces had an 'integrated employee development plan'.

On the structure side, we paid closest attention to the organisation of the personnel function within workplaces and at higher levels. Just 7 per cent of respondents identified themselves as 'human resource managers', less than half of the more traditional 'personnel managers'. Three-fifths of all workplaces, however, had a personnel specialist of some sort, either at the workplace or at a higher level.

When these two indicators of strategy and structure were married, the pattern was stark: these workplaces were the most likely to have high commitment management practices in place. The evidence suggests that both strategy *and* structure are important influences on management style; but it must be acknowledged that, while this was the case, the diffusion of high commitment management practices was not especially widespread. Of the practices we specifically asked about, just 14 per cent of all workplaces had a majority in place, though the size of this minority may be more substantial than commentators had previously thought (Legge, 1995).

For most employers, it might be best to characterise their approach as one of retaining control and doing what they could to contain costs. The widespread use of part-time employees, contractors and of various forms of 'non-standard' labour appeared to be largely motivated by achieving savings in labour costs. Most workplaces also have in place a reasonably sophisticated monitoring regime collecting information on financial aspects of their operations and a high proportion set targets in these areas. Importantly, this information is rarely shared openly with employees (especially in the private sector).

There was comparatively little devolution of authority from senior management to line management, nor from management generally to employees. Chapter 4 showed that line managers typically did not have authority to make decisions on matters such as recruitment, awarding pay increases and dismissals. Direct supervision of employees was the most common mode used to control and monitor the work of individual employees, and while 54 per cent of workplaces made individual employees responsible for monitoring the quality of their own work, less than 1 per cent of workplaces used this as the sole means of monitoring quality.

We are largely unable to say whether there is evidence of greater or lesser strategic behaviour over time. It is reasonable to conclude for most workplaces that the broad approach to management is still one of control with high commitment management practices adopted on an *ad hoc* basis. However, the evidence does justify the large amount of attention devoted to this area in recent years by demonstrating, from both a management and an employee perspective, a close association between high commitment management practices, committed employees and a superior climate of employment relations. As ever, though, a conundrum remains: why, if this is the case, are such practices not more widespread?

Employee representation and participation

In 1979 the number of union members in Britain peaked at 13.2 million. It has fallen each year since, and by 1997 was just 60 per cent of this level.[4] A recent longitudinal study by Disney *et al.* (1998) showed, after controlling for other possible factors, that young people now entering the labour market were less likely to join unions than their counterparts a generation ago. The prospects of renewal are, on the face of it, gloomy. Do we have any evidence from which unions might take heart? The answer is mixed.

Chapter 10 showed that there appears to be a cohort effect when it comes to indicators of union presence and strength at the workplace. Over time, these indicators show a consistent decline among workplaces of the same age. Taking private sector workplaces that had been operating for ten to 24 years in 1980, 47 per cent of these recognised trade unions. At each subsequent survey, each new cohort of workplaces of the same vintage were less likely to have recognised unions, such that by 1998 only 22 per cent of these workplaces did so. The proportion was even lower among new private sector workplaces (i.e. less than five years old) where just 18 per cent recognised unions.

Still, unions have a foothold in just over half of workplaces, and in five out of six of these workplaces there is union recognition. These workplaces are, on the whole, larger than average such that 62 per cent of employees work in workplaces with union recognition. Thus, an engagement with a union presence is still part of the work experience for two out of three employees, even if only half that number are actually union members. This leaves plenty of scope for new recruitment, if unions are able to persuade these employees to become members.

We were able to probe this issue further with a series of questions put to individual employees. We asked who, ideally, would best represent their interests over a range of workplace issues, either themselves or a trade union. There are weaknesses with hypothetical questions in surveys. For many employees the situation posed will be so divorced from their own experience that they are unable to contemplate alternative scenarios. However, if we compare employees in broadly similar situations, that is to say in the same workplaces, then some of these weaknesses are less evident. In Chapter 9 we found a fair degree of resistance to union representation among non-union members in recognised workplaces. They were much more likely to follow the stance of employees in workplaces without recognised unions than of their fellow employees who were union members. Thus, on the critical issue of pay, less than a third of non-union members in recognised workplaces thought their interests would best be served by a trade union, compared with around three-quarters of union members. When it came to disciplinary issues, the differences were even greater. On the other hand, a somewhat more positive picture emerges when the questions were couched in the here and now rather than the ideal. About half of those who were non-members in unionised workplaces thought that unions took notice of members' problems and complaints and were taken seriously by management. On these matters their views were more in accordance with union members, although members were more positive, especially on the key issue of whether unions made a difference at the workplace (46 per cent compared with 28 per cent). We conclude from this that there is a potential, but largely sceptical, pool of new recruits in workplaces where unions are already recognised.

To overcome this scepticism may require tackling the issue of whether unions *do* make a difference to the way the workplace is run. Our evidence suggests that, for a substantial proportion of unionised workplaces, this may be doubtful. Many workplaces have a union presence which is either inactive or neglected. How this arises is difficult to establish, as there is a mutual association between an active union presence and a supportive management stance. Among recognised workplaces with lay union representatives, we showed in Chapter 9 that almost a third of the (most senior) representatives spent less than one hour per week on trade union activities. We also showed in Chapter 5 that the scope of joint negotiations over aspects of employment relations at the workplace was quite limited for all but a small proportion of workplaces. Only a fifth of managers in workplaces with lay union representatives negotiate with them over pay and one or more non-pay issues. Half of all workplaces with lay union representatives on site did not negotiate over *any* of the nine matters we asked about. An organised union presence does not necessarily translate into a union voice at work.

On the other hand, there was evidence that, where was a strong union voice, it was more likely to be welcomed by management than resisted. Not only this, but these workplaces were also disproportionately found among those with a large number of high commitment management practices – though there was no distinct union 'effect' on the climate of employment relations when this was more rigorously explored in Chapter 12.

But what of the half of workplaces where there was no union presence? Here, as shown in Chapter 5, employees fare even less favourably in having a 'voice' at work. Continuing the pattern found in earlier surveys, mechanisms for collective consultation were more likely to be found in unionised workplaces. Just a third of workplaces without any union members had a consultative committee in place at the workplace or at a higher level in the organisation, compared with three-quarters of unionised workplaces. The sometimes predicted advent of employee representatives in workplaces without union members has simply not materialised. In 1990, 11 per cent had them and in 1998 the proportion was little (12 per cent) different. Non-union workplaces were also less likely, as shown in Chapter 4, to have in place various forms of direct participation with employees.

To sum up, if a 'representation gap' defined in this way existed in 1990 (Towers, 1997), it was even bigger by 1998. Moreover, to couch this in terms which have more direct meaning, there was an enormous gap between the percentage of workplace management who said they consulted employees about changes at the workplace (70 per cent) and the percentage of employees who agreed with them (30 per cent). Whatever the aspirations and intent of management, these simply do not match the experience of most employees. It is to them we now turn.

Towards a new policy goal in employment relations: improving job satisfaction

In Chapter 8 we reported our findings on job satisfaction. On the basis of this measure, of every ten employees, roughly five were found to be satisfied or very satisfied with their job, two were dissatisfied and three were neither satisfied or dissatisfied. Why is this of interest?

One philosopher has recently opined that 'the existing organization of work produces a far-reaching and disturbing squandering of human moral, intellectual and economic potential' (Murphy, 1993: 1), pointing to the paradox that both liberal capitalism and Soviet communism relied on Taylorist modes of production. It is not the Taylorist division of labour as such that is the problem, according to Murphy, but the 'divorce of conception from execution' in undertaking work (p. 9). Our evidence, presented in Chapters 7 and 8, shows a very strong association between job influence and job satisfaction, which provides some support for this argument. Indeed, there is a long pedigree of research findings from social psychologists which have found the same result (Warr, 1998).

One conclusion to draw from this would be to design better jobs. However, it is misplaced to couch this just in terms of the individual job or worker, if only because they are rarely responsible for structuring the labour process. The unit of analysis must switch here to the workplace. Chapter 8 explored factors that helped explain why job satisfaction differed from one person to the next. If we take explicit account of where people work, we find that 14 per cent of the total variation in job satisfaction arose across workplaces. This is the first stage in attempting to measure how much it matters where people work, as opposed to other factors like the work they do, the hours they work, their age and so on, all of which vary within workplaces. Another way of capturing this is to look at the distribution of satisfied workers across workplaces. All employees said they were satisfied or very satisfied with their job in just 7 per cent of workplaces. At the other end of the scale, less than 1 per cent of workplaces had no satisfied workers. Thus, most workplaces have a mix of satisfied and dissatisfied workers, but the mix varies. Where people work may have some bearing on their satisfaction *independently* of the work they do and the expectations they hold. Not only this, but the extremely close link between job satisfaction and employee commitment suggests, from the analysis of employment relations climate in Chapter 12, that there are real gains for employers and employees in facing up to the implicit or 'psychological' aspects of the employment contract.

Broadly conceived, the main focus of public policy in the field of employment relations since the mid-1960s has been to reduce conflict at work, to find ways of making the system less adversarial. It would be blithe to suggest that the 'problem' has now been resolved, but it is worth putting it in perspective. In 1998 the average number of incidents of industrial action of all kinds was 2 per 100 workplaces, and 94 per cent of workplaces had experienced no industrial action of any kind in the previous five years. On the other hand, all but 7 per cent of workplaces had some workers who were not satisfied with their jobs. It may be time to acknowledge the social and economic consequences of this, to put in place a dual public policy focus – of promoting individual well-being as well as workplace well-being, for the two appear to be inter-dependent. It is apt to end here with a view from just one of the employees who took part in the survey. When asked to add anything about their work, they wrote:

> I enjoy caring for the elderly and find this type of work satisfying. However, it is spoiled by the fact that staff are given very little consideration and are expected to be more available for work than for family. I am happy to be flexible as the nature of this work requires it and provides part of the satisfaction, but staff are expected to give and give and receive little in return which eventually becomes very demoralising.

Employment relations in 1999 and beyond … to the next WERS

It is an unfortunate fact that research can be out of date by the time the findings worm their way into the world. Hence one of the reasons for that hardy perennial, the call for further research. Large-scale surveys may be more prone to this than other research methods because of the sheer amount of time it takes to marshal and present the information in a digestible form. Conscious of this, we went faster by adding extra staff resources to the project. We were also helped by the use of computer-aided interviewing which produced 'cleaner' data at an earlier stage than conventional paper methods.

The speed of our reporting will not prevent some, where they find it expedient, to dismiss the findings as irrelevant because they are out of date. Such a view would be misplaced. The intervening months between survey fieldwork finishing and this book appearing have seen the regulatory landscape of British employment relations radically altered by the introduction of universal minimum employment standards on earnings, hours of work and paid leave. The danger here, though, is in overstating the impact of statutory regulation, for the fact is that employment relations tend to change relatively slowly and often in ways independent of the law (Brown *et al.*, 1997). Even, to take an example, the much-quoted fall in union density since 1979 averages out at just over 1 percentage point each year. Over time the scale of this might be enough to constitute a transformation, but from one year to the next numbers are relatively stable. Moreover, patterns exhibit even stronger stability. Many of the differences found here between unionised and non-union workplaces, for example, were evident in 1980. So the findings in this book should be regarded as a lasting description on the state of contemporary employment relations until such time as the next survey in the series is undertaken.

There will be much to investigate in a future survey. Besides the already noted universal minimum standards of employment, there are other developments which can be foreseen. Increasing European integration is likely to further shape the course of British employment relations. Whether or not the UK joins the European Monetary Union, for example, its ramifications will be felt here (Sisson *et al.*, 1999). The Employment Relations Bill, on its merry dance through Parliament at the time of writing, may help to stem or reverse the decline in union membership by giving unions a statutory route by which to win recognition from recalcitrant employers. The consequences of all of this for employment relations are, at this stage, speculative. Only a further survey will allow the claims and counter-claims made to be empirically examined.

Before looking too far ahead, it is worth reflecting on what has been achieved with this survey. Like previous surveys in the series, WERS 98 must be rated a success in producing a large-scale nationally representative sample of workplaces with which to replenish and accumulate our knowledge of workplace employment relations. Unlike past surveys, the sample this time is also nationally representative of employees in those same workplaces. The matched data set has been used to demonstrable effect throughout this book: in exploring gender differences in earnings; comparing the views of union members and non-members on representation at work, conditional on where they worked; and by compiling an aggregate measure of employee commitment at the workplace level and showing that this was associated with the climate of employment relations. It also showed how variable employment relations were within a workplace, according to occupation; indeed, this was something of a theme recurring throughout the book, taking advantage of changes to questionnaire design that gave a sharper occupational focus.

In reviewing the book produced by our predecessors on the 1990 survey (Millward *et al.*, 1992), Sisson suggested ways of 'doing better next time' (1993: 209). Many of these suggestions were, in the event, taken up. Rather than being seen as reactive, we conclude this time by offering up three suggestions of our own for the next survey in the series.

First, we have largely skirted around conceptual problems to do with the definition of workplace and employee. Late-twentieth-century ('turbo') capitalism is characterised by ever more variety in the contractual arrangements under which work is done. The distinction between sourcing externally from the market or producing internally to the firm has become blurred. Many large organisations, including some in the public sector, have created internal quasi-market structures. In the BBC, for example, in-house production units compete directly against independent producers in supplying programmes. Should these internal units be regarded as distinct workplaces in their own right? It depends, but the number of complex cases appears to be increasing over time, making it harder to place boundaries around the conceptual construct of a workplace.[5]

Similar problems are evident with identifying the workforce. In Chapter 3 it was shown that nine in ten workplaces engage contractors for workplace-based activities, over half employ people on fixed-term contracts, and over a quarter hire workers on a temporary basis from employment agencies. Many workplaces have 'standard' employees working alongside contractors, people on fixed-term contracts, agency workers and possibly also freelancers and casual employees. Where the number of these 'non-standard' workers begins to constitute a significant proportion of all those working at a workplace, it is not clear that one can so easily ask survey respondents to think only in terms of those with a strict contract of employment. Both of these developments raise ever greater challenges for survey designers in attempting to construct an analytical framework which is sufficiently adaptive to usefully get to grips with the employment relationship and changes in it over time.

Second, there is a strong case to be made for removing altogether the employment size threshold for the survey. The principal virtue of this is that it would allow for national estimates covering all workplaces and all employees.[6] The analysis of small business employment relations in Chapter 11 showed some distinctive patterns. We cannot simply extrapolate survey findings based on a sub-set of workplaces to others outside the scope of the survey. There are awkward problems raised for survey designers as well as many practical difficulties in surveying very small workplaces, though it must be acknowledged that these were readily surmountable in going down to 10 employees. There are also now precedents of (smaller-scale) surveys of employers without an employment threshold that have successfully found ways through these problems (Forth *et al.*, 1997).

Our third recommendation is to tackle the question of regional diversity. All official labour market statistics are now presented for the United Kingdom as a whole (i.e. rather than Great Britain). There is no satisfactory reason why Northern Ireland continues to be excluded from the scope of this survey, other than the extra resources required to include it have yet to be found. This argument becomes less tenable now that devolved administrations are in place in Wales and Scotland. However, it must be recognised that the resource questions are non-trivial. It would be relatively straightforward to select a full UK sample, but this would generate so few workplaces in Northern Ireland that they could not be analysed as a distinct group.[7] Thus, to incorporate a regional dimension by, at minimum, allowing results to be presented individually for each country in the union would require substantial over-sampling in Northern Ireland, Wales and Scotland. Besides the desirable policy reasons for having regional breakdowns, it might also be merited on analytical grounds. Research using past surveys in the series, for example, has shown that a north–south 'divide' exists in employment relations even after taking into account the differences in industrial structure (Beaumont and Harris, 1989).

Whatever the shape of any future WERS, we know that the series will continue to inform and enrich our understanding of the contemporary employment relationship.

Notes

1 This position is not without its critics. Kelly (1997: 35), for example, adopting a long-term Marxist perspective, suggests that we may be at the advent of a turning point and 'the consequent shift in the balance of power will soon provide new opportunities for trade union collective organization, mobilization and action'.

2 Better described as the post-World War II system, which was relatively stable from 1945–79 though subject to variations in the locus of power (Fox, 1985).

3 This is the percentage of employees within the scope of the New Earnings Survey covered by one of a specified list of major collective agreements. Note that the survey is not representative of employees

as a whole, given that it excludes many employees whose earnings are below the PAYE threshold, and that these figures do not cover all employees whose pay is subject to collective bargaining.

4 Based on the membership data collected by the Certification Officer.

5 We have no data counting the number of complex cases of workplace definition, but Colin Airey of SCPR, who has been project director for each of the four surveys, is convinced that the 1998 survey had many more such cases than previous surveys.

6 By definition, the threshold would be one employee. There might also be a case for adding the (small number of) industries presently excluded from the survey.

7 A similar situation (though not so pronounced) applies for Wales.

Technical appendix

This technical appendix outlines both the design and the conduct of the 1998 survey. It also provides information about the statistical reliability of the results and how to access the data. For an in-depth coverage of these issues, the reader is referred to two documents: *A survey in transition: the design of the 1998 Workplace Employee Relations Survey*, by Mark Cully; and *The Workplace Employee Relations Survey 1998 (WERS): 1998 Technical Report (cross-section and panel samples)* by Airey *et al*. Both are available through the DTI's employment relations research web site (http://www.dti.gov.uk/emar).

WERS 98 is the fourth in a series of surveys previously known as the Workplace Industrial Relations Surveys (WIRS). The first three surveys were conducted in 1980, 1984 and 1990. Each surveyed a cross-section of workplaces in Great Britain with 25 or more employees. The scope of the fourth survey was widened to include workplaces with 10 or more employees. The various elements to the survey which we now briefly summarise were outlined in Figure 1.1 in Chapter 1.

One or more respondents were interviewed at the selected workplace, each being interviewed as a role-holder with specific responsibilities. The management respondent was defined as 'the senior manager dealing with personnel, staff or employee relations' at the workplace – the breakdown of respondents in terms of their management role is discussed in Chapter 4. Interviews were also sought with worker representatives at each of these workplaces. Eligibility for the worker representative interview was defined by the Computer Aided Personal Interview (CAPI) program during the course of the management interview. Interviewers sought interviews with the senior representative of the largest recognised trade union or staff association (in terms of number of members at the site). If a workplace did not recognise unions for the purpose of negotiating pay and conditions for any section of the workforce, but did operate a formal consultative committee of employees and managers, then the senior employee representative of the committee was sought. Of course many workplaces had no worker representative (of either sort) and in these workplaces no worker representative interview took place.

For the first time in the series, employees were also included in the ambit of the survey. A random selection of 25 was made at each workplace (subject to management's agreement) and self-completion questionnaires, along with freepost reply envelopes, were left for the selected employees. At workplaces with fewer than 25 employees, all employees were surveyed.

In 1984 and 1990 interviews were carried out with workplaces which had taken part in the previous surveys. This panel element was repeated in WERS 98 on a larger-than-ever scale. Only the management respondent, defined in the same terms as above, was interviewed; there were no worker representative interviews; and there was no employee survey. The panel survey also set out to trace the present status of all the workplaces surveyed in 1990, but not selected in 1998. Just knowing, for example, that some workplaces had closed down or had halved their workforce is very important retrospective information, as the responses from 1990 can be examined for any predictive patterns.

The sampling frame and the sample

Cross-section sample of workplaces

The sampling frame for the WERS 98 cross-section survey was the Inter-Departmental Business Register (IDBR) which is maintained by the Office for National Statistics (ONS), and is used for most major official surveys of employers. Its lineage is from the Census of Employment, the sampling frame in all previous surveys in the WIRS series.

Consistent with the previous surveys, the unit of observation was the workplace, which in most instances directly corresponded with the IDBR's 'local unit'. The definition of a workplace used was: an individual place (or places) of employment at a single address, covering all employees with a contract of employment for the identified employer.

The scope of the survey was all British workplaces with 10 or more employees, excluding those within the following 1992 Standard Industrial Classification (SIC 92) division groups: A (agriculture, hunting, forestry); B (fishing); C: (mining and quarrying); P (private households with employed persons); and Q (extra-territorial organisations and bodies). Apart from these population exclusions, all eligible addresses from the 1990 WIRS were deleted from the IDBR sampling frame whenever a match could be found between the IDBR and the 1987 Census of Employment records, the sampling frame for the previous survey. This was to avoid duplication in sample selection between cross-section and panel surveys and amounted to 1,036 exclusions, leaving a frame of 340,375 workplaces from which to draw the sample[1]. The distribution of these workplaces by industrial classification and size of workplace is shown in Table A1.

Within each cell of Table A1, a simple random sample of workplaces was selected. Sampling fractions increased with employment size, in part to give sufficient numbers within each size band for separate analyses, but also to allow reasonably efficient employee-based estimates to be derived. They ranged from one in 545 in workplaces with less than 25 employees to one in 21 for workplaces with 500 or more employees. There was also some over-sampling in certain SIC 92 major groups – E (electricity, gas and water supply), F (construction), H (hotels

Table A1 Number of workplaces within the sampling frame, by 1992 Standard Industrial Classification major groups and workplace size

				Workplace size			
	10–24 employees	25–49 employees	50–99 employees	100–199 employees	200–499 employees	500 or more employees	Total number of workplaces
Industry							
Manufacturing	25,195	11,502	6,742	4,402	2,653	801	51,295
Electricity, gas and water	340	228	176	144	135	58	1,081
Construction	8,811	3,100	1,448	659	274	64	14,356
Wholesale and retail	45,179	13,031	5,317	2,601	1,537	212	67,877
Hotels and restaurants	23,741	5,928	1,890	762	213	56	32,590
Transport and communications	8,577	3,748	2,248	1,285	686	250	16,794
Financial services	9,072	2,960	1,589	750	454	192	15,017
Other business services	23,544	8,271	4,235	2,572	1,304	415	40,341
Public administration	6,224	3,744	2,612	1,559	931	306	15,376
Education	13,299	10,096	4,163	1,824	509	262	30,153
Health	21,019	9,519	3,778	1,295	704	469	36,784
Other community services	12,312	3,785	1,636	660	254	64	18,711
Total	197,313	75,912	35,834	18,513	9,654	3,149	340,375

and restaurants), J (financial services) and O (other community services). The aim of this was to achieve sample sizes of around 100–150 workplaces in each of these groups. This was accommodated by decreasing the sampling fraction within group D (manufacturing).

The selected sample is shown in Table A2. Compared with previous surveys in the series, there is a smaller number of large workplaces. In 1990, 1,007 workplaces with more than 500 employees were selected, compared with a little under half this number in 1998. Less priority was attached to producing separate estimates for very large workplaces and a uniform sampling fraction was therefore adopted for workplaces with 500 or more employees.

Selection of employees for the Survey of Employees

Upon obtaining the agreement of a manager to allow employees to participate in the survey of employees, interviewers asked them for a list of all employees. They then selected a random sample of 25 employees from the list. The same procedure was used in all workplaces apart from those with 25 or fewer employees – here all employees were selected to participate. The decision to select a fixed number of employees from each workplace was influenced by several practical considerations. The fixed sample size approach was simple for interviewers to handle. It could be described with certainty to those with the authority to allow employees to participate without having prior knowledge of the number of employees in the workplace. The fixed sample size approach also gives control over the final sample sizes, both overall and within individual workplaces. With a variable sample size approach, larger workplaces with more employees than expected could potentially be asked to provide a very large sample of employees.

The 1990–98 panel sample

The fundamental requirement for the WERS 98 panel sample was that it should be representative of surviving workplaces that participated in the 1990 survey. An initial analysis provided by ONS suggested that 55 per cent of those workplaces were likely to have survived from 1990 to 1998. SCPR's initial work on the sample of apparent deaths, however, showed that the proportion of surviving workplaces was likely to substantially exceed this amount. For example, some of the workplaces which appeared to have ceased operating were major hospitals and industrial workplaces. It was apparent that changes associated with privatisation of former public utilities and the organisation of health services had led to old records being dropped, rather than the records being updated with current details.

The panel sample was thus drawn as a stratified random sample from the 2,061 productive interviews at workplaces with 25 or more employees from the 1990 WIRS. Workplaces were stratified into groups defined in terms of the number of employees at the time of the 1990 interview and a 63 per cent sample of workplaces was selected within each group. Finally, owing to uncertainty about the extent of survival, it was felt desirable to draw a reserve sample. With this

Table A2 Sample sizes, by 1992 Standard Industrial Classification major groups and workplace size

Industry	Workplace size						Total number of workplaces
	10–24 employees	25–49 employees	50–99 employees	100–199 employees	200–499 employees	500 or more employees	
Manufacturing	28	56	66	85	111	80	426
Electricity, gas and water	2	7	11	19	38	36	113
Construction	27	40	37	33	30	15	182
Wholesale and retail	78	100	83	79	100	31	471
Hotels and restaurants	50	53	34	27	16	9	189
Transport and communications	15	29	35	39	45	36	199
Financial services	18	27	29	27	35	33	169
Other business services	44	65	68	80	86	61	404
Public administration	10	29	41	48	61	46	235
Education	22	78	65	55	33	38	291
Health	35	74	59	39	46	72	325
Other community services	33	45	38	31	25	16	188
Total	362	603	566	562	626	473	3192

precaution, a sample of about 1,300 cases was felt appropriate to achieve a total of 1,000 interviews.

Piloting and developmental work

The piloting and development stages of WERS 98 took place between May and September 1997. In total 62 workplaces were visited and cross-section interviews conducted with managers. Within these, 16 interviews were achieved with worker representatives. In the same period, 35 interviews with managers using the panel questionnaire also took place. The employee survey was tested in 43 of these workplaces.

The main objective of the piloting was to test the design of the face-to-face and self-completion questionnaires and to hone the contact procedures. Particular attention was paid to elements new to the survey series: the use of CAPI in the face-to-face interviews; the self-completion Survey of Employees Questionnaire (SEQ); and the 'feeding forward' of data from the 1990 questionnaires in the panel survey. These were areas where the research team had little prior experience to call upon. There was also considerable uncertainty over the feasibility of conducting a survey of employees as part of the overall project, despite its success in similar circumstances in Australia. Following each of the pilot surveys, the research team made considerable modifications to the wording, ordering and routing of the questions. Many deletions were made to each of the CAPI questionnaires as their interview lengths at pilot all exceeded their target duration.

In all cases in Pilot 1, an attempt was made to select a sample of employees and distribute a questionnaire. Two different reminder strategies were also piloted and we eventually settled on the first of these, which entailed sending a reminder letter 2–3 weeks after the initial placement, directed to the management respondent with additional questionnaires for the (named) non-responders.

The employee survey also benefited from a round of cognitive testing. During the last week of July 1997, interviews were conducted in three workplaces. In each workplace, between seven and ten employees spent about half an hour with a specially-trained interviewer. Respondents were asked to answer pilot questions 'out loud' with the interviewer probing how and why they gave the answers they did. The results of this exercise were used to assess the effectiveness of question wording, the range of answers offered, and to determine priorities for streamlining the questionnaire.

An essential feature of the panel questionnaire was the 'feeding forward' of data from the 1990 questionnaires. In order to replicate this feature in the pilot surveys, the only possible source of addresses was the 1984–90 panel of some 540 or so 'trading sector' cases. At this point the panel sample had yet to be drawn and using the 1984–90 panel addressees would not use up workplaces from either the 1998 cross-section or panel samples. The development work for the 1998 panel study therefore excluded public sector cases, as these had not formed part of the panel sample in 1990.

Fieldwork

Fieldwork began in the middle of October 1997. Prior to fieldwork, each of the 156 interviewers working on the survey took part in a two-day training course run jointly by the research team and SCPR during October and November. While training concentrated on the use of CAPI and administering the survey, a substantial proportion of it was also devoted to introductory concepts in employment relations.

After training, the interviewers were issued with their allotment of the sampled workplaces which they were to contact. These had been divided into two 'waves' (each containing both cross-section and panel addresses). Wave 1 workplaces, accounting for around three-quarters of the total, could, in the view of the research team, be directly approached by interviewers at workplace level. The following contact procedures were used. First the interviewer telephoned the workplace to ascertain the name and job title of the appropriate management respondent. The interviewer then sent an official letter from the DTI explaining the nature of the survey and asking for their co-operation. A further telephone call was made to arrange an interview. In advance of this, the management respondent received the 'Employee Profile Questionnaire' (cross-section) or Basic Workforce Data Sheet (panel) and a Statement of Anonymity Procedures. The EPQ and BWDS were designed to collect factual information that would most likely require reference to workplace records. This included, for example, the total number of employees and a breakdown by their gender and occupation.

Wave 2 addresses were those which belonged to organisations where past experience suggested that an approach at head office level was needed in order to gain agreement for a subsequent approach to the workplace. A letter from the DTI was sent to the Personnel/Employee Relations Director at the head office of each organisation explaining the purpose of the survey and asking for the name and telephone number of an appropriate contact at each site. Once the information was obtained, interviewers then followed the contact procedure as per Wave 1 workplaces, but with the added benefit of being armed with an appropriate contact name (rather than trawling for it themselves) as well as having the tacit approval of a manager's head office. Indeed, most head offices had relayed their approval in the meantime to the respondent. All agreements with government departments and executive agencies were negotiated by the DTI research team, who were able to use their 'colleague' status to facilitate co-operation.

The work generated during Wave 2 was substantial, involving considerable amounts of the time of the research teams at the DTI and SCPR. Nonetheless, it paid off handsomely – of organisations with five or more workplaces selected to take part in the survey only a handful refused to take part.

The research team established a freephone facility so that any potential respondent with a query about the survey could be dealt with immediately by a member of the team. Over the course of fieldwork, almost 400 queries were handled through this line. In addition, reluctant participants were, if deemed appropriate by SCPR, given some gentle persuasion by the DTI research team to reconsider and, our records suggest, about half of the 400 or so workplaces contacted in this way eventually took part in the survey. All of this helped to contribute to the overall success of the fieldwork, with the survey meeting the benchmark of past surveys in the series – testimony to the hard work of SCPR staff and the DTI research team, but most of all to the efforts of the SCPR interviewers.

Once permission to interview had been secured, the burden in a sense switched to the respondents. On average, cross-section management interviews lasted for 108 minutes, worker representative interviews 47 minutes, while the panel management interview averaged 66 minutes. However these figures mask considerable variation. For example, 29 per cent of cross-section management interviews lasted two hours or longer, while 30 per cent of those for the panel took 75 minutes or longer. The duration mainly varied according to the size of the workplace.

Fieldwork outcomes

Fieldwork drew to a close in June 1998, eight months after it began. This mainly reflected a long tail, principally Wave 2 contacts where liaison between the research team and head offices had proved time-consuming. Half of both the 2,193 cross-section and the 882 panel interviews with managers had been completed by the end of February 1998. Table A3 summarises the overall yield from the selected sample for the cross-section survey and panel survey.

Cross-section management interviews

We can see from Table A3 that, from the sample of 3,192 workplaces selected from the IDBR, 463 addresses were classified as ineligible or out-of-scope. These included 158 found to have closed down between the last updating of the IDBR and the time of interview; 185 which had fallen below the survey threshold of 10 employees at the time of interview; 45 found to be vacant or at premises which had been demolished or where the workplace had moved leaving no trace of a new address; and 75 workplaces excluded for a variety of other reasons.

This left 2,729 workplaces classified as within the scope of the survey. From this, 536 workplaces were classified as non-productive including: 422 refusals to participate; 82 where effective contact was never established; and 32 where the interview was postponed and/or transferred to another location on so many occasions that fieldwork was closed down before an effective conclusion had been reached.

Overall, the yield of interviews from the sample of 3,192 workplaces selected from the IDBR was 2,193 or 69 per cent. Among workplaces classified as having 25 or more employees, the yield was 71 per cent. By way of comparison, in 1990, the sample of workplaces yielded 68 per cent. Only 50 per cent of 1998 workplaces classified as having 10–24 employees yielded a productive interview. One in three proved to be out-of-scope – the great majority of cases having fewer than 10 employees at the time of interview.

Table A3 Summary of fieldwork

	Cross-section: management interviews*	Cross-section: worker representative interviews	Panel: management interviews**		
			Number of workplaces		
Selected sample		3,192		1,157		1,301
Minus total ineligible or out of scope	463				261
Total eligible and in scope		2,729				1,040
Minus					
Refusals	422		125		96
Non-contactables	82		34		24
Other non-participating workplaces	32		51		38
Total unproductives		536		210		158
Achieved interviews		2,193		947		882

* The final data set excludes two achieved interviews that were conducted at workplaces within the mining industry.
** The final data set excludes 36 achieved interviews that were conducted at workplaces where we were unable to confirm that the definition of a 'continuing workplace' had been met.

Excluding workplaces that proved to be out-of-scope, the overall response rate for the survey was 80.4 per cent. Among workplaces sampled as having 25 or more employees it was 80.8 per cent. This is slightly lower than the comparable figure in 1990 of 82.7 per cent.

Cross-section worker representative interviews

There was no eligible worker representative at 1,036 (47 per cent) of the 2,193 workplaces where management interviews were obtained. Among workplaces with 10–24 employees, only 24 per cent proved to have an eligible employee representative. In contrast 81 per cent of workplaces with 500 or more employees offered eligible representatives.

Of the remaining 1,157 workplaces, interviews were achieved with 947 worker representatives. This was a response rate of 81.9 per cent. Of the 125 refusals, only 8 of these were from the worker representatives themselves; the remaining 117 were made at the management level. 877 of the interviews achieved were with representatives of recognised trade unions; 70 were with non-union representatives.

Cross-section Survey of Employees (SEQ)

Managers in 86 per cent of cases agreed that employees at the workplace could participate in the survey of employees. However, in nearly 5 per cent of these workplaces, no employee questionnaires were ever received.

There is a strong association between the size of the workplace and management's willingness to participate in the SEQ procedures. Small workplaces (which were less likely to participate in the WERS project overall), surprisingly, proved more likely to agree to the SEQ. However, employees from the smallest workplaces (those with fewer than 50 employees) were less likely than others to return their questionnaires. The level of corporate 'blanket' refusals accounts for half of all refusals, while the main reason management gave for not agreeing to the SEQ was an unwillingness to ask their employees.

Overall, there was a return of some sort in respect of 67 per cent of the 44,283 questionnaires placed. In 64 per cent of cases (28,237) the outcome was a completed questionnaire; the remaining 3 per cent were made up of refusals (1.3 per cent), out-of-scope placements (0.8 per cent) and others (0.7 per cent).

The 1990–98 panel management interviews

Referring back to table A3, we can see that of the issued sample of 1,301 addresses, 261 (20 per cent) were classified as out-of-scope. Over half of these (136) were identified as having closed down, with closure implicit for a further 33 (not traced, derelict etc.). Overall, the productive response was 85 per cent, two-and-a-half percentage points lower than for the 1990 panel. The extent to which workplaces proved to be out-of-scope was closely associated with the size of the workplace in 1990; 32 per cent of workplaces with fewer than 100 employees in 1990 were out-of-scope, while this was true for only 8 per cent of workplaces with 1,000 or more employees.

Of the 760 workplaces surveyed in 1990 and not selected for the panel survey, 83 per cent were identified as continuing workplaces with 25 employees or more. Within the 83 per cent, 53 per cent were at the same address and under the same ownership and 17 per cent were at the same address with a different owner. In total, 62 per cent of workplaces were found to have been in the same ownership since 1990. The remaining 17 per cent of 1990 addresses were found either to have closed down (11.5 per cent) or currently to have fewer than 25 employees (5.2 per cent). The number of workplaces where interviewers were unable to establish any information (1 no trace; 3 refusals) was insignificant.

Coding and editing the data

Coding and editing of the survey questionnaires was carried out by SCPR's experienced data-processing team aided by the SCPR and DTI research teams. WERS 98 saw an improvement in the efficiency of the post-interview operations largely owing to the use of CAPI in data collection. Nevertheless there was still a considerable amount of work involved in preparing the data, including processing 'fact sheets', performing other edits, coding of open and 'other specify' answers, and some overcoding.

Editing is a much simpler process in CAPI surveys because so much of the potential for error is removed at the design and testing stage. Whereas in a paper questionnaire it is difficult to correct internal inconsistencies at the time of the interview, within a CAPI programme such checks are possible. For example, if a management respondent said at one point in the interview that there were no professional employees at the workplace, but elsewhere said that there were, the interviewer would be made aware of this inconsistency and asked to clarify. This feature of CAPI resulted in a relatively small number of new checks introduced for editors.

It was important to be alerted to cases where there was an apparent mismatch between the sampled size or SIC classification of the sampled workplace and the information obtained within the interview. In such cases the interviewer might have interviewed at the wrong workplace or about the wrong set of employees. Fact sheets contained an array of such information taken from the sampling frame and data collected at the interview. Cross checks were performed during the production of the fact sheets so that failing cases were automatically flagged for attention. One task that had been onerous in previous WIRS surveys was the handling of employee numbers sub-divided by gender, hours of work and occupation, which were recorded on the form sent out prior to interview. The CAPI program contained a number of checks within the 45 cell EPQ matrix to ensure that the data collected were as consistent as possible. Only nine of the productive cross-section interviews generated a query arising from this grid at the data processing stage.

Additional checks were included on the panel survey fact sheets to verify that the interviews had been carried out at the same workplace in both 1990 and 1998, and to identify inconsistent data within the 1998 interview. Checks on the validity of the surveyed workplace in 1998 consisted of comparisons with the workplace's employment numbers, industry, workforce composition and union status in 1990.

However, the in-built checks within CAPI were occasionally ineffectual. On closer inspection of the cross-section data, the research team found a large number of workplaces that, although being publicly listed (or part of an organisation that was), recorded themselves as being part of the public sector. The public sector check did not pick these cases up. They were identified by looking at the name of the organisation to which the workplace belonged and therefore required each case to be looked at individually. Only a few subsequent questions in the interview were routed on the answer to this question, therefore, only a small amount of additional data had to be collected by re-contacting the workplace.

Overcodes served two purposes during the coding and editing stages. They identified cases where a (major) change has been made to an interview after its completion, or where the research team had reason to be concerned about a particular set of responses. For example, overcodes were added to cases in which further investigation generated continued concerns about the consistency of definition of the workplace. This had a particular resonance for the panel survey where 36 of the 882 productive interviews were subsequently excluded from the analysis of the panel data set because the research team was unable to confirm that the workplace interviewed in 1998 was essentially the same as that interviewed in 1990.

Overall, 29 per cent of all cases from the cross-section survey and 38 per cent from the panel survey were referred to the SCPR and sponsor research teams to resolve potential anomalies or to clarify an answer. Plausible explanations for the differences were usually obtained either by telephoning the interviewer or the respondent. Once these problems had been resolved, the information was then sent back to the editors in the data-processing team.

Weighting the cross-section sample

Sample of workplaces

To derive unbiased estimates from the sample of workplaces, the data had first to be weighted to compensate for the fact that workplaces had differing probabilities of selection for the survey. The weights derived are calculated as the inverse of the *estimated* probability of selection, scaled back to the achieved sample size after a process of trimming for extreme values.

The probability of selection for any workplace was determined by three factors: the SIC major group and size band as classified on the IDBR; whether the IDBR local unit was a workplace according to the definition applied in the survey; and the probability that the workplace was not selected for the 1990 WIRS. The third factor is included because the 1990 WIRS sample was excluded from the 1998 WERS cross-section sample to avoid overlap with the panel sample.

Experience from previous WIRS suggested there may be occasions where the IDBR local unit would be several workplaces, or a sub-section of a workplace. Of the three cases that fell into the first category in 1998, one workplace was selected at random from those covered by the IDBR local unit. There were also 76 IDBR local units which were found to be sub-sections of a workplace. In each of the 76 cases the true probability of selection was computed.[2] In instances where the IDBR local unit was a workplace as defined in the survey, the probability of selection is simply that of the sampling fraction.

In some instances, the surveyed workplace was found to have a very different number of employees to that recorded on the IDBR. The inverse probability weight for a workplace would then be very different to the weights applied to workplaces of a similar size. For example, a workplace with 1,000 employees in SIC major group D would have an inverse probability weight of 10 if the IDBR employee count was similar for the actual number of employees, but would have an inverse probability weight of 52 if the IDBR gave an employee count of between 100 and 199. Although the use of inverse probability weights gives unbiased estimates, the effect of this potentially large variation in weights within SIC and size groups is to increase standard errors considerably. To avoid this, relatively large or small weights were trimmed. This is the first time this has been done in the survey series.

Finally, the workplace weights were scaled to equal the achieved sample size of 2,193, although the un-scaled weights were kept so that grossed estimates for workplaces could be derived.

Sample of employees

As with the workplace sample, to derive unbiased estimates of the population of employees based on data from the SEQ, the sample had to be weighted by the inverse of the probability of selection.

In practice, some workplaces did not agree to co-operate with the employee survey and some employees, although they received an SEQ, failed to return it. A non-response analysis was undertaken, the objective being to estimate the probability of response, and to adjust the employee weight accordingly. The probability that an employee returned a completed SEQ was estimated by comparing numbers of full and part-time workers by gender and occupation from the returned SEQs, with the numbers that would have been expected if all had responded. This was based on estimates of workforce composition in workplaces with 10 or more employees taken from the EPQ data. Overall, those in part-time work (particularly men) and those in craft and skilled service, personal and protective service, sales and operative and assembly occupations were less likely than average to return a completed questionnaire. The probability of responding was estimated using a rim weighting procedure, the marginals (or 'rims') being derived from the aggregated workplace questionnaires.

Having derived estimates of the probability of response, the inverse probability weight was calculated in the usual way. Finally, the employee weights were scaled to the total SEQ sample size of 28,240.

Weighting the panel sample

The weights applied to the panel data were calculated as the inverse of the probability of being selected for *and* agreeing to take part in the survey. To estimate the probability of responding to the panel survey, a logistic regression model was fitted to the data using independent variables selected from the 1990 management questionnaire.[3]

Just two of these variables were found to be significant predictors of response: legal status (trading public corporation/nationalised industry) and the union-related limits on managers' ability to organise work as they pleased. Both were associated with a greater likelihood of response to the panel survey. The model-predicted probability of responding was used directly in the calculation of the panel weight.

Sampling errors[4]

Sampling error refers to any difference between the characteristics of the workplaces we surveyed and the characteristics of the population. Statistical theory allows us to quantify this through the calculation of standard errors and confidence intervals. Thus, if a new sample had been drawn we would be confident (given a 95 per cent confidence interval) that 19 times out of 20 an estimate would fall within a given range.

Cross-section sample of workplaces

The standard errors of any sample survey are affected by the sample design, particularly by the effects of sampling weights, clustering and stratification. As already described, the design for the cross-section sample was a one-stage stratified design with unequal selection probabilities per workplace. It is important to take these design factors (sampling weights and stratification) into account when calculating correct estimates of standard errors, valid p-values and confidence intervals. Ignoring it, by assuming simple random sampling, results in estimated standard errors that may be too small.

Table A4 gives approximate standard errors for various percentages and sample sizes based on an 'average' design effect. So an estimate of a 95 per cent confidence interval would be plus or minus twice the standard error presented in the table. For example, an estimate that around 60 per cent of workplaces have a certain characteristic, based on a sub-sample size of around 750, would have an associated standard error of around 2.68 percentage points, so a 95 per cent confidence

Table A4 Approximate standard errors for various percentages and sample sizes for the management cross-section data

	Sample size								
	100	*250*	*500*	*750*	*1,000*	*1,250*	*1,500*	*1,750*	*2,000*
Estimate %									
10	4.50	2.85	2.01	1.64	1.42	1.27	1.16	1.08	1.01
20	6.00	3.79	2.68	2.19	1.90	1.70	1.55	1.43	1.34
30	6.87	4.35	3.07	2.51	2.17	1.94	1.77	1.64	1.54
40	7.35	4.65	3.29	2.68	2.32	2.08	1.90	1.76	1.64
50	7.50	4.74	3.35	2.74	2.37	2.12	1.94	1.79	1.68
60	7.35	4.65	3.29	2.68	2.32	2.08	1.90	1.76	1.64
70	6.87	4.35	3.07	2.51	2.17	1.94	1.77	1.64	1.54
80	6.00	3.79	2.68	2.19	1.90	1.70	1.55	1.43	1.34
90	4.50	2.85	2.01	1.64	1.42	1.27	1.16	1.08	1.01

Table A5 Approximate standard errors for various percentages and sample sizes for the employee data

	Sample size							
	500	*1,000*	*2,000*	*5,000*	*10,000*	*15,000*	*20,000*	*30,000*
Estimate %								
10	2.28	1.61	1.14	0.72	0.51	0.42	0.36	0.29
20	3.04	2.15	1.52	0.96	0.68	0.56	0.48	0.39
30	3.48	2.46	1.74	1.10	0.78	0.64	0.55	0.45
40	3.72	2.63	1.86	1.18	0.83	0.68	0.59	0.48
50	3.80	2.69	1.90	1.20	0.85	0.69	0.60	0.49
60	3.72	2.63	1.86	1.18	0.83	0.68	0.59	0.48
70	3.48	2.46	1.74	1.10	0.78	0.64	0.55	0.45
80	3.04	2.15	1.52	0.96	0.68	0.56	0.48	0.39
90	2.28	1.61	1.14	0.72	0.51	0.42	0.36	0.29

interval would be 60 per cent plus or minus 5.36, that is 54.6 per cent to 65.4 per cent.

This provides a useful rule-of-thumb guide to the precision of survey estimates. However, using an 'average' design effect is a simplification which could lead to severe distortions for some variables. Where possible, the reader is advised to peruse tables 8A and 8B in 'The Workplace Employee Relations Survey 1998 (WERS 98): Technical Report' and identify variables similar to the particular estimate of interest.

Sample of employees

In general, the design factors associated with estimates for employees are likely to be slightly greater than those for workplaces, due to the clustering of employees within workplaces. This is counter-balanced by the much larger sample size of employees. Table A5 presents some guidance to the likely size of standard errors for estimates based on the employee data. These figures are based on an assumption of an average design factor of 1.7. While useful as a rule-of-thumb, the same caveats as above apply.

Accessing the data

All the WERS data sets and accompanying documentation (including the full Technical Report) are publicly available from:

The Data Archive,
University of Essex,
Wivenhoe Park,
Colchester, Essex,
CO4 3SQ UK.
Telephone: 01206 872001
Facsimile: 01206 872003
Email: archive@essex.ac.uk
Internet: http://dawww.essex.ac.uk

Notes

1   Subsequently, however, limitations in the matching process were discovered, and 47 'overlap' workplaces were identified in the cross-section sample. 38 of these were withdrawn and no interview was attempted. In the remaining 9 cases the cross-section interview had been completed before the duplication was identified and therefore a panel interview could not take place.

2   It was subsequently discovered that, in about 15 cases, the sampled workplace was a sub-section of a workplace but the other sub-sections had a different reporting unit. These were not identified at the time as potentially problematic. Consequently, the weights for these workplaces do not reflect the fact that these workplaces had more than one chance of selection for the survey.

3   Namely: location of interview (workplace or elsewhere); region; workplace size; legal status; whether independent or part of a larger organisation; whether manager is specialist or non-specialist; whether a union is recognised; relative financial performance; where decisions on senior appointments are made; where decisions on union recognition are made; whether a member of an employers' association; management views on union membership; whether there are any joint consultative committees of employees and managers; any workforce reductions in previous 12 months due to lack of demand; whether opposition from union representatives limits organisation of work; whether lack of management expertise limits organisation of work; proportion of staff from ethnic minority groups; workplace UK or foreign-owned; similarity of workplace and other subsidiaries in the organisation; rating of management/employee relations; industry (SIC80, one digit).

4   *Britain at Work* in the main reports findings from the cross-section of WERS 98, with the exception of Chapter 10 which analyses data from each of the cross-section surveys (1980, 1984, 1990 and 1998) and the 1990–98 panel survey. The companion volume to this text *All Change at Work?* (Millward *et al.*, 2000) is the main repository of analysis for both the time series and panel data. Readers interested in the standard errors relating to those data sets should therefore refer to the companion volume or the technical report.

Bibliography

Abowd, J., Kramarz, F. and Margolis, D. (1998) 'High Wage Workers and High Wage Firms', *Econometrica*, 67, 2: 251–333.

Ackroyd, S. and Procter, S. (1998) 'British Manufacturing Organisation and Workplace Industrial Relations: Some Attributes of the New Flexible Firm', *British Journal of Industrial Relations* 36, 2: 164–183.

Airey, C., Hales, J., Hamilton, R., McKernan, A. and Purdon, S. (1999) *The Workplace Employee Relations Survey, 1998 (WERS): 1998 Technical Report (cross-section and panel samples)*, London: Social and Community Planning Research.

Allen, J. and Du Gay, P. (1994) 'Industry and the Rest: the Economic Identity of Services', *Work, Employment and Society*, 8, 2: 255–271.

Anderman, S. (1986) 'Unfair Dismissals and Redundancy', in Lewis, R. (ed.) *Labour Law in Britain*, Oxford: Blackwell.

Atkinson, J. (1984) 'Manpower Strategies for Flexible Organisations', *Personnel Management*, August: 28–31.

Atkinson, J. and Hillage, J. (1994) 'Employers Policies and Attitudes Towards Check-Off', *Manpower Commentary* Series, 271.

Atkinson, J. and Meager, N. (1994) 'Running to Stand Still: the Small Firm in the Labour Market', in Atkinson, J. and Storey, D. (eds) *Employment, the Small Firm and the Labour Market*, London: Routledge.

Bacon, N. and Storey, J. (1993) 'Individualization of the Employment Relationship and the Implications for Trade Unions', *Employee Relations*, 19, 2: 5–17.

Bailey, R. (1996) 'Public Sector Industrial Relations', in Beardwell, I. (ed.) *Contemporary Industrial Relations: A Critical Analysis*, Oxford: Oxford University Press.

Bassett, P. (1986) *Strike-Free: New Industrial Relations in Britain*, London: Macmillan.

Batstone, E., Boraston, I. and Frenkel, S. (1977) *Shop Stewards in Action*, Oxford: Blackwell.

Beatson, M. (1995) 'Labour Market Flexibility', *Employment Department Research Series*, Employment Department Publication, 48.

Beaumont, P. and Harris, R. (1989) 'The North-South Divide in Britain: The Case of Union Recognition', *Oxford Bulletin of Economics and Statistics*, 51, 4: 413–428.

Ben-Ner, A. and Jones, D. (1995) 'Employee Participation, Ownership and Productivity: A Theoretical Framework', *Industrial Relations*, 34, 4: 532–554.

Berry-Lound, D. (1990) *Work and the Family: Carer-Friendly Employment Practice*, London: IDN.

Blanchflower, D. and Oswald, A. (1988) 'Profit-Related Pay: Prose Discovered?', *Economic Journal*, 98, 392: 720–730.

Brannen, J., Moss, P., Owen, C. and Wale, C. (1997) 'Mothers, Fathers and Employment: Parents and the Labour Market in Britain, 1984 to 1994', *Department for Education and Employment Research Report*, Department for Education and Employment, 10.

Braverman, H. (1974) *Labour and Monopoly Capital: the Degradation of Work in the Twentieth Century*, New York: Monthly Review Press.

Bridgewood, A. and Savage, P. (1993) *General Household Survey 1991*, London: Office of Population Censuses and Surveys.

Brown, J. (1997) 'Managerial Disclosure of Financial Information to Employees: a Historical and Comparative Review', *The Journal of Industrial Relations*, 39, 2: 263–286.

Brown, W. and Rea, D. (1995) 'The Changing Nature of the Employment Contract', *Scottish Journal of Political Economy*, 42, 3: 363–377.

Brown, W., Marginson, P. and Walsh, J. (1995) 'Management: Pay Determination and Collective Bargaining', in Edwards, P. (ed.) *Industrial Relations: Theory and Practice in Britain*, Oxford: Blackwell.

Brown, W. and Walsh, J. (1991) 'Pay Determination in Britain in the 1980s: The Anatomy of Decentralization', *Oxford Review of Economic Policy*, 7,1: 44–59.

Brown, W., Ebsworth, R. and Terry, M. (1978) 'Factors Shaping Shop Steward Organisation in Britain', *British Journal of Industrial Relations*, 16, 2: 139–159.

Brown, W., Deakin, S. and Ryan, P. (1997) 'The Effects of British Industrial Relations Legislation 1979–97', *National Institute Economic Review*, 161: 69–83.

Brown, W., Deakin, S., Hudson, M., Pratten, C. and Ryan, P. (1998) 'The Individualisation of Employment Contracts in Britain', *Department of Trade and Industry Employment Relations Research Series*, London: Department of Trade and Industry, 4. Available on line at http://www.dti.gov.uk/emar.

Burchell, B., Deakin, S. and Honey, S. (1999) 'The Employment Status of Individuals in Non-Standard Employment', *Department of Trade and Industry Employment Relations Research Series*, London: Department of Trade and Industry, 6. Available on line at http://www.dti.gov.uk/emar.

Clark, A. (1996) 'Job Satisfaction in Britain', *British Journal of Industrial Relations*, 34, 2: 189–217.

Claydon, T. (1996) 'Union Derecognition: a Re-Examination', in Beardwell, I. (ed.) *Contemporary Industrial Relations: A Critical Analysis*, Oxford: Oxford University Press.

Cockburn, C. (1983) *Brothers: Male Dominance and Technological Change*, London: Pluto Press.

Colling, T. and Ferner, A. (1992) 'The Limits of Autonomy: Devolution, Line Managers and Industrial Relations in Privatised Companies', *Journal of Management Studies*, 29, 2: 209–227.

Collinson, M., Rees, C. and Edwards, P. with Inness, L. (1998) 'Involving Employees in Total Quality Management', *Department of Trade and Industry Employment Relations Research Series*, London: Department of Trade and Industry, 1. Available on line at http://www.dti.gov.uk/emar.

Cooke, W. (1997) 'The Influence of Industrial Relations Factors on U.S. Foreign Direct Investment Abroad', *Industrial and Labor Relations Review*, 51, 1: 3–17.

Crompton, R. (1997) *Women and Work in Modern Britain*, Oxford: Oxford University Press.

Cully, M. (1998) *A Survey in Transition: the Design of the 1998 Workplace Employee Relations Survey*, London: Department of Trade and Industry. Available on line at http://www. dti.gov.uk/emar.

Cully, M. and Maginson, P. (1995) 'The Workplace Industrial Relations Surveys: Donovan and the Burden of Continuity', *Warwick Papers in Industrial Relations*, 55.

Cully, M. and Woodland, S. (1998) 'Trade Union Membership and Recognition', *Labour Market Trends*, 106, 7: 353–364.

Cully, M., Woodland, S., O'Reilly, A., Dix, G., Millward, N., Bryson, A. and Forth, J. (1998) *The 1998 Workplace Employee Relations Survey: First Findings*, London: Department of Trade and Industry. Available on line at http://www.dti.gov.uk/emar.

Davies, N. and Teasdale, P. (1994) *The Cost to the British Economy of Work Accidents And Work-Related Ill Health*, HSE Books.

Deakin, S. and Morris, G. (1995) *Labour Law*, London: Butterworths.

Department for Education and Employment (1998) *National Child Care Strategy*.

Department of Trade and Industry (1998a) *Fairness at Work*, Cm 3968.

Department of Trade and Industry (1998b) *Our Competitive Future: Building the Knowledge Driven Economy*, Cm 4176.

De Vaus, D. (1996) *Surveys in Social Research*, London: University College London Press.

Dex, S. and McCulloch, A. (1997) *Flexible Employment: the Future of Britain's Jobs*, Basingstoke: Macmillan.

Dickens, L. and Bain, G. (1986) 'A Duty to Bargain? Union Recognition and Information Disclosure', in Lewis, R. (ed.) *Labour Law in Britain*, Oxford: Blackwell.

Dickens, L. and Hall, M. (1995) 'The State: Labour Law and Industrial Relations', in Edwards, P. (ed.) *Industrial Relations: Theory and Practice in Britain*, Oxford: Blackwell.

Disney, R., Gosling, A. and Machin, S. (1995) 'British Unions in Decline: Determinants of the 1980s Fall in Union Recognition', *Industrial and Labor Relations Review*, 48, 3: 403–419.

Disney, R., Gosling, A., Machin, S. and McCrae, J. (1998) 'The Dynamics of Union Membership in Britain', *Department of Trade and Industry Employment*

Relations Research Series, London: Department of Trade and Industry, 3. Available on line at http://www.dti.gov.uk/emar.

Dunn, S. and Wright, M. (1993) 'Managing Without the Closed Shop', in Metcalf, D. and Milner, S. (eds) *New Perspectives on Industrial Disputes*, London: Routledge.

Earnshaw, J., Goodman, J., Harrison, R. and Marchington, M. (1998) 'Industrial Tribunals, Workplace Disciplinary Procedures and Employment Practice', *Department of Trade and Industry Employment Relations Research Series*, London: Department of Trade and Industry, 2. Available on line at http://www.dti.gov.uk/emar.

Edwards, P. (1986), *Conflict at Work: A Materialist Analysis of Workplace Relations*, Oxford: Blackwell.

Edwards, P. and Marginson, P. (1988) 'Differences in Perception Between Establishment and Higher Level Managers', in Marginson, P., Edwards, P., Martin, R., Purcell, J. and Sisson, K. (eds) *Beyond the Workplace: Managing Industrial Relations in the Multi-Establishment Enterprise*, London: Blackwell.

Edwards, P. and Scullion, H. (1982), *The Social Organization of Industrial Conflict: Control and Resistance in the Workplace*, Oxford: Blackwell.

Edwards, P., Hall, M., Hyman, R., Marginson, P., Sisson, K., Waddington, J. and Winchester, D. (1992) 'Great Britain: Still Muddling Through', in Ferner, A. and Hyman, R. (eds) *Industrial Relations in the New Europe*, Oxford: Blackwell.

Elgar, J. and Simpson, B. (1993) 'The Impact of the Law on Industrial Disputes in the 1980s' in Metcalf, D. and Milner, S. (eds) *New Perspectives on Industrial Disputes*, London: Routledge.

Ezzamel, M., Lilley, S., Wilkinson, A. and Willmott, H. (1996) 'Practice and Practicalities in Human Resource Management', *Human Resource Management Journal*, 6, 1: 63–80.

Felstead, A., Burchell, B. and Green, F. (1998), 'Insecurity at Work', *New Economy*, 5, 3: 180–184.

Fernie, S. and Metcalf, D. (1995) 'Participation, Contingent Pay, Representation and Performance: Evidence from Great Britain', *British Journal of Industrial Relations*, 33, 3: 379–415.

Fernie, S., Metcalf, D. and Woodland, S. (1994) 'Lost Your Voice?', *New Economy*, 1, 4: 231–237.

Flanders, A. (1964) *The Fawley Productivity Agreements*, London: Faber and Faber.

Forth, J., Lissenburgh, S., Callender, C. and Millward, N. (1997) 'Family Friendly Working Arrangements in Britain 1996', *Department for Education and Employment Research Report*, 16.

Fox, A. (1985) *History and Heritage: The Social Origins of the British Industrial Relations System*, London: Allen and Unwin.

Freeman, R. and Medoff, J. (1984) *What Do Unions Do?*, New York: Basic Books.

Gallie, D., White, M., Cheng, Y. and Tomlinson M. (1998) *Restructuring the Employment Relationship*, Oxford: Oxford University Press.

Gennard, J. and Kelly, J. (1995) 'Human Resource Management: The Views of Personnel Directors', *Human Resource Management Journal*, 5, 1: 15–32.

Glynn, S. and Gospel, H. (1993) 'Britain's Low Skill Equilibrium: a Problem of Demand?', *Industrial Relations Journal*, 24, 2: 112–125.

Godfrey, G. and Marchington, M. (1996) 'Shop Stewards in the 1990s: a Research Note', *Industrial Relations Journal*, 27, 4: 339–344.

Gospel, H. (1992) *Markets, Firms, and the Management of Labour in Modern Britain*, Cambridge: Cambridge University Press.

Green, F., Machin, S. and Wilkinson, D. (1999) 'Trade Unions and Training Practices in British Workplaces', *Industrial and Labor Relations Review*, 52, 2: 179–195.

Gregg, P. and Wadsworth, J. (1995), 'A Short History of Labour Turnover, Job Tenure, and Job Security, 1975–93', *Oxford Review of Economic Policy*, 11, 1: 73–90.

Groshen, E. (1991) 'Five Reasons Why Wages Vary Among Employers', *Industrial Relations*, 30, 3: 350–381.

Guest, D. (1987) 'Human Resource Management and Industrial Relations', *Journal of Management Studies*, 24, 5: 503–522.

Guest, D. (1995) 'Human Resource Management, Trade Unions and Industrial Relations', in Storey, J. (ed.) *Human Resource Management: a Critical Text*, London: Routledge.

Guest, D. and Conway, N. (1998) 'Fairness at Work and the Psychological Contract', *Issues in People Management*, London: Institute of Personnel and Development.

Guest, D. and Hoque, K. (1996) 'Human Resource Management and the New Industrial Relations', in Beardwell, I. (ed.) *Contemporary Industrial Relations: a Critical Analysis*, Oxford: Oxford University Press.

Guest, D. and Peccei, R. (1994) 'The Nature and Causes of Effective Human Resource Management', *British Journal of Industrial Relations*, 32, 2: 219–242.

Guest, D. and Rosenthal, P. (1993) 'Industrial Relations in Greenfield Sites', in Metcalf, D. and Milner, S. (eds) *New Perspectives on Industrial Disputes*, London: Routledge.

Guest, D., Conway, N., Briner, R. and Dickman, M. (1996) 'The State of the Psychological Contract in Employment', *Issues in People Management*, London: Institute of Personnel and Development.

Hakim, C. (1990) 'Core and Periphery in Employers' Workforce Strategies: Evidence from the 1987 ELUS Survey', *Work, Employment and Society*, 4, 2: 157–188.

Hakim, C. (1996) *Key Issues in Women's Work*, London: Athlone Press.

Hall, M. (1996) 'Beyond Recognition? Employee Representation and EU Law', *Industrial Law Journal*, 25, 1: 15–27.

Hampson, I., Ewer, P. and Smith, M. (1994) 'Post-Fordism and Workplace Change: Towards a Critical Research Agenda', *Journal of Industrial Relations*, 36, 2: 231–257.

Health and Safety Executive (1996) *A Guide to the Health and Safety (Consultation with Employees) Regulations 1996*, HSE Books.

Healy, G. (1997) 'The Industrial Relations of Appraisal: the Case of Teachers', *Industrial Relations Journal*, 28, 3: 206–220.

Hendry, C., Jones, A., Arthur, M. and Pettigrew, A. (1991) *Human Resource Development in Small to Medium Sized Enterprises*, Sheffield: Department of Employment.

Humphries, J. and Rubery, J. (1992) 'Women's Employment in the 1980s: Integration, Differentiation and Polarisation', in Michie, J. (ed.) *1979–1991: The Economic Legacy*, London: Academic Press.

Hyman, R. (1987) 'Strategy or Structure: Capital, Labour and Control', *Work, Employment and Society*, 1, 1: 25–56.

Hyman, R. (1997) 'The Future of Employee Representation', *British Journal of Industrial Relations*, 35, 3: 309–336.

Ichniowski, C., Kochan, T., Levin, D., Olson, C. and Strauss, G. (1996) 'What Works at Work: Overview and Assessment', *Industrial Relations*, 35, 3: 299–333.

Incomes Data Services (1998) *Pay Systems and Pay Structures and the Relationship to Low Pay: A Research Paper for the Low Pay Commission*, London: IDS.

Institute of Personnel and Development (1995) *Personnel and the Line: Developing the New Relationship*, London: IPD.

Institute of Personnel and Development (1998) *Getting Fit, Staying Fit: Developing Lean and Responsive Organisations*, London: IPD.

International Survey Research (1997) *Transition and Transformation: Employee Satisfaction in the '90s*, London: ISR.

Jenkins, R. (1989) 'Discrimination and Equal Opportunity in Employment: Ethnicity and "Race" in the United Kingdom', in Gallie, D. (ed.) *Employment in Britain*, Oxford: Blackwell.

Jewson, N., Mason, D., Drewett, A. and Rossiter, W. (1995) 'Formal Equal Opportunities Policies and Employment Best Practice', *Employment Department Research Series*, Employment Department Publication, 69.

Kalleberg, A., Knoke, D., Marsden, P. and Spaeth, J. (1996) *Organisations in America: Analysing their Structures and Human Resource Practices*, Thousand Oaks, California: Sage.

Kelly, J. (1997) 'Long Waves in Industrial Relations: Mobilisation and Counter-Mobilisation in Historical Perspective', *Historical Studies in Industrial Relations*, 4: 3–35.

Kessler, S. and Bayliss, F. (1998) *Contemporary British Industrial Relations*, Basingstoke: Macmillan.

Kochan, T., Katz, H. and McKersie, R. (1986) *The Transformation of American Industrial Relations*, New York: Basic Books.

Labour Research Department (1998) 'Are women out of proportion?', *Labour Research*, 87, 3: 12–14.

Legge, K. (1995) *Human Resource Management: Rhetorics and Realities,* London: Macmillan Press.

Lincoln, J. and Kalleberg, A. (1990) *Culture, Control and Commitment*, Cambridge: Cambridge University Press.

Locke, E. (1976) 'The Nature and Causes of Job Satisfaction', in Dunnette, M. (ed.) *Handbook of Industrial and Organisational Psychology*, Chicago: Rand McNally.

Lockwood, D. (1975) 'Sources of Variation in Working Class Images of Society', in Bulmer, M. (ed.) *Working Class Images of Society*, London: Routledge.

Lowe, J. (1992) 'Locating the Line: The Front-Line Supervisor and Human Resource Management', in Blyton P. and Turnbull, P. (eds) *Reassessing Human Resource Management*, London: Sage Publications.

McCarthy, W. (1994) 'Of Hats and Cattle: or The Limits of Macro-Survey Research in Industrial Relations', *Industrial Relations Journal*, 25, 4: 315–322.

Machin, S. (1995) 'Plant Closures and Unionisation in British Establishments', *British Journal of Industrial Relations*, 33, 1: 55–68.

Machin, S. and Stewart, M. (1996) 'Trade Unions and Financial Performance', *Oxford Economic Papers*, 48, 2: 213–241.

Machin, S., Stewart, M. and Van Reenen, J. (1993) 'Multiple Unionism, Fragmented Bargaining and Economic Outcomes in Unionised UK Establishments', in Metcalf, D. and Milner, S. (eds) *New Perspectives on Industrial Disputes*, London: Routledge.

Makin, P., Cooper, C. and Cox, C. (1996) *Organizations and the Psychological Contract: Managing People at Work*, Leicester: The British Psychological Society.

Marchington, M., Goodman, J., Wilkinson, A. and Ackers, P. (1992) 'New Developments in Employee Involvement', *Employment Department Research Series*, Employment Department Publication, 2.

Marginson, P. (1984) 'The Distinctive Effects of Plant and Company Size on Workplace Industrial Relations', *British Journal of Industrial Relations*, 22, 1: 1–14.

Marginson, P., Edwards, P., Martin, R., Purcell, J. and Sisson, K. (1988) *Beyond the Workplace: Managing Industrial Relations in the Multi-Establishment Enterprise,* London: Blackwell.

Marginson, P., Edwards, P., Armstrong, P. and Purcell, J. with Hubbard, N. (1993) 'The Control of Industrial Relations in Large Companies: An Initial Analysis of the Second Company Level Industrial Relations Survey', *Warwick Papers in Industrial Relations*, Warwick: Industrial Relations Research Unit, 45.

Marginson, P., Gilman, M., Jacobi, O. and Krieger, H. (1998) *Negotiating European Works Councils: an Analysis of Agreements Under Article 13*, European Foundation for the Improvement of Living and Working Conditions, Luxembourg: European Commission.

Metcalf, H. (1990) 'Retraining Women Employees: Measures to Counteract Labour Shortages', *Institute for Manpower Studies Report*, 190.

Milkman, R. (1998) 'The New American Workplace: High Road or Low?', in Thompson, P. and Warhurst, C. (eds) *Workplaces of the Future*, Basingstoke: Macmillan.

Millward, N. (1994) *The New Industrial Relations?*, London: Policy Studies Institute.

Millward, N., Bryson, A. and Forth, J. (2000) *All Change at Work?*, London: Routledge.

Millward, N., Stevens, M., Smart, D. and Hawes W. (1992) *Workplace Industrial Relations in Transition: The ED/ESRC/PSI/ACAS Surveys*, Aldershot: Dartmouth.

Morehead, A., Steele, M., Alexander, M., Stephen, K. and Duffin, L. (1997) *Changes at Work*, Melbourne: Longman.

Mowday, T., Porter, L. and Steers, R. (1982) *Employee-Organization Linkages: the Psychology of Commitment, Absenteeism and Turnover*, London: Academic Press.

Murikami, T. (1997) 'The Autonomy of Teams in the Car Industry: A Cross National Comparison', *Work, Employment and Society*, 11, 4: 749–758.

Murphy, J. (1993) *The Moral Economy of Labor: Aristotelian Themes in Economic Theory*, New Haven: Yale University Press.

Newby, H. (1977) *The Deferential Worker*, London: Penguin.

Newton, T. and Findlay, P. (1996) 'Playing God? The Performance of Appraisal', *Human Resource Management Journal*, 6, 3: 42–58.

Nichols, T. (1986) *The British Worker Question: A New Look at Workers and Productivity in Manufacturing*, London: Routledge.

Nichols, T., Dennis, A. and Guy, W. (1995) 'Size of Employment Unit and Injury Rates in British Manufacturing: a Secondary Analysis of WIRS 1990 Data', *Industrial Relations Journal*, 26, 1: 45–56.

Nolan, P. and Brown, W. (1983) 'Competition and Workplace Wage Determination', *Oxford Bulletin of Economics and Statistics*, 45, 3: 269–287.

Office of Population Censuses and Surveys (1990) *Standard Occupation Classification Volume 1*.

Osterman, P. (1994) 'How Common is Workplace Transformation and Who Adopts It?', *Industrial and Labor Relations Review*, 47, 2: 173–188.

Parcel, T., Kaufman, T. and Jolly, L. (1991) 'Going Up the Ladder: Multiplicity Sampling to Create Linked Macro-to-Micro Organizational Samples', in Marsden, P. (ed.) *Sociological Methodology*, 21: 43–79.

Patterson, M., West, M., Lawthorn, R. and Nickell, S. (1997) 'Impact of People Management Practices on Business Performance', *Issues in People Management*, London: Institute of Personnel and Development.

Pendleton, A. (1997) 'Characteristics of Workplaces with Financial Participation: Evidence from the Workplace Industrial Relations Survey', *Industrial Relations Journal*, 28, 2: 103–119.

Phelps Brown, H. (1990) 'The Counter-Revolution of Our Time', *Industrial Relations*, 29, 1: 1–14.

Piore, M. and Sabel, C. (1984) *The Second Industrial Divide: Possibilities for Prosperity*, New York: Basic Books.

Poole, M. and Mansfield, R. (1993) 'Patterns of Continuity and Change in Managerial Attitudes and Behaviour in Industrial Relations 1980–90', *British Journal of Industrial Relations*, 31, 1: 11–36.

Porter, M. (1990) *The Competitive Advantage of Nations*, London: Routledge.

Price, L. and Price, R. (1995) 'Change and Continuity in the Status Divide', in Sisson, K. (ed.) *Personnel Management: a Comprehensive Guide to Theory and*

Practice in Britain, Oxford: Blackwell.

Purcell, J. (1993) 'The End of Institutional Industrial Relations', *Political Quarterly*, 64, 1: 6–23.

Purcell, J. and Sisson, K. (1983) 'Strategies and Practices in the Management of Industrial Relations', in Bain, G. (ed.) *Industrial Relations in Britain*, Oxford: Blackwell.

Rainbird, H. (1994) 'Continuing Training', in Sisson, K. (ed.) *Personnel Management: a Comprehensive Guide to Theory and Practice in Britain*, Oxford: Blackwell.

Rainnie, A. (1989) *Industrial Relations in Small Firms*, London: Routledge.

Ramsey, H. (1977) 'Guides to Control: Workers' Participation in Sociological and Historical Perspective', *Sociology*, 11, 3: 481–506.

Regalia, I. (1996) 'How the Social Partners View Direct Participation: a Comparative Study of 15 European Countries', *European Journal of Industrial Relations*, 2, 2: 211–234.

Robinson, S. and Rousseau, D. (1994) 'Violating the Psychological Contract: Not the Exception but the Norm', *Journal of Organisational Behaviour*, 15, 3: 245–259.

Rogers, J. and Streeck, W. (1995) *Works Councils: Consultation, Representation and Co-operation in Industrial Relations*, Chicago: University of Chicago.

Scase, R. (1995) 'Employment Relations in Small Firms' in Edwards, P. (ed.) *Industrial Relations: Theory and Practice in Britain*, Oxford: Blackwell.

Scott, M., Roberts, I., Holroyd, G. and Sawbridge, D. (1989) 'Management and Industrial Relations in Small Firms', *Department of Employment Research Paper*, Employment Department Publication, 70.

Sewell, G. and Wilkinson, B. (1992) 'Empowerment or Emasculation? Shopfloor Surveillance in a Total Quality Organisation', in Blyton P. and Turnbull, P. (eds) *Reassessing Human Resource Management*, London: Sage Publications.

Sisson, K. (1987) *The Management of Collective Bargaining: An International Comparison*, Oxford: Blackwell.

Sisson, K. (1990) 'Introducing the Human Resource Management Journal', *Human Resource Management Journal*, 1, 1: 1–11.

Sisson, K. (1993) 'In Search of HRM', *British Journal of Industrial Relations*, 31, 2: 201–210.

Sisson, K. (1994) 'Personnel Management: Paradigms, Practice and Prospects', in Sisson, K. (ed.) *Personnel Management*, 2nd Edition, Oxford: Blackwell.

Sisson, K. and Marginson, P. (1995) 'Management: Systems, Structures and Strategy', in Edwards P. (ed.) *Industrial Relations: Theory and Practice in Britain*, Oxford: Blackwell.

Sisson, K., Arrowsmith, J., Gilman, M. and Hall, M. (1999) 'A Preliminary Review of the Industrial Relations Implications of Economic and Monetary Union', *Warwick Papers in Industrial Relations*, Warwick: Industrial Relations Research Unit, 62.

Sly, F. (1996) 'Women in the Labour Market', *Employment Gazette*, 93, 10: 483–502.

Smith, J., Edwards, P. and Hall, M. (1999) 'Redundancy Consultation: A Study of Current Practice and the Effects of the 1995 Regulations', *Department of Trade and Industry Employment Relations Research Series*, London: Department of Trade and Industry, 5. Available on line at http://www.dti.gov.uk/emar.

Spector, P. (1997) *Job Satisfaction: Application, Assessment, Causes and Consequences*, London: Sage

Stevens, G. (1999) 'Workplace Injuries in Small and Large Manufacturing Workplaces 1994/5–1995/6', *Labour Market Trends*, 107, 1: 19–26.

Stewart, M. and Swaffield, K. (1996) 'Constraints on the Desired Hours of Work of British Men', *Warwick Economic Research Papers*, University of Warwick, 468.

Storey, J. (1992) *Developments in the Management of Human Resources*, Oxford: Blackwell.

Storey, D. and Westhead, P. (1997) 'Management Training in Small Firms: a Case of Market Failure?', *Human Resource Management Journal*, 7, 2: 61–71.

Taylor, P. and Walker, A. (1994) 'The Ageing Workforce: Employers' Attitudes Towards Older People', *Work, Employment and Society*, 8, 4: 569–591.

Terry, M. (1995) 'Trade Unions: Shop Stewards and the Workplace', in Edwards, P. (ed.) *Industrial Relations: Theory and Practice in Britain*, London: Blackwell.

Thornley, C. (1998) 'Contesting Local Pay: The Decentralisation of Collective Bargaining in the NHS', *British Journal of Industrial Relations*, 36, 3: 413–434.

Towers, B. (1997) *The Representation Gap: Change and Reform in the British and American Workplace*, Oxford: Oxford University Press.

Trades Union Congress (1998), 'Focus on Balloting and Industrial Action', *Trade Union Trends Survey*, 98, 5.

Trades Union Congress (1999) 'Focus on Recognition', *Trade Union Trends Survey*, 99, 1.

VandenHeuvel, A. (1994) 'Public and Private Sector Absence: Does it Differ?', *The Journal of Industrial Relations*, 36, 4: 530–545.

Wajcman, J. (1998) *Managing Like a Man: Women and Men in Corporate Management*, University Park, PA: Pennsylvania State University Press.

Warr, P. (1998) 'Well-being and the Workplace', in Kahneman, D., Diener, E. and Schwarz, N. (eds) *Foundations of Hedonic Psychology: Scientific Perspectives on Enjoyment and Suffering*, New York: Russell Sage.

Watson, G. and Fothergill, B. (1993) 'Part-Time Employment and Attitudes to Part-Time Work', *Employment Gazette*, 101, 5: 239–248.

Williamson, O., Wachter, M. and Harris J. (1975) 'Understanding the Employment Relationship', *Bell Journal of Economics*, 6, 1: 250–278.

Wood, S. and De Menezes, L. (1998) 'High Commitment Management in the U.K.: Evidence from the Workplace Industrial Relations Survey and Employers' Manpower and Skills Practices Survey', *Human Relations*, 51, 4: 485–515.

Working Time Regulations 1998, *Statutory Instruments 1998*, 1833.

Wright Mills, C. (1959) *Sociological Imagination*, New York: Oxford University Press.

Zabalza, A. and Tzannatos, Z. (1985), *Women and Equal Pay: The Effects of Legislation on Female Employment and Wages in Britain*, Cambridge: Cambridge University Press.

Index